Sound and Glory

DYNE-AMERICAN PUBLICATIONS, INC.
2070 Naamans Road, Suite 103
Wilmington, Delaware 19810

Title: "SOUND AND GLORY"
Printed in the United States

FIRST AMERICAN EDITION 1990

Editor: David Hirschberg

Consults: Marshall Lytle, Ralph Jones, Frank and Florence Beecher, Chris Gardner, Joey Ambrose, Dick Richards, John Grande, Susan Hirschberg, B. David Behringer, John Allums, Rex Zario, James Allsman, Duke Snow, Bill Turner, Kenny Denton, James Myers and Frank Acierno.

Design and Layout: J.J. von Hoelle and Ellen Coppola

Typesetting: Anette Ruff – PaMar Graphics, Inc.; Wilmington, DE

Art Work: Laura Haley

Photo Preparation: Chien T. Sung, Wilmington, DE

British research staff: Pauline Shayler and Maeve Wright.
German research staff: Gertrude Kuebler and Mark von Trataner.
Mexican research staff: Annette Nunez, Denise Gregoire and Padro Velegus.

Book, torch and motto seal on page five is the registered trademark of Dyne-American Publications, Inc.

ISBN: Hardcover: 1-878970-00-3 Softcover: 1-878970-01-1

Library of Congress number: 90-082945

The incredible story of Bill Haley, the Father of Rock'n'Roll and the music that shook the world

by John W. Haley & John von Hoelle

DYNE-AMERICAN PUBLISHING

This work is dedicated to the brothers, sisters and daughter of John W. Haley:

Sharyn Ann Haley
Joan Patricia Haley
Doreen Debra Haley
William John Haley
James Steven Haley
Scott Robert Haley
Martha Maria Haley
Pedro Antonio Haley
Linda Georgina Haley
Loyd Edgar Gill

and

Jacqueline Ann Haley

also to the children of John von Hoelle:

Eric John von Hoelle
Christopher David von Hoelle
Timothy Mark von Hoelle
R. Andrew von Hoelle
Ellen Ann von Hoelle-Coppola

CONTENTS

WE'RE GONNA' ROCK AROUND THE CLOCK TONIGHT!

words & music by Max C. Freedman
Arr. Harry Filler

2

RHYTHMIC

VOICE

ONE, TWO, THREE O'-CLOCK, FOUR O'-CLOCK, ROCK,
FIVE, SIX, SEV-EN O'CLOCK, EIGHT O'CLOCK ROCK
NINE, TEN E-LEV-EN O'CLOCK
TWELVE O'CLOCK, ROCK WE'RE GONNA ROCK A ROUND THE CLOCK TO NIGHT!

CHORUS

1. PUT YOUR GLAD RAGS ON AND JOIN ME HON WE'LL HAVE SOME FUN WHEN THE
2. WHEN THE CLOCK STRIKES 2 AND 3 AND 4 IF THE BAND SLOWS DOWN WE'LL
3. WHEN THE CHIMES RING 5 AND 6 AND 7, WE'LL BE ROCK-IN' UP IN
4. WHEN IT'S EIGHT, NINE, TEN E-LEV-EN TOO, I'LL BE GO-IN' STRONG AND
5. WHEN THE CLOCK STRIKE 12, WE'LL COOL OFF, THEN START A ROCK-IN' 'ROUND THE

1. CLOCK STRIKES ONE, WE'RE GON-NA ROCK A-ROUND THE CLOCK TO-NIGHT, WE'RE GON-NA
2. YELL FOR MORE.
3. SEV-ENTH HEAV'N.
4. SO WILL YOU.
5. CLOCK A-GAIN.

CHORUS

ROCK, ROCK, ROCK 'TIL BROAD DAY-LIGHT, WE'RE GON-NA ROCK, GON-NA ROCK A-ROUND THE CLOCK TO-NIGHT!

An early hand written score of "Rock Around The Clock" 1953

Courtesy® Haley Family Collection

FOREWORD

To understand the genius of Bill Haley and his music, one needs to understand his conception of Rock'n'Roll. For many in the early 1950's, the formula of this new style of music was very difficult to comprehend. Looking at its form written on a sheet of music, it seems deceptively simple, for in classic rock'n'roll, such as *Rock Around the Clock* or *Shake, Rattle and Roll*, it's neither the words nor the notes which bring this unique sound to life—it's the performance.

The words and notes are but the skeleton, to which accomplished musicians add their body and soul. It is this well-rehearsed performance that breathes life and vitality into Rock'n'Roll. In Bill Haley's band, skilled and talented musicians forced their instruments to the very edge of chaos. Their fingers flying over strings and keys so fast their hands become almost a blur, while reed instruments honk and wail as if in total agony. A highly controlled, syncopated chorus of sounds, all driven by a wild, primitive, but always thundering beat. A bastardly, irreverent symphony of hypnotic rhythms, totally integrating a vast spectrum of musical forms and pushed to the razor's edge by sheer energy and will. Bill Haley created a music of awesome power, with the vitality to conquer generations still unborn.

This was Bill Haley's brand of Rock'n'Roll, and this was the sound he used to first rock the world on an incredible afternoon in the spring of 1952.

Courtesy© Haley Family Collection

"Bill Haley – The man who started it all."

John Lennon

Bill Haley, My Father

Over the last decades, many books and articles have been written about the early years of rock'n'roll and my father. Unfortunately, a great deal of the information contained in these publications has been incorrect and/or misleading. Many people who are aware of these fallacies have suggested that I write a more accurate account of my father's unique career and a little more of the private side of his life.

When he died in Texas in 1981, he was working on his autobiography, but unfortunately, he did not live to finish it. When he was inducted into the Rock and Roll Hall of Fame in 1987, I decided it was time to share his story with his millions of fans.

In researching this book, I came to appreciate my father's struggles and accomplishments in a new light. I found he was a true pioneer in every sense of the word. I was grateful to have his personal diaries, private papers and most of his business documents for reference.

I wish to thank many of the Comets, whose friendships I hold dear. Their efforts and personal stories have greatly enriched this book. I also wish to thank the many colleagues and friends of my father to whom I am indebted. Their kind contributions were greatly appreciated and we have gratefully listed their names in our "Acknowledgments".

My father climbed out of poverty to great wealth and international acclaim. Many times he stumbled and fell, and became disillusioned, but he always got up and tried again. This is his story, and the story of the musicians and other talented people who helped him along the way.

He never lost faith in his music and this is his most lasting gift to all of us. When asked in an interview just before his death: "How would you like to be remembered?" He rubbed his chin thoughtfully, and said quietly: "Well. . . . as an entertainer. . . . the fellow who started it all. . . and I hope contributed to the happiness, perhaps, of the world, a little bit."

In this spirit, I hope you will enjoy reading his story.

John William Haley

ACKNOWLEDGEMENTS

Bill Haley was a very complex man. He was also a very private man. He had the unique ability to say what he thought you wanted to hear and to be what he thought you wanted him to be. A few people we interviewed believed Bill to be a not very bright, but lucky country boy who stumbled into his success. However, to many other associates who knew him better, Bill Haley was a talented musician, composer, bandleader and shrewd businessman who made millions of dollars during his lifetime and controlled a half dozen corporations.

To a very large group of early rock enthusiasts, Bill Haley is the "Father of Rock'n'Roll". To them, there were only three great innovations of music in the past one hundred and fifty years; Strauss' waltzes, Handy's blues and Haley's Rock. To other so-called "music critics" Bill only imitated or combined already established musical forms and his only contribution was to make them more popular. This work became the search for the real Bill Haley—was he really the "Father of Rock'n'Roll" and what were his real contributions to the world of popular music?

We found the "real" Bill Haley was very difficult to separate from Bill Haley the myth. A myth which he, and his organizations, had carefully created. To add to the confusion of information on his life, Bill Haley himself told interviewers over the years he was born in three different cities, in three separate years. After he passed thirty, and younger, more dashing performers began to share the stage and fame of rock'n'roll with him, he began the legend of his going on the road at the age of fifteen, to better cover his already thirteen year old career. Reality and legend became one with the public and the press, and few outsiders knew the difference.

As Bill became the first international rock superstar, he tried to play down the significance of his early hillbilly roots. His managers felt these country origins were "un-cool" or too "square" for the "Pied Piper of Rock n'Roll".

After losing his first fortune to the cruelties and misadventures of fate and unsound investments, he set about to make a make a second fortune far greater, but this time without the knowledge of his associates. He concealed from the public and many of his closest colleagues the full extent of his far-flung international financial affairs.

Bill Haley had few life-long friends, the two great exceptions being Jack Howard and Rudy Pompilli. Although Bill's music was known and loved by millions, no one person we interviewed could give us an accurate, overall view of him. He seemed to have never let anyone get too familiar or know too much. He always remained a bit mysterious and kept much of his financial, family and personal affairs secret from his three wives, his musicians and his many business associates.

To find a clearer picture of the real Bill Haley, we interviewed over ninety people who knew Bill at some point in his life. It was only after ten years of documentary research and three years of fascinating personal interviews in Europe, Mexico and the United States, that the real story of Bill Haley's remarkable life, triumphs and ordeals came slowly into focus.

We are indebted to many gracious people for loaning us their home movies, rare photographs, tapes, documents and valuable insights. They each opened a window of understanding to the complex personality of Bill Haley. We would like to extend our warmest thanks and appreciation for their most welcomed efforts.

To the following schoolmates, neighbors, and friends whose interviews gave us a precious insight into the boyhood of Bill Haley, we offer a special thank you: James Otis, Frank Gray, Wilfred Davis, Joe Lauginiger, Charles Griffin, Naomi Austin, Dorothy Heavlow, Robert Miles, Albert McCann, Frances Booth, George Booth, Florence Appel, Bill Gray, Mary Thomas, Reece Thomas, and Jayne Davis.

For first hand information about the critical and lean years from 1945 to 1950, we would like to acknowledge these fine people: Duke Snow, Dick Aydelotte, Harvy Smith, Peggy White

Moriarty, Robert Thornton, Frances Chandler Riley, Naomi Allsman, Dick Holmes, Ruth Kayser, Conrad Parsons, Richard Sipps, David Shanzer, Amos Stolzfus, Earl Phillips, Michael Testa, Flo Thomas Caldwell, Charles Wayne, Neil Drummond, Dorothy Wright, Leonard Brown, James Colletti, John Muntz, Charles McCune and Joseph Piccirilli.

For the important early years of 1950 to 1954, in which Bill and his musicians developed rock'n'roll, we wish to thank these generous people whose interviews gave this period fresh understanding: Arretta Keefer, Samuel Sgro, Harry West, Sharyn Ann Haley, Janet Cedrone Alvarez, Carlos Alvarez, Danny Vanore, Kenn Petzke, Ronald Beeks, Clifford Redden, Edward Farmer, John Buzzell, Jay Rubinsky, Patricia Miller, Frank Pingatore, Carl Russell, Paul Miller, Jim Miller, Norma Joseph, Phyllis Miller and Billy Williamson.

The glory years of 1955 to 1958 were made more revealing due to the contributions of these friends and associates of Bill Haley: Shirly Emery, Brian Lee Hart, Elsie Lightcap, Tony Liquori, Jack Ketrick, Ruth Sipps, Joseph "Lucky Taylor" Costello, Ben Giliberto and Philip Malatesta.

For the years 1959 to 1981, which we cover in our epilogue, we wish to thank: Bill Turner, John "Bam Bam" Lane, Ann Pompilli, Denman Stanfield, Lakena Keffala, Joann Hensley Fartanoni, James Acierno, Chris Gardner, Stuart Colman, Denise Gregoire, Herbert Kamitz and Kenny Denton.

We wish to offer our warmest appreciation to the following very key individuals whose rare and most personal contributions make this work an historical treatise of the early development of rock'n'roll as well as the story of Bill Haley:

To Rosario Lefavi, President of the Arcade, Arzee and Rex Zario Music Companies and former C.E.O. of Bill Haley's publishing companies. Mr. Lefavi graciously gave us unlimited access to the detailed financial and business files of Cowboy Records, (1946-1951); Haley-Howard Publications, (1951-1955); Sea Breeze Music Inc., (1955-1976); Valley Brook Publications, Inc. (1955-1985); Jack Howard Publications, (1944-1985); Clymax Records (1957-59); Arcade Music Company, (1953-present); Bill Haley International, (1956-1960); Bill Haley & Comets Inc. (1956-1963); Worldwide Management Co., (1957-1958); Industrial Mechanics, Inc., (1956-1958), and thousands of rare Bill Haley, Four Aces of Western Swing, Comet and Saddlemen performance contracts, telegrams, photographs and other rare documents.

To John Grande, Bill's partner and co-founder of the Saddlemen and the Comets. His many hours recalling details and setting us straight on conditions of the time were immensely important to our story.

To Joseph D'Ambrosio, the Comets' first saxophonist, whose brilliant golden horn gave the band its world renowned sound. His thoughtful input was most welcomed.

To William "Billy" Gussak, Bill's early session drummer, whose fascinating stories of the early Essex and Decca recording sessions are priceless.

To Dick Richards, the Comet's multi-talented stage drummer, whose advice and goodwill opened many doors to our research.

To James E. Myers, President of Myers Music and the co-author of Bill's greatest song, *Rock Around the Clock*. Jimmy's many hours of interviews furnished us with unique, first hand information and documents on the early history of Rock'n' roll, Bill Haley and the Philadelphia recording industry.

To Vincent "Catfish" Broomall, the Comets' astute band boy and road manager. His revealing interviews gave us one of the best behind-the-scenes overviews of the years from 1953 to 1958.

To Ralph Jones, the Comets' famous drummer, whose home movies, private photos and recollections added a great deal of warmth and depth to our story.

To Marshall Lytle, bass player for both the Saddlemen and the Comets, whose kind interviews, home movies and vivid recollections were greatly appreciated.

To Milton Gabler, the man who brilliantly recorded over one hundred Bill Haley songs at Decca Records; his detailed interview and technical remembrances were most welcomed.

To Ralph Brownlowe, whose expertise in identifying vintage instruments in photos was indispensable.

To Al "Rex" Piccirilli, Bill's flamboyant bass player, whose back-slap techniques became one of the basic beats of Bill's early rockabilly. His many hours of explaining the early years of rock and politics within the Saddlemen and the Comets were of great help to this story.

To George Gray, the husband of Bill Haley's sister. He lived with the Haley family for the first three years of his marriage to Peggy Haley. His recollections of family events from 1942 to the late 1950's were indispensable.

To James "Slim" Allsman, one of the lead guitarists in Bill Haley's Four Aces of Western Swing. Our very special gratitude for his many hours of interviews and bringing us many of Bill's early musicians and for his loans of rare photographs of Bill's early groups.

To Frank Beecher, Bill's brilliant lead guitarist, whose style contributed so much to the Comets' legend. Frank and his wife, Florence, gave a great deal of time and input on this project.

To Scott Haley, Bill Haley's youngest son by his second marriage. His many hours of interviews shed a great deal of light on the private side of his father. Scott's family stories, newspaper clippings and family dates became indispensable.

To Gertrude Kuebler, for her many hours in translating hundreds of foreign newspaper accounts and other documents pertaining to Bill's European tours.

To Lloyd Roach, Sal April, Jon Rafal, Ian Alexander and all the staff at radio station WCZN, successor to WPWA, at 1590 on the AM dial. This great group of people was very instrumental in helping us locate many of Bill Haley's early associates through their many broadcast appeals and special "Bill Haley Birthday Bash" programs.

To David Hirschberg, our editor, whose friendship, wise counsel and extensive editorial guidance were indispensable and always available. His attention to historical and technical detail was, to say the least, painstaking and thoroughly comprehensive.

To the late John "Jack" Howard, Bill Haley's manager, business partner and friend, whose personal files contained the largest amount of information to be found on Bill Haley's personal and financial affairs from the years 1943 to 1976.

To the late Dorothy Crowe Haley, Bill's first wife, for her records, scrapbooks, photographs, and the many stories as told to her children.

We also wish to thank the staff of the Library of Congress and the Federal Bureau of Investigation, Washington D.C. for their kind assistance with the many government documents released to us under the Freedom of Information Act; the staff of the Chester Musicians Union, to which Bill and most of his early band members belonged; Widener University, for use of their microfilm archives on early Chester and Delaware County newspapers of the 1940's and 1950's; and the Bethel Historical Society, for access to Bill Haley's early school records and documents pertaining to life in Booth's Corner during the 1930's and 1940's.

Discography Acknowledgments

Bill Haley's incredible six hundred plus discography listed in the back of this book is one of the most comprehensive ever compiled. We wish to gratefully thank the following dedicated collectors and friends for their many hours of research in helping make this list possible: Paul Miller (Holiday/Essex/Somerset/Pye Records), Michelle Manganaro (Vogue Records), Alan Whaley (Sonet/Crescendo/Janus Records), Maria Nunez (Orfeon/Dimsa/Maya Records), Milt Gabler (Decca/MCA/Coral/Brunswick Records), Suzanne Coston (Warner Brothers Records), Rex Zario (Cowboy/Arzee/Arcade/Claire/Roller Coaster/Bear-Polydor Records), Jim Myers (Atlantic/Keystone/Center Records), Rick Whitesell, Stan Mayo, David Hirschberg, Chris Gardner, Denise Gregoire, Adam Komorowski, Kenny Denton, Stuart Colman, John Beecher, Ron Beeks and especially Bill's greatest European fan, Herbert Kamitz.

INTRODUCTION

Today it is difficult to imagine the world of music without the pulsating rhythms and hypnotic beat of the sound that came to be called "Rock'n'Roll". Since its creation in the early 1950's, legends have been made, fortunes spent and commercial empires built by its performers and promoters. Through concerts, recordings and videos, the youth of five continents have danced and clapped to its wild, intoxicating sounds.

In less than forty years, Rock'n'Roll has overcome enormous obstacles of social, political and religious scorn to become a multi-billion dollar, world-wide industry. These past four decades of often bitter hostility and controversy have also made Rock'n'Roll one of the most misunderstood musical artforms ever created. It is amusing that in the Soviet Union Rock'n'Roll was considered "Capitalism's most decadent music" while at the same time the ultra-right KKK believed it to be a "Nigger-loving Communist plot to destroy the minds and morals of our American youth". Denounced by many church and civic leaders of the day, Rock'n'Roll musicians were under constant pressure and ridicule from newspapers, television and the pulpits across the nation. Never in the history of music was there such a wall of hate and contempt as was built around this "vulgar and shameless sound of promiscuous sex". The heavy toll on the minds and souls of many of its early performers was tremendous. "Everybody hates us. . . except the kids", was how Bill Haley once expressed his frustration.

However, the new, irrepressible sound would not die. The greater the protest, the wilder became the beat. Its often torn and bloody banner was lifted from near oblivion many times by gifted singers and musicians. Renewed and revitalized by each succeeding generation as their own, Rock'n'Roll proved to be a formidable foe to its detractors and the battle cry of each new generation. It became a catalyst, and then the anthem, to nations of rebellious and restless youth. It heralded the loss of an age of teenage innocence, and neither America nor the world would ever be the same.

"Sound and Glory" is not the history of Rock'n'Roll, but the story of its birth from a cauldron of musical experience by a most unlikely man, a man whom we can only now begin to appreciate. This is the story of the early years of Rock through the eyes and ears of the people who were there. The untold story of a shy, young country boy who strummed an old cracked guitar and dreamed of one day being another Gene Autry but instead, and against all odds, became the first international Rock'n'Roll superstar. This is the story of Bill Haley, the man who tore down the barriers of musical prejudice and segregation and became the "Father of Rock 'n'Roll". This is also the story of his unique gift to the world, that magnificent celebration of sound we all know as classic Rock'n'Roll.

John J. von Hoelle
Booth's Corner, Pa.

"If one can hear the seeds of the coming hurricane, in the gentle stirring of a warm summer's breeze . . . then the seeds of Rock'n'Roll can be heard in the classic strumming of the Spanish guitar... in the wild, foot-stompin' rhythms of the old Gaelic Jigs... and in the distant, hypnotic cadences of ancient Africa."

John von Hoelle

CHAPTER ONE

THE EARLY YEARS 1925-1943

"as is bent the twig—so grows the tree."

Courtesy J. Ketrick

Bill Haley, age 6 months, in his father's arms.

It is believed by many enthusiasts that Rock'n' Roll was born of rhythm and blues in the legendary night clubs of New Orleans, St. Louis, Harlem, and Chicago. Other knowledgeable music historians refer to its rich Country-Western origins, which in turn owe their heritage to even earlier Scotch-Irish traditions. Still others would argue that Rock'n'Roll isn't a musical form at all, just a lot of wild, synchronized noises created to infuriate ones elders. They would tell you that if hell had a band, Rock-'n'Roll would be their tune!

To many, rock music may be loud, garish, throbbing and irreverent. Millions love it and even more millions hate it. However, it's difficult to ignore. It has saturated our culture and contains the power and energy to arouse the deepest passions.

Where did this unbridled celebration of sound come from? What musicians dared to break with long-held traditions and tear down the walls of musical prejudice? When did Rock'n'Roll become popular, and why? The answers begin in the historical records of the fourth decade of the twentieth century. A time within the living memory of many of us. A time before there was such a word as Rock-'n'Roll. A time when such music was unknown.

It was 2:30 on a hot, sultry afternoon in the noisy blue-collar suburb of Detroit called Highland Park. A seven pound, eight ounce boy was born in a small, second floor apartment on Florence Avenue to William and Maude Haley. The date was July 6th, 1925. The little boy would be named William John Clifton Haley, but one day he would become the musical legend known as Bill Haley, and with his Comets, he would rock the concert halls of the world with the thunder of his sound and the glory of his music.

The baby was the second born to the Haleys. Margaret, their daughter, was born two years earlier. William Sr. had moved to Detroit from Firebrick, Kentucky, where he found work in a nearby service station. The Roaring Twenties were in full swing and times were good to the thirty-five year old father. He enjoyed his work as a mechanic and his wife gave piano lessons in their home at 25¢ an hour. Maude Haley was a woman of strong religious convictions and gentle kindness. She had come to America with her family from Ulverston in Lancashire, England before the First World War. She had studied classical piano in Great Britain, and played the organ with such grace she was often asked to play at her church services.

Her American husband, part Cherokee indian, was a quiet man from the hills of eastern Kentucky. He had to quit school early to find work. His father had died young and his mother desperately needed his income to raise the younger children. William Sr. struggled with this burden until the last of his brothers and sisters were educated and on their own. Only then, after he was thirty years old, did he marry.

James Otis, who worked with William Sr. said: *". . he had a bad speech impediment which made him shy of talking very much. He was very good with his hands, a born mechanic . . . could fix almost anything. He kept to himself and, you know, I seldom saw him smile. I guess you would call him a real hillbilly at heart, but I tell you, he could play both the mandolin and banjo. He couldn't read no music, but he could pick out any tune he wanted. He had an ear for good country music. I think that's where little Billy got his ear for them foot-stomping hillbilly tunes."*

William Sr. was viewed by his son's boyhood friends as being a peaceful man of few words. They say he was a gentle, hard working but quiet man. The Great Depression had left a bit of sadness in his eyes, and a sense of doom, at times, descended on him. The lack of a good education and the hard life he had known in his youth gave him few grand illusions or great expectations. His quiet strength of character and deep love of playing lively hillbilly music pulled him through many periods of personal depression.

In 1929, two events happened that would change the course of history for four-year old Bill Haley. The first was a bungled inner-ear operation which severed his optic nerve and would leave the little boy blind in his left eye for the rest of his life. This handicap was not noticed by his parents until one day when he and his father were looking up at an airplane. William Sr. was shading both his eyes from the sun; little Billy was only shading one of his eyes. This wild, un-focused eye would have profound effects on the opportunities and personality of Bill Haley in the years to come.

The second event was the crash of the New York Stock Market. The widespread depression it created would lead to the loss of William Sr.'s job in the early 1930's. Depressed and unable to find work in Detroit, the young mechanic packed the family's belongings in an old Ford Model T and drove 550 miles to the little town of Boothwyn, Pa. where his wife's mother and family lived. He had received word from his wife's brother, Frank Green, of a possible job opening in a local viscose factory in nearby Marcus Hook. With family help, William secured a position paying 25¢ an hour. After several months living with their in-laws, the Haleys moved to a small, second floor apartment on Shaw Terrace in crowded downtown Chester, Pa.

In 1933, the Haley family moved to a five room bungalow in the little cross-roads village of Booth's Corner, Pa. The small house was on Kirk Road near its intersection with Foulk Road, just behind the old Auction Mart. Before long, Maude and William turned it into a comfortable home for their two children: ten year old Margaret, whom everyone called "Peggy", and seven year old Billy.

Booth's Corner was in the rolling green hills of Bethel Township, about five miles from Chester and twenty miles south-west of Philadelphia. Here the young Bill Haley found a way of life far different from the congested city streets he had known back in Detroit and Chester. Great open fields and small farms dotted the quiet but beautiful countryside.

Haley family home on Kirk Road, Booth's Corner.

His new neighbors raised hogs, chickens, horses and God-fearing families. This was a place where brilliant, orange day-lilies grew wild along the roads edged with low gray-stone walls. A down-home piece of God's country where people took pride in their work, their church, their family and their simple but honest country ways. This way of life was to have a profound effect on Bill Haley and his music in the years to come. Bill was to say later that these were his "Tom Sawyer" years. He so loved the tranquil peace of this quiet countryside that when he became very wealthy and was the Rock'n'Roll idol of the world, he would choose this place, the very land his father had plowed, to build his dream home, his beloved "Melody Manor".

Like the other boys in the village, "Billy", as his mother liked to call him, swam in the nearby water holes which fed into Naaman's Creek. He fished the streams and explored the many woods and meadows he found about his new world.

Bill Haley's school records are still preserved in the Bethel Historical Society's archives. They show him attending the one-room Chelsea school in the fourth, fifth and sixth grades. His teachers were Sara Jane Zebley and Sara Brodhead. They also show him to be one of the brightest kids in the school. He had an "A" average with only two days absent for the full year of 1933-34. By 1936, his grades had slipped to a "B" average.

Just across Naaman's Creek Road, near the Davis Farm, was a large pasture the kids would use as a ball field when their chores were done. Here games of baseball, football and hockey would be played with all the skill and will each boy could muster. The older boys lorded over the younger ones, but they always made room for them on the teams. In a village as small as Booth's Corner, every kid was needed just to fill basic positions.

Here a young boy could show what he was made of. Home runs with bases loaded or long catches for a winning touchdown created the heroes of the day. Here dreams of being the next Babe Ruth or Knute Rockne filled a young mans fantasies. But for the visually impaired 12 year old Bill Haley, this was not to be.

Blind in one eye and near-sighted in the other, the young Bill Haley had poor over-all vision and no depth perception at all. With this condition it made it almost impossible for him to catch a ball flying through the air or hit one with a bat. He was too young to understand this handicap and at an early age withdrew from competitive sports altogether, leaving him very self-conscious and with a deep, life long feeling of inferiority. To mask this feeling, the young Bill Haley withdrew from association with other boys his age. He became a quiet loner, and to many people, awkwardly shy.

Frank Gray and Wilfred Davis, two long time residents, remember Bill and the ball games well. *"Us boys would gather in the old field next to the Davis farm after our chores were done. But Saturdays were the best days. We'd choose up sides and play ball. Everybody brought their own equipment. Bill would come over and play sometimes, but he wasn't a very good ball player. He couldn't catch nothing. He got a lot of kidding. When he would miss an easy catch, they would give him a lot of hell. No one understood back then what having only one eye meant. Bill was always the last to get picked when they chose up teams. I remember one fight Bill and Joe Lauginiger got into. Joe had called him a "one eyed Susan". Bill flew into him and the dust went flying! Afterwards, Bill spent a hour on his hands and knees looking in the grass for a button Joe tore off his shirt. You see, he didn't want his mother to know he was fighting again. He was very self-conscious about his eye and sometimes it was the object of ridicule from some of the older boys. Bill was a bit of a loner, quiet, but good natured. He would sometimes give us boys cigarettes and let us ride his bicycle."*

Another boy from the village got into a fight with Bill after school one day. He was two years older and doesn't remember the reason. However, he

Courtesy N. Allsman

Bill Haley (age 11) front row left. Photo taken on Shaw Terrace with his sister Peggy, top row right, and the Austin sisters.

punched Bill in the right eye during the fistfight. Bill was about twelve or thirteen years old at the time. As his one good eye became swollen he became completely blind. Bill fell to the ground covering his eyes and cried, *"I can't see...I can't see!"* The older boy, known as a bit of a bully among the local kids, said to him, *"I only popped you in one eye!"*. Bill replied with tears streaming down his cheeks: *"I'm blind in my other eye. I can't see nuttin'! Please take me home!"*

"Gee, I felt awful, I didn't know he was blind in that eye. I picked him up and led him home. When I got there, I banged on his front door and ran away. I've felt bad about that day ever since. Many years later, when he was one of the richest men in the town, I had to ask him for a donation for our local fire department. With a big grin, he said he'd do a concert and donate all the profits to the fire hall if I promised not to punch him in the eye again! Hell, by then he was big enough to throw me out the window! He turned out to be a hell of a nice guy."

Charlie Griffin, another local boy, remembers stealing Bill's bicycle a couple of times. *"I was one of the town ruffians back then. Bill was always pretty good about it. At least when I took his bike, he always knew where he could find it!"* Charlie, Ike McCann and the other guys also remember chewing on raw garlic so their parents wouldn't find out they had been smoking the cigarettes Bill gave them. The free cigarettes also seemed to buy Bill a little peace and respect from the big guys. But the missing tobacco also created a great deal of friction between Bill and his father. It was the cause of more than one trip to the proverbial woodshed.

Naomi Austin Allsman remembers Bill always walking down the road with his hands in his pockets and his cowboy hat pulled down to his eyebrows, as if to hide his bad eye under the wide brim. *"The kids teased him a lot about it, and Bill was in more than his share of fights. His mom would forbid him to fight, but sometimes he couldn't just walk away. She played the organ at church and told him it didn't look right for him to always be in trouble. Sometimes when he got home after one of his battles, his father would give him another wooping for his un-Christian behavior. I think this was one of the reasons Bill was the way he was. He couldn't win: if he stood up to them, he got into fights, if he walked away, they would make even more fun of him. So Bill began to keep to himself. I always liked him — he would do anything for you".*

Now alone much of the time, Bill became known as a bit of a day-dreamer. The long, languid summer days were filled with visions of knights in their shining armor defending their ladies and the castles of his mother's England. Bill loved to read stories of high adventure and daring heroes. His part Indian heritage lead him to read books on Geronimo, Crazy Horse and Sitting Bull. He wished the great Indian nations were still the masters of the wild West and he was one of their great war chiefs. He longed to be famous and have everybody in the world know his name. So much for the dreams of Bill Haley and a million other adolescent boys.

By the time Bill was thirteen, his new fantasy was to become a singing cowboy like the ones he idolized every Saturday afternoon at the movie houses in nearby Marcus Hook or Chester.

Joseph Lauginiger, a school mate of Bill, remembers the Christmas of 1938 when Bill received his first real guitar from his parents. It was not new and had a funny green color, but to an excited thirteen year old, it was a priceless treasure. His father taught him to play the basic chords and notes by ear. This second-hand guitar and the music it would create became a love affair Bill would hold for the rest of his life.

He soon realized he had his father's talent and ear for music. He found he could listen to a tune on the radio and pick it out on his guitar, note for note. From his mother he learned to sing a pretty fair ballad.

The Haley family often played and sang together on Sunday evenings. Bill on his guitar, his mother on her old, upright piano and his father on his mandolin. Peggy, Bill's older sister, would tap on top of the piano and sing in her beautiful soprano voice. Sometimes she would play along with her mother in a piano duet. They would sing and play their father's lively toe-tapping music of the Kentucky hills or Mrs. Haley's favorite hand-clapping gospel hymns. Their songs always had a distinctive beat and earthy rhythm to them. Once when a haughty neighbor wondered if such "music" was appropate for Sunday evenings, Mrs. Haley replied in her most proper British accent: *"I presume you are not referring to our gospel hymns, so you must be concerned about the propriety of my husband's Kentucky music. As you well know, Mrs. Booth, the Bible tells us to make a joyful NOISE unto the Lord, and this my family surely does!"* Nobody EVER argued scripture with Mrs. Haley, NOBODY.

Bill Haley and his guitar were now inseparable. He carried it to school, to work, anywhere he went. When he was on his bike, dashing madly down the dusty country roads, his guitar would be slung over his back.

One day while walking in the woods, a group of village kids came upon Bill strumming his guitar and loudly singing a popular ballad. *"We all just sat down and listened to him for about twenty minutes. After Billy sang each song he would bow as if pretending the trees were his audience. Then one of the girls coughed or something, and Billy, who didn't know we were there, looked startled and ran home. I guess he was a little embarrassed. You know, he wasn't a bad singer. That's the first time we ever heard him sing. It's kind of funny now to think this might have been Bill Haley's first concert, us four girls and a thousand trees!"*

News of Bill's ability to sing and play the guitar spread through the village grapevine. The dual reputation as a loner and a shy singer of country-western songs created an almost irresistible mystique about him among many of the village girls.

Dorothy Heavlow, a neighbor of the Haleys, remembers, *"All of us girls had a terrible crush on him. He was about fourteen at the time. He had this one girl friend who was just mad about him. He would kiss her quickly, once each day, as she waited downstairs at the old school across from the old Auction Mart. We all thought that was very daring back then. He was building a reputation as a ladies man even then!"*

At eleven years old Bill was just a skinny little kid, but by his fifteenth birthday he had grown into a hulking six foot one inch tall one hundred and seventy-five pound young man! Few bullies were now brave or foolish enough to call attention or to tease him about his bad eye. And nobody called him "Frog Eyes" to his face.

In June of 1940, just before his fifteen birthday, he left school after finishing the eighth grade and went to work bottling water at Bethel Springs. This company sold pure spring water and fruit flavored soft drinks in a three state area. Here Bill worked for 35¢ an hour, filling large five gallon glass bottles with spring water. That summer he met two other young men, Bob Miles and Albert (Ike) McCann while working at the Springs. The three boys soon became close pals. These two buddies were the first real friends Bill ever had.

In July of 1941 Bill received his driver's license and Mr. Smith, the owner of Bethel Springs, let him drive one of the company trucks. Bob Miles fondly remembers the many trips to Ocean City, Rehoboth and the many sea-side hotels he and Bill would deliver their spring water to. *"Bill was an awful driver, you took your life in your hands when you rode with him. I don't know why Mr. Smith ever let him drive those big trucks."* Bill's old hot-rod, a 1935 Plymouth was named "Curly Fenders" by his buddies in honor of his near disastrous driving skills.

Bill's new found popularity among the girls was also noticed by his two friends. Where Bill tended to be a bit shy around adults and most other guys, with the local young ladies he was considered quite bold. He was even known to have kissed a few in public just for the hell of it! Bill had grown into a fine looking young man who towered over most of the other swains of Booth's Corner.

One very touching story about Bill Haley when he was about sixteen years old was fondly recalled by a former sweetheart. She is now married to a prominent Booth's Corner resident and this event remains one of the highlights of her teenage years. It also gives a unique insight into the psyche of the young man and his character.

"Billy came up to me after school one spring afternoon. He was driving one of the big old trucks from Bethel Springs. We talked for a few minutes while my girl friends, who were standing near by, giggled and whispered about us. Billy had his hands in his pockets and was drawing circles in the dirt with the toe of his boot when he asked me if I would go out with him on Friday night. All the girls had a big crush on him, and I was surprised he would ask me for a date. He was very polite, his mother had taught him good manners. She was an English lady. But I had heard he was quite a ladies man and could be very bold when he was alone with a girl. But I was sixteen, adventuresome, and a bit of a rebel myself. Besides, I had never been out with a boy who had a car! To the shock of myself and my girl friends I said yes, I would meet him in front of the firehall about six. A lot of the boys around here didn't think much about Billy, he got into a lot of fights. He smoked, drank and drove that old water truck through town like a locomotive, which didn't make him too popular with the grown-ups either. Everybody was talking about how crazy he was. I just thought he was showing off a bit. Well, I dared not tell my parents that I had a date with him! In fact, if my father knew I had a date with a boy in a car, he would have skinned me alive! They were very strict!

"That Friday night I met Billy and we drove over to Boothwyn. We went into the drug store and he ordered two large chocolate ice cream sodas! I was becoming a bit nervous because I had relatives here and didn't want to be seen, and it was in the Depression, and ice cream sodas cost a lot of money. I began to wonder what Billy was expecting for all this money he was spending on me! I had told myself I was just going to let him kiss me on the cheek when we said good-bye, if he was nice. I had also practiced several responses my girl friends shared with me, should Billy get too fresh! I thought I was ready to handle myself if things were to get out of control. I was a little bit scared, but my curiosity and sense of adventure seemed to push me along.

"After we finished our ice cream sodas, Billy drove to an isolated country road everybody called "Cherry Tree Lane". It was a notorious "lover's lane" back then. There were no houses, no lights, nobody around! Billy parked the car and sat there for a minute or two saying nothing. At least, I told myself, he didn't tell me he was out of gas. Again I started to get a little nervous—the suspense was killing me! He then turned toward me, without saying a word, and raised his right arm behind my head as if to pull me towards him. I think I just froze! I know I closed my eyes and in panic, locked my hands together in my lap, awaiting his powerful grip. But he didn't grab me. He didn't even touch me! In the dark, he was groping for his guitar which was behind me on the back seat!

He spent the next hour playing his guitar and singing me songs! One of my favorites was "You Are My Sunshine". I told him that he sang just like Gene Autry. He told me about his dreams of being "somebody" one day, and he didn't want to end up in a factory like his pa. He then put his guitar back on the back seat and started to drive me home. I asked him to drop me off at the Auction Mart instead. When we got back, Billy got out of the car and walked around and opened my door just like in the movies. His mother taught him some fine English manners. He then thanked me for a swell time. He looked a little embarrassed, as if he hadn't done something right. His hands were again in his pockets and he just looked down at the ground. He seemed so shy. It seemed to me odd, William Haley, Bethel's great cassanova shy! I don't know what got into me but I stretched up on my toes to reach his cheek and quickly kissed him. Then I ran home wishing I had given him a big hug.

"On Saturday, my girl friends wouldn't believe me when I told them Billy was the sweetest, kindest boy I had ever met. He was a real gentleman. He talked to me like I was important. In doing that, he made you feel important. That was his talent, the charming way which he made you feel good. As I look back now, it seems like he may have wanted to impress me. Well, he did and always has, and that was forty six summers ago! Billy has always been very special to me."

Haley family home near Johnson's Corner.

Late in 1941, William Haley Sr. purchased a modest four room cottage that had once been a chicken coop and five acres of land in Booth's Corner near the intersection of Bethel and Foulk Roads. This property lay just behind the old one-room school house on the corner. For several years before this, the Haleys had been renting a small white-frame house about four miles away, near the Brandywine Summit Camp, just off Beaver Vally Road. Bill had attended the Johnson's Corner school on Concord Pike with his sister Peggy.

Bill's father, true to his hillbilly heritage, had cleared off several acres and planted a sizeable garden. He raised a variety of vegetables and several hundred chickens. The excess produce, poultry and eggs were sold to supplement the income he earned working at the American Viscose rayon factory in Marcus Hook.

Florence Appel, their neighbor, was Peggy Haley's best friend. The two girls were the same age and walked the half-mile together to school each day, with Billy usually tagging along. Florence remembers Bill often practising with his guitar on the side porch of their home and Mrs. Haley calling out many times: *"Billy, did you feed the chickens yet?"*

Haley family home on Foulk Road, Booth's Corner.

Bill Haley, with some prodding from friends, entered the Siloam Methodist Church's "Amateur Musical Contest". This event was one of the highlights of the Church's social season. It was held upstairs in the old Redmen's Lodge Hall, just across Foulk Road from the Siloam Cemetery. Here, Bill Haley found himself and Frank Gray in a tie for first place. The judges asked each boy to play his best tune so they could decide the winner. The great two-story wooden hall had over a hundred and fifty in the audience, mostly parents and friends. Frank Gray recalls: *"I was so nervous my mouth was almost too dry to blow on my harmonica, but Bill was worse off than me. He had cracked his guitar falling off his bicycle that afternoon and it sounded none too good. He also said two of his strings got busted when he went to visit the outhouse during break. Well, when the time come, I went out there and played my best tune, "The Wreck of the Old*

97". Bill went on after me and was so nervous he forgot the words to his song. So he just tried to play some old hillbilly tune with only four strings on that cracked guitar. He didn't sound none too good at all. That was my one claim to fame, the day I beat out Bill Haley in a talent contest. Boy, was I glad he couldn't sing so good that night! Years later, when he was a big star, we would joke about him losing out to me that night. Then one day he came up to me at the fire hall and said he might not have lost if "someone" hadn't cut his guitar strings! Boy, that really floored me—how did he find out about that?"

The loss must have been a major disappointment for Bill, for it would be two years before he would get up the courage to play in public again.

The Japanese attack on Pearl Harbor in December created a great outpouring of patriotic fervor in the little village of Booth's Corner as well as the rest of the nation. Every able-bodied young man wanted to get into uniform. Bill and his two friends Bob and Ike were no exceptions. The three friends could not wait to sign up as soon as they were of age. They would talk for hours about their friends in the service and worry that the war might be over before they got a chance to fight.

In January of 1942, the three close friends quit their jobs at Bethel Springs and went to work for 50¢ an hour at another local firm, A.H.Wirtz Co. This company manufactured bakelite air craft parts at the time. This job lasted only a few months due to some misguided, youthful highjinks. Bill and his two buddies were fired for locking their male supervisor in the ladies room. When Bob Miles was asked *"What was the supervisor doing in the ladies room?"* he mischievously smiled and answered, *"I guess he was looking for us. He was ALWAYS looking for us!"*

One night several months later, Bill and Bob Miles were drag-racing their souped-up hot rods down Chester Pike near Darby. Bill's car lost control on a sharp turn, jumped the curb, and blew out all four tires before landing in a grassy ravine. Bill, quite shaken, asked his girl friend if she was hurt. The terrified young girl just cried hysterically. Bob pulled his car over and ran back to check on his friends.

The next morning he drove Bill back to the car and helped him replace the four blown tires. Always short on cash, Bill had stopped at an auto salvage yard and bought a set of used tires and wheels. After the car was returned to the road Bill turned to Bob and said: *"Next time I'll beat ya!" "That'll be the day"*, Bob laughed. He knew with the girls Bill was the champ, but with cars, Bill Haley was a one man destruction derby. Bob would also say, *"the day Bill Haley got his driver's license, the people of Booth's Corner began walking on the telephone lines! Boy, did Bill like to drive fast. I don't know anybody who liked to drive as much as Bill."*

Soon after, all three boys found work in the massive Baldwin Locomotive Works in Eddystone, Pa. On weekends they often cruised the streets of Chester in one of their old cars looking for adventure. It has always been perceived by the young men of small towns that city girls were a bit more accommodating than their country cousins. This universal piece of wisdom drove Bill Haley and his two companions to the bright lights of Chester on many a Saturday night. This bustling city became the magnet for many of their amorous sorties. Bill would usually sit in the back seat and play his guitar. If they got lucky and found a couple of girls willing to be seen with a bunch of country boys, Bill would sing one of his best songs to break the ice. His quiet country charm, good looks and singing ability proved to be irresistible, even to the city girls. Both Bob and Ike recall, *"Bill had a way with girls, like he always knew what to say, and when to say it."*

Six months later Ike McCann was called for service in the Army, and Bob Miles shortly after, into the Marines. Bill, who tried to enlist, was rejected due to his blind eye. He argued with the recruiting officer that he could fight as good as any man, with one eye and one arm tied behind his back but the Army was not impressed with Bill Haley's bravado. They told him to go home and become an umpire! This was a bitter disappointment to him, as he watched his two best friends leave for combat duty; Ike in Europe and Bob in the Pacific. In hurt or in anger Bill took a train as far as his money would take him, three hundred miles to the city of Wheeling, West Virginia. Here, using his middle names, John Clifton, he tried to join the Marines. He again failed the eye examination and was given a second 4F rating. He returned home eight days later, feeling completely useless. He would later say: *"This was one of the lowest points in my life, I felt devastated!"* The reality of his handicap hit home for the first time. Bill felt he was being punished because of an error made by a clumsy doctor so many years ago in Detroit. He now viewed his semi-blindness as not just an embarrassment but as a hated curse. His always fragile self-esteem now fell to a new low. He missed his two best friends and all the good times they had shared. He wrote them many times and would read their letters from the battlefields of Europe and the South Pacific over and over. When

Bob Miles in his Marine uniform.

Bob Miles was shot while fighting in an island jungle, Bill was the only person he told back home. Bob later recovered from his wounds and never did tell his parents or his wife of his injury. Bill also hated it when people would ask him: *"Why is a fine young man like you not in the service?"*

With the war in high gear, the Baldwin factory produced the tanks and great locomotives which pulled America's trains, so vital to the war effort. Due to his large frame and poor eyesight, Bill was given the job of tightening the large three-inch bolts on the boilers, a task requiring great strength and stamina. His massive steel open-end wrench weighed over ten pounds. He became very proud of his work in the defense plant and was glad he could contribute something to the war effort.

His many hours of overtime often extended long into the night. Proudly he would show his calloused hands to his girl friends. America also needed good, strong men in her factories as well as in her armies and this helped the seventeen year old Bill Haley come to terms with himself and his handicap.

In the summer of 1943, another little noticed event would forever alter the direction of Bill Haley's life and set him on a course seeking his fame and fortune as a Country-Western singer.

In Booth's Corner at this time was a unique institution called the "Sale" by all the locals. Its full name was the Booth's Corner Auction Mart and was founded in 1932 by George Phillips. Here, every Friday from noon to midnight, thousands of shoppers, merchants, farmers, con-men and the curious would gather to buy, sell or just exchange the latest news and gossip of the week.

In the center of this vast assembly was a great wooden barn full of little stalls filled with every conceivable type of merchandise one could ever want. Attached to this large barn were more "in-door" stands. These were rented out for three to five dollars a day. Outside of this rambling complex of sheds, other "outside" merchants sold their wares from the ground or off the back of trucks or wagons. They each paid Mr. Phillips a dollar for the privilege.

The whole affair resembled a combined carnival, country auction and flea market all rolled into one. Here you could buy almost anything from live chickens, hogs, cattle and sheep to fresh baked Amish breads, cakes and pies. The farmers came to sell their produce by the bushel or the pound and buy needed tools, clothing and other necessities.

Other "merchants" offered gold-plated trinkets, girly magazines, miracle hair tonics or the latest in genuine snake oil, guaranteed to cure anything that ailed you if you could down a couple of swigs a day! Word had it from many of the old-timers that if you could drink a bottle of the "tonic" a day, you wouldn't care what ailed you!

The tantalizing aromas of barbecued chicken, fresh roasting peanuts, popcorn and red candy apples filled the air along with the sounds of children and adults trying their luck at the games of chance or testing the latest rides.

Thus, "Meet you at the Sale" was a common phrase as friends and neighbors made this Friday night ritual the main attraction in Bethel Township. Attracted to this boisterous, colorful atmosphere was Bill Haley. In fact, he was one of the regulars and in his earlier days had often picked up some extra money unloading the large produce trucks for a quarter. During the holidays, he even sold Christmas trees with Earl Phillips, the owner's colorful son.

Sometimes, Bill Ormsby, the crusty old assistant manager and head maintenance man, would hire Bill and a couple of other boys to clean up around the market grounds and burn the trash on Saturday mornings. Little did Bill know that this vibrant country market would offer him his first opportunity to become the cowboy singer he had been secretly dreaming of. It was in this noisy, circus-like atmosphere that the seventeen year old Bill Haley would first perform in public for an audience of over a thousand—although he would not even be aware of it!

Throughout the market, hung from its wooden rafters and strung through several large oak trees, were a series of loudspeakers. The merchants used them to call out their many specials during the day.

Bill Ormsby would also announce baseball scores, local events, lost kids, or just "Jacob McKay, your father says to get back to the wagon or you're walking home!"

The microphone for this system was in the market's office. One evening the wily Ormsby, as a practical joke, invited the shy young Haley into this room on the pretext of wanting to hear this great voice he was supposed to have. Ormsby knew Bill could play the guitar, but he had never heard him sing. For an inducement of ten cents, Ormsby coaxed the bashful young man to sing him a song, in the total privacy of his office. Unknown to Bill, Ormsby had turned on the microphone and had quietly spread the word to the market's denizens of Bill Haley's debut.

Bill sat down in one of the old wooden chairs, unslung his guitar, and strummed several chords. He had known Ormsby for years and was a little flattered this old boss had asked him to sing. Plus nobody ever paid him to sing before and ten cents is ten cents! Ormsby asked Bill if he knew *Has Anybody Seen My Gal?* Bill not only played that song but followed it up with the beautiful ballad *My Old Kentucky Home*. Bill sang both songs with such skill and feeling that Ormsby was very impressed. His practical joke had backfired, for the kid really could sing! Many people in the market that evening thought the radio was on and Gene Autry was singing.

That night Bill found himself sort of a celebrity and a "somebody" for the first time in his life. People came up to him and wanted to shake his hand. Over six feet tall, dressed in his straw cowboy hat and boots and holding a green guitar, Bill Haley was easy to spot. Ormsby gave him a big slap on the back and told him he had real talent. He also said he ought to share it and not be so shy about it.

Bill had made such a hit that the following Friday night Mr. Phillips told him he would pay him a silver dollar to sing a few songs to gather the crowd for his big auction. Bill Haley's natural shyness gave way to a greater need, the burning desire to be recognized as somebody special. This could be what he had prayed for! They actually wanted him to perform for their customers!

Within a month he was standing on a stage made of two old wooden tables set up under the great oak tree, out in front of the market. A long string of naked lightbulbs dangled from its lower branches attracting squadrons of moths and mosquitoes in their haze. Here, with a big grin, Bill would sing and play his guitar for about half an hour to gather the curious crowd.

These early performances were remembered by many local residents as being long on enthusiasm and a bit short on "stage presence". Bill's awkwardness was translated in his stiff delivery. His large "farm hand" frame never seem to quite move in rhythm to his music, but his youthful innocence and warm country voice won over many in the passing crowds.

As his popularity grew and hundreds gathered to hear him sing, Bill summoned up the courage and told Mr. Phillips that one dollar was not much, considering the crowds he was drawing. After much soul searching, breast beating and heated discussion, Phillips agreed to a much deserved raise.

Bill Haley had successfully negotiated his first professional contract! He ran home full of excitement *"Ma, Mr. Phillips is going to pay me three dollars to sing for a half hour, they must think I'm pretty good!"* Mrs. Haley encourage her beloved son in this new adventure. She saw in him a new found confidence and a sense of excitement when he was performing before people. She was often heard saying: *"Singing is good for my Billy"*.

By fall his fee had risen to five dollars for an hour performance as Bill became a very popular, regular attraction for the market. Many residents still remember him strolling down the crowded hallways of the market playing his guitar. His dream of being a singing cowboy had come true even if his stage was often an old wooden table or the back of a flatbed truck. Who cared if he had to sell a few watermelons or sacks of potatoes to the crowd afterwards. People could buy their produce anywhere, but they came here to hear the kid from Booth's Corner who sounded just like Gene Autry!

Deep in the woods behind his parent's home one can almost hear the excited, exuberant youth yelling out to his silent audience of trees:

"look out world, here I come!"

Bill and Pop Guthrie
Performing at "the Sale"

CHAPTER TWO

THE DREAM BECOMES REALITY: 1943-1944

"In smilin', singin' and clownin' a boy finds his way."

By September of 1943, the eighteen year old Bill Haley had become a real, certified singing cowboy—at least in appearance. He now sported a white, ten gallon hat, a fancy pair of western boots and a bright red cowboy suit with white fringe and trimmings that would bring tears to a Montana Santa Claus. His detractors would call him a "phony drug store cowboy" and taunt him, *"Hey dude, where did you park your horse?"* Sometimes they had even been known to throw tomatoes at him when he was performing, but woe to he who was seen. Disrespect to an American cowboy in full uniform was like spitting on the American flag, to Bill's way of thinking. More than one obnoxious critic suffered a black eye and a physical, if not moral, lesson in manners for his insolence. Behind Bill's baby face, quiet country manners and soft tenor voice was a fist of iron if you were foolish enough to get his dander up!

Bill's second-hand cowboy outfit was custom-made by Rodeo Ben who operated one of the most famous western-wear emporiums in the East. This was the same Philadelphia tailoring establishment that outfitted Roy Rogers, Gene Autry and a host of other country-western entertainers of the day. A gaily embroidered and appliqued western outfit with contrasting piping and fringe could cost over three times that of a custom-made business suit. Bill wore his "cowboy" suit with all the pride of a U.S. Marine.

From his make-shift stage at the Booth's Corner Market, Bill Haley began to receive many offers to play on week-ends at birthday parties, picnics and church events. He also began to attract about him a group of other talented friends who helped him with his growing number of engagements.

These young people, from fourteen to seventeen years old, formed a loose group which Bill could call upon when needed. He named them his "Texas Range Riders". Bill Gray would play the fiddle, Dorothy Heavlow the accordion and George Gray, Ray McCann or Duke Snow the guitar. Seldom did this band of enthusiastic amateurs ever get the opportunity to all play together as a group. However, each remembers his little shows with Bill with great fondness.

Although Bill would get from three to five dollars a performance, he usually paid off his helpers in cigarettes, candy or a wild ride in his battered-up old car. A big hug and a kiss on the cheek would usually suffice for the girls. As Duke Snow would say: *"We played many times just for the fun of it. We all looked up to him. To us kids he was already a big star."*

One older partner many customers remember playing with Bill was an old carpenter named Ben "Pop" Guthrie. The sight of the teenage Bill Haley playing his guitar, acting as straight man, and singing to the accompaniment of Guthrie's "fancy fiddling" was a real treat to many of the Friday night shoppers. Ben Guthrie's influence with his young protege would have far reaching consequences.

Guthrie taught the eager youngster how to break up his singing routine with some old-fashioned, country-style humor. The old man was a veteran of many years with the earthy minstrel shows. Many old-timers still remember with a chuckle the "put-ons" Bill and Pop Guthrie would perform. They always seemed to be fussin' or cutting each other up.

Bill would climb up on the wooden tables, which were his stage, and help Guthrie up with a pull of his big hand. They would then play a real fast tune like *She'll Be Coming Round The Mountain* to get the crowd's attention. Then Bill, holding his cowboy hat in his hand, would say to the passing crowd, *"Good evening everybody, my name is Bill Haley-and I'm gonna play y'all some music with my boy here"*, waving his hat towards old Pop Guthrie. The gathering crowd would laugh at the suggestion, as the two performers went into another fast tempo tune.

At this point Pop Guthrie would usually crack a joke about Bill's playing ability. A typical remark would be, *"My grannie can play faster than him and she's been dead for eight years."* Guthrie would sometimes speed up his fiddling till it was a faster tempo than Bill's guitar pickin'. Bill would come back with: *"Pop, I hear tell you is always brushing your teeth with gun powder!"* To which Guthrie would mockingly frown and reply: *"Why do you say that, boy?"* Then Bill, with his big grin, would say to the audience: *"Cause you is always shootin' off your mouth!"* The crowd would laugh and clap their hands. They now would number about two to three hundred. After another tune or two, Guthrie would ask Bill if he was getting a little tired trying to keep up with him. He would then offer the younger man an old wooden chair which was usually kept in the market office. Bill would thank him profusely, wiping his brow as he made a big production of sitting down for a well earned rest. Then, as Guthrie grinned at the audience like he was going to pull something, Bill would bolt out of the chair holding his butt as if he were stung by a bee! The crowd would roar as the old fiddler removed an imaginary thumbtack from the chair. As Bill continued to jump about the stage, Pop would go into their next song. Bill would mumble to the audience, as Pop grinned, *"If you can't even trust your partner, who can you trust?"* No one ever knew who was having more fun, the audience or these two zany mis-matched country clowns. The colorful Haley-Guthrie routines remain fond memories of many of the old-time residents of Booth's Corner.

Another comic routine Bill would sometimes do when he performed solo was to stop abruptly right in the middle of a tune after deliberately making an error. With a quizzical look on his face he would examine his guitar and then closely look at his fingers. His actions would draw the curious attention of the audience. He seemed oblivious to them as he pretended to chew off his nails. Using several small pieces of cardboard he had earlier placed in his mouth, he would spit out the "fingernails" and shyly look up and say: *"I was wondering why I was playing so bad."* Again the crowd of country folk would break into side-splitting laughter. There was no pretense of glory here, just plain old down home humor and good old country music. Bill Haley's love of hillbilly slapstick comedy would be an intrinsic part of his stage shows for the next thirty years.

These little put-ons were the seeds of the great showmanship Bill would later develop with his world famous Comets. Many believe Bill found a safe retreat in comedy. This was a place he could hide, should the audience ever find out his perceived shortcomings as a musician. Thus, at this point in his career, we find a young, inexperienced but talented singer and musician, hiding in the gimmicky guise of the clowning, hillbilly guitar picker.

Bill continued to work weekdays at the Baldwin Works for 75¢ an hour, but he eagerly awaited the coming of each weekend. The small fees he collected for his performances only seemed to fire his desire to one day really be somebody important. For now, he would bask in the admiration on the faces of his audience.

By the autumn of 1943, Bill had come to the notice of Arlee Ellsworth, a former prize-fighter, miner and evangelist with the Billy Sunday and Aimee McPherson tent shows. Professionally, the colorful Ellsworth was now heading a very popular seven-member country-western band known as "Cousin Lee and His Boys". He also had his own twice-daily radio show on WDEL in nearby Wilmington, Delaware. On Sundays, he operated the very successful "Cousin Lee's Radio Park" which he founded a mile down the road from Booth's Corner Auction Mart. To the locals, this was their equivalent to the "Grand Ole Opry".

Radio Park was one of a half dozen small amusement parks which dotted the Delaware River Valley during the war years. They were Meccas for music-loving families on Sunday afternoons from May till October. The mainstay of these parks were concerts featuring well known Country and Western bands as well as popular stars of Nashville and Hollywood. The term "Country-Western" was not used in the mid-1940's. At this time, this type of music was referred to as either "Hillbilly" or "Cowboy" music. Stars like Tex Ritter, Gene Autry and Roy Rogers would croon "Cowboy" songs, while artists like Jesse Rogers, Hank Williams and Hankshaw Hawkins would usually sing "Hillbilly" tunes. Along with these headliners, Cousin Lee would invite talented local artists to fill out the program.

Many families would bring their picnics, sit on the ground and listen to the entertainment. They could also sit on rows of wooden benches arranged in front of the stage. For the admission of 50¢, they could hear some of the best cowboy and hillbilly music in America. One could have a treasured picture taken with stars like Roy Rogers or Hank Williams or talk to many other favorite personalities who walked about the park to meet their fans. You could also buy at one of the concession stands western novelties and photographs of the stars. These were sold by a thin, young man named Jack Howard. In the years to come, Jack Howard was to help promote and manage Bill Haley's career. The two men would become life-long friends and business partners.

Years later Howard recalled in the Comet Fan Club News how he first met Bill Haley: *"I was doing publicity work for Cousin Lee...and I happened to come across a young lad working behind a baseball pitch concession stand (at Radio Park) who had the friendliest smile I had ever encountered....it was this*

©DAP

Cousin Lee (between girls) and his band.

winning personality smile that started a friendship that never ended. I stood watching this young fellow time and time again, until one day I decided to strike up a conversation with him, only to find that this personality went a lot deeper than just a smile. It was only a short time before I learned that he could sing and play the guitar. He invited me to visit him at his home one evening when he had to perform at a country market place. It was really a surprise to hear this fellow sing and entertain the folks who came each week to do their marketing.

"With my enthusiasm, I went back to the park operator (Cousin Lee) and finally convinced him to give Bill a chance to perform on his stage. I can still remember it to this day over 10,000 people had come to see the first appearance in the East of Roy Rogers and the Sons of the Pioneers in person... Bill was called up to do a few numbers. He was so excited and elated that he had a hard time trying to make the words come out, but, after the first couple of lines he began to feel that 10,000 people were no different than a hundred".

Bill Haley had been to Radio Park many times to work or be part of the audience, but on this day he was going to perform. That raised platform, standing in the shade of those tall whispering pines, must have seemed like a shrine to the young man. In the crowd that assembled on that beautiful Indian-summer afternoon were his proud parents and most of the population of Bethel Township. Most of them came to see the famous movie star Roy Rogers, but a few waited for Bill's turn on the stage with great expectation. Some came to applaud their hometown boy, who now shared the old wooden stage made sacred by the shoe leather of Elton Britt, Red Foley and Hank Williams. However others, much to the nature of human cruelty, came to watch him be humiliated by the real pros. For now he stood with the legends of Nashville and Hollywood, and not plucking a guitar so he could hustle a crowd to sell sacks of potatoes or melons. Those who wished Bill no good will, be it from jealousy or envy, could remember with sly smiles his other disastrous debut at the Siloam Church's

Dorothy Crowe, age 18, Bill's first love. ©DAP

TONIGHT

DANCING

8:30 P. M.—12 MIDNIGHT

PARISH HOUSE

MUSIC BY

COUSIN LEE AND BOYS

No One Allowed on Dance Floor Dressed In Work Clothes

Admission 50c

amateur contest. They waited with glee for the big boys to show this local yokel how it's really done. Besides, who did he think he was anyway, his father wern't nuttin' but a part-time chicken farmer and everybody these parts knowed Bill Haley was nuttin' but a phony, one-eyed, drug-store cowboy!

Bill Haley's performance that Sunday afternoon at Radio Park was a stunner! After a rough start, he surprised both friend and foe alike. His clear diction and self-taught style of yodeling on several western ballads was a real crowd-pleaser. He sang with an air of confidence most people had never seen before. When it was all over Roy Rogers personally came up on the stage with Cousin Lee and congratulated Bill, shaking his hand before thousands in admiration.

Bill Haley found his path to glory that day. On that crude wooden stage he felt he was king of the world. A sense of pride and power he could not explain came over him like a magic spell. Bill discovered he had the ability to entertain thousands! The applause and praise given after his performance dispelled any second-thoughts he may have had and the shrewd Cousin Lee, with a good eye for new talent, quickly signed the eighteen year old lad to a one year contract at $40.00 a week. That was ten whole dollars a week more than he was making tightening bolts at Baldwins!

Bill became a regular with Cousin Lee's band and spent much of the next year traveling throughout Delaware, Maryland, New Jersey and Pennsylvania. He quit his job at the Baldwin plant and from this time on performed on a full time basis.

During most of this time eighteen year old Bill played all the numerous parks in the tri-state area, such as Sunset, Rainbow, Riverside and Lenape Parks, or the 101, Sleepy Hollow and Circle A Ranches. He shared the stage with the best in the business. During the winter months the band played in any hall that could accommodate over a hundred people. The popularity of Cousin Lee's band left the boys little free time, and since they were on salary, the shrewd Ellsworth kept them on a very tight schedule.

It was at one of these Saturday night dances, in the old Parish Hall in Salem, New Jersey, that Bill met the first great love of his life, Dorothy Crowe. That night is remembered by Peggy White, whose best friend Dorothy had attracted the attention of Bill's winks from the stage. Both girls were extraordinarily beautiful, but the dark-haired, half-Crow Indian Dorothy became the object of Bill's interest.

After the dance, Bill, Dorothy, Peggy and her date all went out together. Peggy recalls: *"I think the two of them fell in love that night. 'Dottie', as we all called her, was only seventeen and still in High School. Bill told Dottie he was going to make it big one day, and everybody was going to know his name. We all laughed, but Dottie was so much in love with her singing cowboy she floated on air from then to the day they were married two years later. Bill was very handsome in his white stetson.*

He had such great manners and a warm personality. He was her Prince Charming—there was never a question about that. He would call her from wherever he was playing and we would go sometimes fifty miles to watch him play. When he smiled at you, it made you feel good all over. And how he could talk! He made his dreams become your dreams."

That year, with the help of Cousin Lee, Bill polished his style and added a great deal of material to his repertoire. Cousin Lee also had a bad eye and maybe in sympathy took the promising young performer under his wing. He used Bill's self-taught yodeling skills as an important facet of his show and featured his new singing star as "Silver Yodeling Bill".

Many local residents recall watching Bill sing Cousin Lee's theme song *Keep Smiling* with his big boyish grin. Bill Haley became known as the smilingest cowboy in the band as he belted out the prophetic words:

When ev'ry thing goes wrong, keep smiling
When ev'ry thing goes wrong, just laugh
Throw back your shoulder, stick out your chin
Long as you can smile, you're bound to win.

When ev'ry thing goes wrong, keep happy
Never let your troubles get you down
Ev'ry thing will be all right
And this old world will look bright
If you can smile, smile, smile.

With this new handle, Bill dreamed of becoming one of the circuit's best yodelers. One Sunday afternoon at Radio Park he met the great Elton Britt. Elton was considered one of the finest yodelers in the nation. As Bill listened to him from the side of the stage, he was in awe of Britt's ability to create even the most difficult trick yodels with such ease. After the show Bill approached the master and asked him for some advice, pointing out that he was a yodeler also.

Duke Snow, who was there at the time, recalled: *"Bill was standing there, with some beer in a paper cup, asking Elton for some advice when Britt said: Son, never drink beer if you want to be a good yodeler. It gives you gas. A first class yodeler only drinks whiskey! And if you can't afford good whiskey, drink port wine!"*. Duke recalled that from then on he never saw Bill Haley drink a beer before a performance. The fear of making a fool of himself on stage and destroying his career with one loud and mighty burp was enough to cause Bill to heed Britt's good advice.

"Brother Wayne" ©DAP

During his tenure with Cousin Lee, Bill was befriended by Wayne Wright, the band's fiddler. Under the stage name "Brother Wayne" this slightly older, quiet and gentle North Carolinian became the closest thing Bill ever had to a big brother. Brother Wayne was well known for his warm smile and hearty handshakes. His fellow musicians said he could play the violin with the skill of a concert virtuoso.

Wright took "a likin" to the younger Bill Haley and invited him to co-host his half hour country-western radio show on WSNJ in Bridgeton, New Jersey. He taught his new friend the finer points of radio broadcasting—a skill Bill would fall back on many times in the future. The careers of these two musicians would often intertwine over the next five years. When Bill was down and out, it was Brother Wayne and his gracious wife Dottie who offered the struggling young entertainer a home-cooked meal and a bed many a night.

By early 1945, Bill was itching to break away from Cousin Lee's local country-western circuit and go for the big time. He also felt his pay was not in line with his contributions as the "kid star" of the band.

Just after Christmas, Bill received word that Kenny Roberts was being drafted by the Navy. Roberts was the lead singer and yodeler for a very popular Country-Western band called the Down Homers. Everett Hinderer, who used the stage name Shorty Cook, ran the outfit which was based out of Fort Wayne, Indiana. The Down Homers were broadcasted from station WOWO in Fort

Early ad (circa 1944)

Wayne. WOWO hosted a very popular country-style hoedown on Saturday nights called the Hoosier Hop at the Quimby Auditorium. The Hoosier Hop was recorded and later broadcasted Tuesday nights nationwide by the ABC network.

This was the opportunity Bill wanted—a chance to yodel and sing with a famous band and be heard across the nation.

Bill, never one to save much money, asked his sweetheart Dottie for a loan so he could go and audition for Kenny Roberts' place. He told her this was his chance to break into the big time and really become somebody.

Dorothy by now had graduated from Salem High School and was working in the office for the du Pont Company at their nearby Deepwater plant. She was still living at home with her father, John Crowe, a police officer in her home town of Salem. Dorothy had always been very close to her father. He was a proud, honest and caring man. He was the most decorated veteran of WW I in his county. For valor in France he received, among many other awards, the American Distinguished Service Cross and the French Croix de Guerre. As the district commander of the V.F.W. and the American Legion, Dottie's father was a true hero and a highly respected public figure.

John Crowe took a dim view of his daughter's infatuation with an itinerant, guitar-playing musician. Very much against her father's wishes, Dottie loaned Bill the money he needed. Bill promised to return rich and famous and marry her. The eager young woman now joined millions of other wartime romantics as she waited the return of her sweetheart, for sometimes both soldiers and aspiring musicians seek glory and fame in foreign fields.

Brother Wayne and Bill Haley at WSNJ.

CHAPTER THREE

THE ODYSSEY: 1945-1946

"Few become Prophets in their own lands."

Kenny Roberts

With an enthusiasm born of great expectations, Bill auditioned for Shorty Cook and was hired on the spot, joining the Down Homers on the road in Hartford, Connecticut. He worked with Kenny Roberts for a week learning as quickly as he could. Not only would he have to sing in high tenor and yodel in Roberts' style, he also had to learn to play Roberts' bass fiddle.

Bill's ear for music and basic intelligence impressed both Roberts and Cook, as he became a valued member of the Down Homers. Bill would write home to his sister: *"Listen Tuesday night to the Hoosier Hop—I'm going to be singing and yodeling and they're going to be hearing me from New York to California!"*

Bill Haley, as a member of the Down Homers and later the Range Drifters, began a two year odyssey which took him from Chicago to New Orleans, and New England to St. Louis. These travels exposed Bill's ear to the unique beats and rhythms of America's diverse regions. These hard-driving, rich and vibrant musical forms awed and excited him. His talented ear for music mentally recorded each new sound, and his one good eye, the techniques required to create it.

In late 1945, Shorty Cook signed a deal with Tom Saffady, President of the newly founded Vogue Recording Company of Detroit, Michigan. Saffady had invented a unique process which could produce a colorful picture within a 78 rpm record. His artists created beautiful full-color "mood-scenes" for each side. A small, black and white photograph of the performers would then be worked into the picture discs like a tiny cameo. These early picture discs were to be Bill Haley's and the Down Homers' first records.

On January 27, 1946 the Down Homers recorded five tunes for their first record contract: *Out Where The West Wind Blows/You'll Come Walking Back/Who's Gonna Kiss You When I'm Gone/Boogie Woogie Yodel* and *Baby I Found Out All About You*. On the two records which were eventually released Bill played rhythm guitar. Kenny Roberts had returned from the Navy and did the yodelling. These early 78 rpm Vogue recordings of Bill Haley with the Down Homers are among the rarest of Haley's country-western discs. They bring in bids of over $500.00 from savvy record collectors.

Bill Haley's first records; Vogue picture disc.

The DownHomers, left to right; Bill Haley, Shorty Cook, Bob Mason, Guy Campbell and Lloyd Cornell.

It was with the Down Homers that Bill wrote his first cowboy ballad, co-authored with Shorty Cook, *Four Leaf Clover Blues*:

I'm just a hard-luck gambler
whose luck is running bad
I'm just a hard-luck gambler
whose mighty blue and sad

I've got the four leaf clover blues
I've got the four leaf clover blues
I want to gamble all the time and never, never lose

Want to roll them bones, and hear the losers moan
Cause baby needs a new pair of shoes
I'm a wild and reckless gambling man
Got the four leaf clover blues
Hey, got the four leaf clover blues

You can have your poker games
You can have your dice
I'll take my four leaf clover
and gamble all my life

Don't want wealth or riches
I don't want grief or strife
I'll take my four leaf clover
and gamble all my life

I'll travel over this country
I just keep rovin' on
If I lose my four leaf clover
I'll know my luck is gone

I've got the four leaf clover blues
Hey, got the four leaf clover blues

Bill Haley as he appeared on a DownHomer song book, age 20. ©DAP

Bill would record the tune later in 1948 with one of his own bands. This would be the first of more than 150 songs he would write or co-write over the next thirty-five years.

The Range Drifters, left to right; Brother Wayne, Bill Haley, Bob Mason and Lloyd Cornell.

In early 1946, after a year with the Down Homers, the ever-ambitious Bill believed he was ready for his own band. He figured he could play just about every popular cowboy tune known, over three hundred by his own count. He had three solid years of experience behind him and soon realized that he couldn't get rich playing in other people's bands. He had also promised his sweetheart, back in Salem, New Jersey, that he was going to be a star and so far he was still just another hired hand in Shorty Cook's band.

He proceeded to form his own band. Unfortunately, he started with two other ambitious musicians in Shorty's band, Bob Mason and Lloyd Cornell. After a stormy confrontation with Shorty over salary, Bill and the other two band members quit. Shorty was furious.

With high hopes and visions born of youth, Bill and his new partners named their band "The Range Drifters". For the fourth member, they recruited Bill's old radio partner Wayne Wright (Brother Wayne) from whom Bill had been renting a room in nearby Tuscola, Ill. The all string band consisted of a rhythm and lead guitarist, a fiddler and a bassist.

In Chicago, Brother Wayne found a spot for the group on WLS's "National Barn Dance" road show. Here Bill got the opportunity to play with stars like Lulu Belle and Scotty and his idols Red Foley and Hank Williams. Both artists gave Bill welcomed advice on show business and many of its finer points. Bill is remembered as "a nice, amiable kid forever asking questions." Red Foley, who took the young yodeller under his wing, made a strong impression on the young man. Foley came from the same hill country in Kentucky as Bill's father. Bill soon adopted Foley's easy style of singing country ballads.

The band left Chicago in the spring of 1946 and began touring without much success. They found getting work more difficult than doing it. Plus Shorty Cook had put out the word on the "band jumpers" and Shorty had a lot of friends in this neck of the woods.

During this time Bill would realize another lifelong dream of being a champion yodeler by winning the 1946 Indiana State Fair's Yodelling Championship. This award would one day be displayed proudly with all his gold records and international awards on the wall of his basement den at Melody Manor.

To get away from Cook's influence, the band, minus Brother Wayne, headed south to the honkytonks of the Oklahoma oil fields, where one of the boys were from. Times were hard in the country at the time. Millions of men were being discharged from the service and jobs were few and far between. Working for as little as $20 a night, the band often lived on canned beans, black coffee and soda crackers. Bill quickly learned the hard side of the itinerant, country-western musician and the dangers of the loose women who haunted their nocturnal lives.

To make ends meet, they bummed precious cigarettes and shots of whiskey off drunken fans and the ever present peroxide-blondes Bill was attracted to. More than once they had to sneak out of their cheap hotel rooms early in the morning to avoid angry husbands, sheriffs or their overdue rent.

Bill, now just twenty-one years old, discovers early the wild side of life, that free booze and the always-available illicit sex are just some of the many "fringe benefits" for a fast-moving, hard-drinking band of good-looking, singing cowboys.

Here in the rough, red-neck bars of Tulsa, Bill found his slow country ballads and the syrupy Yankee-style cowboy music out of place. Besides, the patrons had the bad habit of throwing their empty beer bottles at the band. When Bill complained to one of the bar owners, he was told he should be glad the customers don't hate his music, cause then the beer bottles they throw would be full!

These hard working, hard drinking, oil-soaked roustabouts wanted their country music with a jazzy, hard edge on it. They didn't come to hear no lullabies from a bunch of yankees! Bill quickly adapted to the mongrel, jazz-hillbilly sound made famous by artist like Bob Wills and his Texas Playboys.

After their experiences in Oklahoma, the Range Drifters were glad to work for several weeks in the more refined atmosphere of St. Louis. At least here the audience didn't throw beer bottles at them.

Many evenings when the band wasn't playing, Bill would slip off and visit the legendary black jazz clubs of East St.Louis. The special "rhythm and blues" style unique to that city fascinated him. He also fell in love with the singing style of Lena Horne and collected her records for many years afterwards

It was here in St. Louis that Bill Haley first heard the live but mournful wail of the blues saxophone and the hypnotic rhythms of the black jazz artists. These performers struck him with a deep respect that he would hold for the rest of his life.

In Texas, Bill would encounter two other variations of country-western music. While playing in the San Antonio area the band would come across their first "Tex-Mex" style of Latin beat country music. Rich in the influence of the Spanish guitar, this vibrant, fast moving music was practically unknown, at this time, in most other parts of America.

Bill Haley, age 20, note the trademark cowlick on forehead.

Moving on to Dallas, the band would hear yet another form of cowboy music called "Western Swing". This was the Spade Cooley style of "Big Band" country music, a form of "cowboy jump" with a kick and drive in its beat that Bill loved to hear. Bill Haley was to later say that this Western Jump had a great influence in his later search for his "sound".

The band next headed for New Orleans. If Bill thought the music of St. Louis, Texas or Oklahoma was unique, this Cajun city, with its brazen Dixieland sounds, would awaken him to the power and vitality of another major regional American music. Bill loved Basin Street, its little jazz clubs and the spontaneity of its music. He would spend hours listening to the syncopated chorus of sounds and enjoy the pure celebration of its music. The drive and energy of this music curiously reminded him of his father's foot-stomping Kentucky mountain tunes which he and his family had played so many years ago.

Like an Old Testament prophet wandering in the wilderness in search of the meaning of life, Bill Haley's wanderings filled the great cauldron of his mind with the music heritages of the nation. His ear recorded all he heard, and for the first time in his life, he felt something was missing in the musical culture of many Americans. He felt a lot of people didn't know about the great variety and richness of the nation's many regional musical styles. How come he had never heard Dixieland or Cowboy-blues in his part of the country? There was something else missing. There was a music, a missing concept, an empty void, which gnawed at Bill's sub-conscious. In this vacuum, Bill Haley would one day create a sound that would encompass all the music styles before it. However, it would be four more years before he would be able to gather all its elements and create it, and with its power and energy harnessed, he would capture the imagination of the world.

Meanwhile, Bill left the Range Drifters. The lack of decent bookings, the in-fighting and arguments over the direction of the band's musical format took its toll. Bill felt they were becoming a third rate group and were going nowhere. His dream of a band that could encompass the best of many musical traditions faded away.

Out of money and confused about his own abilities and goals, the twenty one year old Bill Haley wandered about the American Mid-West doing an array of odd jobs from working on a dude ranch to singing for a meal in rowdy road house diners. One night, while "buskin" (playing for small change) before a small audience in a roadside cafe, Bill was asked by a man who called himself "Dr. Protheroe" to share his table. The gentleman ran a dubious traveling medicine show and was in need of a "drummer". Seeing the obviously hungry young musician, he asked Bill if he would like to work for him. The "Doctor" said he needed someone to drum up the crowd. To Bill this was just like what he used to do for the auction back in Booth's Corner. Bill was also in no position to be choosy. The next few weeks he found himself standing on the tailgate of a gaudy painted trailer playing his guitar and doing his comic gags to gather the crowd at small fairs and rural farmer's markets all over the mid-West. Old Doc Protheroe would then step out and begin to pitch his "Miraclé Tonic", which he told the audience helped this poor, little orphan boy, pointing to the ever-smiling, six foot, one hundred seventy pound Bill Haley, *"put some meat on his bones"*.

Many years later, when audiences of tens-of-thousands where sent into a frenzy by the thundering beat and pulsating rhythm of his music, Bill would recall this experience in a newspaper article for the London Daily Mirror: *"I wandered into a cafe to see whether they would let me play and sing in return for a square meal and in there I met a guy called Doc Protheroe. This Doc Protheroe was one of the old medicine showmen...he put on a show to gather a crowd and then sold them medicine.*

"The medicine he sold was good for anything from toothache to lumbago. The Doc was a pretty convincing fella and talker, and he staked me to a meal while we did a deal. If I could draw the customers, he said, we'd team up as a traveling show. I did an audition for him... never in my life have I been so anxious to make good...and we struck a bargain. So off we went with the caravan, round the countryside. Every place we saw a likely collection of people we would drop the back of the caravan and I'd begin to play and sing until the crowd gathered. Then the Doc would suddenly pitch in and sell them the magic cure for all their ills."

All went well until Bill, while mixing up some of the elixir, drank a bit too much of it and got too sick to perform. The good doctor dumped Bill along the road somewhere in western Ohio. Bewildered and ill from the effects of the oily mixture of molasses, sulfur, gin and other secret ingredients, Bill hopped a freight train and rode on the dangerous under-carriage to Fort Wayne, Indiana and asked Shorty Cook if he could rejoin the Downhomers.

According to Cook, *"Bill came knocking at my door late one night with his hat in his hand. His clothing was dirty, and he looked like something the cat dragged in. He told me he'd made a big mistake and wanted to know if I would take him back in the band. He said he'd do anything. I told him I thought he was a pretty good yodeler but his voice weren't all that great. With the war over, good country singers were a dime a dozen. He was all right singing with a bunch of guys, but on his own, he weren't no Hank Williams. He looked so bad, I loaned him forty bucks to go home and think about his future. I just didn't think he had the talent or the push to be anything special. He didn't just want to make a living, he wanted to be a star. This just goes to show you how much I know, but back in '46, Bill Haley weren't no stand up and knock' em dead performer."*

A gaunt and lean Bill Haley posing for a fan in the summer of 1946. ©DAP

CHAPTER FOUR

THE DISILLUSIONMENT: 1946-1947

"Failure is a harsh teacher".

Courtesy© Haley Family Collection

Dottie Crowe just after her marriage to Bill Haley in 1946.

Bill returned to his parents' home in Booth's Corner in September of 1946. He was ill, disillusioned and so broke he had to walk from the train station in Marcus Hook four miles to Booth's Corner. His only request to his mother was not to tell anyone he was home, not even his fiance Dottie. Bill fell into bed and slept thirty hours. Over the next two weeks Mrs. Haley slowly nursed her itinerant son back to health.

At the age of twenty-one, Bill felt he wasn't going to make it big as a cowboy singer. Bill was to later say, *"I returned with the idea of getting out of show business. I had had a pretty decent career, but I wasn't getting anywhere. I needed to get a steady job, forget my foolish ideas, and accomplish something that was real. The road can be hard on a kid if he's not careful. I needed a rest, I wanted someplace to hide. All I could think of is I'm a failure, and now everybody is going to know it."*

Somehow Dottie found out Bill was back home. Maybe Mrs. Haley called her, for Bill was getting more depressed each day. He had not left the house in several weeks. At first, Dottie was hurt and could not understand Bill's actions, but Mrs. Haley's kind words won over the young girl. When she asked Dottie to give Bill all the love and understanding she could muster, Dottie proved.to be a strong and courageous young woman. Bill was plagued with self-doubt and he desperately needed someone to help restore his shattered self-esteem.

Dottie told Bill she didn't care about him being a big star. She would love him whatever he did. She attacked Bill's arguments on what some people had said about him. *"What does Shorty Cook know about talent anyway. Red Foley said you had talent. Cousin Lee said you were the best yodeler he ever had, and you could play for him anytime you wanted to!"*

During the next weeks Dottie saw Bill almost every night. She had succeeded in restoring in him some of his pride, self worth and the will to go on. Their long walks and quiet conversations loosened the grip of depression which had descended on Bill's mind. By late November, Bill began to be some of his old self again. However, he started to look for another career. He still found it difficult to face many of the people in Booth's Corner. He imagined many of his earlier tormentors laughing behind his back. He wanted to get out of the area for a while and start over again, someplace where no one knew him.

A letter from his old friend Brother Wayne told Bill that the radio station he was working on needed another disc-jockey. The station, located 400 miles away in Keene, New Hampshire, appealed to Bill. With money borrowed from his family, he drove up for an interview. The station hired him as a disc jockey for $30.00 a week. Bill would sit in the small operations room and spin the week's most popular tunes, sometimes play his guitar and sing, read the news and the station's commercials with his best monotoned voice. By night he would sleep on the Waynes' living-room studio-couch, as once again Brother Wayne and his wife Dottie boarded the struggling young musician turned disc-jockey.

Several weeks later Bill received word from his sister, Peggy, that she believed Dottie was pregnant. The news was somewhat of a relief to Bill. He loved Dorothy in his own strange way but had felt he had no right to ask her to marry him. He was not making much money and was very far from his promised goals. But the news of the coming baby triggered a basic sense of responsibility in him. Bill called Dottie and asked her on the phone to marry him. He never mentioned he knew about her pregnancy. Dottie, with tears of joy, accepted Bill's rather unorthodox telephone proposal, packed her few belongings, told her father and best friend Peggy White the good news and took a bus to Brattleboro, Vermont. With Brother Wayne and his wife as witnesses, Bill and Dottie were married there on December, 11th 1946 by a Justice of the Peace.

That snowy winter in New England became a healing time for Bill. With Dottie by his side, he received the peace and serenity he now wanted so badly. The young couple rented a small three room apartment near the station. The long nights gave him time to write some of his most beautiful ballads.

In the spring of 1947, Bill and Dottie moved to Hartford, Connecticut where Bill took a better paying position with radio station WTIC. Shortly after, they moved again to a third station, WLBR, in Lebanon, Pennsylvania.

Here among the gentle Amish people and the lush green country side of Lancaster County, Dottie gave birth to their first child, Sharyn-Ann, in June of 1947.

These were lean times for the young couple. Bill was broadcasting six evenings a week. His agenda included doing the evening news, playing recorded music and reading the commercials. Dottie worked during the day at a local store to help bring in a little extra money. As Dottie came in from her job, Bill would leave for the station.

One quiet afternoon, while watching his little daughter, Bill wrote the beautiful and tender ballad *Rose of My Heart* as she lay peacefully asleep in her crib. He left the song on the kitchen table for his wife to see.

Ev'ry cowboy has a gal he likes to call his own,
A gal he has loved from the start,
Now I've got myself a gal,
As sweet as any rose,
I call her the rose of my heart

Rose of my heart, I'm lonely tonight,
Because we are so far apart,
But please don't worry, darlin',
I'll soon come to you,
Sweet little rose of my heart

By September of 1947, Bill Haley had recovered from what he felt was his failure to become a big time singing star. Since Lebanon was only sixty miles from Booth's Corner, Bill, Dottie and Sharyn-Ann would often visit Bill's parents' little farm. The proud grandparents would load up the young couple's car with fresh vegetables, eggs and chickens. On these visits back home, many of the locals would come up to Bill and want to shake his hand. Bill found he was still very much a celebrity in the little cross-roads village. Many had heard him sing and yodel on their radios when he was with the National Barn Dance and the Hooser Hop. These little heart-felt appreciations meant a lot to him.

Courtesy© Haley Family Collection

Bill, Dottie and Sharyn Ann at Radio Park, 1948.

With a new sense of confidence, Bill began to develop some of his earlier ambition again. He no longer wanted to be just another disc jockey, but now wanted to get into radio management, so he could have some control over programming.

Bill loved the rhythm, beat and the vitality of the nation's many regional sounds. However, when he would play some of his personal collection of "race" records on the air, he encountered severe criticism from the radio's head office.

Each time he tried to introduce to his listeners some of the traditional sounds of New Orleans, St. Louis or Chicago, the management would come down on him for playing those "jig-a-boo records". He was warned that "race" music had no place on their station! This ongoing friction with management over his "peculiar and excessive interest in unauthorized music" was one of the major reasons for Bill's brief sojourns with three stations in just ten months.

Bill believed he had discovered a bold, exciting and untapped concept for radio programming. However, he needed a new, open-minded station to try out his format. His break came in October, when his father told him of a new station about to go on the air in Chester, Pennsylvania. Excited and eager for a chance, Bill called the station's new owner and made an appointment for his crucial interview.

©DAP

Bill Haley with his black Gibson LG-2, 1947.

WPWA business card, 1948.

Bill Haley as Musical Director with fan, Frances Chandler, in front of radio station WPWA, 1949. Left to right; Bashful Barney and Brother Wayne.

Courtesy F. Chandler-Riley

CHAPTER FIVE

A NEW HORIZON: 1947-1949

"Disc-jockey, bandleader, husband and bum."

Lou Pollar was a gutsy, forty-five year old enterprising businessman in the Chester area. He had just received his federal license to broadcast at 1590 kilocycles on the AM dial, from dawn to dusk. His new venture was a little 250 watt station with the call letters WPWA. The station could broadcast in the area bounded by Philadelphia to the north, Wilmington, Delaware, to the south, and across the Delaware River to Bridgeport in New Jersey. This was a heavy industrial region populated largely by blue-collar workers who earned their wages operating the great shipyards, refineries, and mills that flanked the western shore of the Delaware River.

Lou Pollar knew his audience. They were the same customers that made his other businesses flourish. First generation Poles, Italians, Greeks, Ukrainians and a couple hundred thousand black and white Americans, many of whom had migrated to the area during the war from the South. This great mass of humanity was packed into tiny row houses and modest little apartments as far as the eye could see. The only thing they had in common was the American Dream, a radio and a love of music with some life and spirit to it.

Pollar also knew he had to compete with the large network stations and their star-studded, high-powered programming. All he needed was a way to get Chester's attention. What he needed was a new format, something different, but what? It was a good thing this station wasn't his only source of income. But what the hell, he told himself, this was just a toy anyhow. He always wanted to own a radio station, and now he had one!

Pollar had been advertising for some good, experienced people to help him run the station and take care of the day to day operations. His crucial interview with Bill Haley on that November afternoon in 1947 was one more important step closer to the development of the birth of Rock'n'Roll.

Bill Haley put on a white shirt and, with much frustration, knotted a hated tie. His dad told him not to take any chances, Mr. Pollar always wore a suit and might be a stickler for conventions. As Bill drove the sixty miles from Lebanon to Chester, he reviewed all his points in selling himself and his ideas to Pollar.

Whatever the twenty-two year old Bill Haley said to Pollar that day must have sounded good. His concept of having programs with all types of music appealed to Pollar's vison of his audience. The benign bigotry, prevalent in many of the other radio stations' programming, always rubbed against Pollar's basic sense of justice, and it did not set well with his deep Jewish traditions.

Bill said he would use live and recorded hillbilly and cowboy music to get the new white Southern listeners, the European folk music for the first generation immigrants and rhythm and blues, Dixieland, jazz and Be-Bop for the blacks. What Bill didn't tell Pollar was how popular he thought the "race" music would be to their white audience.

Lou Pollar took an instant liking to the young man and hired him on the spot. Being a shrewd businessman, he also liked the concept of a radio station that could sell advertising to both the black and white populations. This broader foundation, he surmised, would give the station a better financial base.

Bill Haley was hired as the station's Musical Director. His main responsibility would be to fill the dawn-to-dusk air waves allotted to WPWA with interesting and entertaining programs. Pollar also wanted good basic news, weather and sports shows as part of the schedule. The key word with any program was it must be low cost. Other than these guidelines, Pollar gave Bill, and the station manager, wide discretion on program content and station format.

Since the station was small, Pollar also got the eager young man to agree to be the record librarian, custodian, ad salesman, and if needed, the newscaster, announcer and disc jockey, plus writer and reader of many of the station's commercials. Later, Bill would renegotiate himself out of some of these duties, but for now he felt he had received a rare opportunity to do his own thing.

Bill threw his all energy and soul into WPWA. He would work twelve to sixteen hours a day, six days a week. He interviewed dozens of local people, always looking for good ideas and new talent. Each Sunday he would go to Radio Park and invite celebrities to do a special half hour program. Bill would interview them and ask them to sing or play their latest tunes.

One by one, they put together a schedule of basic programs. They hired a burly, ex-Navy Commander named James Ferguson to do a show on sports with commentary. A popular morning show, from six to eight, was called the "Alarm Clock Club". Bill, with his cheery, "Good Morning, Good Buddies" voice, often did this show himself. Upbeat music, news, and weather reports were broadcast along with time checks every five minutes.

Although many of the station's programs were not much different from their competitors, WPWA's rich mix of live and recorded ethnic music such as polkas, pop, jazz, rhythm and blues and country-western caught the ears of Chester's great coalition of minorities.

One program inaugurated in late 1948 was beginning to get a lot of notice. It was called "Judge Rhythm's Court", and was hosted by "Shorty the Bailiff". Shorty was a forty year old white man named James Reeves. His gift for dialects gave many people the impression he was a black man. His two hour show played predominantly "race" records, presumably to a Black audience. Bill loved this show and a year later, one of its theme songs, *We're Gonna Rock the Joint,* would have a tremendous impact on his career.

Chester's Black community held Reeves in the highest regard, but Haley felt a large percentage of the audience were young whites who loved the beat and drive of the rhythm and blues sounds as much as he did. But for now, Judge Rhythm's Court was *"just a little show the station put on for our colored friends."* This patronizing rationale seemed to quiet the critics and the show was tolerated by the local rednecks, without noticeable loss of sponsors or listeners.

By the summer of 1948, Bill Haley not only had his own show in the mornings but also hosted a mid-day "Ladies Aid" program which gave tips on fashion, health and cooking. Later in the year he added a third, "Western Swing" show to his schedule. This all live-music program followed Judge Rhythm's Court. Bill deliberately used this time slot to best capitalize on the large audience Jim Reeves had created. He felt this was the perfect time and the most receptive audience to introduce his upbeat and lively "Cowboy Jump" music to.

This Western Swing Hour featured some of the best regional country and western artists, who performed just for the publicity. Bill would use the show to introduce many of the tunes he wrote himself. His guests would play or sing along with him. Sally Starr and her husband, Jesse Rogers, Pancake

James "Slim" Allsman Courtesy N. Allsman

Pete Newman, Ray Whitley, Red River Dave, Rusty Keefer, Pee Wee Miller, Fingers Hess, Brother Wayne and Father Polick were just some of the many talented performers who played on Bill's program at one time or another. Bill would also do comic routines, yodel and sing between his commercials. But here and there he would slip into the mix one of his "cowboy jump" tunes to see if there were any favorable reactions. Unfortunately, most people didn't like his mongrelization of their favorite songs and Bill would revert back to standard country-western rhythms.

One of his most frequent guests was a tall, lean "Jimmy Rogers" type of country singer by the name of James "Slim" Allsman. Slim had married Naomi Austin, who was Bill Haley's neighbor back in the 1930's when the family lived on Shaw Terrace. Bill was only twelve years old when he first saw Slim playing his guitar while sitting in his old car, courtin' Naomi.

Allsman remembers, *"Billy wouldn't come up to the car, but would kind of hang around as close as he could so he could hear me play. He never asked me to teach him to play, but I know he was fascinated with the guitar. His family later moved out to Booth's Corner. I went into the Army soon after that, and I didn't see Bill again until after the war.*

He looked me up and came over my house one night with Julian Barnard. He said he wanted to put together a special band to do a new kind of music. He said he had heard music in other places that was more alive than ours. It had a real kick in it. He wanted to mix it with ours and create something really new. He said it would be like mixing Dixieland and Hillbilly. He was real excited about it. I thought he was crazy, and I told him, 'Who's gonna listen to it, if you could do it? Why mess up good country music?' Bill talked way into the night about his idea, but at the time I just couldn't see it. However I told him I'd try to help him out. Bill was a hell of a salesman. I think he could just about talk a person into anything if he had a mind to it. If he wanted to go to the moon in a space ship made of ice cream, he'd have everybody bringing him ice cubes."

James Allsman and Bill renewed their friendship and along with two other local musicians, Albert Constantine on the accordion and Julian "Bashful Barney" Barnard on the bass, they formed a group called the Four Aces of Western Swing.

Barnard was unique among these early singing cowboy-hillbillies. While most of his peers were from poor, hard-working, blue-collar families, Barnard's father was a prominent Philadelphia lawyer and was raised in wealth and comfort. Barney's love of country-western music and his zany comic routines always made him a favorite with the audience, if not with his Orthodox Jewish family! It was also Barney's expensive new car which often hauled Bill and the little band to their shows. Barney's good nature and generosity was tapped more than once by the always-a-little-short Haley.

With this new band, Bill tried to introduce a new style of Western music to the Delaware Valley. Part hillbilly, part Dixieland and part western Swing. Bill's popularity on radio made bookings easier to come by. The band played the Wilson Line excursion boats on the Delaware River and many of the local parks, political functions and taverns in the greater Philadelphia-Wilmington area. The Four Aces of Western Swing also became the "house band" of WPWA.

From his radio show, Bill would plug the group's next performances. These free radio commercials made the band more popular. To further showcase their abilities, he would donate their time and skills to many worthy causes, often to the dismay of the boys in the band. This frequent "no pay for play" may account for the many "fill-in" musicians when his regular boys "couldn't make it" for the "freebees".

©DAP

Julian "Bashful Barney" Barnard

Bill generously gave his own time and talents, often sacrificing the little time he could have spent with his family. It seemed he'd rather perform than take a day off. Few of his fellow musicians felt the same dedication.

It was about this time Slim Allsman bought his first electric guitar. Slim recalls with pride: *"It was a "F" hole Gibson-built Premier arch-top with a built-in electric pick-up and Bigsby vibrato tailpiece. It was a real beauty—with a pearl-inlaid rosewood neck and a golden-maple body. The embedded silver pick-guard would shine like a field of brilliant diamonds when you played it in the spotlight. Everybody I knew came around to look at it—electric guitars were still a bit of a novelty around these parts.But the guy who came around the most was Bill (Haley). He was really fascinated with it. He would come over the house between his radio shows on the pretext of giving me some records or sheet music which promoters had given him. Then he would ask if he could play a few tunes on my Premier. He even borrowed it a couple of times. I*

The Four Aces of Western Swing, left to right: Al Constantine, Tex King, Bill Haley and Bashful Barney.

Slim Allsman's Premier, Bill Haley's first electric guitar.

remember telling him that if anything happened to that guitar his days on earth would be numbered!"

Slim's wife Naomi also recalled with a smile: *"Bill would come over the house a lot of times just before dinner-time and ask if he could play Jimmy's electric guitar. I would get it out from under the bed and Bill would go down in the cellar and plug up the amplifier. For about an hour Bill would be down there making all kinds of strange sounds. It sounded like music from another planet, if you could call it music. Often, Jimmy would come home real tired after a long day's work and find Bill jamming away with his new guitar. Jimmy and I would sit down and eat, and after, I would take a plate down to Bill. One night I remember Jimmy saying that guitar was the most expensive instrument he ever had. Not only did he have to make weekly payments forever—he had to feed it too!"*

Bill's fascination with Allsman's electric guitar opened up a new world of sound for the twenty-three year old musician. The range, power and versatility of this early electrified instrument awed him as he continued to experiment with its new world of magical sounds. Bill would tell Naomi: *"It's like being a god—holding the power of thunder and lighting in your hands".*

However, in the real world of entertainment, Bill's early attempts to blend Dixieland and hillbilly music were usually met with cat calls and many unkind words. The Dixieland sound without brass or percussion instruments was crude and off the mark. Many times in the rough honky-tonk bars of Chester the experimental music angered the crowd and the band would quickly return to its basic country-western sound, if just to finish the set and get paid. It seemed to Bill the public wasn't ready for his kind of mongrel, hard edge, western blues, and more than one irate tavern owner told Haley to *"hold it down on that damn hillbilly-jig-a-boo stuff. Don't you know dude, there ain't no cowboys in Africa!"*

It was also about this time Bill first started to notice a young man in the audience with red wavy hair and a powerful build. Harry Broomall had become one of Bill's most loyal fans as he seemed to be at all the band's engagements. Bill soon began to call him "Reds" and would ask him to run errands and do other small favors for the band-which he seemed eager to do. One night several months later, after he had become the band's unofficial mascot, Reds saved Bill from a beating at the hands of drunken, muscle-bound trouble-maker who didn't like his type of country music. He twice before went up to Bill and told him *"I can fart better than you can sing!"* The third time he approached Bill he said with a drunken slur: *"After this beer I'm gonna beat you like a bull fiddle!"* At this point Broomall grabbed the big gorilla and hauled him out into the back alley for a little lesson in manners. After this incident Reds became Bill's unpaid bodyguard and close friend. He would later serve as Bill's chauffeur and confidant during the halcyon days of the 1950's. James Allsman recalls:

The Arizona Ramblers, Left to right: Slim Allsman, Jack Kenney Carl Russell and Jimmy Collett.

Courtesy C. Russell

"Reds Broomall would do anything for Bill. He didn't even know how to read or write, but he was fiercely loyal to Bill. If Bill gave the word, Reds would take on anybody he thought was a danger to his boss." Years later, when Bill was world famous, Reds would take Bill's children to the beach or out in public, and guard them like a great St. Bernard dog. Jack Haley, Bill's oldest son, has only fond memories of many afternoons he spent under the loving care of this faithful family friend.

For the next year, Bill and the band would play mostly standard cowboy or hillbilly music in public, while they experimented with his other sound in private. But Bill's inability to read music, combined with the lack of the right instruments and the skill to produce the drive and vitality he needed, became a barrier of frustration. He was unable to create the elusive sound and drive he wanted. Bill was like a cook trying to make a half remembered stew, but with neither the pot nor the spices to bring to life his meat, carrots and potatoes.

James Allsman left the band disheartened and joined Carl Russell's and Jimmy Collett's popular "Arizona Ramblers". He later formed his own group and would spend the next forty years playing traditional country-western music from New Jersey to Florida. In the years to come he would occasionally join Bill and the Saddlemen in recording sessions and on stage as a bass player or lead guitarist.

He was replaced with another excellent lead guitarist, Orville Mitchell, who used the stage name "Tex King". The forty year old Mitchell was a native of West Virginia and sang with a beautiful, country-style baritone voice. He was a another veteran of the country-western circuit and his wide experience and good advice added another professional element to the group.

Soon after, Julian Barnard gave up his place in the band to "Big Al" Thompson. During these frustrating times many other talented musicians also tried their skills with this renegade band and its exasperating but challenging leader. Merle Fritz with his steel guitar, Roy Perky and Jimmy Maise with their fiddles. Ernie Walker, Charlie "Fingers" Hess, Slim Bland, Joseph Piccirilli and Clifford Lytle with their guitars and basses. Even the gifted fiddler-guitarist-song writer, Arrett "Rusty" Keefer tried his hand.

All these men were good, classic country-western musicians, but the sound that vibrated in Bill Haley's head could not be reproduced nor even comprehended by any of them. It would be another year before Bill would realize that completely new techniques and instrumentation would be needed.

While searching for his new sound, Bill and The Four Aces of Western Swing cut their first tracks for Jack Howard's Cowboy label. One tune was the song Bill and Shorty Cook had written several years before called *Four Leaf Clover Blues*. This was backed by their version of Hank Williams' *Too Many Parties Too Many Pals,* sung by Tex King. This rare record is a prize addition to any country-western collection.

Bill had known Jack Howard since the early 1940's. They had both worked at Cousin Lee's Radio Park. In 1942, Howard established a Country-Western music publishing company in Philadelphia.

Jack Howard, Bill's first manager. Courtesy© R. Lefavi

On March 3rd, 1945 he founded the Cowboy record label which became the first record label in the city's history. The corporate documents were witnessed by Jesse Rogers, Pete Newman and Tommy Mason. The loan to finance this venture came from B.M.I. and a mysterious source that surprised many of his associates. Howard was to tell a close friend many years later that he had gotten a loan from the "mob". He also said he had received orders to produce cowboy and hillbilly records for the "boys" who controlled Philadelphia's lucrative juke box industry.

A document found in Howard's files twelve years after his death curiously states: *"I hereby waive and relinquish all royalties on the first five thousand records pressed ...for the sum of one dollar and other good and valuable considerations"*. It is believed that these first five thousand records of each Cowboy pressing ended up in the juke boxes of the powerful Philadelphia crime families.

After Prohibition was repealed in 1932, the powers that be in Philadelphia and other large cities such as Chicago and New York moved some of their cash heavy assets into the "machine" business. By the early 1940's over a quarter of a million slot machines, pin ball machines and juke boxes provided literally tons of nickels, dimes and quarters daily to the coffers of Family members and friends. The mob's juke boxes alone demanded millions of pop records a year to feed low cost music to the nation's working people.

Just before the end of the Second World War, the Godfathers decided they had to get into the music publishing and record pressing business to survive. They accomplished this by financing the start-ups of many small independent record pressing plants.

Due to the demands of the Second World War, the major American record companies were rationed in the amounts of raw materials they could buy for the production of 78 rpm discs. During these years of shortages, 1942 to 1945, they used their allotment to produce mainly the music of the great bands and only the most popular singers. The recording of the less popular ethnic and country-western music was curtailed. Unfortunately for the mob, it was the ethnic and regional music that was the mainstay of their juke boxes and most important to them. By late 1944 many juke boxes were only half full of worn-out records.

The decade from 1945 to 1955 witnessed the founding of more record companies than any other decade in American history. The easy to get loans had a few strings attached. The borrower had to produce, "at cost", popular records on demand for regional juke box distributors. The record pressers were free to make any profit they wanted on everybody else. Records made for delivery for the Mob were never marked down on company inventories. Trusted employees and family members worked "the phantom shift", each pressing forty 78 rpm records an hour for the "midnight" deliveries. The mob also told its new entrepreneurs what kind of music they were to produce. Their juke boxes were not in the fancy night clubs, restaurants, or uptown hotels. They didn't want classic European symphonic music or any songs controlled by ASCAP (American Society of Composers, Authors, and Publishers). This international performing-rights organization scrupulously audited all music played that was listed in its catalogs. The Godfathers wanted no one looking into their books. Who cared whether 20,000 records were pressed or 5,000—they wanted new, unpublished music for their "kind" of people. Their juke boxes were in places where the working people go. The neighborhood taverns, the honky-tonk road houses, the private ethnic and social clubs and the corner drug store-soda shops. They wanted black music for the ghettos, hillbilly music for the southern red necks, and cowboy music which seemed to be popular all over.

Thus it may be said that if black rhythm and blues was the mother of rock'n'roll and white hillbilly-cowboy music its daddy, then America's juke box owning Crime Families were among its unwitting mid-wives.

Although the mob did not have direct control of every new independent, their enormous and combined buying power could make or break any of these small record companies. Jack Howard was one of the little men caught up in the new black market of the record business. For the next four years on the "Cowboy" label and twenty-four years on the "Arcade" label, he would publish for and/or record a treasure trove of the region's early talent. Not only the traditional country and western music, but also some of the earliest rockabilly and rock-'n'roll tunes in the nation.

One of Jack Howard's great claims to fame was to introduce the great Canadian country and western singer Hank Snow to this country. His other was to be the first to record the earliest music of Bill Haley. However for the rock historians, it was Jack Howard who would be the first to record *Rock Around the Clock*.

Hank Snow with Jack Howard

Courtesy© R. Lefavi

Jack Howard in his office at Cowboy Records,1948.

Howard was an unusually driven little man with many eccentricies. He was compelled with an almost profane fascination with all things western and the music of the American cowboy. For all of Howard's shortcomings as a businessman, his love of Country-Western music was to make the city of Philadelphia one of the regional pioneers in recording the nation's new pop, rockabilly and rock'n'roll music. He was a tireless promoter, and although many times exaggerating his importance, his sheer enthusiasm won over many people, including the young Bill Haley. He would leave behind him a body of work which is still being recorded today. Unfortunately, his lack of social graces and business acumen would forever keep him in the minor leagues. However, for now he was one of the few people who saw a potential in Bill Haley's lively style of "cowboy-jump".

Bill and his fast changing "Four Aces of Western Swing" went on to record dozens of tracks for Howard's "Cowboy" label: *Candy Kisses, Tennessee Border, The Covered Wagon Rolled Right Along, Yodel Your Blues Away, Behind the Eight Ball, Foolish Questions, I Wasted A Nickel, Red River Valley, Raining Teardrops In My Eyes, I Dreamed Of An Old Love Affair, I Love You So Much It Hurts, My Bucket's Got A Hole In It, Wreck On The Highway* and many others. Only *Candy Kisses* backed with *Tennessee Border* were released before the label went bust. None of the Cowboy 78 rpm's reached the C/W charts. Billboard Magazine gave them poor reviews. Their sales officially never amounted to more than two to three thousand copies each. The band sold most of these during their band breaks or after performances for badly needed pocket and travel money. Bill also used the recordings as promotional tools for the group on his radio shows.

Bill Haley's first record with the "4 Aces of Western Swing".

©DAP

The Four Aces of Western Swing: left to right: Al Constantine, Bill Haley, Jimmy Maise and Bashful Barney.

In the files of Jack Howard were found copies of letters Bill Haley wrote to other disc jockeys: *"as one Dee Jay to another, I'd appreciate you giving my latest record "Candy Kisses" a spin. I think you will like it."* Signed: *"Your Pal Bill"*. The letter was typed on WPWA stationary.

Few people knew Bill paid Jack Howard for his records at 25¢ each or $62.50 for 250 which was the minimum pressing order. And because Bill was on a tight budget, the band often recorded the masters in his Chester radio station on their primitive acetate disc recording system. Many of these masters still exist and are in the hands of private collectors and publishing companies.

Jack Howard was also out selling Bill Haley's and other Cowboy label records. His distribution system consisted of every record shop which could be reached by Philadelphia's mass-transit system. Jack, who never learned to drive, would lug cartons of his records by bus or subway to dozens of music shops all over the city. He would leave a quantity of each new record in the stores on consignment. On his next visit, he would count his stock and bill the store owner for the records sold. The stores worked on a 30% mark-up. With no up-front cost to them, they welcomed Jack's "rack-jobber" style of merchandising. On these slim profits Howard struggled to make ends meet and keep alive his publishing company.

Bill Haley and The Four Western Aces, left to right: Rusty Keefer, Bashful Barney and Al Constantine. ©DAP

What Bill Haley didn't know, but soon found out, was that he was getting cheated somehow. Through friends, he learned his recordings were finding their way into juke boxes as far west as Detroit, Chicago and St. Louis. When he asked Howard when he was going to get some royalties, he was told to look at it this way: *"The no-royalty juke box sales were like getting "free publicity", and it wasn't "healthy" to ask these guys to be paid for a favor."* Bill knew the score and decided not to have many "favors" done for him in the future. He also vowed to one day own his own publishing company and have control of his music.

Meanwhile, Bill shortened the group's name to Bill Haley and his Western Aces in early 1949. Another local group called the "Four Aces" was becoming very popular and the similarity in names created some confusion to the public. Something else was puzzling Bill—while his group did so-so with his material, other groups were reaching the country-western charts with his songs! Andy Reynolds and his 101 Ranch Boys had a hit on Columbia Records with Bill's song *"Candy and Women"* as did Charlie Stone on the Mercury label. Pete "Pancake" Newman did the same with Bill's *"Four Leaf Clover Blues"* on the RCA Victor label. Bill was beginning to have some doubts about the quality of his band, or maybe it was his own singing ability?

In the summer of 1948 a sex scandal destroyed the credibility and wholesome reputation of Cousin Lee. The old band leader asked Bill if he would take his place and host the Sunday programs at Radio Park. Bill added this challenge to his already crowded schedule. He produced a series of country-western shows at Radio Park but found it difficult to overcome the legacy of ill will created by the park's founder and luckless owner.

Throughout 1948 and the early months of 1949, Bill Haley and his band maintained a grueling schedule. They all held down regular jobs during the day and then often played far into the night. For Bill, as well as the other men in the band, Fridays were especially masochistic. They all worked nine to twelve hours that day. Already tired from their long week they would grab a fast bite to eat, bathe, if they had time, and rush to the site of their next gig. Here they would perform till after 2 am. Bill would drink gallons of black coffee just to stay awake. Even Sundays were spent performing at area parks or other social events. Between his responsibilities at WPWA and the enormous time required traveling, rehearsing and performing with his band, Bill had precious little time with Dottie and Sharyn-Ann. His desire to make it as a leader of a great band with a new sound had become a blinding obsession, driving a cruel wedge between him and his family.

Dottie Wright, the wife of Bill's close friend "Brother Wayne", gave this chilling insight into the conditions at the time: *"Bill wasn't making much money then, none of us were. He poured everything he made back into his music. He even had to pay to get recorded. This was a bit of a joke at the time among some of his rivals. He did a lot of free shows for charity and paid the expenses out of his own pocket. He paid to print up his posters. He was always broke and borrowing money for gas to get to his next job. He would tell everybody he was trying to quit smoking but would bum cigarettes every chance he could. He never ate right...lived on sandwiches and black coffee. He and Dottie were living in a small three-room apartment on the second floor next to the train tracks in Chester. The whole place would shake like an earthquake every time the trains would roar by... which was about every twenty minutes. I don't know how they could get any sleep there. It was pretty bad. One very cold night, Bill was playing late, Dottie came over to our place carrying her baby. She was very shaken and*

EVERGREEN PARK

ST. JOHNS, PENNA. PHONE DRUMS 2661

Sensational Triple Attraction!

Sunday Afternoon and Night

(IN PERSON)

Bill (Jack) Haley

Sensational Recording Artist And Screen And Stage Star. A Real Treat To See And Hear.

PLUS HIS

All Western Sextette

With Music, Songs And Comedy The Real Western Way

FREE -- PICTURES -- FREE

Bill Haley Has Arranged With The Management To Give Away Absolutely Free An 8x10 Photo Of Himself To The First 500 People Entering The Park.

Park date ad 1949, note Bill (Jack) Haley and his "All Western Sextette".

looked so pathetically tired. She was a very beautiful girl but the hard times were grinding her down. She asked if she could please sleep on our couch that night because she couldn't fight the rats in her apartment anymore. She said she was afraid they would bite her baby. She looked terrified. My husband was also out and I told her I would appreciate her company. We put little Sharyn Ann, who was about eighteen months old, in the crib with my baby. I put on some tea and served some cookies I had made earlier. Dottie must have been hungry... she ate over a dozen before I noticed and asked her if she would like some "midnight breakfast". This was a meal we would usually fix for our men when they came home after their shows. Soon after this she left Bill and moved back to her father's home in Salem."

Bill moved into the basement of the radio station. Lou Pollar let him build a little office next to the coal bin. It was just large enough to hold a battered up old wooden desk and a used army cot. Visitors seemed to always remember the place being coated in coal dust. Slim Allsman recalls: *"Sometimes when the boys were rehearsing in Bill's office, the coal truck would arrive with a delivery. The awful noise of a ton of coal tumbling down the metal shute and the cloud of soot it created would cause everybody to flee upstairs."*

Many nights, too tired to drive the forty miles home to Salem, New Jersey, Bill would fall exhausted on the soot-covered little cot in his makeshift, plywood office. Often performing till two in the morning, Bill would be back on the air at 6 AM doing his morning show. His wife Dorothy became more and more angry and frustrated in her role as a musician's widow.

For a short period Bill toyed with the idea of changing his stage name to "Jack Haley". He created another side band of six musicians for special Sunday park dates. This band was billed as "Bill (Jack) Haley and his All Western Sextette". The musicians were the same men who had played at one time or another in his other bands.

Adding to this whirlwind schedule, Bill and Jack Howard, who was by now acting as his part-time manager and booking agent, added a Saturday matinee "Cowboy Stage Show" to their itinerary. This act featured "Yodeling Bill Haley, the Singing Cowboy" doing a medley of western songs up on a stage. Bill would dress in his best cowboy suit and white Stetson, with a six shooter in a hand-tooled leather holster strapped to his leg. Jack Howard would be at his side hamming it up with slapstick and other comic routines to get the kids laughing.

Early leaflet advertising "Yodeling Bill Haley".

This act was usually presented at special matinees at the larger movie houses in the greater Philadelphia area. One of the flyers from this era states: *"Free autographed photographs of Bill Haley the Singing Cowboy, to the first 500 boys and girls."* This was followed on one occasion by the film, *Wild Bill Elliott in the "Last Bandit,* three color cartoons, and Chapter 11 of *Atom Man*, all for 25¢! Bill would receive $15.00 per show from Jack Howard.

In April of 1949, Bill came up with the clever idea of doing a marathon radio program of hillbilly and western music to raise funds for the American Cancer Society. Earlier he had a good friend die a horrible death from the disease and Bill had promised his family to do all he could. With characteristic zeal, he called everybody he knew in the country-western circuit and asked for their support.

On April 16th, 1949 at 6:45 am, Bill went on the air. This was the first time an entire broadcasting day would be devoted to raising funds for cancer research using only country-western music as its draw. By day's end, Bill Haley raised over $16,000 in pledges, an enormous sum for a local disc jockey in those days. Bill received telephone interviews from Hollywood stars such as Melvyn Douglas and Ray Bolger. Milton Berle and Tallulah Bankhead sent him telegrams which he read on the air. Shorty Long and his Santa Fe Rangers, the Sleepy Hollow Ranch Gang, the 101 Ranch Boys, Pee Wee Miller, Jesse Rogers, Sally Starr, Cliff and Marshall Lytle and a host of other local stars made personal appearances. In the nation's newspapers the following day, Bill Haley received coast to coast recognition for his

Bill Haley at one of his theater stage shows. Jack Howard kneeling below Bill.

Courtesy© R. Lefavi

outstanding contributions to the 1949 Cancer Drive. Bill's own Western Aces provided all the back-up music for the entire twelve hour and forty-five minute program.

However even after this unprecedented event with all its national press exposure, success and a decent living still eluded him. Everybody patted him on the back and told him what a swell job he was doing but he still had to bum his cigarettes and use cardboard to hide the holes in the soles of his boots. Bill, mentally and physically drained, disbanded his Western Aces and slipped into another period of depression.

The next few months were another period of re-examination for Bill. He seemed overpowered with a sense of frustration and bewilderment. Friends say this was when he began drinking again. Bill learned early that alcohol brought out the darker side of his personality and usually avoided drinking altogether. However, when he fell into periods of depression, the bottle often became his only nourishment—and the more he drank, the more morose he became. Why was real success always just beyond his grasp? How come with all the power of thousands of radio advertisements, plenty of playing time on the air waves and over a thousand performances, he was still only a local celebrity? Nor, did he feel, were his bands doing any better, after all the practicing and teaching. What was wrong? Was Shorty Cook's assessment back in Fort Wayne right? Was his voice only adequate? Why did his band members keep leaving him? Whatever happened to the new sound he was going to create, that exciting, new sound that eluded him like a frail will-o-the-wisp? The questions ran through his mind like haunted winds, but the answers seemed like phantoms, forever beyond his grasp.

At the request of Jimmy Myers and a session fee of twenty-five dollars, Bill and several fellow musicians record two more songs: *Stand Up and Be Counted* and *Loveless Blues.* These tracks were leased to Center Records, a small independent label from nearby Havre de Grace, Maryland. This record sold a few thousand copies in the mid-Atlantic states but also failed to make it to the country-western charts. Curiously, Bill does not use his regular name on the label. He creates a new pseudonym from his two middle names and is listed as "Johnny Clifton and his String Band".

By day Bill works ten and twelve hours at the station. By night, he would solo or play a duet with another musician in the dingy, third rate honky-tonks of "Bethel Court", Chester's notorious red light district. His marriage to Dottie was almost non-existent. His obsession with "being somebody" and failing to do so, had driven a painful void between him and his young wife. Dorothy could neither understand nor condone his one-sided ambitions or his notorious liaisons with rumored young women who haunted the cheap dives which now seemed to draw him.

Slim Allsman and Duke Snow recall this period of Bill's tribulations: *"Bill was separated from his wife at the time. This one night he was playing at a club called Luke's Musical Bar at Third and Market in Chester. We nicknamed it the "Bucket of Blood". It was one of those cheap joints where fights between the customers were part of the entertainment. It had a graveyard in the back. We used to joke, that was so Luke's customers wouldn't have to be carried far. There was no air conditioning back then and the place smelled of old sweat, stale beer and cheap perfume. On hot summer nights we worked from seven till two in the morning with our sweat-soaked shirts sticking to our bodies like awful. The cigarette haze was so thick that sometimes you couldn't see the end of the bar from the band stand. This place was the pits. They would pay twelve bucks and a bottle of cheap wine. I think Bill played there because they didn't expect much and that's about how he was feeling about himself".*

Courtesy J. Muntz

Duke Snow and "Scrappy".

Slim continues: *"Well, this one night, it was after midnight, Bill was half lit on port wine, with cigarette ashes all over his usually spotless cowboy shirt. After his last set he told me nothing was working right for him. He couldn't seem to get anything going. He said he thought he worked harder than anybody he knew, but had no dough to show for it. He feared ending up in the viscose factory like his dad, as part of the damn machinery. To Bill, that was his idea of hell on earth. He then followed me into the head. As I was standing in front of the urinal making my contribution to the Delaware River, I see this real macho guy punching holes in the wall with his fist. Well, the wall was just made of thin plaster board. So I told him punching holes in this wall was no big thing. To prove it I punched a hole too and I was a lot lighter than this bruiser. Well, Bill was not to be outdone by either of us. So*

LIVE ENTERTAINMT
SOLD OUT
NO spitting on floor
ALL NIGHT LO
please use bathrooms
NO throwing beer bottles
LUKE'S BAR
laura Haley

he clenched that big fist of his and with one mighty swing, punched the wall like a cannonball going through solid timber.

"Well, like I said, nothing was working for Bill at the time and that night at Luke's proved it. Bill's fist hit a two by four stud hidden behind the spot he chose to punch. With a yell you could hear on the other side of hell, Bill's guitar plucking hand became a bloody, mangled mass. It swelled up real bad on him and when we asked the bartender for some ice, the owner Luke, who was an ex-boxer, punched Bill out for bustin' up his wall in the latrine. He confiscated Bill's old Kay guitar, kept his night's pay and threw him out in the street like some old bum. Worse yet, Bill almost got run over by a beer truck! I guess it just wasn't one of Bill's better days! I can still see him sitting in the street with his face and hand all swollen, checking to see if he lost any of his teeth. He was sure a sight to behold. Duke and I picked him up and took him to the Chester Hospital and got him fixed up."

The next six weeks, Bill's hand was in a cast. Unable to play his guitar, Bill had Slim Allsman and some other friends play on his show. *"He felt real stupid when he sobered up,"* said Slim, *"but I think it gave him a chance to rest, and I think he really needed it."*

This "vacation" from his normally brutal schedule of the past twelve months was an unplanned but most welcome pause for Bill at a critical time in his career.

Unbeknownst to Bill Haley, he was just months from an a new opportunity which would lay the foundation for fame and fortune beyond his wildest dreams. But for now, the summer of 1949, Bill was overcome with another round of self doubts and depression. He felt he had blown, in the last four years, more opportunities than most people get in a lifetime. Dog tired and with a throbbing pain in his hand, Bill drove his old panel truck back to Salem, back to Dottie.

The anger melted in Dottie eye's as she saw his little-boy-hurt look and the swollen hand in the white cotton sling. She took him in, like she would so many more times to come. She gave him the comfort, compassion and a sympathetic ear he so desperately needed. After they made love, she would comb her fingers through his sandy brown hair and play with the cowlick that formed a natural spitcurl on his high forehead. Bill's sad, country-boy face and quiet demeanor, when he was down, never failed to bring out the deep love Dottie had for her wayward, exasperating, and often infuriating husband.

It was usually Dorothy who loaned Bill money when he was broke, lifted his spirits when he was down, and encouraged him when he wanted to quit. This beautiful, caring young woman would be his inspiration and his phantom nemesis, for Bill seemed to appreciate her only when all else failed.

The following months the young couple went through a phase of unabashed enjoyment of each others company. Their reconciliation was a dream come true for Dorothy. Even two-year old Sharyn-Ann seemed to love playing with her father. Bill worked days at the station and was home for dinner most evenings. Sometimes late at night, Bill would get up from his bed and write one of his country ballads. One of the songs Bill wrote at this time for Dottie was *My Cute Little Brown Eyed Gal*:

Some fools have silver and gold
But I've got a treasure to hold
They have diamond filled chests
But my treasure's the best
I've got a cute little brown eyed gal

She's my cute little brown eyed gal
I've never had a better pal
When skies are gray,
My troubles fade away
Cause I'm with my little brown eyed gal

This was the real family life Dottie had always dreamed of. She had been the product of a broken home herself. Raised by a caring father, whom she loved very much, Dottie had come to believe that all men were as fine and noble as he. She also naively believed a "good woman" could bring out the goodness in any man. She had prayed her entire young life for a proper family, with a husband, children and caring grandparents. Her only other aspiration was that one day she would have a house of her own. Her husband's obsession for fame was not on her list of priorities.

Dorothy loved Bill when he was himself—shy, gentle and not trying to impress strangers. She disliked many of his phony show business buddies, the fast women who shamelessly threw themselves at him, and the cheap honky-tonk atmosphere of low-class bars. She also felt he was wasting his talents and losing his pride playing in places like Luke's Musical Bar. Many years and tears later, Dorothy's faith in the talents of her husband would bear fruit. Only she had the vision to predict that he would become someone very special, if only because he wanted it so badly.

On one enchanted evening, many years to come, Bill would play a Command Performance before the British Royal Family. This would be no great surprise to Dottie, nor afterwards, when he was introduced to, and shook hands with Her Majesty, Elizabeth II, the Queen of England. At this one sublime moment, William John Clifton Haley felt he was finally given the recognition he had been seeking his whole life.

Yes, Dottie knew her man. Now if she could only learn to harness his tremendous energy and drive, and channel it, so there would be a place in his world for her and Sharyn-Ann. This was her greatest prayer, her most secret wish above all others. However, coming events would deal her an unkind and undeserved fate as she would become one of the tragic heroines of this story.

CHAPTER SIX

THE SEARCH FOR THE SOUND: 1949-1953

"One last try for the golden ring."

While Bill Haley was recovering from his injured hand with Dottie in Salem, another set of events which would have a dramatic influence on Bill's career were being set into motion fifty miles away, just north of Philadelphia.

James "Slim" Allsman was playing in Norristown, Pennsylvania, on radio station WNAR with two new sidekicks in a trio called the "Southern Swingsters". Slim had met these two promising young musicians earlier at the same station. The youngest, a seventeen year old Italian-American lad named Johnny Grande, was a classically trained pianist. However it was the music of the cowboy accordion which attracted him most. Johnny was a street-smart kid with black, wavy hair and a quick smile. His handsome latin features were to earn him the nickname "lover" among his fellow musicians. As a youth, what he lacked in stage experience he made up for in sheer enthusiasm.

The other young man was a twenty-one year old Irish-American named Billy Williamson. This jolly, unassuming, but multi-talented musician played the steel guitar, the fiddle and the bass with the rough grace of the self taught. However it was his own techniques in playing the steel guitar that would one day make him a legend as one of the great "steel lightning flash" guitarists.

Billy and Johnny were close friends, with Billy acting almost like a big brother to his younger pal. When Slim wanted Billy to join his group, he found he had to take the "kid" too. Both young men wanted to be professional musicians and Allsman's invitation to form a group was most welcomed.

Over the next few months Grande practiced his country-western tunes and did his best to keep up his part of the trio. Slim would say, with his big cowboy grin, *"that kid's gonna make it, yes, I think that kid just might make a damn good musician some day! I just hope we don't starve to death first!"*

The three-piece band took every job they could get. They played all the second-rate clubs from Newark, New Jersey to Baltimore, Maryland. After several months of much effort and little money, the trio found it difficult to stay together. Slim would later recall, grinning: *"The boys developed a real bad habit—they were led to believe good musicians should eat at least once a day!"*

Courtesy N. Allsman

The "Southern Swingsters" left to right: Billy Williamson, Slim Allsman and Johnny Grande, circa 1949.

While on the road with Slim, Johnny and Billy had heard Slim talking, with a mixture of admiration and ridicule, about a crazy musician he used to play with named Bill Haley. Slim told his two young companions: *"Would you believe this guy was trying to play hillbilly, Dixieland and Western to a rhythm and blues beat?"* Slim compared that *"to mixing beer, whiskey, red wine and warm milk together. Now I know that might sound like one hell of a milkshake, but I don't want to be the poor fella to have to drink it!"*

However, to John Grande the concept of creating a new kind of hybrid music was intriguing and he

©DAP

Billy Williamson, Bill's partner and steel guitarist.

asked Billy if he knew this Bill Haley guy. Williamson, with a serious expression on his face said: *"Matter of a fact, I do. He's a disc jockey on WPWA in Chester. He was the kid star of a Western outfit and he's played in hot bands all over the country."* Williamson had met Haley a few times at WPWA and had seen him perform at Radio park. *"Man, he had a band,"* said Billy enthusiastically: *"Every guy in it could double and they got a chance to show what they could do. Haley doesn't hog the spotlight himself."* The two men agreed that Williamson should go to Chester and see if Haley was interested in forming a group with them.

The young musician met with Bill Haley at the radio station. The meeting was short and a great disappointment. Williamson told Johnny later that evening: *"Haley didn't have a band anymore and didn't want one either. Too many worries."*

Bill's hand was now out of the cast, but the splintered bones, torn tendons and pulled muscles ached when he tried to play the guitar. Bob Thornton, a friend of Bill's at this time, said: *"Bill's hand never did heal right. This was why he usually played just chords on the rhythm guitar. He lost some of his dexterity and seldom played lead guitar in public much after that. I once even watched him try to play left-handed, but that didn't work out either."* Back in Philadelphia, the persistent, young John Grande wouldn't give up. He talked Billy Williamson into trying to convince Bill Haley one more time, but this time to tell Bill how much they wanted to help him develop the new, hybrid "Cowboy-Jive" sound Allsman had told them about. They also decided to go together. In a magazine article written in 1958, Grande recalled this historic meeting: *"I remember the way Billy introduced me to Haley. 'Johnny can play piano and accordion, Pops, Western or Dixie. He's had eight years of classical music education, too. And, in eight years, one can't help learning something. . . even this guy!' "*

The two men used every persuasion they could think of to win over the stubborn and unconvinced Haley. Bill said: *"You don't know what you're getting into. The road is a hard and unforgiving mistress, and very few make it. Plus, if you work twice as hard as everybody else, and are twice as talented, it don't mean a darn thing. You need to be in the right spot at the right time. Which means, you need twice as much luck as everybody else, too!"* Bill used every reason he could think of to discourage the enthusiasm of the two young musicians. Besides, Bill reasoned, these two kids had no real experience, compared to many of his other partners. So why waste a lot of time and money training them? In six months they too, like all the others, would probably pick up and quit and he would again have nothing to show for all his effort but more frustration.

Johnny Grande, Bill's partner and key music arranger.

©DAP

However, on the other hand, the more established musicians seemed to be unable to accept the new disciplines required to find or mix the new sounds. They seemed too set in their ways. Maybe a couple of wet-behind-the-ears kids with a good, basic foundation in a variety of musics would be more open to new ideas. And this Grande kid could read music—maybe he could help in the complex arrangements that a new music might require. John Grande continues: *"The longer the huddle went on, the more I liked Haley. He looked like a kid with his smooth face and sandy hair and that curl that kept falling down onto his forehead, but Billy was right. Young as he was, this guy had something. Music to him was more than some notes on a page, or sounds dragged out of an instrument. It was direct communication from one person to another. Haley clinched it by saying, 'All my life I've been looking for something I haven't yet found in music. I've always thought if I could get together with some guys who felt the same way I did, we might work it out.' "*

Billy's Irish grin was wide as a jack-o-lantern. *"What are we waiting for, Bill?"* Said Johnny impatiently.

"It's going to be rough," Haley warned. *"I don't know where the loot is coming from."*

"Johnny and I have worked odd jobs before," said Billy. *"But what about you? You got a family."*

"I'll make out," said Bill. *"The way I figure it, I've got to know whether I'm ever going to amount to something in music. This is the time I've got to make my move as a man. Want to go partners?"*

They all shook hands on it. That's all the contract they had for many years to come. Haley was to be the undisputed leader, but only the first among equals when the profits were distributed. The nucleus of the band that would rock the world was forged in friendship and a sense of high adventure, on that remarkable day in the winter of 1949. The excited young musicians then chose a name for their new group, *"Bill Haley and His Saddlemen"*. According to Al Rex, who was with Bill that night, this historic deal was made at Luke's Musical Bar at Third and Market streets in Chester. Flo Thomas, a barmaid at Luke's at the time, recalls: *"Bill's spirits really picked up. I asked him if he had hit the numbers or something. He just said to me: 'Flo, darling, I'm gonna try one more time to hit the big time. Music is all I got. . . if I'm gonna be somebody. . . it's got to be with my music. I've got nothing else going for me.' "*

"Bill had gotten back into Luke's good graces again. Luke had even given him back his guitar in return for some free performances. He even got Reds Broomall to fix up Luke's busted walls. It was hard back then to stay mad at Bill. He was so polite and always a good draw. Even other entertainers would come to hear him at Luke's."

Marshall Lytle and his brother Cliff were two of Bill's admirers. Marshall remembers Bill always introducing them and other local musicians in the audience and getting them to come up on the stage to do a few tunes. This popular rite also gave Bill's voice a few minutes of badly needed rest.

The next months Bill Haley demanded at least two hours rehearsal every day except Sunday. The three men would take popular tunes and play them in many different styles, trying to syncopate the various rhythms and cadences into a new format. They experimented on dozens of little used or half forgotten techniques to build volume and create unique sound effects. They used many of the techniques Bill had observed in his travels around the country. True to Bill's prediction, John Grande, being the only musician who could read music, became the chief arranger and recorder of most of their new material.

In one technique which became dominant, Bill would back-slap the strings on the bass fiddle, the way he saw Pee Wee Miller do it when he played with Cousin Lee. This unusual technique changed the bass from a melodic to a percussion instrument. It gave the early "Rockabilly" music to come some of the drive and power that drums would add later when they would cross over to the unknown dominions of the sound known as "Rock'n'Roll".

Left to right: Bill Haley on fiddle, Johnny Grande, Jimmy Weidow and Al Thompson on bass.

Courtesy R. Kayser

Bill with fan, Jimmy Weidow, lead guitarist, and "Big Al" Thompson.

Courtesy R. Kayser

One of their early bass players was Al Thompson, a large hulk of a man of over four hundred pounds. He had lived across from Bill on Shaw Terrace in Chester. Bill had taught Al how to play the bass and added him to the band as a comic-musician. Al would dress in a ragged pair of cut-off jeans and a too small shirt which made him look like he was bustin' out of his clothes. With his floppy hat, he clowned around playing his great bass as if it were a toy. Bill would sometimes introduce him to the audience as his poor half-wit cousin from Possum Trot, Tennessee. Al Thompson's hilarious comic routines with the bull fiddle became a standard part of the repertoire of the band for many years to come. Bill Haley's unique ability to add slapstick comedy to his performances was a feature that he would keep in his shows for the rest of his life. This was one of his unique gifts as a master showman as well as a bandleader.

Soon after, another talented musician, Albert Piccirilli, who used the stage name Al Rex, took over Thompson's place in the band. Rex had the added talent of an excellent voice as well as a gift for comic routines. His zany stunts earned him the title of the "Milton Berle of the Saddlemen's Show."

With a new enthusiasm and several months of intense practice, Bill felt he had the makings of one of the most versatile bands in the area. These kids were natural musicians and took to music like ducks to water. They could play anything from polkas to Dixieland, Bill's wild Cowboy Jump to Western Swing. Bill advertised the group on the radio every chance he got. He featured them on his program as the "house band" and booked them in as many places as he could find, but he knew he needed a full time manager to really go places.

Al "Rex" Piccirilli, Bill's flamboyant bass player, 1951.

©DAP

On January 24, 1950 Bill signed a contract with Jack Howard to be his "Personal manager and publicity agent". This curious document, witnessed by Eddie Malle, gave Howard a 10% commission on all bookings up to $200.00; 15% from 201.00 to $300.00 and a very generous 25% of all earnings over $300.00.

Jack Howard, in turn, signed an exclusive booking agreement with the Jolly Joyce Agency for the Saddlemen. The contract, dated April 21, 1950, guaranteed free radio plugs for all appearances within a radius of one hundred miles of Chester. It also stated the following prices for the group; $200.00 for Sundays, and $150.00 on all other days. This contract, with its hefty fees, show that Bill was getting ready to break into the main Country-western circuit.

Unfortunately, the money was seldom that good. Records show that on May 17th, 1950, the band played at the Abruzzi and Molise Hall in Chester for a fee of $55.00. That breaks down to about $12.00 per man after Howard's commission was deducted. On Sunday June 18th, the Saddlemen played four forty-five minute shows at the Rocky Springs Park near Lancaster for $75.00. After commissions, union fees and travel expenses, a one hundred and forty mile drive, each man cleared less than twelve dollars.

By August, the band was playing a two week engagement at the Shore Bar, in Cape May, New Jersey. This was the first of a decade-long summer residency for Bill's bands on the popular Atlantic beachfront resorts. This contract offered $350.00 for playing seven days a week, from 9 P.M. to 2 A.M, forty minutes on and twenty minutes off per hour. The week before, they were performing at the Circle A Ranch all day for $81.00. With a little arithmetic one can see the boys in the band usually made as little as $2.00 to $3.00 an hour for their efforts. John Grande recalls: *"Bill connived and contrived to get us some pocket money. . . one show a week, officially, at the station. We sort of drifted into others. In the beginning, we were paid eighteen dollars a week, and my folks thought I had flipped when I told them I was happy about it. I found an outside job with the Wilmark System, a store protective service. I was lucky to have a boss who wanted to see me make it in music. Whenever our bookings were good, I'd quit. When they were bad, he would hire me back. Billy Williamson, at various times, worked in the hosiery mill, a woolen mill, and as a plumber's helper. Haley, at the radio station, worked practically around the clock. When he had his "Country Store" show, at 6:00 A.M., he even slept at the studio.*

"We took any booking we could get, lodge dances, banquets, weddings, little joints that called themselves night clubs. But the important thing was that we rehearsed in the studio every day for two years. The people there, including Mr. Pollar, went out of their way to help us. One of the engineers gave us a big assist by putting our trial runs on tape and playing them back so we could study them. When we were broke, he would sort of delay putting it on the bill. "We were always looking for something different. We'd take a standard, like "Ida," and play it every way we could think of . . . fast, slow, loud, soft, hillbilly, waltz, Dixie, progressive. Haley was like a scientist, putting one thing after another into a test tube. One of the most important of those happened the day we were studying some Count Basie records. Since we didn't have brasses, we fooled around with the strings, trying to get the same effect, trying to build volume. Haley, with the bass, discovered that when he plucked the strings in the accepted way, it came out 'rrom-pahhh'. If he back-slapped them, it changed the accent to 'rrrroom-pah'. That's how the heavy backbeat became the basic form in our new sound. As Bill experimented with the band, he would say to us, 'We've got to get them on their feet. Make them move. Make them feel the rhythm.' American music was in a period where vocalists were the top attraction. Nobody danced anymore. The big band sound had died and the dance halls were empty. Thousands of good musicians were out of work. Bill Haley wanted to get the nation back on its feet.

"Every time we did get a club date," Grande continued, *"We watched every minute to see what effect our new music had on people. Once we thought the secret was to play it loud. If people couldn't talk across a table, maybe they would get up and dance. We peaked up our amplifiers . . . and got thrown out of more joints that way. The owners didn't like it when people danced instead of buying drinks. Volume alone wasn't the answer."*

The secret was to be found in their mixture of rhythm, beat and drive. The actual formula was still elusive. However, they knew that they had tapped into something unique.

In the summer of 1950, through the efforts of Jimmy Myers, Bill Haley and his Saddlemen cut their first records. They were on Ed Wilson's Keystone label, a small Philadelphia independent publisher. The songs were standard western swing tunes: *Deal Me A Hand / Ten Gallon Stetson* and *Susan Van Dusan / I'm Not To Blame.* These rare 78 rpm records recently brought bids of over $500.00 each from astute collectors. They are the first recordings of the band that would become the nucleus of the world famous Comets.

At Jack Howard's request, Bill does a promotional record for Reno Browne. Browne was an attractive blonde, Western movie star who had starred in several low-budget films for Monogram Pictures. Bill's vocals on this Cowboy label record, *My Sweet*

©DAP

First known photo of Bill Haley and his Saddlemen, spring 1950. Left to right: Billy Williamson, Johnny Grande, Slim Allsman and Bill with his head down. Note poster on wall.

Bill Haley and the Saddlemen's first record, 1950.

Bill Haley's last Cowboy recording 1950.

Little Girl From Nevada / My Palomino And I are credited to "Reno Browne and Her Buckaroos featuring Bill Haley on vocals". Label credits notwithstanding, the "Buckaroos" are actually the Saddlemen. The release was favorably reviewed in Billboard on December 2, 1950: *"Bill Haley chants a zippy western rhythm tune with presence and projection, lively combo underneath."*

In October, four other Saddlemen tracks are also leased by Myers Music to the larger New York, "Atlantic" label: *Why Do I Cry Over You? / I'm Gonna Dry Every Tear With A Kiss* and *Teardrops From My Eyes / Loveless Blues.* Only the first two tracks are released.

Like Bill's earlier efforts, these recordings enjoyed only a limited success, selling but a few thousand copies in the mid-Atlantic states. Bill continued recording standard Country-Western songs because they helped pay the bills, and no one seemed to want to record his primitive cowboy-jive sound. The money the band made from their "cowboy" music kept the dream alive while they continued the search for their new hybrid, breakthrough sound.

These were rough times for the band and for Bill Haley personally. When the guys' morale would get real low, and a sense of frustration prevailed, it was the wit and courage of Billy Williamson who often pulled them through many times. Williamson's comic personality and "All American Boy" looks masked his unique contributions to the group as a first rate songwriter, idea man and excellent lyricist. United with John Grande's arrangement skills, Bill found he couldn't have had two better partners. The combined talents of these three young musicians were to lay the foundations of the world's first true "Rock'n'roll" band. The main problem now was to hang on till their "miracle" came.

Far from the smoke-filled clubs and the open-air park engagements that kept the Saddlemen going, a world shaking event was unfolding which would have another direct effect on the future of the struggling little band. On June 25th, 1950 the armies of North Korea invaded South Korea. America and her United Nations allies were drawn into another bitter Asian war. For Bill Haley and the Saddlemen this conflict created a whole new type of audience. Tens of thousands of young sailors and soldiers were called up. Many of them poured into the garrisons and naval bases around Philadelphia.

One of the band's first breaks came when Jim Myers, an associate of Jack Howard's publishing company, pulled a few strings and got the Saddlemen a two-week engagement at the Spigot Cafe in Philadelphia. Here Haley introduced the new primitive beat of his lively "Cowboy Jive" music to this new audience of young sailors from the nearby naval yard. The Korean War was building up and the ships of the fleet made their scheduled visits to the city's massive naval repair base. Their awaiting crews, made up of thousands of young men from all over the nation, became a new beer drinking, music loving audience which packed the clubs and bars on both sides of the Delaware River. The Spigot contract still exists and spells out the terms of the gig: *"The unit known as Bill Haley and his Saddlemen will perform six hours a night from Monday to Saturday. Saturday from 5 P.M. til midnight, all other nights 7 P.M. til 2 A.M. The sum of $281.25 a week has been agreed."*

Newspaper ad 1951

The young sailors who filled the Spigot Cafe loved Bill Haley's brand of guitar bustin' cowboy-jive. As news of the sailors' response reached the owners of other clubs, the Saddlemen became one of the hot new bands in the area. One very popular club owner, John Anthony, invited the band to play at his club for two weeks at $350.00 a week. Anthony's club was the famous Twin Bar in Gloucester, New Jersey, just across the Delaware River from the Navy yards. Here the band found a home and a base to build an audience that would appreciate their unique sound. Bill Haley and his Saddlemen were soon playing to a packed house. Here Bill and his musicians perfected their early unique "Rockabilly" sound.

At the Twin Bar about ten o'clock every Friday and Saturday night, the Saddlemen would stop playing their country-western music. Bill would then announce to the crowd with a big grin, *"All you hillbillies out there gotta go home now, cause we're gonna play a little something we call Cowboy-Jive. It's a mixture of Western swing, Dixieland, and hard-edge blues. And we're the only band crazy enough to play it. So all you hillbillies cut loose, and let the cool cats swing, cause we're gonna rock this joint tonight".* Then, with their two amplifiers on a full ten, the Saddlemen would create a sound like no other on earth. Bill Haley's version of *"We're Gonna Rock This Joint Tonight"* would vibrate off the walls so hard you could "feel" the music! As the older generation and the lovers of pure country music made it for the doors with their hands over their ears, the young people would pack the large room. Within ten minutes, the placed "rocked" with the craziest music this side of the moon.

The band was to play an unprecedented eighteen months at the Twin Bar. They built up a loyal, enthusiastic following and a growing chorus of criticism. One irate customer remembers complaining that the music was so loud her ears rang for three days. Another said she *"thought it was a shame how they abused their instruments. They were not made to be played like that, I know because I was a music teacher, and no real musicians treat their instruments like that!"*

The steady paychecks, packed rooms and some profits from their records gave the group their first taste of success. Bill found it necessary to give up his management duties at WPWA, but asked Pollar if he could keep his show at the station. Pollar said it was no problem, for his young musical director had become a top radio celebrity and was a valuable asset to the station.

Billy Williamson and Johnny Grande decided the times were good enough to get married. Grande recalls: *"As you might expect from our own long friendship, Billy married an Italian girl and I married an Irish girl. Cathy was a practical nurse at the Delaware County Hospital when she came to hear us in Lima, Pennsylvania, and suddenly, that confirmed bachelor, Billy, wasn't quite so "confirmed" anymore. I met Helen O'Shaughnessy in Philadelphia . . . and when my folks, like good Italians, were still saying I should have a steady job before I thought of getting married, Helen was saying, "I'm a good office worker. That makes one regular income in the family."* We *got married when the band found its first two-week engagement. Billy and Catherine Cafra on November 29, 1950; Helen and I on December 2, 1950. The girls went with us, and our fine friends, Mr. and Mrs. Ralph Caletti, of the Edgemont Inn, Trenton, New Jersey, greeted us with a double wedding cake and a party!"*

Once again Bill felt he was on the verge of a major breakthrough, career-wise. Not only was he doing six radio shows a week, playing to packed clubs every weekend, singing, yodeling and doing comic acts at theater matinees with Jack Howard, he was also writing and publishing his own songs.

Back in Salem, his bewildered young wife Dorothy had given birth to Bill's first son on December 1st of 1950. She named the little boy John William Haley. For months now, she had resigned herself to her lonely existence. She felt lucky to see Bill for a few hours a week. Once more, his career was demanding most of his wakening hours. She cried and wished things were different, but she knew she had little influence over her driven, fame-seeking husband. Her tear-stained pillow was her only company on many a desolate night. Now with a new baby, a three year old, and an absent, seemingly indifferent husband, Dorothy leaned on the strong moral support of her father. It was he who gave her the will and the courage to go on with her empty and lonely marriage.

Meanwhile, in May of 1951, Dave Miller, a young and enterprising ex-Navy man and President of Palda Records, called Jack Howard and asked him if Bill Haley was on contract with any record companies, including Howard's own Cowboy label. Howard said to his knowledge, Haley did not have a recording contract. Miller had caught Bill's radio show and his act at the Twin Bar. He was impressed with Bill's band and their new sound. He called Haley at the radio station and asked him if he would be interested in doing a "Bill Haley" version of a song called *Rocket 88.* It had just been released on the Chess label by Jackie Brenston and was doing well in the black juke boxes.

Dave Miller's genius preceded Sam Phillips of Sun Records by three years in recognizing the potential of a white performer who could sing like a black man. His selection of Bill Haley to do this historic record set into motion events of monumental proportions.

Bill was excited, but he told Miller he would let him know the following day. Bill had just hung up the phone when it rang again. An excited Jack Howard was yelling, *"Bill, you lucky S.O.B., this is the break you've been waiting for! Dave Miller wants to record your kind of stuff! And he might sign you guys to a record contract! He owns his own pressing plant, print shop, and distribution system!"* Howard's enthusiasm only added to Bill's building excitement.

Bill Haley's first record on Dave Miller's Holiday label.

Courtesy P. Miller

Dave Miller, President of Palda Records. Pioneer of Rockabilly recording.

Bill Haley's only comment was he wanted to get paid a little something up front for the arrangement and a percentage for each record sold. Plus he wasn't interested in any "free publicity" from the mob's jukeboxes. If Miller can live with that, they had a deal.

Several days later, Bill and the band were gathered in the small basement office at WPWA. Because the Saddlemen did not have a lead guitarist, Bill asked an old friend, Danny Cedrone, to join them on this important recording. They all listened to the Brenston rhythm and blues version of *Rocket 88.* After rehearsing it for several hours, they added their "cowboy-jive" rhythm and beat arrangement. After several more hours of practice, they went upstairs and cut a demo acetate disc in the station's studio. The next morning Bill delivered it to Miller in Philadelphia.

Miller told Bill he liked the rhythm and arrangement, but he wanted a more predominant beat and a more "negro" sound to the vocals. He also wanted to blow out the sides of the juke boxes like the way the Saddlemen bounced their music off the walls at the Twin Bar. Bill asked Miller if he was concerned about sound distortion and its effect on the music. Miller, who most of the band thought was a bit of an eccentric, pounded angrily on his desk with his fist and screamed sarcastically: *"Who says we're going to record music?"*

©DAP

A pensive Bill Haley with side-burns and stetson.

★★★★★★★★★★★★★★★★★★★★★★★★★★★★★★★★★★★★

BILL HALEY'S Great New HOLIDAY Record

"TEARSTAINS ON MY HEART"
(Published by Haley-Howard Publications—BMI)

"ROCKET 88"
(Published by Hill & Range Music Co.—BMI)

STILL GOING STRONG — "I'M GONNA DRY EVERY TEAR WITH A KISS" backed by "WHY DO I CRY OVER YOU"

— ASK FOR IT — **— PLAY IT —** **— SELL IT —**

★★★★★★★★★★★★★★★★★★★★★★★★★★★★★★★★★★★★

Sample of postcards mailed out by Dave Miller to disc jockeys.

The following day, June 14th, Miller and Howard met with the band in a rented Philadelphia studio. Miller arranged the mikes to amplify the terrific beat of Al Rex's unique back-slaping bass technique. After several more hours and more profane screaming by the demanding Miller, a final disc was cut to his satisfaction. Miller took this sound track and added some attention getting traffic sounds for effect.

Miller backed *Rocket 88* with a tune Bill Haley wrote called *Tearstains On My Heart.* This traditional country-western ballad had been recorded by several other artists on the Cowboy label. The two songs were released on Miller's "Holiday" label the summer of 1951 without any photos or publicity. Miller wanted to see if he had captured the "Black" sound with a white recording artist. Miller was to say many years later, in a radio interview with Stuart Colman, that he had paid Haley $25.00 and each of the sidemen $15.00 for the session.

The record sold a modest 10,000 copies in the first two months, according to Miller's accounting. It became Bill Haley's best selling record to date. Shortly thereafter the Saddlemen signed their first recording contract. The one-sided deal gave the band a royalty of one and a half cents per record sold, after studio and session musician's cost were deducted!

Several months after recording *Rocket 88,* Bill's rebellious bass player, Al Rex, leaves the band and forms his own group. He also takes over Bill's radio show at the Chester station. Meanwhile, Lou Pollar sells WPWA and the station changes its call letters to WDRF.

©DAP

Marshall Lytle as an early Saddlemen.

Bill hires another talented young musician, Marshall Lytle, whom he has known for years. Marshall's older brother Cliff had played with Bill in the Four Western Aces, along with Tex King, who roomed at the Lytle home. Bill was a frequent guest for dinner as the young musician fell under the persuasive charm and enthusiasm of Haley's dreams. Lytle had his own show on WVCH, a com-

The Cowboy Jive Band
BILL HALEY
and The
SADDLEMEN
WPWA Cancer Program Nets $16,000
A total of $16,000 in pledged contributions toward the 1949 Cancer Drive was rolled up by the nearly 13 hour program conducted by Station WPWA on Saturday, it was announced today by the studio.
From 6 a. m. until the station went o.. the air at 6.45 p. m., Bill Haley and his Western Aces spearheaded a continuous program of music, talks by prominent local residents, and messages from nationally-known persons—all for the 1952 Cancer Drive.
Contributions brought or mailed to the studio and pledges given in telephone calls brought the total close to $16,000 today.
There were personal appearances by a number of entertainers, telegrams read from Milton Berle, Tallulah Bankhead and others, and recorded telephone interviews with such stars as Ray Bolger and Melvin Douglas.
Bill Haley
Rhythm Guitar
Billy Williamson
Steel Guitar
Johnny Grande
Accordian and Piano
Marshall Lytle
Bass
POPULAR
HILLBILLY
JIVE
COWBOY
HOLIDAY
RECORDS
DISC-JOCKEY COPY
HALEY-HOWARD PUB.
BMI
(H-108B)
Mfgd. by
PALDA RECORD CO.
PHILA., PENNA.
DOWN DEEP IN MY HEART
(Haley)
BILL HALEY
and the
SADDLEMEN
3 Years on
Radio Station WPWA
Guest Shots on
WFIL-TV
3 Months at
Spigot Musical Bar
Phila.
12 Months at
Twin Bar
Gloucester, N. J.
NIGHT CLUBS
THEATRES
TELEVISION
RECORDS
Extra Added
Attraction
For Outdoor Dates
Lou Graham
Vocalist
The Most Versatile Band in the Land
The Nation's Leading Representative for Hillbilly and Western Artists
JACK HOWARD PROMOTIONS
"IN THE HEART OF THE LARGEST BUYING MARKET IN THE EAST"
122 N. 12th STREET—PHILADELPHIA 7, PA.
CALL LOcust 7-3318—IF NO ANSWER CALL Kingsley 6-1287
YOU NAME THE ACT YOU WANT AND WE'LL LEAVE NO STONE UNTURNED TO SECURE IT FOR YOU

peting Chester radio station, where he also sang and played rhythm guitar. Bill taught the seventeen year old lad how to back-slap the bull fiddle and reproduce Bill's unique "clicking" sound. Marshall recalls: *"Bill asked me come and play the bass for him. I said I didn't know how to play a bass. He said: "I'll teach you". So he spent one hour and taught me the basic chords plus how to back-slap and get a shuffle beat. The day I joined the Saddlemen, I bought a bass. That night I joined them at the Twin Bar as the youngest member of the band. Bill had to pencil a thin mustache on my face to make me look older. I was under age at the time."*

Marshall also recalls his fingers were so sore and bloody, he had to wrap tape around them to pound the strings of his bass fiddle. Later, when thick callouses formed on his hands the bandaids were no longer necessary.

For the Saddlemen's next record on the Holiday label Miller selected a Haley styled "cowboy-jive" tune called *Green Tree Boogie.* He backed this one again with a traditional western ballad called *Down Deep In My Heart,* both written by Bill Haley. Danny Cedrone's partner Bob Scaltrito did the lead guitar work for these two tunes.

In August at Dave Miller's request, Bill Haley recorded two unusual country-blues duets with Loretta Glendenning; *Pretty Baby* and *I'm Crying,* also on the Holiday label. The Saddlemen also recorded without Bill on the vocals, backing Curly Herdman on the Abbey label with Bill's song *Rose Of My Heart* b/w *Barnyard Special.*

That summer Haley adds another popular young Hank Williams style singer to his show by the name of Lou Graham. The band would cut three records on Ivan Ballen's Gotham label with Lou on vocals; *Two-Timin' Blues / Long-Gone Daddy; My Heart Tells Me / Please Make Up Your Mind;* and *I'm Lonesome / A Sweet Bunch Of Roses.* A promotion flyer designed by Jack Howard stated, *"Lou Graham is available as an extra attraction for outdoor dates with the Saddlemen".*

In American popular music, Johnny Ray was singing his passionate *Cry* and *The Little Cloud That Cried,* and Hank Williams, his immortal *Cold, Cold Heart.* Clara Anne Fowler, better known as Patti Page, topped the Hit Parade with her classic rendition of *Tennessee Waltz.*

In October, Bill and his Saddlemen record two Christmas songs; *A Year Ago This Christmas* written by Bill backed with *I Don't Want To Be Alone This Christmas* for the Holiday label.

The year 1951 was prolific when one looks at the songs Bill Haley wrote and had recorded. To his already hectic schedule as a bandleader, disc jockey and songwriter, Bill made one more important, far-seeing decision. In January he had bought into Jack Howard's music publishing company and became a full partner. The firm's name was changed to Haley-Howard Publications. Their address was 122 North 12th Street in Philadelphia. This contract still exists, and in paragraph five, the shrewd and savvy Haley wrote in, *"I, Bill Haley, reserve the right to have the last word in the selection of all song material that is contracted for both publishing and/or recording with any of the singers or performers that may be under contract to HALEY-HOWARD PUBLICATIONS, with the final approval of the negotiating company".* Bill's many years in the broadcasting and live music field would serve him well in the years to come.

Bill's hands-on experience in the music business had taught him the importance of controlling his own works. He became the first rock musician to shrewdly recognize the potential value of writing, publishing and recording his own material. Six years later the gifted Buddy Holly would follow this example set by Bill Haley. A decade later, Brian Epstein, the Beatles' manager, would give John Lennon and Paul McCartney the same advice. However in 1951, Bill Haley was already deeply involved in all aspects of the music scene.

If Bill and the Saddlemen thought 1951 was a good year, 1952 proved to be even more rewarding. Their steady stream of records enjoyed a popular run in the mid-Atlantic states, and as far west as Cleveland, Ohio. The jukebox industry was still their biggest customers. Although none of these records reached the national charts, they proved to be money makers for Dave Miller. The demand for live performances kept the Saddlemen playing the parks and clubs from Baltimore to the New Jersey shore.

In January, Bill and the Saddlemen recorded their last release on the Holiday label. The first song *Jukebox Cannonball* was a pure Haley hillbilly-jump version of a classic country standard *Wabash Cannonball.* The other side, written by Bill, *Sundown Boogie,* was a fine example of his early "cowboy-jive", rockabilly musical style. Bill's old friend Rusty Keefer joined the band with his fiddle on this recording date.

Arrett "Rusty" Keefer was a popular local country-western musician. He played the fiddle, guitar and the bass with the best of them. But his greatest gift was his prolific ability to write some of the best tunes in the business. In the years to come, Keefer would become one of Bill's chief songwriters and would collaborate with the Comets on some of their best country and rock songs.

Jack Howard and Bill Haley ©DAP

★★★★★★★★★★★★★★★★★★★★★★★★★★★★★★★★★

HUNDREDS OF DISC JOCKEYS SAY

HALEY HAS HIT

WITH HIS GREAT RECORD OF

"ICY HEART"

B/W "ROCK THE JOINT"

BILL HALEY'S GETTING HOT

HE'S EXCLUSIVE WITH *Essex* RECORDS

★★★★★★★★★★★★★★★★★★★★★★★★★★★★★★★★★

Sample of postcards which Dave Miller sent out to disc jockeys.

Courtesy J. Cedrone

Early that spring, Dave Miller asked Bill if he could record the Saddlemen's wild version of *Rock The Joint* for his new Essex label. Bill had been playing it as his theme song for over a year in their live performances. Jack Howard had suggested recording the tune and Miller noticed how the younger crowd went crazy over it.

Haley's primitive hillbilly-boogie music was steadily developing into a more urban, hard-edge Rockabilly sound. Dave Miller pushed the not so subtle changes. He wanted to record this new heavier beat and its driving rhythm.

This ground-breaking song was cut using Bill's own arrangement. He poured all the power and energy he could muster into that recording session. Forcing a strong rhythm from the piano and guitars and a driving beat from Lytle's bass, Bill and his Saddleman create their first true rock song. Haley's clear diction added another sharp cadence to this classic early rock'n'roll tune. The verses and chorus were alternated with letter-perfect solos by Grande, Williamson and Danny Cedrone, who was asked again by Bill to play the lead guitar on this important recording. Cedrone's brilliant and fiery jazz inspired solo was so impressive Bill Haley would have him repeat it note for note when he recorded *Rock Around the Clock* two years later. Cedrone, who had his own group called the "Esquire Boys", would go down in Rock history as one of the first true rock guitarists. As a lasting tribute to Cedrone's unique style and skill Bill Haley would gauge all other lead guitarists by this musician's genius. Long after Danny's untimely death, when Bill had become an international superstar, he would tell all other young, aspiring guitarists who wanted to join his band *"When you can play like Cedrone, come back and see me."* On the other side of *Rock The Joint* the Saddlemen recorded *Icy Heart*, a song inspired by Hank Williams' *Cold, Cold Heart*. It was a moderate beat country ballad in classic Saddlemen style. Billboard gave *Rock The Joint* the following cautious review in its April 26, 1952 issue: *". . .jumpy opus is an odd mixture of country-western and rhythm and blues. Nevertheless, Bill Haley and the Saddlemen manage to generate a sense of excitement."*

Danny Cedrone, the Comets' lead guitarist on many early recordings.

As Bill's career as an entertainer, songwriter and publisher began to rise, his six year old marriage to Dorothy became practically non-existent. For most of the past year he seldom saw his wife. When Bill did go home to Salem, only forty miles away, his trips were more like visits than homecomings.

Bill's birthday July 6, 1952. Ruth Kayser presents a home-baked cake to the Saddlemen.

Courtesy M. Lytle

One poignant evening in the summer of 1952, Bill made one of his unannounced "little visits". Awkwardly, he told Dottie he had gotten a young girl into "trouble". Dorothy broke down and cried at first, but in seeing the futility of protest, she told her wayward husband he could have a divorce if he remembered his responsibility to their two children.

She knew he was having affairs, but the sudden reality of something like this happening caught her off guard. She asked who was the "lucky" girl and did she know her? Bill just stared at the floor almost too ashamed to talk. He said his girl friend's name was Joan Cupchak, but everybody called her "Cuppy". She lived up in Camden. Painfully embarrassed, Bill told Dottie she had probably seen her around the Twin Bar. He then went on to tell her he first met the nineteen year old blonde when she went up to John Grande, after a performance, and asked to meet Bill Haley and get his autograph. Grande made the fateful introduction.

Dorothy's first reaction was hurt and anger at the "other woman", but this soon turned into pity and a prayer for her. Dorothy knew many women found her husband irresistible. The lucky ones got the one night stands. The ones that married him became the true "victims" for even Cuppy would soon find she couldn't compete with Bill's greatest love—music and the adoration it could create. Bill received his divorce on November 14th, 1952. He promptly married his very pregnant girl friend four days later on November 18th, 1952.

That summer all America would hear Bill Haley and his "crazy" new sound with its pounding beat. As requests for the Saddlemen's new sound grew, Bill realized the band needed a full time manager. They needed a strong business manager to better handle the publicity, bookings and the cash flow, a man who knew show business and could be a full time promoter, disciplinarian, critic, adviser, and tough contract negotiator.

The first man Bill asked was James E. Myers, who had been an associate with Jack Howard in Howard Publications Inc. Jim Myers was a prolific song writer, band leader and now President of his own publishing company, Myers Music. He knew his way around the entertainment business. The two men had known each other since 1947, when Myers had asked Haley, then a disc jockey at WPWA, to spin a couple of his records on the air. Haley would give Myers' records air time, and Jim would give Bill access to recording studios, contacts in the record business and some of his songs. The two ambitious men became business associates,

James E. Myers, aka Jimmy deKnight, President of Myers Music. Courtesy J. Myers

with common goals. Bill's former recordings on Center, Keystone, and Atlantic Records were partly due to Jim Myers' wide contacts in the publishing business.

However, at this time Myers told Bill he could help more on the publishing end of the business than traveling with the band. Jim felt his talents were more in writing, recording and publishing songs than in promoting live performances. Besides, he and Max Freedman were working on a new pop tune called *Rock Around the Clock* which he hoped Bill would record for him.

Bill then asked another radio associate, James H. Ferguson, who had been helping him with advice and publicity for some time already. Jim worked at WPWA with Bill, doing a sports commentary show each morning. Ferguson, who everybody called "Lord Jim", got the nickname from his early days when he sailed the seven seas as a cadet on a large sailing ship. The numerous short stories he wrote to his friends back home reminded them of the exotic tales of the "Lord Jim" of literary fame. Ferguson had spent the war years as a Lt. Commander of a navy salvage vessel in the Pacific.

James Ferguson was also the publisher of a small weekly newsletter called "Lord Jim's Letter". The paper was distributed free to local taverns, restaurants, and other establishments. It featured short stories and articles about local people, happenings and coming attractions in Chester's taverns and restaurants. Lord Jim thought of himself as the "Walter Winchell" of Chester. He filled his little paper with gossip and spicy little tidbits on the area's sports and entertainment personalities. If a retailer or bar owner would buy an advertisement in his paper, Lord Jim would make sure a favorable article would follow on how good their food or the music was. Sometimes when their food and music were terrible, Lord Jim would find something else good to say, even if it was just how big the drinks were. He also, for a small fee, would write a favorable article on anyone who wanted to see their name in print.

Lord Jim was also well known as a fast talking scoundrel, a character right out of a Damon Runyon novel. To many of the barroom denizens in the Chester area he was a likeable rogue with a very large frame and a great, booming belly laugh, especially when he told one of his many off-color jokes. His powerful slap on the back was the dread of many a smaller soul who were slow to get the punch line of his latest crude joke. As an ex-prize fighter and bar owner, Ferguson always seemed to move in and out of Chester's shadowy underworld. So everybody laughed at Lord Jim's jokes, and privately, everybody laughed at Lord Jim's pretensions.

With his large ten cent cigars, he would try to put on the airs of being somebody important to know, a friend of the rich and famous, but would lose all credibility by his complete disregard of basic civil conventions. He seldom wore socks, even when he wore a business suit, and his gaudy ties always seemed to record his last ten meals. When asked once by an embarrassed Bill Haley to please get a new tie for an important meeting with some Decca record executives, Lord Jim smiled and said. *"Not to worry, I always look good in everything I eat!"*

Jim Ferguson also personally knew and had an uncanny likeness to another celebrated manager, Col. Tom Parker. Parker would one day make another young man named Elvis Presley a show-business legend. Both of these managers were cast from the same mold. They both had the same round, fat, cigar-chewing face, the same build, the same garish mannerisms, and the same questionable ethics. Both would proudly tell you they were just a couple of old con-men and refer to the days when carnival and fight promoters would hype and exaggerate the greatness of their shows to attract the suckers. But at this stage in his career, Bill

James Ferguson, "Lord Jim", Bill's crafty manager,

Haley felt he needed a good "carny-man" and Jim "Fast Fergie" Ferguson saw some potential big bucks to be made in this little band with its loud but unique new sound. In fact, Lord Jim saw a potential goldmine! Unfortunately, Bill Haley was one of the few people in Chester who did not see Ferguson for what he really was.

Johnny Grande tells it like this: *"We got our fourth partner, Jim Ferguson, who was our promotion and business manager, in an off-handed way. Jim was a big, colorful character who had been all over the world, commanding a Navy vessel. "Lord Jim", as everybody called him, published a little newspaper and was a sports commentator at WPWA. He took an interest in us and helped us. When we felt low, he encouraged us. We were his hobby. . . until eventually we took up so much of his time, we asked him if he would let us be his business. . . if he would become a partner. Jim is the one who foraged around, and got us bookings, guided us through the times when we didn't fit anywhere."*

Late in 1952, inspired by his adopted theme song *Rock The Joint*, Bill Haley would write the quintessential rock song, *Rock A Beatin' Boogie* which would later be recorded by Danny Cedrone and his group the Esquire Boys. Bill Haley tells this story in an article published in 1955: *"I was sitting at the kitchen table trying to write this tune. The first lyric was easy, 'Rock, rock, rock everybody!' Then I wrote 'Stomp, stomp, stomp everybody!' But it didn't fit. I then wrote in, 'Roll, roll, roll everybody!' It sounded better, I liked the two R's sound of rock and roll. The rest is history!"* This "Rock" classic was also recorded on Okeh label by a black group called the Treniers a few months later. Bill himself would not record the song until 1955. Only his recorded version has the above quoted introduction.

This historic tune would become one of the theme songs for the famous "Moon Dog Show", which launched the career of rock's greatest prophet, Alan Freed on Cleveland's radio station WJW. Freed's opening yell was to chant Bill Haley's opening lyrics: *"Rock, Rock, Rock Everybody. . . .Roll, Roll, Roll, Everybody"* as he pounded a phone book in unison with the revolutionary song. Alan Freed later would often say on the air: *"Tonight kids, we're gonna Rock'n'roll".* Eventually the term "Rock'n'roll" came to differentiate Haley's new sound from the shuffling beat of traditional black rhythm and blues music. Later, to cash in on the growing rock'n' roll craze, any tune with the most remote beat was dubbed "rock'n'roll, as dozens of choregraphed-harmonizing groups and finger-snapping soloists would use rock's bandwagon to break into the pop music field.

The word "rock" had a long history in the English language as a metaphor for *"to shake up, to disturb or to incite".* Shakespeare used it in his play "Venus and Adonis" when he wrote *"My throbbing heart shall rock thee day and night".* The verb "Roll" was a medieval metaphor which meant "having sex". Writers for hundreds of years have used the phrases "They had a roll in the hay" or "I rolled her in the clover". In an old English sea chanty we can find the lyrics:

"Oh do, me Johnny Bowker. . .
Come Rock'n'Roll me over"

In the old Cockney slang "Bowker" and "over" rhyme. The combination of the two verbs became a popular euphemism for wild, shake'um up, illicit sex. Centuries later the phrase was adopted into the slang of the American Negro jazz musicians who are now thought to have created it. Alan Freed is given the credit for coining the phrase "Rock 'n'Roll" when referring to this new method of playing music. Although he began as a rhythm and blues disc jockey, he was one of the first to popularized Bill's new and exciting format of musical expression. His late-night record show became a pulpit for his nocturnal ravings and hip-jive talk—as he preached the gospel of Rock to tens of thousands of eager young converts.

It is but a footnote in history that a white country boy from rural Pennsylvania should write one of the first true rock'n'roll songs, *Rock A Beatin' Boogie*, and that would be recorded by a popular and talented black group (The Treniers). It is also ironic that when he did record his own song with the Comets three years later, it would be labeled a "cover" version. The word "cover" was a record business term for earthy black music, cleaned up and recorded by white artists for a larger and more predominant teen audience.

The year 1952 saw Tex Ritter's haunting lyrics; *"Do not forsake me O'my darling"* from *High Noon* become one of the top songs on the *Hit Parade*. Hank Williams continued his string of classics with his cajun-jumper called *Jambalaya* and Kitty Wells sang her immortal ode to bar room sweethearts in *It Wasn't God Who Made Honky-Tonk Angels.*

With the release of *Rock the Joint* Bill Haley and his Saddlemen had developed and recorded for the first time a very distinctive new sound. By electrifying and magnifying it on their high powered amplifiers, they created a strange unfocused music of raw, almost savage power. Its very essence troubled some people. Their beat and rhythm was wilder, and more driven, than anything then offered from a traditional Western Swing band. They played with such frenzy that their instruments seemed to groan in agony. The term, "guitar bustin'" meant just that, as strings often twanged into the air and the bass shattered. The Saddlemen played their instruments with a wild abandon, as if they were going crazy. Many thought they were just a bunch of crazy musicians horsing around. Although they made it seem very spontaneous, it was often well planned and well rehearsed.

Many professional musicians would shake their heads in disbelief, but Haley's seemingly bizarre techniques and hard driving sounds found a new, enthusiastic audience, who were looking for something totally different. However, many people believed the band to be just a freak attraction, and scoffed at any suggestion that this "crazy hillbilly-nigger" music might be a new musical form.

The Saddlemen and their sound were so far from the mainstream of traditional Country-Western music that they looked totally out of place in their gaudy cowboy suits. This was noted by their new manager.

Lord Jim, who was watching the band with an old friend and former club owner, Sam Sgro, remarked: *"Sam, how do you like my boys?"* Sgro replied: *"Jim, they got a good sound and a solid beat, but what's with the cowboy suits?"* Sgro wasn't the first to point out how inappropriate the cowboy costumes were to this "real gone" band. Lord Jim also wondered who ever thought up the name "Cowboy-Jive". These guys were playing hard-edge, electric country blues, and there ought to be a better name than "Cowboy-Jive". Lord Jim had a long "dutch-uncle" talk with Bill and the guys that night. *"If you boys want to play in the uptown lounges some day, or want to be taken as serious musicians, you got to get out of those cowboy suits. I know you guys love hillbilly music, but that's not where the big bucks are. You guys have got something. You don't sound like nothing I've ever heard. But I do know this, it ain't hillbilly, it ain't cowboy and it ain't jazz. And you guys are too pale to be a rhythm and blues combo. In fact, what you guys do ain't even music to most people. And we ain't gonna make any money on the damn jukebox sales. But the younger people seem to like it, and that's a start. We've got to find an audience other then the sailors. This war ain't gonna last forever, and sailors don't buy records. We've gotta reach the kids and get on the charts. It's the kids who buy records, and hell, you'll never reach them in beer joints."*

Bill, looking very interested, said *"Any suggestions boys"?*

"Yes, but I don't know if you guys will go for it," said Lord Jim, as he looked each of them in the face. *"If the kids won't come to you, why don't you go where they are . . . . . in the schools?"* Grande recalls, *"We knew that score, no dough! But Haley had an idea and we took a vote. That's how it happened, we played the high-school assemblies. It was tough to do at the time, but it proved the smartest thing we ever tried. The kids taught us. We tried our experiments on them. When their shoulders starting moving, their feet tapping and their hands clapping, we knew that particular tune or style was worth keeping in the act. It was Haley's ear, the Haley sensitivity to his audience which brought us our first hit."*

By July, Dave Miller called Bill to say *Icy Heart / Rock the Joint* was a hit on the jukeboxes, and he wanted Bill and Jack Howard to go on a promotional tour of influential radio stations and plug the record on the air waves. With a bundle of twenty-five dollar U.S. Savings Bonds, Bill and Jack Howard took off on a promotional tour to see major disc jockeys who could find time to play the Essex record and interview Haley on the air. It was one of the customs of the time for disc jockeys to be given a small "thank you" remuneration, in the form of a savings bond, for their much appreciated courtesy and hospitality.

Later, these small gestures of "goodwill" grew into a vicious system of power influence. Influential disc-jockeys and TV personalities demanded substantial cash payments, percentages of royalties, sexual favors and other considerations to give new records air time. They became all-powerful St. Peters of the golden gate to the heaven of the national charts. Few new artists, recording on small, independent labels, could break into the big time without the blessing and/or the bribery of these gate-keepers of stardom. By the late 1950's, this scandal would reach the halls of Congress, and the wide-spread practice would one day be outlawed as "Payola". However in 1952, it was the custom and Miller and Haley played the game as did most of their competitors.

Bill and Howard had been visiting mostly country-western disc-jockeys urging them to play *Icy Heart*. Bill was even planning on being invited to perform at the Grand Ole Opry, a tradition for artists with best selling country-western records. He had even just talked to Hank Williams at his home. Hank told him how proud he was of Bill finally making it to Nashville. The Grand Ole Opry was a dream Bill had had since childhood. It was ironic that just as he was about to achieve his ten year ambition as a country-western singer, his "other" sound would soon catapult him to an un-dreamed of superstar status.

Bill Haley was in a motel in Nashville when he received a urgent phone call from Miller, who told him it wasn't *Icy Heart* that was selling, but the flip side, *Rock the Joint!* Bill quickly back-tracked to Chicago and Cleveland then down to Richmond, Washington and Baltimore. Everywhere they went the "Pop" disc-jockeys were saying, *"Man, you've got a record there!"* According to Haley over 200,000 copies were eventually sold. At last he was recognized across the land. Jukeboxes and radio stations fueled a teenage buying frenzy, and a new music was to come of age.

With its new name, courtesy of Alan Freed's Moon Dog Rock'n'Roll House Party radio show, Bill Haley's new format for the celebration of sound was given wings. No longer a negro music wailing deep in the souls and ghettos of the nation's subculture. No longer a country-western music played by hillbillies in cowboy hats. Neither black nor white, but a powerfully new American music.

Alan Freed, one of Rock's greatest impresarios.

Created from the blood, sweat and best traditions of both, but bowing to none. Soon the youth of five continents would fall before its thundering beat and hypnotic rhythms. A new, exciting, renegade music form had been born, but there would be hell to pay. Rock music was a bastard sound. The old music establishment had traditionally looked down on Rock's lowly un-wed parents, its black rhythm and blues mother and the red-neck hillbilly-jump daddy. But that was mild compared to the ridicule and scorn they would heap on the offspring. Yes, O'yes sir! There was going to be hell to pay!

The lyrics alone would condemn it. Didn't the opening lines of *Rock the Joint* foretell the wanton destruction of private property that was to come? And didn't police, teachers and churchmen say it would lead to the moral decay of the nation's young people? This wasn't your usual teenage swoon-moon music about stolen kisses on the cheek, under the old apple tree. This would be interpreted as a deliberate call for wanton destruction, an invitation to mayhem and lawlessness on an unprecedented scale:

"We're gonna tear down the mailbox,
Rip up the floor,
Smash out the windows,
And knock down the door!
We're gonna rock this joint tonight!"

Unbeknownst to the so-called powers that be, Bill Haley had opened a musical Pandora's Box and the virus would spread until the breeze became a cultural hurricane. Bill Haley's disciples had yet to catch the bug, but his infectious rhythms and beat would soon be seducing their dormant talents.

In that spring of 1952, when Bill Haley was recording *Rock the Joint*, twenty-one year old Chuck Berry was a hairdresser in St. Louis, thinking about joining a little rhythm and blues combo to make some extra money. In 1955 he would record his first hit on the Chess label, *Maybellene*.

Twenty-three year old Ellas Bates (Bo Diddley) was also three years away from his first hit record. Down in Lubbock, Texas, fourteen year old Buddy Holly, still in junior high school, was dreaming of forming his own band some day. Twenty year old Richard Penniman (Little Richard) was working odd jobs in Macon, Georgia, still three years away from his first hit song, "Tutti Frutti". Twenty-three year old Antoine "Fats" Domino known for his "New Orleans sound", would not adapt his pounding boogie-woogie piano style to a more rock beat until 1955.

Another unknown, sixteen year old Jerry Lee Lewis was under the influence of the soft country music style of Gene Autry. He had just been expelled from a fundamentalist Bible school in Waxahachie, Texas. His talents and future were yet to be awakened.

Down in Memphis, Tennessee that spring of 1952, a seventeen year old boy named Elvis Presley was in the eleventh grade. He had promised his mother he was going to be a truck driver, because they made good money. He also promised her he would get her out of the hated public housing project their poverty had forced them to live in. He swore to her she would never again be on public welfare.

Over the next three years Bill Haley's remarkable string of hit rock'n'roll songs would alter the careers of thousands of musicians and vocal artists the world over. For the above six young men, Bill Haley's new sound would forever alter their destinies.

A remarkable cultural revolution was about to take place as the nation elected Dwight David Eisenhower as it s 34th President. Bill Haley had opened the door and torn down the barriers of musical prejudice, but like another pioneer-explorer, Christopher Columbus, Haley had little idea of the vast new worlds he had discovered and/or revealed nor the magnitude of its influence on the culture of the world in the second half of the twentieth century.

On his return to Chester the following week after the *Rock the Joint* promotional tour, Bill called the guys in the band about the good news. He then set

For Bookings Call LOcust 7-3318

BILL HALEY

and the

SADDLEMEN

STARS of STAGE, RADIO and RECORDS

Personal Management 122 North 12th Street
JACK HOWARD PROMOTIONS Phila. 7, Pa.

Bill's business card, 1951.

up the last recording session on which his group was called the Saddlemen. They would record two songs, *Dance with a Dolly* and *Rocking Chair On The Moon*. The first tune was a western-jump standard based on the popular song *Buffalo Gal*. The second, written by Bill, was a modified rockabilly song with a slower pace and beat than *Rock the Joint*. Bill gave his bodyguard Harry Broomall a co-writer credit on the tune as a reward for his loyalty.

The Saddlemen had begun to wear sport coats and ties when they were playing their new sound. Even for their many country-western performances they had already abandoned their flashy movie-cowboy costumes and adopted a more conservative western suit with white Stetsons that made them look more like wealthy Dallas oil men.

The record sales of *Rock the Joint* caused a change in Bill Haley's perspective of his music. Before, he had used his recordings as merchandising tools to promote his band. Now Dave Miller had shown him another way to fame and fortune through the power of record distribution. In the future, the band would become the machine to make the records which would reach more people than ten thousand live performances.

Meanwhile, Lord Jim was on the road nailing posters on telephone poles up and down the highways, advertising each new performance. Jack Howard had designed the posters that Ferguson plastered all over town. Lord Jim played up the group's new sound in his newsletter; while Bill wrote more songs to feature his new beat. Things were starting to cook now.

With their new, exciting sound and sharp looking outfits the name "Saddlemen" no longer seemed appropriate. According to Marshall Lytle, it was Bob Johnson, Program Director at WPWA who first suggested the name "Haley's Comets" for a new handle. *"Ya'know, with a name like Haley, you guys should call your group the Comets!"* Bill had been told many times his music was "far out" and the idea of a blazing comet searing across the skies appealed to him.

The family of Dave Miller also claim it was their brother Dave, with his unique knack for merchandising, who came up with the catchy name. In any event, soon after, Bill met with Billy Williamson, Johnny Grande, Lord Jim and their junior partner, Marshall Lytle and voted to adopt the snazzy new name. Thus just before the Thanksgiving holidays in 1952, the world's first true Rock'n'Roll band changed their name and their image for the last time. Off came the cowboy boots and the white Stetsons. With some regrets and more than a little apprehension, the four young musicians, turned their backs on their beloved country/western music and bravely faced an unknown future as "Bill Haley and his Comets".

First photo of Bill Haley and his Comets, December 1952.

©DAP

Courtesy© Cash Box Magazine

Dave Miller, Bill Haley and Monty Kelly on cover of Cash Box Magazine, Sept. 1953.

CHAPTER SEVEN

THE SOUND AND THE GLORY: 1953-1955

"The golden years of discovery"

For Bill Haley, the year 1953 would begin with a personal tragedy shared by all fans of country-western music the world over. About eight o'clock in the evening, after playing till the early hours of dawn at a New Years Eve bash, Bill Haley sat at his kitchen table with tears in his eyes. He tried to hold a cup a black coffee and a cigarette in his trembling hands. He had just heard on the radio about the tragic death of his mentor and idol, Hank Williams. The "Hillbilly Shakespeare" had just been found dead in the back seat of his automobile. He was twenty-nine years old, just two years older than Bill.

Haley remembered Hank's kind words and encouragement when he needed them. He also knew of the perils of driving dead tired, late at night, on unfamiliar icy roads. Bill played Hank's records for days in a strange daze of melancholy. Only when he heard Hank's newest hit, *I'll Never Get Out of This World Alive* did he smile and tell Bob Thornton *"That skinny hillbilly knew he was burning out. Now at least he'll never have to worry about being a has-been. He was the greatest and there will never be anyone like him, never!"* That night at a local bar Bill, Bob Thornton and some friends raised a glass to their fallen hero and made a fitting toast, *"Hank old boy, may ye get to heaven a half hour before the Devil knows you're there"*. They all knew of Hank's legendary vices, drinking and wenching included, and this old Irish saying was their only way to help a fallen friend charm the angels as he had won the hearts of the common people here on earth.

If most of the members of the Chester's musician's union thought Bill Haley and his rag-tag band had gone over the edge in 1952, the year 1953 would prove them right. It just depended on your definition of edge! Bill Haley was the talk of the town, and his band was taking a lot of ridicule, some of it good-natured, most of it not. But the year would bring the final fusion of two new instruments, the drums and the tenor saxophone, to the Comets' new sound. With these new "non-traditional" instruments, the band finally left the realm of the hillbilly sound behind them.

Just how difficult times were this first year is recalled by John Grande. *"We were playing a gig in New England, when the band invited Jack Howard to dinner before the show. After everyone had finished, we, one by one excused themselves, telling Jack we had to go to the "head". The band was so broke and too hungry to miss another meal. We all left by the back door and went around to the front window. There sat poor Jack—for twenty minutes he watched that men's room door—praying. Finally a nervous manager went over to him and presented the rather hefty bill. Jack trembled as he counted out his last bit of folding money—swearing under his breath. Later, when money wasn't so tight, we would all laugh about this stunt, especially because Jack was always very careful with his money."*

No one quite knew what to do with the band and this lead to some friction among Bill's advisors and publishers. Thus, they compromised and continued recording their "rock'n'roll" songs backed with their traditional country-western or what came to be known as "rockabilly". Many of the early Holiday and Essex releases set the pattern for the earthy "back-slap bass" rockabilly style that was later popularized by Elvis Presley and others. Some misinformed music historians have attributed this unique style to Presley, Buddy Holly or Carl Perkins. However, in fact, these classic Bill Haley recordings (1950-1953) pre-date any Presley, Holly, or Perkins work.

Early in 1953, while playing at the Golden Slipper in Aston, Bill was asked by Bill Falls, the club owner, if he would let his son accompany the Comets with his drums. Mr. Falls said his son could pick up the beat from the bass and would get a big kick out of it. Bill, wanting to please the club owner, agreed. Later that night, guest lead guitarist Slim Allsman mentioned to Bill: *"Those drums don't sound bad"*. Bill replied, *"You know, they sound real good!"* Shortly after that, Bill hired his first road drummer, a youngster named Charlie Higler, for a two week engagement at the Blue Mirror Club in Washington D.C. Later that spring Bill also used drummer Earl Famous for a two week gig at the Gray Stone Tavern.

Several weeks later he re-hired Higler at the Broomall Cafe. He played for the Comets during

Rare 1953 photo of the Comets showing their new drummer, Charlie Higler, second from left.

©DAP

The Comets' first record.

Billy Gussak, the legendary session drummer of the Comets Courtesy W. Gussak

most of the summer of 1953. In the fall Higler is replaced by Richard Boccelli, who uses the stage name Dick Richards. Richards, a former teacher and football player, had played drums off and on for several years. At the time he joined the Comets he was half of a lounge act called Richards and Lee, alternating sets with Bill and his Comets at the Hofbrau in Wildwood, New Jersey. Richards also proves to be an excellent baritone singer, an additional asset for the struggling band. Richards recalls: *"When Bill approached me to join his band he told me: 'We're on to something. We know we've got something new here.' I didn't believe it at first but after I joined I realized we had something that WAS completely different".*

By early spring Dave Miller was ready for another record. The jukeboxes were getting hungry. Bill wanted to test his new driving drum beat and "doctored" a song he knew called *Tennessee Jive*, turning it into *Real Rock Drive*.

The Comets couple *Real Rock Drive* with *Stop Beatin' Around the Mulberry Bush*, for their third Essex release. Miller likes the added vitality the drums make and tells Bill to be ready to record some more in a month.

For this session, Bill used drummer Billy Gussak at Miller's suggestion. Gussak was a superbly trained musician and his innovative techniques add the cadence and drive both Miller and Bill want. Gussak becomes Bill's main session drummer for the next three years.

Gussak was a student of the Juilliard School of Music, and was trained in the conservatoral style of classical music. His Russian-Jewish parents dreamed their son would one day be a classical musician like Gussak's father, who had studied violin at the famed Odessa Conservatory. However, as a young man, Gussak was attracted to the drums by listening to the sounds of Eddie Dougherty, a black drummer, who played in Harlem's famous Shim Sham Club. Billy would even slip into the back of the local black Baptist church just to feel the rhythms and beat of their music. *"My people had nothing like it at the time. I guess you can say I was inspired by Eddie's drumming and the rhythms of that beautiful Negro spiritual music."* Billy Gussak went on to be one of the most sought after drummers in the country. He played for Sid Caesar and Arthur Godfrey on their top rated television shows as well as on C.B.S.'s Hit Parade and on such pop hits as *Hernando's Hideaway* by Archie Bleyer and *Mr. Sandman* by the Chordettes. His unique ability to keep almost perfect time became indispensable to Bill Haley and his very complex music. Gussak's cadence became the vital heartbeat of the Comets' early recorded music.

On the personal side, Bill's new wife, "Cuppy" gave birth to their first daughter on March 15th, 1953. The little girl was named Joan, after her mother. The young couple lived in a small apartment in Norwood, Pa. Bill and the band were still doing free performances in the high schools to test their songs, a form of "market-testing" long before the practice became popular. From these high school concerts and interviews with hundreds of teenagers, Bill Haley writes down dozens of jive and buzz words used by his new and enthusiastic audience. They become the basis of his next hit song, *Crazy, Man, Crazy.*

In an interview printed on Nov. 10th 1953 in the Philadelphia Evening Bulletin, Bill Haley said, when asked if he knew *Crazy, Man, Crazy* was going to be a national hit: *"I knew I was on the right track because the kids began clapping in rhythm and yelling 'Go! Go! Go!' as they dug that beat. That's what we were selling . . . a beat the kids could dance to. It's the kids who buy the records today . . . they can make or break you.*

"We went out to school assemblies . . . . I play as many school dates as possible . . . and made it a point to talk to the kids, ask them questions, listen to the phrases they used, like 'Man, that music's gone,' and 'Dig that crazy rhythm!'

"That's how 'Crazy, Man, Crazy' got to be written. I had a date to cut a record, and the day before the cutting, I hadn't decided what to play. I wanted to do something new, different. I had taken down a whole list of expressions I had heard kids use. Among them I had written: 'crazy man'."

"The kids use crazy to mean anything exceptional, good. Like a necktie a boy's wearing. You like it. You say to him, 'That's crazy, man . . . crazy.' You say a thing's crazy, you mean it's just wonderful.

So I wrote down.the phrase, Crazy, Man, Crazy . . ...and then the other words tumbled into place:

"When I go out and I want a treat,
I find me a band with a solid beat.
I grab my chick and we dance about,
When they start rockin' . . . boy,
We start to shout:
Crazy, Man, Crazy . . ."

"I beat out the rhythm on the kitchen table . . . I could hear the music in my ear . . . and I was never more sure of a hit in my life. The kids would go for it, I just knew it.

"I yelled into my wife and starting singing the words. She said: 'Shh! You'll wake the baby!' But she liked it. I called up my manager, Jim Ferguson . . . and sang him the song. 'It's 3 A.M.,' he said. 'Can't you pick a better time to write your hits?'

"I called Dave Miller, president of Essex Records, in New York. He went wild over the number. He started planning a big campaign right then. So we waxed it the next day and things have been moving for us ever since."

Marshall Lytle also recalls the day *Crazy, Man Crazy* was created: *"We had just finished a gig at Eddystone High School and as we were loading our instruments in the car we asked the kids how they liked our music. One kid answered 'like crazy, man, crazy!' Bill quickly wrote down the teenage expression. We were always looking for catchy words or phrases to write songs with. We left and went directly to Bill's apartment for lunch. While Cuppy was making us something to eat, Bill started strumming his guitar with several tunes, playing around with the crazy-man-crazy idea. I joined in and we began throwing tunes and lyrics together. After several hours we worked out our first song to hit the national charts."*

The musicians Bill Haley assembled at the Coastal Studios in New York to record his first national hit were: Art Ryerson, lead guitar; Billy Gussak, drums; Billy Williamson, steel guitar; Marshall Lytle, bass; Johnny Grande, piano; and Bill on the rhythm guitar. The flip side of *Crazy, Man, Crazy* was *Whatcha Gonna Do*, also written by Bill Haley. Bill's good friend and brilliant lead guitarist, Danny Cedrone was not on this or the Comets' next three records due to the growing popularity of his own band.

In an interview on Stuart Colman's Radio London "Echoes" program, Dave Miller mentioned that Tommy Dowd, later to become the legendary producer at Atlantic Records was his engineer on *Crazy, Man Crazy*. And in the great shouting chorus of *"GO GO GO"* at the record's end, in addition to all the Comets, was Dave Miller himself, Jerry Blaine, the President of Jubilee Records, the building's janitors and many curious on-lookers pressed into service.

True to his word, Dave Miller heavily promoted *Crazy, Man, Crazy* the spring and summer of '53 as *"the new hot music for real cool cats"*. The trade publications took note: on May 2, the disc was listed as Billboard's *"Best Buy"* and Cash Box's *"Sleeper of the Week"*. The song roared to the nation's top twenty charts and established Bill Haley and his Comets as one of the hottest bands in the land. Cash Box Magazine's annual reader's poll listed the Comets as one of the *"Best Small Instrumental Groups of 1953"*.

The nationally known Ralph Marterie Orchestra covered the song on the Mercury label and added to Bill's prestige as a song writer and stylist.

Bill now wanted to record a song given to him a few months back by Jim Myers. Myers had told Bill the song had been written with him in mind. Bill loved its catchy tune and sat down and worked out the arrangement for the Comets. The band had been playing it all summer at Wildwood, on the New Jersey shore. The crowds went wild over it and it became the Comets' most requested tune. The song was *Rock Around the Clock* written by Max C. Freedman, a 58 year old postal clerk and veteran lyricist with songs like *Sioux City Sue*, and *Song of India* to his credit and James E. Myers under the name Jimmy DeKnight. The song had originally been written as a pop tune with the title *Round The Clock*. The word "rock" was becoming a "buzzword" in music publishing and Jimmy Myers added the words: *"We're Gonna Rock"* and *"Tonight"* to the title. He then had Harry Filler create a three-part arrangement which was published in 1953 by Myers Music. But Dave Miller would have no part of it. Twice Bill took the song to the recording studio and twice Dave Miller literally tore it up. Miller and Jim Myers, both music business veterans, had had some serious altercations over the distributions of Cowboy Records and Miller did not want to record anything associated with Myers. This decision would turn out to be one of the most embarrassing errors in Miller's long and distinguished career as a pioneer in the recording business.

Meanwhile, the Comets recorded four more records in 1953 on the Essex label. The first was the followup to *Crazy, Man Crazy* called *Fractured* written by Bill and Billy Williamson, backed with *Pat-A-Cake*, also written by Bill but with Marshall Lytle as coauthor. On the label, Bill's co-authors names were accidentally switched.

Their next session produced *Live It Up* backed with *Farewell, So Long, Goodbye*, both written by Bill Haley. This was the first Comet recording in which Tony Lance's baritone saxophone is played.

The seventh Essex record released was *I'll Be True/Ten Little Indians* with Cliff Leeman playing the tom toms and snare in place of Billy Gussak, Bill's favorite drummer, who couldn't make this session.

In November, believing the baritone sound too heavy, Bill switches to the tenor sax and finds the last ingredient in his elusive, new sound: the wailing sexuality of the jazz-blues saxophone.

In nineteen-year-old Joey Ambrose (D'Ambrosio) he finds a young, raucous musician who could do justice to the offscale "blue" notes Bill had first heard in St Louis so many years before. Joey was born and raised in North Philadelphia and had studied alto and tenor saxophone with local legends Carmen "Spags" Spagnola and Mike Guera, Benny Goodman's clarinet teacher. Joey had at first been a fan of Charlie Parker's progressive jazz, but was soon won over by the great rhythm and blues tenor honkers such as Red Prysock, Tiny Bradshaw and Flip Phillips.

Max Freedman (in suit). The man who wrote "Rock Around The Clock". ©DAP

He began his professional career playing in Philadelphia's small bars and strip joints, where the teenager perfected his rhythm and blues technique and learned to "walk the bar", following the strippers with his moaning and wailing sax.

Ambrose recalls: *"I auditioned for the Comets job at Dick Richards' house and was hired on a try-out basis. Bill still wasn't sure he wanted to add me on a permanent basis. Then a few weeks later we did a teenage dance in Baltimore and I went into the audience during my solo and did some antics. Then Marshall did the same thing. The kids went wild and after the show Bill told me I was now a full-time Comet, and told me to keep the antics in the act."*

Years later Big Joe Turner, the Boss of the Blues, was to tell Bill Haley in his dressing room after a show, *"That boy (Ambrose) was the palest nigger to ever blow a blue note."* Turner meant it as a compliment, and Bill, who would become one of Turner's greatest fans and lifelong friends, took it with pride.

Courtesy© Haley Family Collection

The 1954 Comets, left to right: Billy Williamson, Johnny Grande, Joey Ambrose, Marshall Lytle and Dick Richards.

Joey's first record with the Comets was Haley's totally off-the-wall ode to insanity called *Straight-jacket* and their last on the Essex label. This song was the "B" side of Bill's arrangement of the Glen Miller standard, *Chattanooga Choo-Choo*. The vocal chorus, which consisted of four members of the Ray Charles singers, was added to this record by Dave Miller to imitate Glen Miller's Modernairs.

On stage Bill continued to showcase the multiple talents of his musicians. The unique chemistry and versatility of these six young men was to produce a very special bond among them. When Marshall Lytle would sing, Bill would play the bass. When Billy Williamson sang, in his high tenor, Bill would go over and play the electric lead. When Dick Richards sang in his rich baritone, Joey would play the drums. Johnny Grande would switch between the accordion and the piano, when available. Haley, Williamson and Lytle could play lead guitar when required. Bill's ability to share the spotlight with his musicians was greatly appreciated by all of them. Most band leaders had kept their sidemen in the background.

In Philadelphia, Jack Howard, while in partnership with Bill Haley (Haley-Howard Publications) establishes another publishing company called "Arcade Music Inc." This firm in which Bill is a silent, but controlling partner, becomes affiliated with ASCAP. Their new company cuts the first version of *Rock Around the Clock* on Haley's new "Arcade" label. The song is performed by an old friend of Bill's, Paschal Vennitti, using the stage name "Sonny Dae and his Knights". Unfortunately the disc sank quickly without a trace and *Rock Around the Clock* would have to sleep another year before Bill Haley and his Comets could record it with their unique beat and vitality.

By Autumn of 1953 Bill and the Comets' *Crazy, Man, Crazy* could be heard on jukeboxes and radios across the nation and across the seas. In Great Britain it was released on the London label in August. By October it was covered by Lita Rosa and the Ted Heath Band on the British Decca label. With these early records, the seeds of Bill Haley's style of rock'n'roll crossed the Atlantic Ocean and invaded England. A decade later, highly-charged English rock bands, led by the Beatles, and honed in Hamburg, would mount a "Rock Renaissance". This awesome new power would re-invade America and eventually put all the world once again under the spell of Bill Haley's new hybrid sound.

In 1953 however, the music industry didn't know what to call his music. The kids just called it "Bill Haley's Music" and no one was more flattered than Bill himself. *Crazy, Man Crazy* had now sold over 750,000 copies. Cash Box Magazine featured Bill and Dave Miller on its front cover. With his new popularity, Bill also noticed *Rocket 88*, *Rock the Joint* and several other of his "Rockabilly" songs had roared back to life in the record stores and on the jukeboxes. People starting treating him like a star and he loved it.

In an interview with British disc jockey Roger Scott, Bill Haley was asked: *"Why didn't you record Rock a Beatin' Boogie in 1953?"* Bill answered, *"Well as I recall back, we were ridin' high you see . . . we had Rocket 88' on the jukebox, we had 'Rock the Joint', 'Crazy, Man, Crazy' and all my buddies were comin' round sayin' 'Hey Bill, you've got that magic touch at the moment, so write us one. Danny Cedrone who was very very close to me, Danny had recorded this, (Rock a Beatin' Boogie) and I also gave it to the Treniers and I hoped they would have a hit record with it. Being a friend I didn't think it was right for me to come out and record it myself over top of them. Neither of the records hit really big, but it was a help to the groups . . . "*

Although the juke boxes played their songs from coast to coast, the stage Comets still had a difficult time away from their base in Philadelphia. The first months of 1954 prove to be as awkward and confusing as 1953 had been. For Bill Haley and his newly christened Comets, their little combo with the big beat still didn't seem to fit anywhere. They were booked into the Preview Lounge in Chicago, after pulling a lot of strings. The club was a Dixieland-jazz room which had just played host to the legendary sounds of Dizzy Gillespie. On the first night the audience didn't know what to make of Bill's hybrid music. On the second night, an embarrassed manager had to ask the Comets to leave! After this fiasco, it became difficult to book the band in the "uptown jazz clubs". It seemed jazz enthusiasts were not too enthusiastic about the Bill Haley sound!

Desperate for work, Lord Jim, working through a friend in Miami, booked the Comets for a much-needed two week engagement. When they got there, they found their booking canceled. The club owner didn't like their music and refused to let them play. The band had used all their funds to get to Florida, which was a thousand mile trip. Stranded and out of gas and food money, Lord Jim goes into a little club on the Tamiami Trail and talks the skeptical owner into a ninety/ten percentage deal for the band. They even have to build the stage they were to perform on. For the next three weeks the Comets have to clean up the place and play

The Comets on stage 1953. Left to right: Marshall Lytle, Johnny Grande, Joey Ambrose, Bill Haley, Dick Richards and Billy Williamson.

Courtesy D. Hirschberg

forty performances for enough money just to get home! At one point Marshall Lytle remembers: *"things were so bad I had to split a hamburger and a bowl of chili with Dick and Joey.. and that was all we had to eat that whole day!"*

It is interesting to note that in the spring of 1954 Bill Haley believes he has peaked, career-wise. In a later interview he admits, *"This was an era that for us, I suppose like any group with their first hit record, I felt at this time, 'gee I've had my career', I was ready to retire. I thought I've had 4 or 5 records'. . .I was completely unprepared for what happened next."*

What happened next was an incredible string of events of almost ludicrous proportions. Looking back now, these events seem like a divine comedy of errors which almost doomed Bill Haley's career and the greatest rock song ever recorded.

By early 1954 the major record companies where starting to show interest in Haley's new sound. The sales of *Crazy, Man Crazy* had.been very impressive. Jim Myers still had faith in his song, *Rock Around the Clock* and its hit potential. He desperately wanted it to be recorded on a major record label. In March, Myers was making the rounds in New York with his song. Mitch Miller at Columbia expressed some interest, as did Steve Sholes at RCA. But with Milt Gabler at Decca ·Records he hit pay-dirt.

Decca was one of the giant "Big Three" American record companies along with Columbia and RCA. Decca had been founded in 1934 by Jack Kapp with a sizeable investment of capital provided by the British Decca Recording Company. Kapp had earlier been running the old Brunswick Record Company, but the Depression years in America had plunged sales and profits to near bankruptcy. British Decca gave Kapp the rights to the "Decca" name, financial support and use of any English masters the new firm may need for their catalog.

American Decca became one of the Big Three by several shrewd marketing strategies. First they encouraged radio stations to play their records on the air, at a time when other record companies were complaining about the "free" and unauthorized use of their records on the air waves. Second they signed up outstanding talent such as Bing Crosby, who to date is the artist with the greatest number of records sold in the world (Over 400,000,000), Guy Lombardo, Tommy and Jimmy Dorsey and other big name entertainers. Their third major marketing strategy was to recognize and exploit the vast potential of "minority" music. "Minority" music would be hillbilly, cowboy, folk and "race" tunes. Under their 7000 Series which later became their *Sepia Series*, an impressive array of jazz, Dixieland, country-jive, rhythm and blues and electric blues was recorded. By the early 1950's Decca had built a solid reputation for discovering new talent and having the courage to record new trends in music before its major rivals.

Milt Gabler was a top jazz and rhythm and blues producer and A/R man at Decca. He had been watching the Bill Haley sound grow in popularity for several months now. Myers played Gabler several of Haley's Essex records and a demo of a Haley version of *Rock Around the Clock*. Gabler seemed impressed on how the small combo got its big beat and drive. Over lunch, and much influenced by Jimmy Myers' enthusiasm, he made the historic decision to record this new hybrid music. Gabler had a unique gift to spot talent and coming trends in popular music. He had recorded the genius of Louis Armstrong, Billie Holiday, Ella Fitzgerald, Louis Jordan and other artists who were to become musical legends in their day. However this odd "Bill Haley sound" was new to him. It seemed raw, erotic and powerful and it wasn't like anything he had heard before. The lunch ended with a handshake and a verbal agreement between Myers and Gabler to record two songs, one chosen by Gabler and the other by Myers.

Jimmy Myers was ecstatic. On his return to Philadelphia he told Bill Haley of the deal and that Milt Gabler of Decca Records wanted to see him. Bill told Myers he was still under contract with Essex and Dave Miller would never let him go without a deal. Would Decca buy-out his contract with Essex?

Myers knew Miller would kill any deal he was part of and asked to read the Haley-Miller contract. He was looking for a loop-hole when he found it was due to expire April 8th, just two weeks away. Also, Dave Miller's right to renew the contract had expired on March 8th. The two men decided to wait until the contract ran out and not to worry about a Decca buy-out. Dave Miller, the President of Palda/Essex/Holiday Records, was busy in Germany recording a new classical series on his Somerset label and was unaware of the coming loss of one of his best selling artists. For Jimmy Myers, this was sweet revenge for Miller's black-balling his *Rock Around the Clock* for almost two years.

On April 1st, 1954, April's Fools Day, Myers, Gabler and Bill Haley met in Decca's New York offices. The three men discussed a contract for four records a year, a standard royalty of 5% of sales, $5000.00 in advance royalties, and the understanding that Decca would mail out each release to two thousand disc-jockeys with full support publicity.

Palda RECORD CO.

8406 LYONS AVENUE, PHILADELPHIA 42, PA.
Phone: SAratoga 9-4137

AGREEMENT

This agreement entered into this day of April 8th 1952 by and between Palda Record Co. of Phila., Pa. hereinafter referred to as the "Company" and William Haley of Boothwyn, PA. referred to as the"artist."

Whereas the company is engaged in the manufacture and sale of phonograph records and is desirous of recording and exploiting for sale records featuring the talents of the artist the following is mutually agreed.

The artist will render his vocal talents exclusively for recording purposes to the company for a period of two years from above date. Also, the company reserves the right to a renewal of this agreement for an additional period of one year upon notifying the artist in writing of its desire for renewal at least 30 days prior to the expiration of this agreement.

The artist will not record for any other company or person for the duration of this agreement. The artist furthur agrees not to record any selection recorded for the company for any company of person for a period of five years from the termination of this agreement.

The company agrees to pay the artist a total royalty of one and one half cents (.01½) per double face record sold featuring the vocal talents of the artist. However, the company will deduct from the aggragate royalties due the artist all sums paid to musicians used in accompaniment of the artist on said recordings.

(The company agrees that is is good standing at this date with the American Federations of Musicians and will comply with all the Federations rules to the best interests of the artist.)

Royalty statements with remittances for amounts due the artist will be rendered him each calender quarter of the year.

The company will release a minimum of four double face records (8 sides) each year, for the duration of this agreement featuring the talents of the artist. However, this a minimum of releases and at the discretion of the company more releases may be made featuring the artist. The company agrees that the artist reserves the right to select three (3) selections out of every eight (8) siedes recorded for the company.

The artist agrees that the company may use his name and photograph in the course of promotion. W.H. JH

Whereas, this agreement is transferable and the company reserves the right to its sales or transfer, it is agreed that all provisions of this agreement must be met by any firm or person that may succeed to its rights.

The company agrees that it will to the best of its abilities promote and exploit the artist.

The artist or his assigned representative have the right to an examination of the company's sales records at anytime during normal business hours for the duration of this agreement.

William Haley — William H aley
Jack Howard — Jack Howard -Manager
David L. Miller — PALDA RECORD CO.

Photostat of Bill Haley's original recording contract with Dave Miller.

Plus full page ads in Billboard and Cash Box magazines! This was the kind of marketing power Bill Haley wanted. Bill was also impressed by the fact that Red Foley, one of his idols, was also on the label. With the deal set and signed, the three men shook hands and agreed on a recording date four days after the Essex contract was due to expire.

Bill Haley returned home to prepare for the upcoming recording session with the Comets. While they had been performing *Rock Around The Clock* for over a year, Bill wanted to put together a unique arrangement for this all-important recording.

Joey Ambrose has a vivid recollection of the rehearsals: *"We worked on the arrangement of "Rock Around The Clock" at Bill's home. All of the Comets were there, plus Danny Cedrone who would be our lead guitarist. Danny was an accomplished musician and we all looked to him for advice.*

"First we all listened to Sonny Dae's recording. Then we decided the record would have more 'bounce' if we added stacatto riffs throughout the song. The voicing on the riffs was three parts — sax, lead guitar and steel. Danny, Billy and I worked it out on the spot and it sounded great.

"Marshall suggested that Danny use as his guitar solo the terrific solo from 'Rock The Joint'. The second break was supposed to be a sax solo, but the song was building to a point where I thought we'd get more excitement out of it by doing something the whole band could join in on. That's what rhythm and blues combos would often do. So we came up with that second riff. All of this was worked out before we went to New York to do the session".

The date set for the session was April 12th, 1954. The studio for this legendary recording would be a former ballroom in Manhattan called the Pythian Temple. Decca had been using this huge auditorium-like hall for years. Its cavernous high ceiling and great walnut-paneled walls created a natural reverberation chamber which added a unique strength and volume to any music played there. Gabler had recorded some of his best work here in what Decca called their Studio A. Decca had also just installed their new "state-of-the-art" high fidelity recording equipment, thus ending their monotone sound forever.

On the appointed day and long past the eleven o'clock starting time, Gabler paced up and down the great ballroom, looking at his watch. He was smoking one of Jimmy Myers' Havana cigars, cursing under his breath. Myers was apprehensive as the proverbial bride waiting at the altar for a no-show bride-groom. This couldn't be happening! Neither Bill Haley nor any of the Comets had shown up yet! Didn't they know this was the biggest break of their careers? Did they forget? *"Where in the hell are they?"* Gabler fumed. *"Don't they have telephones in Chester?"* Calls to Haley's and Lord Jim's home went unanswered. It was now near noon.

Precious studio time was being wasted. Two sound engineers and Billy Gussak were standing by, trading show business stories. With arms waving in the air, Gabler finally exploded at Jimmy Myers: *"Why didn't the bastards at least call?"* Finally Gabler received the message from his office, the Comets were on their way. They should get to New York about 1:00 P.M.

To cool down Gabler, Myers suggested lunch to get Milt's mind off the clock. They left word to call them at once if the boys showed up. Gabler wanted to know what kind of two-bit band Myers was pushing.

Meanwhile on one of the most important days in his life Bill Haley and his Comets run into an incredible bit of bad luck. They were stuck on a muddy sand bar in the middle of the Delaware River! The Chester-Bridgeport ferry had run aground mid-river during low tide. Bill had gotten little sleep the night before in his excitement. After all these years of work only to be done in by a mud bank was too much. Bill was never much of a religious man, but against Mother Nature he needed all the help he could get. Bill Haley told friends later that he prayed for help and promised the good Lord something very personal. The Lord must have been with him because with the help of a rising tide and a local tug boat, the ferry was finally freed from the river mud and shortly docked on the New Jersey shore. Bill frantically called the Decca office and told them of his delay. He said he would be there in two hours and to hold the studio, please! Bill's mad, death-defying ninety-mile race to New York City was one of pure courage for the ashen-faced Comets. At just after one o'clock in the afternoon, the Comets, their instruments and the equipment tumbled out of their caravan in front of the studio on West 70th Street. Jim Myers and Milt Gabler had just returned from lunch. Bill apologized to Gabler for the embarrassing delay and thanked him for being so patient. Gabler looked at his watch again and told Bill *"The next time we have a recording date, take the bridge!"* Gabler wanted to cancel the session, saying there wasn't time left to do it right. Bill pleaded that his band already had *Rock Around the Clock* down pat and they could learn Gabler's song in an hour. Gabler reluctantly agreed, and said he would give it a go. The Comets, stiff and cramped from their long

©DAP

Bill reviewing lyrics with Milt Gabler while Lord Jim (in glasses) looks on.

drive, had also not eaten since early morning. Lord Jim went out to get some sandwiches and coffee while they hastily set up their equipment.

Gabler wanted Bill to stand on the floor down in front of a four-foot high wooden stage with his own microphone, facing the band. The band was arranged up on the stage with microphones placed about their instruments. The stage with its lower ceiling formed a natural shell. Other mikes were placed about the room to pick up the natural echo and unique acoustical characteristics of the great hall. Gabler handed Bill the sheet music for their first recording, *Thirteen Women*. The song was a strange, off-beat, novelty tune about thirteen women and one man left alive after an atomic bomb attack. A far cry from the happier material the Comets were used to doing. However, Milt Gabler owned a piece of it and Bill felt he was not in any position to argue the point. They rehearsed *Thirteen Women* for about an hour and a half before they began recording. They had to do six takes and playbacks before Gabler was satisfied. Bill wasn't too crazy about the tune but if that's what Mr. Gabler wanted — so be it!

Jimmy Myers anxiously looked at his watch. It was after four and the engineers had told him they break off at five! The boys now had only forty minutes to record his song. To get it down on tape it would have to be pushed. Jim was hurt, all this time spent and now his song was going to get the "bum's rush".

Gabler also was looking at the clock on the studio wall. *"I hope you guys don't need any rehearsal time with the 'Clock' song. We've only got time for a couple of takes."*

With all that had happened that day to the Comets, the next half hour was a true miracle in music. Tired, hungry, under extreme pressure and having wasted most of the afternoon on what several thought was a weird song, they now had to cut what Gabler called "the Clock song" in two takes.

Bill had earlier reviewed the song's arrangement with the session drummer, Billy Gussak, between takes of *Thirteen Women*. He had stressed the importance of Gussak's lightning snare drum rim shots to the piece. This unique technique had been developed by Gussak to enhance the clicky-click sound Marshall Lytle created while back-slapping his bass.

It was 4:30 P.M. before the first note was played of the song that would one day rock the world. Billy Gussak hit two sharp-rim shots and Bill Haley shouts out the immortal words which would become forever the international anthem of Rock'n'Roll:

"One-two-three o'clock, four o'clock ROCK!"

Gussak hit another double rim shot and Bill shouts the next verse in a higher scale:

"Five-six-seven o'clock, eight o'clock ROCK!"

Another two rim shots crack through the air and Bill sings the next lyric in a higher scale:

"Nine-ten-eleven o'clock, twelve o'clock ROCK!"
"We're gonna ROCK a-round the CLOCK tonight!"

Bill singing at Pythian Temple recording session. Note the Comets are not playing. ©DAP

Then all hell breaks loose. The Comets come into their own sound and glory as their guitars, saxophone and piano cut full out into a wild orgy of sounds, all powered by the driving beat of Marshall Lytle's back slap bass. Danny Cedrone establishes himself for posterity as the first of the great rock lead guitarists. His fluid style and speed inspired unborn generations with his awesome signature solo, taken note for note from his earlier work on "Rock the Joint".

Joey Ambrose's tenor sax fires short staccato bursts as Grande's pounding piano strengthens the bass line. Billy Williamson's steel guitar meshes perfectly with the sax and the guitars in this joyous celebration of pure sound.

Billy Gussak ends the song with a mad flourish on the drums. Gussak recalls: *"I put that in because I had just done a session the day before where the producer only wanted me to play straight time. I was very frustrated because I always liked to throw in something extra—just beating time is boring. I made up my mind that at this session I'd get my licks in".*

For one inspired, fabulous and sublime moment in time, Bill Haley and his Comets create the perfect rock song, never to be equaled again. A song so perfect, so classic it would sell tens of millions of records over the next four decades. The song would be recorded by over two hundred artists but none would capture the Comets' special magic that was recorded on that spring day in New York City.

Decca's gray-haired sound engineer, Larry McIntire, waved to Gabler. The song might have to be re-recorded. The sounds made by the Comets had drove the control gauges into the "red zones", indicating they had "peaked-out" the new high-fidelity sound system and had created what was believed to be "tonal distortions". Gabler played back the tape. The band was great but Bill's voice had been completely over-powered by the Comets' amplified instruments. Gabler told Bill to go through the song again. This time Gabler cut off the band's mikes and had Bill again face the boys up on the stage. With Bill singing into the only "live" mike, a second tape was recorded as the band replayed *Rock Around the Clock* one last time.

Their studio time was up—they had already gone into overtime. The large clock on the wall showed 5:40 P.M. Gabler called it a wrap. Bill and the band left the hall without hearing a final playback of their "clock song". The two perplexed engineers shook their heads. They doubted if a good record could be cut with such distortion. It might sound like a lot of useless noise. Gabler, tired from a long and exasperating day, decided he would review the tapes in the morning. The greatest rock song ever recorded lay almost neglected, dissected on two reels on a studio table.

The Comets returned to Chester about midnight. Bill was quiet and seemed troubled. The session hadn't gone as well as he had wished. He didn't think he had made much of an impression on the intimidating Gabler. He wished he had gone up to New York the night before, then he and the band could have gotten a good night's sleep. He now blamed himself for blowing this critical recording session. Once again the self-doubts filled his mind as he tried to fall asleep. He was exhausted. Now the hard part—waiting to see if Decca would use the session tapes for a record release.

Gabler recalls that early the next morning April 13, 1954 he took the first tape of *the Clock*, in which the band was so loud they had drowned out Bill's vocal, and had it overdubbed onto the second tape. On the second tape, Bill's voice had come through loud and clear. The two tapes were synchronized to produce a third which Gabler used to cut the master. Bill Haley's new music and Gabler's unique recording techniques were combined to created a rock masterpiece. However, the genius of this recording would not be recognized for almost another year.

BILL HALEY

and his COMETS

DECCA 29124

THIRTEEN WOMEN

and

(We're Gonna)

ROCK AROUND THE CLOCK

America's Fastest Selling Records

On May 6th Decca mailed out 2000 copies to disc-jockeys across the nation, as per their agreement. The suspense was killing Jim Myers. He would call Decca each week and ask about sales. It was beginning to look like *Rock Around the Clock* was not going to be a hit. Gabler set June 7th for another Haley recording date. He had invested five thousand dollars up front in Haley, and he was going to get his money back one way or another!

Meanwhile Myers discovers what he believes to be a tragic mistake while talking to some disc-jockey friends of his. Decca had mailed out the records with all the publicity directed at *Thirteen Women* which had been put on the "A" side of the record! The "new release" ads in Billboard and Cashbox Magazines showed *Thirteen Women* as the major tune and relegated *Rock Around The Clock* to a small block down in the bottom corner of the ad! The DJ's gave *Thirteen Women* a few spins and got little reaction. Since the "B" side was usually the throw-away side, many hadn't even bothered to play it! Besides, Decca called *Rock Around the Clock* a "fox trot" on the label and nobody, they reasoned, listens to fox trots anymore!

Myers began to call all his contacts in the business; disc-jockeys, radio station owners, and friends and asked them to play his song which, in error, was put on "B" side. He finds out many of them have thrown out or given away the record already. He asks Gabler for another release and more samples so he could personally give them out to the DJ's. He begins a two thousand mile trek from New York to Richmond, Virginia, west to Chicago, Cleveland, Detroit and Buffalo, paying the expenses out of his own pocket. He tells the DJ's to give the song another chance, it will be a hit. Jim Myers, as publisher and co-writer turns his faith in *Rock Around the Clock* into a personal crusade.

In May, Bill's wife Joan gives birth to a little girl which they name Doreen. She is Bill's fourth child and Cuppy's second. Bill's family has now grown to three daughters and one son. The new baby helps relieve some of the disappointment Bill feels, due to the apparent failure of his first Decca record.

On July 7th, the Comets are back in New York at the Pythian Temple. Panama Francis mans the drums, Danny Cedrone is the lead guitarist, Joey Ambrose, tenor sax; Johnny Grande, piano; Marshall Lytle, bass and Billy Williamson, steel guitar. Dick Richards is also on hand to help with the vocal chorus.

Milt Gabler had earlier sent Bill the words and music of Joe Turner's rhythm and blues tune called *Shake, Rattle and Roll*, written by Jessie Stone, using the penname Charles E. Calhoun. He also tells Bill to "clean it up". The original Calhoun lyrics were far too sexually suggestive for the teen audience Gabler wanted to hit. The song's raw, earthy language had to be changed before the song could be played on the white radio stations. Bill, a former DJ himself, knows the problem, and with John Grande's help rewrites the "sexually suggestive" lyrics;

Calhoun version:

"Get out of that bed and wash your face and hands.
Get into the kitchen, make some noise with the pots and pans."

Bill Haley's version:

"Get out in that kitchen and rattle those pots and pans.
Roll my breakfast, cause I'm a hungry man."

The second verse was the main one the Decca censors wanted re-written, for it left little to the imagination.

Calhoun version:

"When you wear your dresses the sun comes shining through.
I can't believe my eyes that all of this belongs to you!"

Bill Haley's version:

"wearing those dresses, your hair's done up so nice.
You look so warm, but your heart is cold as ice."

Bill's love of black rhythms and beats coupled with his other love of country-western music creates in this one song the great paradox of Rock-'n'Roll. Big Joe Turner's version, as released by Ahmet Ertegun/Jerry Wexler on the Atlantic label, was pure rhythm and blues. Bill Haley's version is pure, classic Rock'n'Roll. The Haley version outsold the Turner version by millions. The Comets' arrangement was exciting and fresh. The whole band jams away in unison, guitars, bass, piano, drums and sax. Bill sings one of his best vocal performances ever recorded, as the entire band backs him with exuberant shouts of "Go-Go-Go".

Bill's unique vocal treatment (trying to create the texture of the great R&B shouters) was no accident. He carefully rehearsed it at home and in his car while driving to the session. Dave Miller's concept

Bill listening to play-back with Milt Gabler at the Pythian Temple, New York.

of white rhythm and blues sung by a hillbilly was about to pay off.

In an interview with Roger Scott many years later, Bill said; *"... as I mentioned earlier, I was a great champion for rhythm and blues, (and) for black artists. Ruth Brown, I remember, I was a great fan of hers. Big Joe Turner... I idolised Joe... I hadn't met him at that time, we were later to become the closest friends that we are today... and I consider him one of my best friends. Joe had recorded 'Shake, Rattle and Roll' and it was a 'race' record, as I said... it was frowned upon. 'Who's gonna listen to those things?' was the attitude (back then). I hate to say it, but this was the prejudice that was going on at the time. I loved the song and I loved to hear Joe Turner sing. I'd sit for hours, (listening). So I thought well, I love that song so I'll do it. That was really why I did the tune 'Shake, Rattle and Roll'."*

For the flip side of the record the Comets record another Jimmy Myers song called *ABC Boogie*. Bill had made a verbal deal with Myers to record one of his songs at each Decca session.

Gabler was very pleased this time with Bill and the Comets. He joked with the band and seemed in a much better mood. As Bill listened to the playbacks he too was impressed with the crisp sounds and the hard driving big beat of his band. He also wondered why Gabler was so quiet about his first record. It had now been out for a month. Maybe Gabler didn't like to talk about his mistakes? Anyway Bill felt good about this one, it had "hit"written all over it. Decca put its full force behind it in the trade papers. If rock'n'roll had a future with the public, one of these records had to get on the charts. Decca was doing its job, but the non-explosion of *Rock Around the Clock* puzzled Bill.

Ten days later Bill was stunned to learn that his brilliant lead guitarist, Danny Cedrone died of a heart attack after mysteriously falling down a flight of stairs. Cedrone, whose fiery guitar solos and powerful riffs had added so much to the Comets' dynamic sound,was not only one of Bill Haley's best musicians but also one of his closest friends. Cedrone would never know the impact his "Clock" solo would have on the world of rock music. At his funeral several days later in South Philadelphia, Bill Haley openly wept in the street after the viewing. This was only the first of several personal tragedies that would beset Bill Haley as he approched the peak of his success.

Shake, Rattle and Roll received extremely favorable reviews upon its release. Billboard placed the disc in its coveted "Spotlight" position, although crediting the artist as "Bill Haley's Orchestra." Noted Billboard: *"This one is especially recommended for (juke box) operators, and the pulsating manner in which the orchestra plays and shouts this tune could help the disc attract a bit of coins."*

By July, the Comets were back on the Jersey shore creating their wild and crazy music to the vacationing crowds of sun-worshippers. *Shake, Rattle and Roll* was on the national charts and Bill Haley and his Comets had their first million seller! Also the indefatigable Jimmy Myers' one man crusade was beginning to pay off. *Rock Around the Clock* sales had reached 75,000 records.

Bill Haley's music now shares the charts with the best "pop tunes" in the nation: Kitty Kallen's *Little Things Mean A Lot*, The Crew-Cuts' *Sh-Boom* and Rosemary Clooney's beautiful *Hey There*. By September the Comets are flooded with offers for per-

Dave Miller at his Miller International record factory in Germany.

Courtesy P. Miller

sonal appearances. Their fee rises from $600.00 to $2000.00 a performance!

On July 6th 1954 the Comets and his family throw Bill Haley a big surprise party. Today he is twenty-nine years old. He receives an eighteen-foot speed boat. Bill loves to fish and will spend many hours with friends on the craft which he christens "THE COMET". Five hundred miles away in Memphis, Tennessee, on this exact day, a new young singer named Elvis Presley records his first pressing on the Sun label. Backed by Bill Black and Scotty Moore, Elvis sings *That's All Right* and *Blue Moon of Kentucky*. Elvis Presley and Bill Haley's paths would soon cross and their dates with destiny would enrich and forever change the world of popular music.

Three weeks later, the second of a series of tragic deaths would befall Bill Haley. His little girl, Doreen, is found dead in her crib in what is known now as Sudden Infant Death Syndrome. She is but two months old. Bill and his wife are inconsolable. The Comets continue to honor their club dates, but Bill is not with them.

Dave Miller, watching Bill Haley's popularity growing to star status, capitalizes on his treasure house of Haley's earlier recordings. He re-releases on his Essex and Transworld labels eight of Haley's songs on singles, sixteen others on EP (extended play-four songs per record) and twelve others on an LP which he calls "Rock With Bill Haley and the Comets". He also unearths from his vaults two rehearsal tapes of an unreleased Comet tune from 1953, Sy Oliver's *Yes Indeed*, and issues them on his Transworld label. By year's end he has more titles in the stores than Decca! It has been said of Dave Miller that he made more money on Bill Haley's music after Bill left him than he did when Haley was one of his artists. Miller was a shrewd operator and a promotional genius, and in the long run, he may have had the last laugh.

History will record that it was the big hearted but demanding Dave Miller who drove Bill Haley into adding the heavier beat to his sound. It was the always searching Miller who suggested adding Gussak's drums to Bill's traditional cowboy band, thus opening the door to the final fusion of country-western and rhythm and blues instrumentation. It was Dave Miller, years before Sam Phillips at Sun Records, who first realized the potential profits of a hybrid, black/white sound hidden in the anonymous grooves of a record. Dave Miller's contribution to the development of Bill's sound and the birth of Rock'n'Roll are incalculable.

After the demise of his Palda Records in 1956, the undaunted Miller founded a new record company which he called Miller International. With his characteristic vision and drive this enterprise became one of the leading independent manufacturers of records in Europe. Over the next two decades he would produce over 200,000,000 records before merging his company with the global entertaining giant, MCA.

Meanwhile, on September 21st 1954, Bill is back at the Pythian Temple in New York. Gabler was proud as a peacock with his new found star and treated Bill accordingly. Gabler felt with his recording techniques and Bill's new, exciting ideas and arrangements, they had a winning team. He recalls: *"Haley's kind of music had a tremendous kick to it. The Pythian Temple was made for the Comets. It had a natural reverb to it. We got a great natural sound in there. The Comets always set up so they could play off one another. They could "feel" each other's vibes. They had to hear a song before they could play it. I think only Johnny Grande could read music. We used to cook up an arrangement right there on the session. In a couple of hours you would think they had played it for months. They were all "head" musicians. . . it was all ear harmony and when they got cookin' there was none better. They were a rockin' little band."*

Bill was excited about the two new songs he wanted to record. The first was written by a black man and a white woman, Beverly Ross and Julius Dixon's classic *Dim Dim the Lights*. Bill's friend Rusty Keefer contributed the bass vocal intro on this number. On the flip side was a song by Frank Pingatore called *Happy Baby*. Pingatore, an aspiring young composer, had been Bill's barber. He had also helped Bill with several of his previous arrangements. Bill recognized early his talents and began to use his work. Frank was to become the first to organize the Comets' music and manage their publishing companies.

Gabler overdubbed the Comets clapping in unison over the chorus. The use of a "clap track" was yet another of Gabler's innovative techniques that would continue to be used to the present day.

This recording session was also Frank "Franny" Beecher's first with the Comets. Beecher was a friend of Billy Williamson and was recruited to replace the late Danny Cedrone as lead guitarist. His memorable ad-lib guitar solo and smooth runs on *Happy Baby* had greatly enhanced the arrangement and impressed Haley. Within a few weeks, he had adapted remarkably well and would go on to be a first-rate rock musician. Although Beecher began his career as a country-western guitarist with the Buckaroo Ramblers, his years playing with the Buddy Greco and Benny Goodman bands were his honing grounds. In 1949 he played with Goodman at President Truman's Inaugural Ball. Frank had admired the techniques of Charlie Christian's jazz guitar and had used many of his methods. However with the Comets, Frank Beecher and his electric guitar mixed the earthy sounds of the western guitar with the eloquence of jazz and created his own unique style.

Frank recalled his first session with the Comets: *"Bill Haley had definite ideas of how his music was to sound and how his sidemen were to play. Once I knew what he wanted, I knew what to contribute. So I explored the possibilities offered by what he liked. Once I got with it, I knew what I had to do, so I just did it. I didn't copy anybody or even attempt to. Once I learned rock and roll music, I just played what I felt."* Beecher went on to say, *"although there was no chord work at all on the early records, on the job I'd slip a few things in here and there. I'd get a look once in a while from Bill."*

Franny Beecher and his first country-western band the "Buckaroo Ramblers". Left to right: Beecher, Brother Wayne, Jean Domerick, Sam Boccella, Joe Denick and John "Smoky" DiDomenico. Courtesy F. Beecher

The Comets had been without a full-time lead guitarist on their stage shows. Billy Williamson filled in the spot with his steel guitar and when needed, Marshall Lytle or Bill himself picked out the melody on their guitars. However when recording, Bill Haley had used Art Ryerson or Danny Cedrone. Franny Beecher would soon join the "stage Comets" and give them a sound closer to the one millions now heard on their records.

Frank "Franny" Beecher 1955: Comets' new lead guitarist. ©DAP

At the end of the session Milt Gabler went over to Bill and the boys and broke the latest figures. Their recording of *Shake, Rattle and Roll* had sold an incredible two and a half million copies in the last eight weeks! *"You boys are going to be rich . . . I think we've got one hell of a hit!"*

The four partners who owned the Comet organization, Bill Haley, Billy Williamson, Johnny Grande and Jim Ferguson split up the first royalty check from Decca, just over $5000.00 each. Ferguson, the small-time hustler from Chester, swaggers with his new-found wealth and importance. He now can afford the best in Havana cigars, old Scotch and young women. The race tracks and bookies become his home and best friends. He also becomes a "soft-touch" to many of his old bar room buddies. He loved to flash a large bank-roll and publicly peel off a fifty dollar bill to a pan-handling pal.

Haley's other two partners, John and Billy, put down-payments on new homes for their families. Bill finds a contractor to build him an eleven room ranch house on his father's five and a half acre farm in Booth's Corner. The Comets and friends help Bill clear the land of trees and rubble. Marshall Lytle's home movie camera records the boys, clad in jeans, hard at work with axe, saw and shovel. The "dream house" is only eighty feet from the converted little chicken house that was once his boyhood home. Bill would never tear down this eye-sore beside his dream home. Later he would say: *"I left it there just in case I forget where I came from."* Even today, the two houses stand side by side in stark contrast.

Bill lays out the driveway, patio, stone terraces and barbecue pit himself. He also lays out a curious narrow concrete walkway which leads from the back of the house over a small creek down into the woods for several hundred yards. After meandering through the tall oaks, it leaves the woods and returns to the main house by another route, again crossing the creek over a second arched, wooden bridge and back to the front of the house. The woods were the same ones he used to hide in when he played and sang his boyhood songs. In the turbulent years to come, Bill would walk with hands behind his back, along his "Sidewalk to Nowhere" to think out his problems in the beloved woods of his boyhood.

Bill Haley would name his new home "Melody Manor" after his old idol Gene Autry's "Melody Ranch". Construction was to be completed by the following spring at a cost of almost $100,000. 00.

By September, Decca released *Rock Around the Clock* and *Shake, Rattle and Roll* in Britain on its Brunswick label. The songs would go on to inspire thousands of British youths to discover hidden talents. In an interview just before his tragic death, John Lennon recalled that as a fourteen year old boy he was lying on his bed in his aunt's apartment, and *Rock Around The Clock* came over the radio. *"I loved it . . . it just grabbed me, like mentally . . . That afternoon I borrowed a few bob and bought the record. That was when I knew I wanted to go into pop music. Soon after my aunt bought me a*

This rare photo was taken during the building of "Melody Manor". Left to right: Bill's father, his sister Peggy, unknown, his mother Maude, unknown, Cuppy, Bill, and Reds Broomall. 1955.

Courtesy© Haley Family Collection

Courtesy© Haley Family Collection

Bill and his sister Peggy and Cuppy on left.

guitar." In 1968 Lennon and Brian Epstein would visit Haley backstage at the Royal Albert Hall. The two rock superstars traded autographed photos. Lennon gave Bill an autographed photo signed with the following inscription: *"To Bill, You Started It All!"*

In late September, Elvis Presley makes his first and only appearance on the Grand Ole Opry. He sings *Blue Moon of Kentucky*. James Denny, the Opry's Talent Coordinator advises Elvis after his performance to *"go back to driving trucks"*. Elvis is crushed and angered. Denny would be named Billboard's Man of the Year!

Meanwhile *Shake, Rattle and Roll* stays on the charts for 27 weeks. Royalty checks roll in from both Decca and Essex in unprecedented amounts. The Comets are booked solid for the next ten months. Their fees run from $2500.00 to $5,000.00 a performance. Everything they seemed to touch turned to gold. By October of 1954, Bill tells Bob Thornton: *"I think I must be dreaming, this can't be happenin'. I'm just a simple country boy. . . but I hope I never have to wake up!"*

About this time the Comets are featured in a film short subject called "Roundup Of Rhythm", released by Universal-International Pictures. They are shown performing three songs, *Skake, Rattle and Roll, Crazy, Man Crazy* and their instrumental version of *Straightjacket*. The film represents the first visual documentation of Haley's new sound and stage antics as well as his talent as a lead guitarist. His guitar-boogie solo dispels doubts of those who believe he could only play rhythm guitar.

Bill is home for five days and back out on the road. This time a thirteen one-nighter road tour of the mid-west. This Hank Snow/Tom Parker live road show is a unique blend of Country, Rockabilly and Rock'n'roll. He and the Comets will play to over 85,000 fans. While on this tour, Tom Parker, Hank Snow's partner, asks Haley's manager Jim Ferguson if they could add one more act. The two "carny" men are old acquaintances. Ferguson tells Bill: *"Parker says he's got this kid he wants to polish up a bit. His manager is a disc jockey in Memphis named Bob Neal, but Parker says he may want to take the kid over. The kid needs to go on the road with some real pros. He bombed out in Nashville, but they didn't understand him. I think he's got some real potential. Can we fit him in on the tour?"*

Both Ferguson and Haley know Parker as having been the manager of stars like Hank Snow and Eddy Arnold. Bill decides to do The Colonel a favor and let the kid on for a few shows. The Kid from Memphis joins the road show in Omaha, Nebraska. He follows Hank Snow and sings mostly ballads and a new, raw form of southern rockabilly. His best tune, according to Haley, was *That's Alright Mama*. Elvis Presley tells the Comets that he had cut a record on it several months ago. They wish him luck even though, at the time, they have never heard the record.

In an interview over a decade later, Haley recalls Elvis coming to see him back stage in Oklahoma, City. *"He was just standing there. . . we were about to go on. He came up to me and said what a fan he was. He seemed like a nice kid to me. He said he wanted to learn the business and Colonel Parker had said I was one of the best to learn it from. He reminded me a little of myself, going up to Hank Williams and Red Foley with almost the same words. Several nights later after his set, he asked me what I thought of his singing. I had watched him and so I told him I thought he had a lot of natural rhythm. Show a little more of your feeling, son..don't look so scared. Let'um know what you got. Let um feel your music.*

"For a couple of days we buddied around together. I was curious to see what the Colonel saw in him. I asked him how he got to meet the Colonel. He told me the Colonel knew a lot of the right people in the music business. He asked what I thought the best guitar was. I told him I always liked the Gibson L-7 myself. He loved my car and I let him drive it for a while on our way to Tulsa. He said to me, "One day I'm gonna buy me a Cadillac and I'm gonna buy one for my mamma too!"

"After about a week he got lonesome and would talk about his mother. Being on the road away from his family tended to get him low. He asked me if I was ever on the Grand Ole Opry. I said no, but I was once, almost. Then I got into Rock'n'Roll and ain't sang much hillbilly since. Now, with my drums and sax man, I don't think they would even let me in town! He grinned with a funny kind of smile and said "I don't need um' too". He was only a nineteen year old kid then and had a lot of spunk. His eagerness to learn reminded me of myself, back when I was his age. He told me his favorite song was "Crazy, Man Crazy", and after he heard it he knew he wanted to be a singer too. I told him it was my first big hit. I wished him luck. He left us in Tulsa, and we finished the tour. The thing I remember most about Elvis was the way he looked. At first, I thought he was just another star-struck youngster with a guitar. His long hair, it was kinda sandy-blonde then, his clothes and the hulking way he carried himself, at first, put me off. And if he hadn't been recommended by Parker, I probably would have never talked to him. But when you got to know him a little bit, he was really a very nice, polite young man. He always called me "Sir", even after I told him to call me Bill. He had more than just talent. I think he was hungry to be "somebody" to make it big, except he wanted it, it seemed, for his Mother. At the time, I kinda' thought that was unusual."

Although it was Bill Haley's recollection in this interview that this event occurred in late 1954, the Comets interviewed say it happened in 1955.

It would be hard to imagine a greater year for Bill Haley and his Comets than 1954. Their music was being played not only throughout America, but around the world. However it was 1955 which marked the beginning of three "golden years" of unabashed wealth and stardom for the band.

The year begins with the dissolving of the handshake partnership of Bill, John Grande, Billy Williamson and Lord Jim. The complexities of taxes, personal liabilities and international agreements call for a more formal organization. They incorporate the band under the name 'Bill Haley and his Comets, Inc.' Bill was named President, Williamson, vice-President, and John Grande, Secretary-Treasurer. James Ferguson is made an associate with a special arrangement.

At the same time, Bill, Grande and Williamson incorporate "Seabreeze Music Inc." This music publishing company was to be affiliated with B.M.I. (Broadcast Music Inc.). The song catalogs and copyrights of Bill Haley's other publishing company, Haley-Howard Publications, became their opening inventory. Robert Hayes and Frank Pingatore were appointed to run the day to day operations.

On January 5th Bill and the Comets drove to New York for another recording session. Bill and his two musician partners, Johnny Grande and Billy Williamson had written their first song to be published under the Seabreeze copyright, *Birth of the Boogie*. Former big band drummer Cliff Leeman would replace Billy Gussak for this session. Dick Richards does the eight bar tom-tom introduction.

The other song they recorded that day was a tune called *Mambo Rock,* capitalizing on the current Mambo craze and proving Bill Haley's theory any song could be converted into a rock'n'roll tune.

On January 26th, 1955 the Comets' song *Dim Dim the Lights* hits the national Rhythm and Blues charts. It would be the first "race" record by a white artist to be so honored.

Meanwhile in Hollywood, MGM Studios was finishing a movie based on Evan Hunter's novel 'Blackboard Jungle". It starred Glenn Ford, Anne Francis and newcomer Sidney Portier. The film was a violent teenage saga about switchblade-knife carrying high school punks and the attempted rape of a teacher in her own school. Its graphic portrayal of rampant juvenile delinquents, dancing in a wild, sexual orgy to tunes of Patti Page or Eddie Fisher wouldn't quite fit the part. A whole new sound track was needed for the film. Director Richard Brooks and Producer Pandro Berman wanted a harder, more threatening music. Coming home one day after shooting, Brooks finds his teenage daughter listening to *Rock Around the Clock*. That's what he wanted for his theme song! It had the power and energy to grab an audience's attention. It pounded the ear drums like some savage, tor-

Courtesy MGM

mented demon. *"Whose music is that?"* he asked his daughter, *"Gee Dad, where have you been? That's Bill Haley's music!"*

The next day Brooks called Jimmy Myers at Myers Music, the publisher of *Rock Around the Clock,* and Decca Records. He received the rights to use the song in his soundtrack. Gabler laughed in a recent interview as he remembered giving MGM *Rock Around The Clock* for one dollar, *"hoping they could rejuvenate its disappointing sales." Blackboard Jungle* was released in March of 1955. From that day on, Rock'n'Roll's perception in the minds of millions of adults was changed forever.

John Rockwell, noted New York Times music critic, has a vivid recollection of first hearing the tune: *"Those of us who were there will never forget its impact. This writer, a teenager at the time, first heard it in a movie theater—it was the theme song of the film Blackboard Jungle—and recalls the shared feeling of thrilled, almost bewildered excitement among that crowd as one of the high points of his life."*

Although the film would sell millions of records for Decca, Bill Haley's happy, joyous, and sometimes comical music become embedded in the minds of the social guardians as a grave danger to America's youth. Giant posters printed by MGM Studios show an evil black and white silhouette of a crazed young hood holding a switchblade knife. In large bold print it says: *"BLACKBOARD JUNGLE, A Drama of Teen-Age Terror!"* The big screen's graphic portrayal of senseless brutality by music-driven teenagers was not lost on the public. This coupling of Haley's new sound and a presumed rise in juvenile delinquency was a tragic development for rock music. However, for now, Bill Haley was unaware of the fire-storm of vicious criticism to come.

On the 25th of April, Bill was again on the road when he learns his mother has died of complications due to her diabetes. She had been ill off and on for several years. Her frail body could no longer endure. She and Bill's father lived next to Melody Manor and their son had seen that they wanted for nothing. Bill went home and buried his beloved mother in a nearby cemetery, alongside her parents.

This gentle English lady with her soft Lancashire accent had always encouraged her son's music. She had come to a strange, new land and struggled to raise her family in the hardest of times. She had married late in life, cleaned houses, took in wash, and sold eggs to make ends meet. Her husband grinded out his life in the mills and factories about Chester. She wanted more for her son. She loved

Bill Haley and Frank Pingatore at Steel Pier, Atlantic City publicity for "Two Hound Dogs". Note "Reds" Broomall in dark suit behind Bill.

music, any kind, and when people would criticize her husband's hillbilly playing, or her son's Rock-'n'Roll, her answer was always the same; *"The Bible says to make a joyful noise unto the Lord and the men in this family make the best there is!"* Maude Green Haley was the quiet, driving spirit of the Haleys. Though she died thousands of miles from her birthplace in the little town of Ulverston, her gift to the world was her unprejudiced love of everyone's music, which she passed on to her only son. Bill, with his sister Peggy at his side, bade a last farewell to their mother in the beautiful cemetery high on a hill overlooking the Delaware River.

Bill mourned the death of his mother far more than he let anyone know. It drew him closer to his family than ever before. He hires an elderly couple, Doc and Delores Anderson, to stay with his ill and failing father. William Sr.'s early years in the coal mines of Kentucky and his heavy smoking had left his lungs weak and frequent coughing was the only way he could clear them.

Commitments force Bill on the road again. This time a ten day string of one-nighters in the New England states. On the way back, May 10th, the band stops in New York to record their fifth Decca record. Bill chooses another Charles E. Calhoun song *Razzle Dazzle* and *Two Hound Dogs* written by Frank Pingatore and himself. Billy Gussak is again the session drummer. Gabler tells Haley that *Rock Around the Clock* is back on the national charts, and sales have gone over a million! The historic record would stay on the charts from May till October, an unprecedented six months. The management at Decca is ecstatic!

Franny Beecher now comes aboard the Comet team as their full time lead guitarist. Bill sets his salary at $175.00 a week plus expenses.

The Comets now get to experience Franny's notorious practical jokes on a regular basis. Whether is was short-sheeting their beds, secretly setting fire to guitar picks or just spinning tall yarns, Franny could always be counted on to do something to relieve the tension of life on the road.

Up until this time Bill Haley had affiliated himself primarily with the B.M.I. performing-rights organization for the collection of his song royalties. There was another larger and older performing-rights group which was the arch-rival of BMI called ASCAP (American Society of Composers', Authors, and Publishers). Any publishing firm who belonged to BMI could not be a member of ASCAP. Most ASCAP songs Bill had recorded were written by Jim Myers and listed in the catalogs of Myers Music which was a member of ASCAP.

To gain entree and become a member of the elite ASCAP, Bill Haley, John Grande and Billy Williamson form another music publishing company on May 16, 1955, "Valley Brook Publishing, Inc.", so named after an area near Bill's boyhood home in Booth's Corner. This firm became associated with ASCAP by the end of the month. Over the next three years Valley Brook and Seabreeze would hold the publishing rights to hundreds' of songs. Most were written by Bill, the Comets, their wives or their staff writers. Frank Pingatore, who by now is a close friend and staff writer for Bill, takes over the management of both companies. His skills as an arranger and musician during the past two years were invaluable.

Both companies were quartered in the new rented offices of the Comet organization located at 112 East 5th Street in Chester.

On May 21, 1955, Decca releases Bill's first 10″ long play album, *Shake, Rattle and Roll,* Containing eight tracks, this rare collectible for some reason depicts only five of the Comets on its cover.

Another feature film is released with Bill Haley's music on the sound track. *Running Wild* with Mamie Van Doren, Keenan Wynn and William Campbell includes scenes of teenagers dancing to a juke box playing *Razzle Dazzle*. The film was made for the teenage drive-in crowd and was released by Universal-International Pictures. Bill's picture is used in the advertising of the film although he does not appear in the movie.

When the Comets returned home in late June *Rock Around the Clock* was the number one song in the nation. It stayed there for an incredible eight weeks! Decca announces in the trade papers that Bill Haley and his Comets have sold over three million records in the past thirteen months!

On July 28th Bill's wife "Cuppy" gives birth to a boy. This is Bill's fifth child and the third by his new wife. They name him William Haley Jr, although he is actually the third of the line with the name William.

Dave Miller continues to capitalize on Haley's old recordings and re-releases on his various labels another series of albums, extended plays and singles. Miller also heavily promotes Haley's sound aggressively in England and Europe on the London label.

In August, Bill Haley files a lawsuit against Dave Miller's Palda Records. He asks the court for an injunction that would bar Miller from issuing recordings Haley made while under contract to Essex-Holiday. Miller is also releasing bootleg copies of Bill's *Rock Around the Clock* on his 45's. The suit describes those recordings as "inferior quality to said plaintiff's current releases." The suit is later dropped when Miller's company files for bankruptcy the following year.

The Comets continue playing to capacity crowds in the nation's largest theaters and auditoriums. The Comets' share of the gate-receipts for playing a long weekend at Steel Pier in Atlantic City, New Jersey is just over $27,000 in cash! They accept offers to appear on Sammy Kaye's and Milton Berle's network show. Later even Ed Sullivan books them for his coast-to-coast television show. The Comets' fee rises to as high as $10,000.00 a performance in a frenzy of demands.

Decca's subsidiary Brunswick releases to British and European audiences twelve of Bill's new songs, on four singles and one extended play records. Vince "Catfish" Broomall, the band boy for the Comets, remembers one of the royalty checks from Decca being just over $17,000.00. From this check, Bill promises to give each Comet their first bonus of $1,000.00 each.

While appearing at the Chicago Theater before thousands each day, Bill is told by his accountants that it would be best, tax-wise, not to use their own cars for tours anymore. Up to this time, the Comets were driving their own personal vehicles with Harry "Reds" Broomall and his young nephew, Vincent "Catfish" Broomall driving a paneled truck containing the instruments and equipment.

Bill Haley and Patti Page, Chicago 1955.

With this tax advice in mind, (spending some of the enormous profits before taxes as business expenses), Bill and his three partners went to a Chicago Cadillac dealership one afternoon to check on their truck which had been banged up in an minor accident on their way to the city.

Catfish remembers the day well: *"We went there because that's where our truck was towed. While waiting around the showroom for an estimate, the kid who had towed us in showed us some of the new 1955 models that just came in. They were the most beautiful cars I'd ever seen. They were so long they looked like battleships! Bill and Lord Jim, Johnny and Billy Williamson were not dressed up. They had on some old clothes and looked like some hay-seeds just off the wagon. None of the regular salesmen approached us, even when the kid ran over and told the sales manager we might be interested in buying a Cadillac. In fact, the manager, after looking us over, wasn't very impressed, and told the kid, 'YOU sell them a car!' The kid, who knew who we were, said 'If I do, can I have the commission?' The Sales Manager told him: 'You sell those bums a Cadillac and you can have the commission plus I'll buy you lunch too!'*

"The kid comes back and tells Bill what his boss had said. Bill Haley walks over to the showpiece of the room, a fully-loaded yellow Cadillac Coupe de Ville, and says: 'I'll take that one'. Johnny Grande takes a beautiful white convertible, Billy Williamson picks a dark blue sedan and Lord Jim selects a handsome silver-grey El Dorado.

"Bill tells the flabbergasted sales manager he wants the cars delivered tomorrow and his bank would wire the payment in cash before five o'clock. He also tells the man to be sure the kid gets his commission, or else! Bill loved it when he had these kinds of opportunities to show "the snobs" he was not some dumb hayseed who just fell off the turnip wagon. He was in high spirits for the rest of the tour."

In September the Comets suffered their first major crisis—the departure of three band members in a salary dispute. As thousands of dollars poured weekly into the pockets of Ferguson and the three partners; Haley, Grande, and Williamson, three of the original band members, Ambrose, Lytle and Richards remained on a flat salary of $175.00 a week, plus some expenses.

This un-equal sharing of the enormous profits the Comets were earning created a dangerous friction among the non-partners in the band. The initial hurt feelings grew into bitter resentment as their repeated requests for a more equitable profit-sharing plan was ignored by their manager, Lord Jim.

Haley's decision to let Ferguson handle the salary negotiations proved disastrous. Lord Jim's smug belief that no musician was dumb enough to quit the Comets proved to be a grave error. His unique ability to provoke resentment split the world's first rock band down the middle.

Marshall Lytle, Dick Richards, and Joey Ambrose walked into the Comets' office in Chester, just after

"The Jodimars," left to right: Marshall Lytle, Dick Richards, Max Daffner, Joey Ambrose, Chuck "Fingers" Hess.

Courtesy D. Hirschberg

Labor Day, and asked for their last pay check. Bill Haley received the news from Sam Sgro, his office manager. *"Lord Jim was too scared to tell Haley—Bill was furious!"* recalled Harry West, one of Haley's assistants. *"Lord Jim at first had told Haley the guys wanted to become full partners and that's why he turned them down, to protect the partnership. Why cut them in on the pie, they were just sidemen. Later, Bill found out he had lost half of his band over something that might have been settled with a decent raise and a share of the profits. Lord Jim was always trying for a better deal, only he never knew when to cut the bull-crap. He screwed up more deals for Bill than anyone else I know. Bill thought Ferguson was his "Good Luck" charm. By the time he realized what a liability Lord Jim really was, it was too late."*

In consideration for Bill, the three young rebels gave him two weeks notice and even offered to help train their replacements. After fulfilling their promise the three ex-Comets form their own group and call themselves the "Jodimars"; **JO**ey, **DI**ck and **MARS**hall. They went on to record a series of records for Capitol Records from 1955 to 1957 and continued as a Las Vegas lounge act until 1959. Their Capitol recordings were reissued in Great Britain in the 1970's with great success. In 1989 at the 20th International Rock'n'Roll Festival in Great Britain, they performed as the Jodimars and reunited with Johnny Grande and Frank Beecher to "Rock The Joint" as "The Comets". They brought down the proverbial house with twelve songs and four encores. The power of their music proved ageless.

Shortly after the departure of the Jodimars in September of 1955, Frank Pingatore also leaves the Haley organization and takes over their management. Bill had become furious when he learned Frank had been working with Marshall Lytle in writing material for the new group. Frank had been with Bill for two years. The handsome young Italian-American had helped the Comets with some of their best work and his sound advice and cool instincts would soon be missed.

Jack Howard, Bill's silent partner and co-owner of Arcade Music Company, assumes Frank's job running the Comets' publishing firms. Howard is named vice-President and CEO of the venture, a job he would hold until his death in 1976.

The defection of the Jodimars left Bill in a dilemma. He had major television, club, concert and recording contracts to honor and he needed a good sax man, a bass player and a drummer. They had to be first rate musicians and trained rock-'n'rollers in two weeks! In 1955, these types of musicians were very rare.

Bill first calls Al Rex, his former bass player from the "Saddlemen" days. Al was "MR. Bass" in the Chester area and after leaving the Saddlemen, he took over Bill's radio program at WPWA, started his own band and began writing music. Al was also a very fine singer and could relieve Bill of some of the demands on his voice. In the years to come Al would become one of the most flamboyant of the Comets. His wild antics, many learned from Marshall Lytle, would become legendary around the world.

For his new sax man, Bill hired a renowned jazz musician from Chester, Rudy Pompilli. Rudy had been with the Ralph Marterie Orchestra and was recognized as one of the finest saxophonists in America. Rudy's warmth and charm was to make him one of the most beloved of the Comets. His close friendship with Bill Haley is a touching story all its own. Rudy would go on to serve the longest tenure of any Comet, remaining with Bill for twenty-one years. The drummer Bill hired was Don Raymond. Raymond was a nine year veteran of the Catskill circuit and had played with the Desi Arnaz band. Many critics compared his style with Buddy Rich as his drum solos became a major highlight of the Comets' show. His short but stormy career with the Comets was to last only two months.

Rudy Pompilli with the Ralph Marterie Orchestra.

Courtesy A. Pompilli

With another recording date coming up fast, Bill puts his new band through a relentless schedule of rehearsals. Johnny Grande would piece together the arrangements while Billy Williamson steered and coaxed the sound. Taking full advantage of their two weeks notice, Bill had his new Comets watching his departing Comets from the audience. Within two weeks the new band was back in the Pythian Temple for two days of recording.

On September 22nd they recorded a song written by Bill and Rusty Keefer called *R-O-C-K* and the classic rock song Bill had written in 1953, *Rock-A-Beatin' Boogie*. The following day the Comets record one of their all time great rock pieces, *The Saints Rock'n'Roll*, a tune which Bill adapted from his mother's favorite gospel song. He adds Milt Gabler's name to the credits as a favor to his producer. The other song recorded that day was Winfield Scott's classic *Burn That Candle*. These four records are the first to feature Rudy Pompilli and Al Rex playing as Comets. Cliff Leeman again works his magic on the drums.

With this new lineup, the early, raw rockabilly sound of the Saddlemen-Comets came to an end. Rudy's powerful, jazz-edged saxophone meshed perfectly with Franny Beecher's guitar to create a new, more urban sound for the Comets and change their music forever.

In early October, Bill Randle calls Ferguson and asks him to do a free-bee show for him in Cleveland. Randle, next to Alan Freed, is one of the most powerful disc-jockeys of the mid-fifties rock'n'roll scene. Almost a Command Performance, the Comets agree and travel to Ohio as requested. They find themselves playing in the Brooklyn High School gym headlining a sock hop with The Four Lads, Pat Boone and a nervous twenty year old Elvis Presley. This would be Elvis' first appearance in the North.

Al Rex recalls the night: *"Elvis and us shared the stage. While waiting nervously to do his set, he turned to me and said: 'I hope these Yankees like my music'. I reassured him that he had no problem: "just go out there and do your stuff".* After asking Bill if it would be all right, Elvis sang Haley's version of *Shake, Rattle and Roll* and *Crazy, Man Crazy.*

Bill Haley and Elvis Presley Courtesy Kenn Petzke
Cleveland, Ohio 1955.

The show was a roaring success as the Comets brought the house down. The kids went home ecstatic as Bill headed for a store room converted into a dressing room for him. Still in the gym, Elvis asks Randle if he could get a picture with Bill Haley. The jubilant Elvis is ushered into Haley's make-shift dressing room. Bill greeted him warmly and asked about the Colonel's health. Elvis filled Bill in on all that had happened to him that year. After about a half hour of pleasantries their photograph was taken by Tommy Edwards. Though neither used the titles at the time, this historic photo shows the "Father of Rock'n'Roll" shaking hands with the future "King of Rock'n'Roll".

The following weekend the new Comets began their first grueling four week tour of the southern states, ending up in Texas. They played before over 90,000 people.

On October 14th, while in Texas, Bill gets separated from the rest of the band. Unknown to Bill at the time one of their Cadillacs blows a tire and has no spare. Running late, Bill goes on to Lubbock to find the stadium full. The promoters were getting hysterical. The kids were growing restless and Lord Jim says: *"What can we do?"* The promoter tells Bill, *"You got to go on!"* Bill replies, *"I can't go on, I don't have any instruments..no band.. or anything!"*

The promoter says, *"I've got a couple of local boys that will cover you!"* He then introduces Haley to nineteen year old Buddy Holly and his band. Bill asks them if they knew any of his songs. *"Yes Sir, Mr. Haley,"* Holly answered, *"ALL OF THEM!"* A nervous Bill Haley went on the stage that night for the first time without his Comets. He joked about his band getting lost *"cause they stopped and asked directions from a rancher. He told them Lubbock was just down the road a piece.... and that was a hundred miles ago!"*

Buddy Holly and his band backed Haley for about a half hour before the Comets showed up. Bill later commented to his band, *"If any of you boys ever leave me, I know now where to find some real GOOD rock'n'rollers!"* The trauma of the departed Jodimars is still fresh in his mind.

Bill Haley later tells Milt Gabler about the little rock band in Texas. *"You should hear them before some other producer does."* Bill didn't recommend many artists to Decca. The last time was a kid from Memphis, but nobody at Decca was listening. This time Gabler was quicker on the up-take.

In November, Don Raymond, their drummer for two months, leaves the band after a serious altercation with Bill. Catfish recalls Bill and Raymond ending an argument in a hotel elevator with a round of fisticuffs. The intervention of Reds, Bill's bodyguard, saved both men from serious harm. Needless to say the Comets need another drummer and fast!

Rudy suggests an old pal of his from his home town of Chester. Ralph Jones and Rudy had been members of a legendary Chester combo, Little Ernie's Four Horsemen. Bill calls Ralph Jones long-distance and asks him to join the band. Ralph, who was working as a milkman for Abbott's Dairy asks, *"How much is the pay?"* Bill says *"$250.00 a week salary plus expenses,..and a bonus for all recording sessions."* Ralph, who was making about $90.00 a week, said *"When do you want me?"* The next day he joins the Comets on the road in Ohio. As a classic jazz drummer, Jones had never played Bill's style of rock'n'roll before. His first comment upon walking into the hall where the Comets were rehearsing was: *"O' My God! What are they doing? And WHY are they doing it SO LOUD?"* Within a week, with cotton stuffed in his ears, Ralph was hitting the rim shots like an old pro. Catfish, the Comets band boy, nick-names the new drummer "Poppa Jones". At thirty-two he looks like the oldest Comet. Actually, Franny Beecher is older, but his boyish good looks hide his age well.

The last recording session in 1955 was scheduled for December 12th. The song Bill arranged was Robert Guidry's *Later, Alligator*. The song had previously been recorded by Guidry under the stage name Bobby Charles. Milt Gabler changed the name to *See You Later, Alligator* and it became one of the top songs of 1956. The teenagers adopted the lyrics and *"See you later, alligator....after a while, crocodile"* become embedded in their jive

Ralph Jones, the Comets globe-trotting drummer. ©DAP

vocabulary for years. The record sold over two million copies in its first two months. Bill used Franny Beecher's "chipmunk" voice as the opening line. The other song recorded that day was *The Paper Boy* written by Catherine Cafra, Billy Williamson's wife. This recording was Ralph Jones' first session with the Comets. He became the first stage drummer who was good enough to pass the critical requirements of Haley and Milt Gabler. It was also their first and only Decca record not recorded in the Pythian Temple. Gabler used the studio on the second floor of the Decca building in New York.

The Christmas party Bill threw that year to christen his new home, "Melody Manor" was memorable. He invited all the Comets and their wives, all of his managers, roadmen, office workers and friends. The Comet organization had now grown to over twenty people on the payroll.

Milt Gabler called to wish everybody a Merry Christmas and tell Bill his record sales had gone over five and a half million and that didn't count what Dave Miller was selling! What a year—1955 had been unbelievable and the Comets were booked for the next nine months with a movie contract, eight more records and over one hundred and seventy live performances. This year would be

CLASS OF SERVICE
This is a full-rate Telegram or Cablegram unless its deferred character is indicated by a suitable symbol above or preceding the address.

WESTERN UNION

W. P. MARSHALL, PRESIDENT

1220

SYMBOLS
DL=Day Letter
NL=Night Letter
LT=Int'l Letter Telegram
T=Int'l Victory Ltr.

(28)

The filing time shown in the date line on telegrams and day letters is STANDARD TIME at point of origin. Time of receipt is STANDARD TIME at point of destination

PA283 1955 DEC 2 PM 2 50

P LLH199 LONG DL PD=FAX PHILADELPHIA PENN 2 101PME=
:BILL HALEY & JIM FERGUSON=
FAULK ROAD BOOTHWYN PENN = CHESTER 5-0128 =

TRIED GET YOU AND JIM ON PHONE LINES BUSY. MUST KNOW IMMEDIATELY REGARDING ZARDI'S IN HOLLYWOOD. CAN DOUBLE WHILE MAKING PICTURE IN HOLLYWOOD WEEKS OF JANUARY 6 AND 13, 1956 AT $5000.00 WEEKLY. CLUB CLOSES EARLY NIGHTLY. IF NOT TWO WEEKS, HOW ABOUT ONE WEEK. WOULD TAKE CARE OF YOUR TRANSPORTATION AND LIVING EXPENSES. PLEASE WIRE IMMEDIATELY FOR ME TO ACCEPT. REGARDS/JOLLY JOYCE=

Courtesy© DAP

One of hundreds of telegrams in Comets' files.

BILL HALEY
"Mr. Rock and Roll"

It's Been Quite A Year!

BILL HALEY and his Comets

- **"No. 1 Rhythm & Blues Personality"**
  ... Annual Readers' Poll — 1955 (DOWN BEAT 12/28/55)
- **"No. 1 Instrumental Group"**
  ... Annual Readers' Poll—1955 (RECORD WHIRL, January '56)
- **"No. 1 Favorite Record and Artist"**
  ... "Rock Around The Clock"
  ... Annual Readers' Poll—1955 (RECORD WHIRL, January '56)
- **"No. 1 Small Instrumental Group"**
  ... Annual Poll—1955 (CASH BOX, November 26, '55)
- **"No .1 R&B Artists of the Year"**
  ... Annual United Press Poll
- **"No. 1 Record of 1955"—"Rock Around The Clock"**
  ... Annual Poll — 1955 (CASH BOX November 26, '55)
- **Triple Crown Winner on Billboard Magazine's record popularity charts.**

Personal Director	*Recording Exclusively*	*Exclusive Booking*
James H. Ferguson 801 Barclay Street Chester, Pa.	for **DECCA RECORDS**	**Jolly Joyce Agency** New York Philadelphia

Down Beat Magazine, January 25, 1956

You are cordially invited to attend

Bill Haley and His Comets'

Third Annual

Christmas Party and Brawl

Wednesday evening, the twenty-first of December

nineteen hundred and fifty-five

at seven o'clock p.m.

Melody Manor, Faulk Road, Boothwyn, Pa.

Dress informal

1955 invitation to the Comets' "Christmas Party and Brawl".

the first they would earn over a million dollars.

The year 1955 also witnessed an incredible explosion of black rhythm and blues talent on the popular entertainment scene. For the first time, these artists were given the opportunity to perform before large racially mixed but predominantly young white audiences.

Since Rock'n'Roll and rhythm and blues were kissin' cousins, the love of one usually brought with it an appreciation of the other. Millions of teenagers had discovered the joy and excitement of this new powerful music, whatever you wanted to call it.

In fact, the readers of "Downbeat" magazine voted Bill Haley the 1955 "Rhythm and Blues Personality of the Year." The runners-up were Big Joe Turner, Dinah Washington and Ruth Brown. The 1955 Annual United Press Poll also voted Bill Haley and his Comets as their "R&B Artists of the Year". Bill Haley was the first white man to have ever won these awards. Bill thought them a bit odd. To his way of thinking, he had not recorded any rhythm and blues that year. However he thanked the organizations for the honor and asked them to add Rock'n'Roll as a separate category next year.

Bill Haley's personal love of black music, called by some "his nigger-loving attitude", allowed him to share the stage, without hang-ups, with little-known black entertainers, something most top white stars would not do at the time. Bill and his Comets were often billed as the "Main Attraction" of the stage and road shows. However these Rock-'n'Roll extravaganzas often became the first showcases for lesser known groups and artists such as Bo Diddley, Little Richard, Big Joe Turner, LaVern Baker, Chuck Berry, the Platters, The Five Keys, the Drifters and countless other talented black entertainers.

Bill Haley's hybrid sound had opened the gates and lifted the heavy curtain of prejudice. He would share with the world his love of all musics. His genius for creating a mongrel, powerful sound of incredible life and vitality had torn down the barriers and obliterated the lines defining black and white music. For this he would be both glorified and vilified in the coming years as were few other entertainers in the history of music.

Comets' rare first album, 1955

Courtesy© DAP

The New Comets, December 1955.

CHAPTER EIGHT

THE COMING STORM: 1956-1957

"Sticks and stones may break your bones but names can kill ya!"

By the beginning of 1956, Bill Haley and his Comets were the undisputed kings and pied-pipers of the new, dynamic sound now known around the world as Rock'n'roll. They became the embodiment of the blue-jean, tee-shirt, hot-rod, sock-hop culture of teenage America in the mid 1950's. They became what one newspaper called: *"The Grand Masters of the Big Beat"*. Privately, Bill feels he is losing control and wants to slow down and take some time to think things out. Everything was happening too fast. However his contract commitments compel Bill and the Comets to travel to Hollywood for their first "Rock" movie for Columbia Pictures. They leave on New Years Day. The Comets new drummer, Ralph Jones, becomes the Comets unofficial historian with his ever-present movie camera. His behind-the scenes home films and vivid memories give us a unique insight into the Comets experiences for the next five years. Ralph remembers flying over the Rose Bowl game in the afternoon just before landing in Los Angeles.

The band first record their showcase number *Rudy's Rock* in Columbia's massive "dead room" sound stage. The song had been written by Rudy Pompilli and Ralph Jones several years before. All the other songs used in the film were taped directly from Decca's masters and lip-synced by the Comets. Now audiences around the world will experience the Haley sound on a magnificent soundtrack. The band memorize their lines, shoot their scenes and return home in two weeks.

Sam Katzman, the producer, is eager to cash in on the tremendous popularity of Rock'n'Roll. With the title of *Rock Around the Clock*, he had a screenplay written by Robert Kent and James Gordon. The writers base the story on notes given them by Bill Haley. The story was a fictionalized account of the birth of Rock'n'Roll by Bill Haley ánd the Comets. Booth's Corner becomes Strawberry Springs and Jimmy Myers becomes Steve Hollis, the man who discovers the small band and their sound in a hick town. Hollis, realizing the potential value of Rock-'n'Roll as a teenage dance music, signs up the band to a contract and blazes their way to glory after a few ups and downs. The story is a bit glib, but in the best tradition of the "B" movies of the era.

One can overlook the "cuteness" of the story-line and feast on some of the best Rock'n'Roll music ever played on film. The talent was staggering. Fred Karger's supervision of the sound track was superb. The line-up with the Comets included the Platters, backed by the Ernie Freeman Combo, Freddie Bell and his Bellboys, Tony Martinez and his band and the incredible rock'n'roll dancing of Lisa Gaye, movie star Debra Paget's sister.

The song *Rudy's Rock* is the hit of the film. The movie shares with the world the Comets' unique stage presentation and sound. Many of the practices and techniques developed by the Comets became standards in many other rock bands for years to come. Bill's approach to stage presentation had become very professional and sophisticated. His use of comedy to break up the pulsating, sexual overtones of his sound was pure genius. Al Rex, the bassist, would toss his great instrument in the air, sit on it and play it upside down. Part of the act, but not in the movie, was Al splitting his pants in some wild antic; the audience would roar! Sometimes he would play his bass while lying on it and Rudy, while playing his sax, would go over and sit on him. The audience loved it. The band's comical acrobatics established them as a strong visual act while their music drove the audiences wild with delight. The movie produced a strong, vivid message: Rock'n'Roll was fun, pure and simple "have a good time" fun, nothing more, and done right, nothing less.

In anticipation of the release of the movie *Rock Around the Clock*, Milt Gabler schedules another recording date. Decca has now sold over seven million Bill Haley records. Teenagers line up hours before record stores open to buy the latest releases. Hundreds of Bill Haley fan clubs across the nation receive monthly newsletters from the Comet organization telling the kids the dates of record releases. The magazine also tells them the dates

Courtesy© Columbia Pictures

and places of coming Comet appearances and stories about the band and their families. Jimmie Lynn becomes the editor of the "Comets News Letter". Lynn was a disc jockey at WVCH radio in nearby Chester and a talented songwriter. He became the popular host of a teenage "Bandstand" type of television program in Wilmington, Delaware. His popularity with the kids and his organizational skills were one of the reasons for the very strong network of Bill Haley Fan Clubs all over the United States. In Wilmington, Delaware alone there are over 3,000 members!

As the popularity of Rock'n'Roll grew, the attitudes of many people in the hard-core, anti-rock establishment polarized. They received new converts weekly. The full meaning of the Supreme Court's landmark decision that "separate but equal is not Constitutional" began to dawn on the segregationists as the first black children began to attend white schools. They felt betrayed and their wrath fell on the "nigger-loving Communists" who were destroying America. Thus anything of Negro origin became suspect. They deeply believed the Communists in Washington were using the "dumb-ass niggers" to destroy White-Christian America. Their hatred became a passionate crusade.

The Klan pointed out to Southern school boards and civic authorities that even the internationally recognized and highly esteemed Encyclopedia Britannica Yearbook for 1955 had warned the world about Rock'n'Roll by saying, *"The Rock'n'Roll school in general concentrated on a minimum of melodic line and a maximum of rhythmic noise, deliberately competing with the artistic ideals of the jungle itself."* This, they said, was a fancy way of telling the world Rock'n'Roll was *"savage jungle music"*. And no one needed to explain what race used to live in the jungle!

Bill Haley and his new sound became one of their prime targets. He was portrayed as one of the "Great Corruptors" of a frightening new teen-rock cult. At first, a few misguided ministers, red-neck KKK'ers, and unenlightened police officials began to bemoan the lack of respect and a lost sense of responsibility among many American teenagers. They also observed that the kids seemed to ALWAYS be listening to that *"ROCK'N'ROLL MUSIC!"*

Then some pretzel-brained psychiatrist expressed the view that Rock'n'Roll music had a strange, insidious ability to destroy the morals of young people. He then dragged out some dubious statistics to prove his theory.

With this "proof" in hand, a bunch of fanatics, out of work because the Joseph McCarthy "commie and witch hunt" was over, decided that *"Rock'n'roll

Johnny Johnston with Bill Haley on set of Rock Around the Clock. Courtesy© DAP

must be a damn Communist-nigger plot to destroy the minds and souls of our American youth!"* Thus was launched in America another bitter witch hunt—born of twisted patriotism and long-simmering racism.

Soon politicians, teachers, parents and other self-appointed upholders of the nation's virtue were condemning Bill Haley for corrupting and demoralizing the entire younger generation. At first Bill laughed at the suggestions, but as the attacks became more and more bitter, they began to hurt. What started as a natural dislike for the music by some people, grew into one of the most hostile and controversial campaigns ever launched against a musical art-form. Rock'n'Roll became one of the most misunderstood sounds ever created. Much of the hatred and hysteria aimed at Rock'n'Roll was but a mask to hide the fear and prejudice of its hillbilly and Negro origins. Polite society had never looked with much favor towards either one.

Bill reads a newspaper article sent to him from North Carolina. Two kids got into a fight outside a theater where he was playing, and the media prints *"RIOT AT HALEY ROCK'N'ROLL SHOW—KIDS INJURED!"* He shakes his head in disbelief. All he wanted was a happy, fun loving music Why all this?

He tells the Comets they would have to be very careful from now on. *"They are out to crucify us. One mistake and it could be all over. Be careful talking to the press, and for God's sake—NO teen-*

THE OTTAWA CITIZEN

Second Section | OTTAWA, CANADA, TUESDAY, JULY 17, 1956 | Pages 17 To 32

Inventor Of Rock 'N Roll Defends His Type Of Music For Teenagers

By Bob Blackburn

"If I thought for one second that I was doing anything to harm teenaged kids, I'd quit this business in a minute," the inventor of rock and roll said last night.

The speaker was, as every schoolboy knows, Bill Haley, leader of the group known as The Comets, and the man credited with the origination of the brand of music that currently has parents tearing their hair and youngsters just tearing.

Haley, who naturally has a tremendous amount of contact with the teenagers, says maybe 98 percent of those he meets are perfectly well-behaved—they don't say, "Hey Bill . . ." they say, "Would you please autograph this picture, Mr. Haley."

"There is no way in the world," he thinks, "that this music can have any bad effect on the kids. It does draw them together in one place, and if they're going to do something bad they'll do it. You could say the same thing of a baseball

at the age of six, and right from the start he was particularly fond of dixieland. He started to play professionally when he was 15, playing with, among other things, a travelling medicine show. He also did some busking—i.e. stalking into a bar, planting his hat on the counter, and playing on in the hope that the customers would shower silver into the hat.

It was about the same time that "progressive" jazz was emerging that Haley started rock and roll, although no one had thought of the name at that time.

Admired Progressive Jazz

"I admired progressive jazz and the men who played it," he says, "and I wish I was a fine enough musician to do it myself. But I can't, and I got to thinking that there should be some new music for the people. Progressive jazz, after all is for intellectuals."

He decided to make a combination of four types of music that would appeal to four major segments of the public. His choices: 1) country and western, 2) rhythm and blues

ards. He went at this combination very deliberately, and started turning out the kind of music he's playing today, but that was back around 1950, and althought it was rock and roll then just as much as it is now, no one paid too much attention.

He started out going around the high schools (with the complete approval of the principals, please note) and studying the sort of music the youngsters wanted. His first big record, Crazy, Man, Crazy, was one result. "Go man, go," he points out, "just happened to be what all the kids were saying those days."

Good Happy Rhythm

He proceeded on the assumption that anything simple, basic and down-to-earth has a good chance of becoming a hit. His own definition of rock and roll: "A good, happy rhythm type of music with a solid afterbeat, with down-to-earth lyrics that people will remember." Repetition, he figures, is one of the most important ingredients.

Offstage, Haley is an exceedingly pleasant, serious man who looks even younger than his 31 years (partly because of the

boyish "kiss curl" which he carefully combs over his forehead as part of the act.) He takes his music seriously, and likes to point out that it's no haphazard accumulation of sounds but rather is as carefully arranged as that of any orchestra.

He worries constantly about the bad name rock and roll is getting, and blames some of this on his imitators, many of whom, he says, aren't playing rock and roll at all but call it that. He is unwilling to make any comment on Elvis Presley, and you can interpret his silence as you please.

It's significant that while his group is athletic enough, they do absolutely nothing that could be termed "suggestive."

Meanwhile, he sees no reason to stop what he's doing. He recalled with this reporter, who is of a like age, the days when both used to crowd around bandstands to listen to Ellington and Basie and Shaw and the rest, and behave much the same way. "They didn't call us juvenile delinquents then, though. Nobody had thought of the phrase."

Pickets Hit 'Anti' Line

'Jungle Music' Critics Opposed

BIRMINGHAM, Ala., May 20 (AP)—Pickets staged a white citizens council demonstration outside a rock-and-roll show here today, and prompdy were picketed by young rock-and-roll lovers.

About 25 police officers watched the orderly demonstration outside the Municipal Auditorium, where the show headed by rock-and-roll star Bill Haley was performed.

Negro singer Nat King Cole was attacked by a group of white men in the same auditorium when he appeared at a similar

Haley Fans To Picket In Protest

CHESTER — Bill Haley fans from at least five states are expected to hit the bricks for rock 'n' roll Tuesday night, according to a spokesman for the Chester band leader.

Among the pickets will be some Delaware Countians who will join other Haley fans from throughout the Philadelphia area, Southern New Jersey and northern Delaware in marching at the WCAU

Bill Haley Sounds Off On Off-Color Lyrics

A vigorous campaign against off-color and double-meaning lyrics to modern rhythm and blues music is being waged by Bill Haley, the nation's top rock 'n' roll purveyor who, with his Comets, currently takes off in Columbia Pictures' musical, "Rock Around the Clock," at the Theatre. Haley flatly refuses to play any tune that, as he puts it, "couldn't be sung in my home or at a church festival."

The former country boy from Booth's Corners, Pennsylvania, claims that most of the caustic comments on rock 'n' roll are directed not at the music but at the lyrics of some tunes. Haley adds, "If the words are off-base, I rewrite them."

The music world considers Bill Haley a modern-day wonder. More than six million copies of his recordings have been sold in little over a year, a record unequalled

Jerry Gaghan

Bomb Is Too Much Rock 'n Roll for Haley

THE UNRECONSTRUCTED SOUTH: When Bill Haley and the Comets played their rock-and-roll show the other night in Greenville, S. C., an anonymous tipster phoned police that a time bomb had been placed in the 3,700-seat Textile Hall. . . . The Greenville cops just gave Haley time enough to play "See You Later, Alligator," and then cleared the hall. . . . Several thousand persons outside, seeking admission to the show were denied entrance without being told why. . . . Police roped off the area and waited until about 3.30 in the morning before they found a crude bomb of six sticks of dynamite. An alarm clock time contraption had failed to work, according to Jim Ferguson, Haley's manager. . . . Cancellation of the second show cost the Haley troupe and the Greenville promoter an estimated $5,500, Ferguson said.

HALEY . . . digs dynamite

Haley's war on CBS ... clared Saturday when th... of the musically-famed ... challenged statements ... Garry Moore on his Tuesd... show.

Moore describe... music—of which ... ally conceded to ... —as "insidious."

Haley shot bac... asked for time on ... explain his bran... threatened to org... at CBS studios a... got no answer.

Haley's office ... swer has been ...

"Garry Moore ... rock 'n' roll as ... said in a statem... "But, just the c... roll has been ins... of fans all over ...

"I encourage ... fans to join me in ... unjust criticism."

More than 1,000 ... are expected to p... three demonstration... Haley's office. Th... said more than ... have indicated th... the WCAU studio.

Death of Rock 'n' Rol

Wardner Dougan of ... president of the fed... | people, and on popular numbers in the organization's February | nies al... was co...

Billy Rose Blames Network For Growth of Rock 'n' Roll

New York, Sept. 19—(AP)—Producer Billy Rose said yesterday that it is easier to get good American popular music through the Iron Curtain than through the "electronic curtain" of broadcasters' control over recordings and music publishing.

He accused Broadcast Music, Inc., (BMI), owned by networks and radio stations, of giving the public mainly "obscene junk pretty much on a level with dirty comic magazines" and of being

Rose, like a number of ... nesses earlier, said the netwo... through BMI, the record companies and music publish... firms affiliated with the ... works, can decide what songs ... published, recorded and hear... the air.

Rose, recalling Al Jolson, N... Bayes and Eddie Cantor as onetime "big salesmen of so... said now "it's a set of untal... ed twitchers and ...

THE EVENING BULLETIN | TUESDAY, NOVEMBER 10, 1953

Man, Catch That Crazy Haley Music

6,000 Teen-Agers Shake, Rattle 'N Roll To Blatant, Blaring Music Of The Comets

By JOHN de WOLF

Bill Haley, the mild-mannered, pleasant dance band musician who started it all, listened to the stamping of feet and the chants of wild applause from backstage a few minutes before he went on to

squealed with delight at the simple, suggestive strains of "When The Saints Rock and Roll," "Rock Around The Clock," and "Crazy, Man, Crazy."

And when an exuberant saxo-

known recreation booster; and John Avison, accomplished pianist and conductor of the CBC Concert Orchestra.

What they thought of the show they say below. And though only

Mr. Haley, who says he grosses $1,000,000 on his tours.

"I never thought it would be this popular. What we have to worry about as musicians is that it doesn't get out of hand, so we

Bill Haley Threaten To Picket TV Studio

CHESTER— Bill Haley, leader of Bill Haley and His Comets, today threatened picketing of CBS studios throughout the country Tuesday over a recent referral to rock 'n' roll music as "insidi-

In a later statement, Haley sa... picket lines will be organized ... CBS studios throughout the cou... try if there is no response fro... Moore.

age girls in the hotel rooms, No heavy drinking in public, No kind of behavior that would blow it for us. Don't give them any mud to bury us in." It is interesting to note Bill never had to warn the Comets about marijuana or hard drugs, which were prevalent backstage at many of the large package shows. The world's first rock band never needed the artificial highs to produce its classic rock music.

At this point, recalls Ralph Jones, Bill started doing "bed checks", like a coach checking on his team. But, like many ballplayers, some of the boys would go to bed and await Bill's check, then go out and hit the town. Sometimes Bill would send Catfish to check on the boys. Noting some beds empty after midnight, the young man used discretion and never informed on the roving band members. For his valued silence, the Comets always made sure Catfish never wanted for anything.

Several months before, impresario Irvin Feld signed a $50,000.00 contract with the Comets to head what would be billed as the "Biggest Rock n' Roll Show of 56". Bill was to headline a star-studded program of the top artists in the country. The first leg of the tour begins in Pittsburgh on the 25th of January. They are to finish up in Washington D.C. on the 5th of February. While on this tour, Bill Haley reads in Billboard that RCA is releasing their first recording of Elvis Presley, *Heartbreak Hotel.* Bill says to Lord Jim: *"Hey, that's Parker's kid from Memphis. How about that!"*

The segregationists will try to use this tour to create a public relations nightmare for Bill. The Comets are one of eleven acts on the bill. However, they also were the only white performers and Bill is warned that his career might be in jeopardy if he continued to tour with "niggers". Bill ignors the advice and begins several close relationships on this tour. One of the supporting artists is his idol Big Joe Turner, "The Boss of the Blues". He and Bill become life long friends from this meeting. Many years later in Mexico, they will record several songs together. Also on the tour were The Platters, LaVern Baker, Bo Diddley, Roy Hamilton, the Five Keys, The Turbans, the Drifters and Red Prysock and his Rock'n'Roll Orchestra.

For two glorious weeks Bill Haley thought he had died and gone to hog heaven. He was to later say: *"There was more rhythm and rock on that bus than all Harlem and East St. Louis put together!"* Feld's "Super Attraction" plays to over a hundred thousand fans. But the mixed audiences of black and white kids together brought down the wrath of the segregationists. In the South, the Comets have to play afternoon shows for black audiences and evening shows for white fans. Black artists were not allowed to even be on the stage with white artists. Bill Haley was branded a "Communist-nigger lover". They view his willingness to share the program with negroes as the final proof of his betrayal. Small gangs of klansmen began to cause trouble at the show sites. Extra police were hired to prevent fights and vandalism. Several shows end with fighting youths and overturned cars. Although these events usually happened after the show, the newspapers called them "Rock Riots". The Comets' tour bus was often vandalized in the parking lots during the shows. The letters "KKK" and "Nigger Lovers Go Home" were graffitied on their sides while the tires were slashed. Catfish, Reds and several police officers were often required to guard the Comets' vehicles. Towns began to ban rock shows as the publicity goes from bad to vicious. Bill returns from the tour angry and down. He feels bitter at all the accusations. He feels they are trying to destroy "his music".

Courtesy© DAP

Rare photograph of Bill Haley in session at the Pythian Temple.

The movie *Rock Around the Clock* opens in Washington D.C. on March 14th. The entire Comet organization goes to the premiere. The anti-rock critics pan the script and call the music trite and

Gabler lecturing the Comets at the Pythian Temple. Courtesy© DAP

obnoxious, but the kids love it. They dance in the aisles and clap to its infectious rhythm and beat. The world's first rock musical is a box office smash, although it is banned in many cities.

On March 23rd, the Comets return to New York and the Pythian Temple for a remarkable series of three recording sessions. The idea behind these sessions was to feature the individuality and breadth of talent possessed by each Comet, as Bill featured them during their live appearances. They record a record breaking six songs on the first day in eight hours. The first song is the brilliant sax instrumental called *Rudy's Rock*, a more polished version of the tune performed in the movie. The arrangement is pure, classic Haley and features the legendary talents of Rudy Pompilli. After one hears it, you know why he was chosen the best saxophonist in Down Beat's reader's poll.

The second piece recorded was a song featuring the tremendous guitar playing skills of Franny Beecher. Written by Franny and Johnny Grande, *Goofin' Around* is one long and brilliant rock guitar solo. Its climactic end is pure magic. Billy Williamson gets to highlight his singing talent with Paul Winley and Ethel Byrd's song *Hide and Seek*, which had been an R&B hit for Joe Turner. Billy's R&B vocal style plays on the popular *Hucklebuck* craze, with some excellent solos from Rudy and Franny Beecher.

Tonight's the Night by Bill Haley and Catherine Cafra was a sophisticated melody with a fine dual saxophone and guitar solo. It also hints at the jazz traditions of some of the new Comets. *Hook, Line and Sinker* by Bill Haley, Eddie Khoury and Ron Bonner is a novelty song featuring Rudy's saxophone and Franny's classic guitar solos.

The last song recorded that afternoon was *Hey Then, There Now*, written by Ralph Jones and Rudy. This song, like *Tonight's The Night*, was sung by Al Rex, Franny Beecher and Billy Williamson, billed as the "Comets Trio". It is reminiscent in style of the earlier Comets who had featured a vocal trio on stage shows, consisting of Marshall Lytle, Dick Richards and Billy Willianson. The band returned home for three days rest. Gabler has them scheduled in four days for another session.

On March 27th. they return and record *Blue Comet Blues* by Al Rex and Franny Beecher. This was a pure, classic rock'n'roll guitar instrumental which features the genius of Beecher's theories which were a decade ahead of any other rock guitarist. *Calling All Comets,* another sax instrumental by Bill and Rudy, is another classic of rock adaptation of an earlier rhythm and blues sound. Williamson's brilliant steel guitar electrifies the driving rhythm with Rudy's powerful saxophone out in front.

Their third and last song that day was *Choo Choo Ch'Boogie*, a Haley treatment of an old Louis Jordan great. The Comets changed the arrangement and turned it into another fine classic piece. Bill Haley and his band record some of their finest work that afternoon and evening. The remarkable talents of each member of the band would now be preserved to be enjoyed by the rock fans for generations to come. Bill Haley returned to Melody Manor after midnight tired, but very pleased. He knew he had just recorded some of the best music of his career.

The following day anti-rock forces have a field day. The prestigious New York Times, on March 28th printed an article headlined *"Rock & Roll Called 'Communicable Disease'.* A Hartford, Connecticut phychiatrist, Francis Braceland, called rock music *"cannibalistic and tribalistic....it is insecurity and rebellion. It impels teenagers to wear ducktail haircuts, wear zoot suits and carry on boisterously at rock & roll affairs".* The good doctor was commenting on a "riot" that occurred after some rock fans were thrown out of a local theater.

The Comets were back in the Decca studios a week later on March 30th. They record *Hot Dog Buddy Buddy*, another classic rocker written by Bill himself. The song showcases Ralph Jones' drumming at its best with Franny's superb guitar solos. The entire band joins in this celebration of rock music. The second song recorded is *A Rockin' Little Tune* by Johnny Grande and Billy Williamson. Johnny's accordion gets the prominent place in this unusual instrumental featuring some brilliant solos. The third song recorded was an attempt to adapt a popular folk song from Scotland to a rock arrangement, Bill Haley and Rusty Keefer's *Rockin' Through The Rye*. Rudy's solo is the high point of this hybrid work. This technique would later be repeated, creating a series of rock songs based on popular folk music of many different lands.

The following day an anti-Rock'n'Roll rally is held in Birmingham, Alabama. It is given wide television news coverage. Its spokesman, Asa Carter, head of the racist "Alabama White Citizens Committee" charges the National Association for the Advancement of Colored People (NAACP) was seducing and corrupting white teenage girls by promoting Rock-'n'Roll. He states, *"with its basic heavy beat of the Negroes, it appeals to the base in man, it brings out animalism and vulgarity".* He then went on to say his people were *"initiating a campaign to force radio stations and jukebox owners to boycott this immoral music".*

Bill, Sam Sgro, his office manager, and many other staffers had watched the news clip that night. The following morning at the Comet office in Ches-

Courtesy© DAP

Lord Jim and Bill Haley in their Chester office.

ter, everyone was talking about the program. Bill is remembered saying, *"We don't need this...Why do bigoted idiots like that get all that kind of publicity?"*

Ten days later, Nat "King" Cole is attacked and beaten while singing on stage at the Municipal Hall in Birmingham. His crime: *"singing nigger music to racially mixed audiences".* Five members of the "White Citizens Committee" are arrested for the beating. One was the "Director" of the committee. Things were starting to get ugly as the anti-rock forces find kindred souls within the terror of the Klan. The Comets receive their first real death threats. They are the next scheduled Rock'n'Roll show to perform at the same Birmingham Municipal Hall the following weekend!

Two days later Bob Raiford, a disc jockey for WBT in Charlotte, North Carolina, was fired from his job for denouncing, on the air, the racially motivated attack on Cole. Many southern towns begin banning Rock'n'Roll music at public swimming pools, dances and schools.

Popular band leader Meredith Wilson calls rock *"the music of idiots...rock & roll is dull, ugly, amateurish, immature, trite, banal and stale. It glorifies the mediocre, the nasty, the bawdy, the cheap, the tasteless."*

So called "distinguished academics" like Roosevelt University sociologist S. Kirson Weinberg pontificate that *"Rock'n'Roll music is a manifestation of the insecurities of the age. The effect of the music is*

The Comets attract huge crowds of racially mixed fans.

more predominant in girls." Even Steve Allen on his prime-time television program tries to ridicule rock by reading Gene Vincent's *Be Bop A Lula* lyrics in a slow dead-pan voice to a phony canned laugh track. At this difficult time, his tasteless humor is considered vicious by the pro-rock group. Bill Haley tells Lord Jim, *"Don't you ever book us on that jerk's show!"*

Bill Haley is personally listed as one of the groups banned by a new ordinance in Jersey City. The city fathers felt *"Rock'n'roll music encouraged juvenile delinquency and inspired young females in lewd bathing suits to perform obscene dances on the city's beaches"*.

Even "Time" magazine in an article on Bill Haley's new sound commented in their June 18th issue, *"Rock'n'roll is based on Negro blues, but in a self-conscious style which underlines the primitive qualities of the blues with malice aforethought. Characteristics: an unrelenting, socking syncopation that sounds like a bull-whip; a choleric saxophone honking mating-call sounds; an electric guitar turned up so loud that its sound shatters and splits; a vocal group that shudders and exercises violently to the beat while roughly chanting either a near-nonsense phrase or a moronic lyric in hillbilly idiom."*

Brian Boles, the demi-god of segregationists and founder of the National Association for the Advancement of White People, calls Bill Haley: *"the Judas' goat, because he betrayed for thirty pieces of silver the youth of America with white-washed nigger music!"* He screamed in his speeches that *"Bill Haley and his kind were a disgrace to their race and they would burn in hell-fire forever!"*

The effect of this bitter and unfair criticism on Bill was akin to having a great dark cloud pouring acid on his parade. His old problem of self-doubts began to rear its ugly head again. He had knowingly opened a Pandora's Box of ethnic music, never dreaming it held so much pent-up hate!

In late May, while playing in the Ponce de Leon Park in Atlanta, Georgia, five teenagers are arrested at Bill's concert before an estimated 10,000 fans. Another boy was hit in the head by a flying beer bottle. The show business magazine "Variety" reported this "riot" with extensive coverage.

Unbeknown to the newspapers, the Comets and Bill were continuingly receiving death threats by phone and in the mail. The band was warned more than once: *"If you walk on the stage you'll be shot!"*

Ralph Jones, the Comets' official worrier, remembers: *"Sometimes we were scared to death, but we played anyway. We faced up to 20,000 people, always thinking someone out there might have a gun and shoot us! Sometimes the music and noise was so loud, you couldn't hear a cannon go off! We were even getting bomb scares constantly. At one concert down South the police DID find a bomb! All this was nerve-wracking for us...I don't know how we even could play!"*

Bill begins to carry a gun even on stage and his bodyguard Harry Broomall never leaves his side. The pressure on Bill mounts and he begins to get his first severe case of "crowd nerves," as Lord Jim calls them.

In June, another incident achieved national attention when "Newsweek" printed, *"Even before the joint began to jump there was trouble at the National Guard Armory in Washington, D.C. 5,000 people, mostly teenagers, poured in for some rock' n'roll. Knives flashed and one young man was cut in the arm. Inside 25 special officers waited for Bill Haley and the Comets to swing into the big beat."*

The story goes on to say that another youth was cut over one eye and was rushed to the hospital. This set off a general melee. More teenagers were injured, cars stoned and false fire alarms given. The armory manager, Arthur Bergman, was quoted, *"It's the jungle strain that gets them all worked up!"* Now even more cities across the nation began to ban rock concerts. First in Washington D.C., and then in cities and towns from California to New England.

On June 17th, while on tour in Canada, Bill was told of the death of his father. He had been fighting a losing battle with cancer and tuberculosis. Bill returned home and buried him next to his mother. The memories of his father and their good times came flooding back at the services. It was this wiry old man that had first taught him to play the guitar. It was this quiet, little man's happy foot stompin' music that had lit the fire in Bill's subconscious. The son could still hear his father's old mandolin going "mountain crazy" on a long Sunday evening. Bill buried the mandolin with his father, as a last sign of respect, and with a final whisper, walked away with tears in his eyes. His sister, Peggy, his family and friends were about him. He told a friend later that he never felt so alone. Although he was thirty years old, being an orphan was still painful.

Several weeks later Bill is told his "Rock and Roll Under the Stars" Concert in the Roosevelt Stadium was canceled by Jersey City mayor Bernard Berry. A "rock-riot" the week before in Asbury Park sent twenty-five youths to the hospital and they didn't want to take any chances in their town.

At the Pennsylvania Chiefs of Police Association conference in Pittsburgh that summer, a spokesman said of Rock'n'Roll, *"it is an incentive to teenage unrest..."* Another Pittsburgh officer, Inspector

Jimmy Myers and Bill Haley. Courtesy J. Myers

Fred Good, related to newsmen that *"Wherever there's been teenage trouble lately—Rock'n'Roll has almost always been in the background. The songs are more suggestive than those sung in burlesque houses and the rhythm seems to have some special hypnotic effect which has created ridiculous male hootchie-kootchie dancers."*

Angered by the vicious attacks on what he felt was "his" music, and the canceling of his concerts, Bill Haley began his all-out "Don't Knock the Rock" campaign. He signed to do another movie to be shot in the fall which would show the positive side of Rock'n'Roll.

Returning again to New York on July 12th, Bill and the Comets record the first rock "message" song, titled *Teenager's Mother*. The song was a well-intended ode to the freedom of choice in music. For the "A" side Bill selects Little Richard's *Rip It Up*. This fiery, classic Haley rock'n'roller was Ralph Jones' favorite song. In view of the growing criticism of Rock'n'Roll's "suggestive" nature, Bill tones down the original lyrics, changing *"We're gonna rip it up—and ball tonight"* to *"We're gonna rip it up—at the ball tonight"*.

The attacks in the press continue and Bill finds himself being quoted and mis-quoted almost daily. One of the most popular Bill Haley mis-quotes of the day was *"Everybody hates us...except the kids"*. Although he said many times he did think it, he never remembers saying it to a reporter.

When asked years later why he thought Rock'n'Roll caused so many riots, Bill answered, *"You know, the press is interested in sensationalism. There has been a lot of talk about the riots that took place when we would perform back then. The problem with Elvis, and Fats Domino, and Chuck Berry, and myself was that there were so many kids who wanted to see us that they couldn't get into the place. In ninety-five per cent of the places we worked, if the auditorium seated ten thousand, the promoters would let fourteen thousand kids in. You get that many kids standing on top of each other and something is going to happen. It was the enthusiasm, and this is what caused the riots that took place."*

In Australia, *Rock Around the Clock* reaches number one on their charts. Bill is besieged with offers from promoters to tour the "Down-Under" continent. He turns down $45,000.00 plus expenses for a fifteen day tour of Australia. He informs the promoter the offer is inadequate. The following week, Bill turns down another offer from Milton Berle for $6000.00. Berle wanted Haley and the Comets on his prime-time network show for a 15 minute set. Bill could not find the time—his tour schedule was relentless.

In the summer of 1956, Communism, rock'n'roll, illicit sex and juvenile delinquency all became one related issue in the minds of many Americans. It became the most talked about subject in the nation. Bill finds the attacks from the KKK and other *"stupid, narrow-minded idiots"* easy to dismiss as *"just plain crazy"*. But what bothered him more than any other criticism was that from fellow musicians and performers. Bill felt they, above all people, should know he was not out to destroy "their" music, that he was not *"a puppet whose strings were being pulled by Communists and the NAACP."* How could they say these things? Also how could they say his sound was not music, and his musicians were *"drunken half-trained amateurs whose vices were infecting and demoralizing American youth?"* Bill's anger and hurt grew day by day, headline by vicious headline.

Unknown to Bill at this time was the sinister force united against him and his new sound. Unfortunately he had made a powerful and bitter enemy in J. Edgar Hoover, the dreaded Director of the Federal Bureau of Investigation. The bigoted but Machiavellian Hoover hated rock music and personally believed it was created to undermine the moral fiber of America and spawn juvenile delinquents. Since he had always considered himself the self-appointed watch-dog over the nation's morals, he set about to undermine Rock'n'Roll's influence anyway he could.

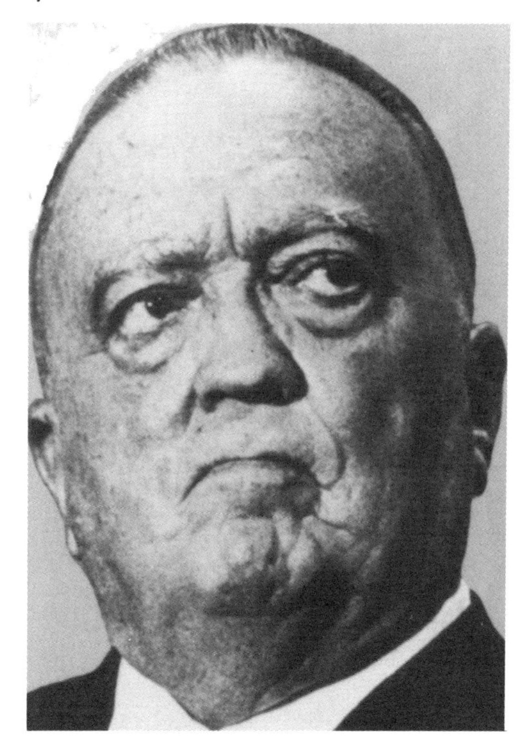

J. Edgar Hoover
Director of F.B.I.

DECODED COPY

[XXX] **Radio** ☐ **Teletype**

FROM LOUISVILLE 11-7-56 NR 071428

TO DIRECTOR URGENT

BILL HALEY AND HIS COMETS, INFORMATION CONCERNING, POLICE COOPERATION MATTER. COLONEL CARL E. HEUSTIS, CHIEF OF POLICE, LOUISVILLE, KENTUCKY, THIS DAY ADVISED THAT ELVIS PRESLEY AND BILL HALEY AND HIS COMETS, RIVALS FOR THE ATTENTION OF QUOTE ROCK AND ROLL UNQUOTE FANS, ARE SIMULTANEOUSLY BOOKED FOR APPEARANCES AT THE JEFFERSON COUNTY ARMORY AND THE KENTUCKY STATE FAIRGROUND EXPOSITION CENTER NOVEMBER 25 NEXT. COLONEL HEUSTIS ADVISED HE HAS RECEIVED INFORMATION THAT THERE HAVE BEEN RIOTS AT JERSEY CITY, NEW JERSEY, ASBURY PARK, NEW JERSEY, SANTA CRUZ, SANTA JOSE, CALIFORNIA, HARTFORD, CONNECTICUT, AND JACKSONVILLE, FLORIDA AS RESULT OF SUCH SIMULTANEOUS APPEARANCES. RIOTS REPORTEDLY RESULTED IN MANY THOUSANDS OF DOLLARS PROPERTY DAMAGE. COLONEL HEUSTIS REQUESTED INFORMATION FROM THIS BUREAU REGARDING ANY SUCH RIOTS IN AN EFFORT TO PREVENT SUCH RECURRENCES HERE. IN VIEW OF THE EXCELLENT COOPERATION BETWEEN LOUISVILLE PD AND THIS OFFICE IT IS REQUESTED THAT THE BUREAU FURNISH AN AIRTEL SUMMARY OF ANY INFORMATION APPEARING IN FILES SUITABLE FOR DISSEMINATION TO COLONEL HEUSTIS.

RECEIVED: 11:05 AM RADIO

11:22 AM CODING UNIT MJM

Mr. Rosen

63-3064

NOV 9 1956

If the intelligence contained in the above message is to be disseminated outside the Bureau, it is suggested that it be suitably paraphrased in order to protect the Bureau's cryptographic systems.

One of many F.B.I. telegrams released under the Freedom of Information Act.

By early 1956 Hoover had become a major player in the growing anti-rock movement. Misusing the enormous power of his office, Hoover personally encouraged and supported the manufacture and distribution of anti-Haley and anti-rock propaganda. His "friends" released a steady stream of dubious statistical and scientific data to "prove" the harmful effects Rock'n'Roll had on young people; especially impressionable teenage girls. This clandestine operation, jokingly code named "Beethoven", leaked and/or magnified any negative Rock'n'Roll stories to the nation's press. They supplied directives to local law enforcement agencies to alert them of the potential dangers of holding Rock'n'Roll concerts in their communities. They created a climate of fear and prejudice which became a feeding frenzy for the country's unsuspecting media. The same dubious tactics Hoover would later use on the N.A.A.C.P. and Dr. Martin Luther King were being honed on unsuspecting Rock'n'Roll performers.

By the summer of 1956 Bill was to learn first-hand that Philadelphia based F.B.I. agents were questioning his friends, neighbors and associates for very personal information. Ruth Sipps recalls telling Bill Haley: *"They wanted to know if he drank a lot, fooled around with young girls or was a member of any communist or negro-rights organizations."* Mrs. Sipps remembers laughing at the agents and saying: *"Bill Haley is as American as President Eisenhower", but the agents didn't seem too impressed".*

Another friend, Bob Thornton, went up to Bill and jokingly asked if he had robbed a bank or something. He told his friend the F.B.I. was asking an awful lot of questions about him.

Puzzled, Bill asked several local police officials about the F.B.I. investigation. He was told not to worry about it, *"the Feds did routine background investigations on all famous people."* The fact that even the F.B.I. thought he was famous flattered Bill and whenever the subject of F.B.I. inquiries arose, Bill would just smile and shrug his shoulders.

Hoover, of course had hoped to find some scandal in Bill's past that he could use to control Haley. Something he could use to tarnish Bill's image as a clean-living family man. This tactic was used many times by the unscrupulous Hoover to destroy a career or blackmail powerful political and entertainment peope. Even Elvis Presley would fall under the power of the cunning manipulator as he became an informer for Hoover's secret files.

Bill would go on battling the anti-rock forces for the rest of his life never realizing the powerful influence Hoover's F.B.I. had in manipulating public opinion. However by the summer of 1956 the seeds had been well sown and it became very fashionable for the rich and famous to publicly criticize rock music and its practitioners.

Bill was deeply hurt when Frank Sinatra, whom he had always admired, was quoted saying: *"Rock-'n'Roll is phony and false, and sung, written and played for the most part by cretinous goons."*

Rosemary Clooney, one of the top recording stars of her era, added in her two cents: *"Maybe there is something to be said for it, but you know, the musicians playing on those rock'n'roll records never tune their horns. They are never with the piano and the records sound like they got a bunch together in a vacant warehouse to perfect their recording technique. Maybe we should keep the big beat of rock' n'roll and get back to music. If our top name orchestras, or possibly one yet to be organized, should develop a big-beat, only blending the harmony, rhythms and melody we have been so accustomed to with our big bands, maybe that would be the answer. I believe that this style of music is just another one of the passing fads."*

Clooney wasn't the only one who hoped Rock-'n'Roll would roll over and die. Many other top professionals in the entertainment business believed it would go the way of the short lived "Skiffle" craze. Skiffle was one of the first English imports. Its fast shuffle and hybrid country-boogie sound came on to the American music scene like a lion and within months disappeared.

Teresa Brewer, another very popular singer among the younger crowd, commented that *"Rock-'n'Roll is simply a beat dressed up to look like a song. When you've heard one, you've heard them all....Can you imagine "Rock Around the Clock" still a favorite 10 years from now? Time is a good test of quality....and it will soon judge Rock'n'Roll's place in American music."* Teresa, How right you were!

Mitch Miller's comment was more to the point: *"Rock'n'Roll is not music, it's a disease".* To which Richard Neville proclaimed, *"Rock'n'Roll is an asylum for emotional imbeciles".* All would one day eat their words, but for now they had the effect of a battering ram on Bill's fragile self-esteem. *"Sticks and stones will break my bones, but names can kill ya",* Bill would say as one insult after another found their mark.

By mid-summer, Elvis Presley had become one of the hottest new singing stars of the year. In the unique logic of youth, if your parents really disapprove of something, it must be fun. Thus Elvis Presley received the growing adoration of millions of teenagers, and the scorn of their elders. He was also beginning to share with Bill Haley the "sticks and stones" of a hostile adult world. His highly

Courtesy© Down Beat Magazine

Front cover of Down Beat Magazine, March 1956.

Courtesy© DAP

Bill at home reading "Billboard".

graphic illustrations of hip thrusts were reviled as nothing more than lewd public displays of the male pelvic thrusts used in sexual gratification! The press started to call him a "Howling Hillbilly" and "Elvis the Pelvis". The anti-rock public loved seeing the hated Presley impaled on the cruel barbs of the press, almost as passionately as his fans pledged their undying love and loyalty.

One night at the office of his accountant, Bill Smith, the subject of Elvis came up. Bill commented to Lord Jim and Bob Miller: *"If the Kid keeps swiveling them hips, the bastards are gonna hang him from the church steeple!"* Lord Jim retorted, *"Well at least you'll have some good company!"*

Bill laughed with a weary half-smile and remarked, *"I hope he makes some money fast...before they get him. All he wants is to buy his momma a cadillac! I tell you this, that boy is a nice kid, I hope they don't eat him alive".*

Lord Jim shows Bill another article clipped from the newspapers, *"Reds Denounce Rock'n'Roll!"* The story, datelined Moscow, quotes the new Russian leader Nikita Khruschev saying: *"Rock'n'Roll is Capitalism's most decadent music."* Bill is said to have shook his head and said, *"Well can you beat that! Now even the damn Communists are jumping on the bandwagon! You know Jim, if it weren't so stupid it would be funny. I oughta' get a medal or something. I think I'm the first S.O.B. to get the Catholics, the Protestants, the Klan, the Communists, the Press, Frank Sinatra, and most adults over twenty-five to agree on something! Who else is left to take a swing at us?"* Lord Jim, who always liked to patronize Bill, said *"You forgot the Arabs. I hear they ain't allowed to play your music from Egypt to Iran! They say that Rock'n'Roll is against their Islamic traditions!"*

Bill is said to have banged his head on the desk and with a self-mocking smile said: *"What's Santa Claus gotta say about Rock'n'Roll?"*

"Jingle Bell Rock anyone?" laughed Lord Jim.

"I don't know what Old St. Nick is got to say", Bob Miller said as a word of caution to Bill, *"but if you guys try to Rock'n'Roll "Silent Night" they might just hold another crucifixion!"*

Billboard magazine in a July article states, *"Elvis Presley is the most controversial entertainer since Liberace."* On the "Steve Allen Show", another prime-time network television program, Elvis is made to look ridiculous as Allen insists Presley wear a tuxedo and sing without emotion or body movement, *Hound Dog*, to a sad faced old hound. Bill Haley was furious. He tells several friends: *"The bastards did that on purpose! They just wanted the kid to look like a jerk! They want to make us all look like jerks! They think Rock'n'Roll is a joke! Don't anyone ever mention' that jazz-freak's name around here again! This whole thing is getting ridiculous, it's getting me sick!"*

Meanwhile the band goes back on tour for three weeks. The auditoriums and theaters are packed with sell-out audiences. The movie "Rock Around the Clock" is creating millions of new fans. For the first time many people who had never attended a Bill Haley Rock'n'Roll show could now see Bill's sound as a happy, good time music. They could see for themselves that there was nothing threatening, lewd or sinister about it.

In the field of merchandising, promoters and other fast thinking entrepreneurs flooded the country with "Rock Around the Clock" hats with the Comets' names stitched on, the first "concert" T-shirts, board games and skirts with Rock'n'Roll motif adornments.

Rock'n'Roll became big business to whole new industries outside the obvious turf of simple entertainment. The recorded sales of electric guitars, amplifiers, sheet music and all the ingredients needed for teens to start their own Rock bands reached unheard of proportions during 1955 and 1956.

At this point in the development of Rock'n'Roll, Bill Haley found himself in a strange position. He was making a fortune playing his type of music. He was in such demand he charged top dollar for each performance. He had ten times over the requests he could possibility fulfill. His publishing companies, Valley Brook and Seabreeze, were turning out dozens of songs and collecting royalties from Bill's mega-hits from around the world. By August, Bill's records had sold over 8,000,000 copies. And yet the press kept asking him *"Do you think Rock-'n'Roll is just a fad?"* or *"How can you justify the damage done to young people who are addicted to your music?"*

To this last question, Bill told the reporter: *"My mother and father were good Christian homespun folks and although I haven't been as close to the church as I would like to have been during the last few years, I feel certain that the teachings of my folks were thorough and that my conscience will not let me travel far from the straight and narrow. So, how could I develop an unhealthy music if I think straight and try to live right? If Rock'n'Roll is wrong, if it's bad for the young folks, and I know it isn't, I will be the first one to stop playing it."*

Bill was most grateful when the late, great Kate Smith, a veteran entertainer and powerful singer, came to his defense with her open-minded opinion: *"Rock'n'Roll is the rhythm of our time. Millions of people...adults, as well as youngsters...have indicated it's a form of music they like to hear, hum, sing and whistle. Frankly, when I first began hearing Rock'n'Roll songs on the various disc jockey programs my reaction was, It's exciting, but it can't last. However, several months ago I began to get the feeling that Rock'n'Roll had lasting qualities."*

When other entertainers such as Sammy Kaye, Benny Goodman and Duke Ellington attacked the "snobbism" of the anti-rock forces, Bill Haley felt, for the first time, his music might be given some credit beyond its original teenage audiences.

Bill began to distance his style of Rock'n'Roll from some of the other "More sexually explicit" variations which were, as he put it, *"only adding fuel to the fire."*

Bill began to point out the happy, care-free and fun-loving nature of his music. He said his brand of Rock'n'Roll was free from the blatant sexuality which he believed could destroy its acceptance by the larger and still undecided adult community.

Renewed with some moral support from a growing list of rock enthusiasts, Bill continues to speak out strongly for his kind of music and distance himself from the more bizarre and suggestive styles.

In another interview at this time he states: *"At the time that the kids are out listening to our music, they're not getting into trouble. When they're home listening to records, they're not getting into mischief. It can only help them, not hurt them. A lot depends on the parents and how they take care of their children, and a lot depends on the entertainers. Bad lyrics can have an effect on teenagers. I have always been careful not to use suggestive lyrics. .....Wherever we appear the public has come out in droves, yet the industry is tearing the music down. If Rock'n'Roll can bring people into the ballrooms and make them dance, why then don't those musicians who call Rock'n'Roll bad music write their own arrangements against the beat and form small units of, say, nine men? I know for a fact that a lot of the musicians who think my music is bad are not working steadily. If the music is bad, as they contend, what's to stop them from making it good by writing their own arrangements?"*

By mid-July the Comets are back on the road with their Rock'n'Roll Extravaganza. They tour eighteen states and play before over 125,000 people. But it's a long hot summer, and before its over, the anti-rock forces launch new and even more brutal attacks.

One night, after a major rock show in the South, the Comets were in their bus getting ready to pull out of the parking lot. It was well past midnight when a black man ran up to the bus and frantically pounded on the door. Al Smithson, the Comets' driver, opened the door and the shaken young man scrambled aboard. All the Comets recognized him at once as he ran to the back of the bus and hid under the boxes and instruments.

About a minute later, as the bus started to pull away, four or five angry red-neck Goliaths ran in front to stop it. One mean-looking goon demanded to know if they had *"a skinny-assed nigger in a pink suit on the bus."* Bill went up front and told the man in his best rebel slang: *"Boy, do we look like a bunch of nigger-loving Communists?"*

The thug smiled with a un-nerving, humorless grin and waved his lead pipe for the bus to get moving. The Klan was out tonight and these formidable-looking psychos were looking for blood.

As the bus rolled out of the parking lot, Bill walked to the back and said in his best black-jive talk, to a trembling Chuck Berry: *"Yo keep messin' with dem women down here Chuck buddy and Beethoven won't be the only dead sucker rolling over!"* Berry swore to Bill he hadn't done anything and he didn't know why those guys were chasing him. Bill told him, *"I know you ain't from the South, but down here, there are guys who would hang you for just looking good!"* Chuck Berry and Rudy Pompilli's legendary double-dates were well known among the Comets and so were Chuck's daring nocturnal sorties.

In September, the Comets were again in Hollywood. Sam Katzman was ready to shoot another

Rock'n'Roll movie. This time they were going to call it "Don't Knock the Rock".

With this film Bill Haley wanted to take on all the fanatics that were bad-mouthing his music. The plot took on all the trappings of a medieval morality play. Nice kids just wanting to have some good clean fun, against a bunch of life-weary, narrow-minded adults who looked so old they could fart dust.

The writers tried to use logic and reason to prove their point. At one part of the story the kids create a play in which they perform many dances from the past and review some of the "wild" music and dances of their parent's generation.

Again the dialogue is weak and the plot thin, but the music alone is worth the price of admission. The massive sound studio at Columbia produces a magnificent sound track which again carries the film although all the characters lip-sync their songs. Sam Katzman has another low-budget, box office hit to add to his "Rock Around the Clock" film which is now playing in theaters around the world.

The Comets play their new songs, *Calling All Comets*, *Goofin' Around* and *Rip It Up*. Newcomer Little Richard's rendition of *Tutti Frutti* and *Long Tall Sally* is one of the highlights of the film. Little Richard establishes a new but wilder style with his flamboyant, super-charged performance. He would go on to be another highly controversial super-star of Rock'n'Roll.

When the film was released, Columbia announced it was: *"The Real Story Behind The Rock'n'Roll Headlines."* The shooting of the Comets' scenes took all of one week!

While at a party in Los Angeles, Bill meets the distinguished composer Dimitri Tiomkin. Tiomkin was an Oscar winning writer who created the musical score for *High Noon* and *Friendly Persuasion*. In Hollywood he is renowned for his powerful, symphonic sounds of beautiful melody. The two men are introduced, almost as a joke. However, they spend over an hour together in deep discussion. Tiomkin, a master of some of the world's most classic music and Bill Haley, the "Attila the Hun of Music with Drums and Guitar". Their all-engrossing conversation creates many wisecracks among the celebrities gathered. Their conversation breaks up only at the party's end. Bill tells the Comets later that Tiomkin was one of the most interesting and intelligent musicians he ever met.

Tiomkin, during a visit to New York, tells reporters who ask him how he feels about Rock'n'Roll, *"Some like Bach, some like Benny Goodman and some like Rock'n'Roll. These are all good for certain moods and they are all aspects of American music. There should be freedom not only for the creators but also for the audience."*

Bill playing the bass. Courtesy© DAP

The Russian born composer was reminding us all that music, like religion, should be a freedom of choice. Wasn't that what America was all about?

The media attacks on Rock'n'Roll go on relentlessly. Down Beat, a pro-jazz magazine, brazenly declares war on Rock'n'Roll in their September 19, 1956 issue. *"QUIT ROCKIN' IT'S TIME TO GET ROLLIN,"* screamed their bold-faced headline. The magazine devotes the entire issue to slanted and questionable viewpoints about Rock'n'Roll. They go on to say: *"If with regret, we've no choice but to admit Rock'n'Roll is part of our national culture, for the present, anyway. To disclaim it is futile; to deny its existence, unrealistic. To eradicate it, or at least to demote it, seems to be a matter of urgency."* They go on to say: *"Our own stand, we hope, is clear from the start. Rock'n'Roll may belong to the teenagers, but the earache is ours. Musical considerations aside, most of us could live happier without that nerve-jangling piano, that neurotic sax, and those jack-hammer rhythms. ROCK'N'ROLL HAS GOT TO GO."*

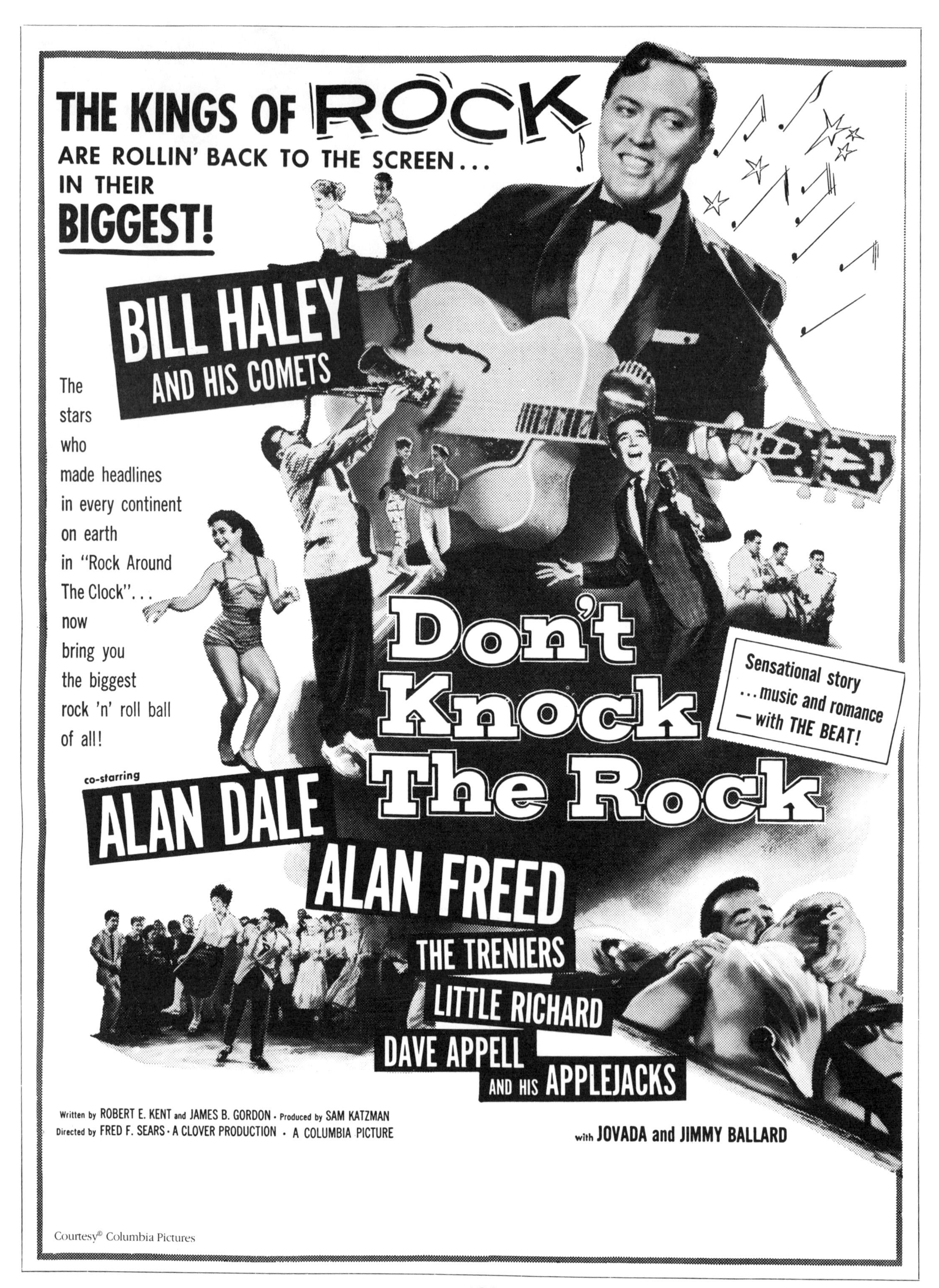
THE KINGS OF ROCK
ARE ROLLIN' BACK TO THE SCREEN...
IN THEIR
BIGGEST!
BILL HALEY
AND HIS COMETS
The stars who made headlines in every continent on earth in "Rock Around The Clock"... now bring you the biggest rock 'n' roll ball of all!
Don't Knock The Rock
Sensational story ...music and romance — with THE BEAT!
co-starring
ALAN DALE
ALAN FREED
THE TRENIERS
LITTLE RICHARD
DAVE APPELL
AND HIS APPLEJACKS
Written by ROBERT E. KENT and JAMES B. GORDON • Produced by SAM KATZMAN
Directed by FRED F. SEARS • A CLOVER PRODUCTION • A COLUMBIA PICTURE
with JOVADA and JIMMY BALLARD

Courtesy© DAP

Rare photo of Bill arguing with Milt Gabler (hand on face). Franny Beecher on electric guitar, Rudy on sax, Billy Williamson on steel above Bill.

In the same issue an article by Les Brown attacks Bill Haley and ends with this contemptuous prophecy: *"England is starting to go rock'n'roll, too, but it's hard to imagine that it will ever become the craze there that it is here. We'll pray for England later. Ourselves first."*

Thank God Les Brown's gift for prophecy was about on the same level as his ability to pray. For it seems neither the Lord nor Britain's incredible rock bands, now only a half generation away, got Mr. Brown's message.

On October 4th, the Comets take a quick break in their road schedule and record *Don't Knock the Rock* at the Pythian Temple. The tune becomes the theme song for the growing pro-rock movement. Decca backed it with *Choo Choo Boogie*, the Louis Jordan number recorded earlier in the year for Bill's 'Rock'n'Roll Stage Show' LP. Four days later, Bill is back home with his wife. Their fourth baby was born and they named him James Steven, after Lord Jim.

Meanwhile, Lee Gordon, one of Australia's most flamboyant promoters, finally succeeded in signing Bill Haley and his Comets to do a tour of Australia in January of 1957. The contract was in the six figures with an up front guarantee, percentage of the gate and all expenses paid, first class. Bill, who didn't like the idea of flying, could no longer pass it up. His partners begged him to sign. Nobody in Rock'n'Roll had ever been offered a lucrative deal like this before!

Less than a week later he would sign another contract for his historic first English tour. With the signing of these two contracts, Bill Haley lays the foundation to become the first international Rock' n'Roll superstar. His new, powerfully exciting music would be unleashed on a global scale never before known. Les Brown's prayers for saving England from Rock'n'Roll would fall on deaf ears.

Meanwhile, he still had thirty-eight performances, six benefits, three network television appearances, and dozens of interviews to do before Christmas.

Bill turns down a guest spot on the top rated Dinah Shore Christmas Show so he can be home for the holidays. *"They don't have enough money to keep me away this time"*, Bill was to tell his family.

Melody Manor the Christmas of 1956 was very special for Bill Haley. The colorful Christmas cards he mailed out inviting family and friends stated: *"You are cordially invited to attend Bill Haley and His Comets' fourth annual Christmas Party and Brawl"!*

The sprawling grounds were covered with multi-colored lights, as Bill had even the largest trees hung with holiday luminations. Inside the brick ranch house were two decorated evergreens, one

Bill Haley lighting cigarette with Bob Hayes on the far right beside Cuppy.

Left to right: Billy Williamson, Bill Haley, Jimmy Lynn, John Grande and Ralph Jones.

Jolly Joyce, Bill Haley (in glasses) behind bar, Lord Jim on right.

Party time at Melody Manor. Left to right: Rudy with his new wife Gladys, Jimmy Lynn and his wife, Cuppy and Jolly Joyce.

Courtesy® Haley Family Collection

Melody Manor

Courtesy© DAP

in the living room and the other in the knotty-pine family room below. Lavish buffets of food and desserts covered the tables as Bill poured drinks from his well-stocked bar. Ralph Jones showed his home movies of the band's tours. The Comets' wives laughed at the off stage antics of their husbands' lives on the road. The women were fond of each other as they shared many a lonely night together. But this evening was different. Everybody was home and well and the future was as bright as ever. They all exchanged Christmas gifts and Bill gave out $1000.00 checks to each Comet and lesser, but still generous bonuses to his other dozen or so employees. Lord Jim read one more headline to the group: *"Haley and his Rock'n'Roll Given Six Months".* They all cracked up with boos and laughter. They all knew the headline well—it was printed in 1954!

For the Comets, the year 1956 had been one of continued creative genius. They had recorded sixteen new songs and some of them were among their best. No less than twelve singles, thirteen extended play and five albums were released on the Decca, Melodisc, Brunswick and London labels. Dave Miller, until his bankruptcy earlier this year, continued to re-release early Saddlemen and Comets songs for the Rock'n'Roll nymphomaniacal youth of the United States, Great Britain, Europe and Australia.

The same songs with different covers and graphics, would be bought and re-bought with the excitement of new albums or singles. Later Decca began doing the same thing as they realize the resaleability of this body of work. What they didn't realize was, they were re-issuing "classics" which were less than four years old! But to imply that Bill Haley's music could become "classic" was a bit too much for holders of the music world's opinion at the time.

Bill and his band had also played over three hundred live performances and starred in two feature films. By any standard, the year had been phenomenal.

However the bitter criticism aimed at his music created a bitter-sweet cloud over Bill's success, and it began to take its toll. Since his father's death, Bill had changed. He became more and more withdrawn, not only from the press and the critics, but from his fans, business associates, and even his band. This new self-imposed detachment was noticed by all. The Comets also noticed a growing emotional change in Bill as he developed a growing phobia of crowds, interviews, parties, and the press in general.

To the Comets, who knew Bill always was a bit shy and insecure, the problem didn't seem great at first. They banded together and did most of the group's PR work. They went to the parties, the interviews, the presentations and made excuses for Bill's frequent absences.

To the press and many business associates, these absences were mis-interpreted as rudeness and arrogance. They had begun to believe that Bill Haley, due to his new-found fame, had become "too good for them". Little did they realize just the opposite was true.

Bill Haley had reached a paradox in his mind. All his life he wanted to be "somebody special". Since

A radiant Bill Haley at the height of his popularity. Courtesy© DAP

Lord Jim and his mother Charlotte. Courtesy© DAP

boyhood he longed for the adoration of the crowd and the loving approval of his peers and elders. As a teenager he believed music could be his avenue to fame and a way out of the mills he so dreaded. All too soon he realized he did not have the playing ability or the strong vocal talent to make it alone as a great country-western singing star. This realization was the cause of his first bout with depression in 1946. Later in 1949, after several false starts, he found the right people and through trial and error, developed his new sound.

He always knew if he could blend country-western and rhythm and blues he could create a new, exciting musical form. This "Musical Holy Grail" became a fixed obsession for Bill. He poured all his time and energy into unlocking its mysteries, abandoning all other interests.

In 1952 he found the key and produced a series of songs that launched a new sound. Now after two brilliant years, with fame and treasure beyond his wildest dreams, the first "King of Rock'n'Roll" wanted desperately the solitude and time to be with his family. Exhausted physically and mentally, Bill needed rest and the peace of mind only the sanctuary of Melody Manor could provide. The hectic schedule of the past six years was exacting its revenge, and he was trying to hold on to the things he loved so much.

But again contract commitments and the pressures and responsibilities of meeting a large payroll forced him into more and more commitments. The fame he so desperately wanted was driving him at a faster and faster pace, till Bill himself thought he was caught in a desperate whirlwind.

As the Comet organization basked that Christmas in the reflected glory of their un-parallelled success, Bill asked Lord Jim if Elvis had gotten his Mama a Cadillac yet. Lord Jim, who spoke to Tom Parker regularly said: *"Hell yes, that boy went out and got his mamma a pink Cadillac a couple months ago—just like yours, Bill!"*

Bill stared at the photograph, hanging on the wall, of himself and Elvis shaking hands. He had another one just like it in his office over his desk. He sipped his bourbon on ice. The little Decca phonograph whirled the Comets' music over the excited conversations about the coming world tour. Rudy was showing off his new wife Gladys as Ralph filled his plate with another helping of his favorite potato salad. What a incredible year it had been. Bill was deep in thought as he pondered what lay ahead. One of his New Years resolutions was to begin a daily diary. He knew now, he and his sound—his music—were going to make history and who better to record it.

Courtesy© DAP

Billy Williamson and his song-writing wife Catherine Cafra.

He tells the gathered clan: *"Some day they're going to write books about us—they're going say a lotta things about us... Those that hate us—will say we were just a fluke-something that shouldn't have happened—a bunch of crazy hillbillies—some might even say we were the worst thing that ever happened to music. Well, I say don't ever let the bastards get you down! And when they say "ROCK-"N"ROLL HAS GOT TO GO", you tell them we're going everywhere—every nation on this rockin' little planet! And when no one can remember their names, the world will still be playing our music."*

Bill then sat down in a large leather over-stuffed chair and in a quieter mood said softly: *"The big joke is, all I wanted was to make a decent living with my guitar—God, I wish my Ma and my Pa could be here tonight."*

They all toast to continued good health and fortune in the comming year. By midnight, Bill had drunk himself into his own world of oblivion—no more worries, no more critics—peace at last—even if it was for just one silent night, one precious night.

The new Comets with their first gold record: "See You Later Alligator". Left to right: Ralph Jones, Rudy Pompilli, Franny Beecher and Al Rex. Photo taken at Melody Manor.

Courtesy© DAP

CHAPTER NINE

NOW TO ROCK THE WORLD: 1957

"Go tell it on the mountain."

On a bitterly cold New Year's Day, Bill, the Comets and their staff began their 11,000 mile trip to Australia. They fly from Philadelphia to Chicago and take the Santa Fe Super Chief to Los Angeles. They arrive in Los Angeles at 8 A.M. and check into the Ambassador Hotel for a sixteen hour lay-over. The following day, Bill takes a tranquilizer and boards a Pan American flight for Hawaii. Bill's fear of flying makes him a bundle of nerves. In Hawaii, Lord Jim's 77 year old mother, Charlotte, takes ill and is left at a local resort hotel with a nurse. After refueling, the flight continues on to Canton Island, then another brief refueling stop in the Fiji Islands. Then, after what to Bill seemed forever, the plane lands in Sydney, Australia on Sunday, the 6th of January.

The group is checked into the Gale Hotel. January is in the middle of Australia's summer and the temperatures soar to over one hundred degrees. Bill retreats to his room after he warns the guys to be careful, anything they do may be reported in the newspapers. The band doesn't want to create any adverse publicity. Bill is very apprehensive about the tour. He has just been informed that two of the cities he will be visiting have banned rock'n'roll music from the airwaves!

Some of the Comets go swimming in the hotel pool, while the others head for the nearby beaches. Freddie Bell, also part of the tour, is the sensation of the beach. The girls flock around him, but one of the most asked questions is *"Where's Bill Haley?"* The Comets wish Bill would come out and meet his adoring fans, but he sits in his room drinking black coffee and nervously chain smoking.

The next morning, Bill and the Comets are hosted to a gala media reception arranged by their promoters and Festival Records. The Australian newspaper reporters, radio and television interviewers treat the visiting American rock'n'roll band like royalty. The Comets are surprised by the warmth and hospitality of the people.

The opening show is a smash hit. More than 7,000 people fill the New Castle Auditorium for two shows. Over 10,000 are turned away. Bill writes in his diary: *"New record here!"* The first two days are filled with interviews and photo sessions for the press. Newspapers and magazines run one story after another to a public who wanted to know "everything" about Bill Haley and his Comets.

One headline reads "THE KING IS HERE" and shows a drawing of Bill with a crown on his head and a scepter in his hand. The all-star Rock'n'roll show also features Bill's close friend Big Joe Turner, "The Boss of the Blues," LaVern Baker, "The Queen of Rock", The Platters and Freddie Bell and the Bell Boys. The Australians would be treated to some of the best Rock'n'Roll talent America had to offer.

The tour moves on to Brisbane, 500 miles north of Sydney. The flight encounters very bad weather and the band lands in the ocean-side city a bit airsick. Bill is visibly shaken and is given several sedatives to calm his nerves. He hates to fly and this nerve wrecking flight was especially hard on him.

In Brisbane, an excited frenzy whipped up by the press packs 10,000 fans into the city's stadium for two shows. Thousands of disappointed fans are turned away. The Comets put on a terrific show and the fame of the extravaganza goes on before them. The Australian Women's Weekly reported Bill Haley and his Comets had packed thousands of fans into Brisbane Stadium and they were *"transformed into a fantastic frenzy".*

The Brisbane Courier Mail reported: *"Whole rows of the audience swayed in unison from side to side stamping and singing in time to the band. The crowds clapped and screamed for more as the show ended."* Bill writes in his little red diary the terse phrase: *"So far, so good".* He is not referring to the tour. He's means he's holding up better than he expected. The Comets play four shows in Brisbane to over 20,000 fans. All shows are sell-outs.

The Australian heat was getting to Bill. He records in his diary on Friday, the 11th of January: *"Flew 1,100 miles to Adelaide, 102 degree temperature. Sore throat and hoarseness".* The sudden change from the icy-cold temperatures back home to the dry heat of a "Down-Under" summer played havoc with Bill's vocal chords. The long and bumpy flight to the beautiful city of Adelaide wore him down. By the 12th of January, Bill was ill with fever and had begun to lose his voice. Despite his sore

Comets play to the largest Australian audiences to ever hear live American Rock'n'Roll

throat and weakened condition, Bill does three of four painful performances at the Tivoli theater. One show is canceled. So enthusiastic was the teenage audience that few realized Bill was not singing. As the Comets played their hit songs, one after another, the kids sang the words in unison. The Comets played their music and also sang the words as they went through their comic act. For three agonizing shows Bill merely lip-syncs to the music. The Comets covered him so well that 12,000 fans were none the wiser. Bill, later that evening, writes in his diary: *"Throat very bad today, had to stop interviews. . . matinee and 2 night shows. . . 7000 people. Feeling real bad. . . hope I get better."* Bill is feverish and beset with chills. The promoter demands the Comets go on with the show, even if Bill just goes through the motions.

On Sunday, the 13th, the group flies 650 miles to Melbourne. Bill sleeps most of the day. A specialist is flown in from Sydney to examine Bill's raw and burning throat. He's given a shot of penicillin and told he must get some rest.

Weakened further with chills and fever, Bill tries to get some sleep between shows. The exuberant Comets go on the town and do the PR work. *"A truly fabulous country. . . the people were so warm. . . They made us feel right at home"*, exclaimed Ralph Jones. *"Man, everything is great. . . the girls were un-real. I never had such a good time!"*, said the seventeen year old band boy Vince Broomall, with a big grin on his handsome face. This was his first trip to a foreign country and he was having an experience of a lifetime. Vince, who the band called Catfish, had been with the band since 1953. His uncle, Harry "Reds" Broomall, Bill's bodyguard, had brought the thirteen year old boy into the Comet organization. The young boy quickly became the Comets' mascot and witnessed first hand the glory years from 1953 to 1958. His prodigious ability to catch fish on his many fishing trips with Bill Haley earned him his nickname.

The young man was in charge of the band's instruments, amplifiers, baggage, and other properties. One of his main jobs was to get all this through customs. The Comets regarded Catfish like the proverbial supply sergeant who could come up with almost anything if the price was right. On the road he was indispensable. He also had a nickname for everybody in the band. Frannie Beecher was the "Hawk", short for "Hawkeye", earned for his prodigious ability to find almost anything lost. Bill of course was "The Chief". Johnny Grande became "Diamond John", due to his flash and charm. Billy Williamson was called "Hoof Head" because of his receding hairline and Al Rex was "Duke". Ralph became "Poppa Jones" and Rudy landed "Scoff". Catfish donned him with this dubious title as a tribute to Rudy's frugal habit of ordering very little during his meals, because he was "on a diet", and then "borrowing" a little food from everybody else's plate.

For the next three days, the Comets play before 40,000 fans at the Melbourne Stadium. All shows are sell-outs with thousands still being turned away at the gate. Bill, still very ill and with fever, performs all five shows. Still unable to sing, Bill lip-syncs the songs as the band's singing covers him. The great stadium reverberates with their wild and crazy music, as the audience sing and clap along with "having a good time" excitement. Bill tersely jots down in his diary: *"Opening show in Melbourne. . . stadium seats 8000 people. Completely sold out. Standing room only... throat still bad."*

On Thursday the tour continues in triumph back to Sydney. Here, in a city which had banned Rock 'n'Roll music on the radio stations, the Comets and their fellow artists play before an unprecedented 84,000 people in five powerful performances! Bill writes in his book: *"Flew 600 miles back to Sydney and then did 2 shows in Sydney Stadium. Holds 12,000 people. . . sold out in advance. . . 24,000 for two shows. Throat improves today."*

On Sunday, Bill relaxes and visits some of Australia's tourist attractions for the first time. He writes in his notes: *"Off today. Went to visit Aboriginal village. Met the champion boomerang thrower of the world. A native. . . he taught me to throw a boomerang. Flew back to Melbourne."*

Comet fever reaches incredible proportions. The next three days they do six more performances before 48,000. Again thousands are turned away at the gate.

On Wednesday, January 23rd Bill and the Comets go to a preview of their movie, "Don't Knock The Rock" in a Melbourne theater. Bill writes: *"preview of our new picture 'Don't Knock the Rock'. Closing day here, turned away 8,000 people. 16,000 for two shows, a new record for here."*

The tour flies back to Sydney on Thursday and plays before 28,000 that evening and another 28,000 on Friday. Saturday again they play a matinee and two night shows at the Sydney Stadium. More than 41,000 Australians pack the huge stadium that day. It is the last concert of the tour. The attendance breaks all records for the great stadium.

That afternoon, a smiling Lord Jim announces: *"Today is my birthday"* and throws a bash that Catfish said must have cost somebody a couple of grand! It was sure one hell of an occasion, the only problem was, this was Lord Jim's third "birthday" in the last twelve months! But no one ever mentioned Lord Jim's faulty memory, his "birthday" parties were always too good to miss. Lord Jim had just three ingredients to insure a successful bash: wine, women and song. Lord Jim's party also marked the end of a very profitable tour. It had been one of the most successful musical programs ever to tour Australia.

More than 300,000 people were introduced first hand to Bill Haley's unique brand of Rock'n'Roll. He became a legend in that country that still lives today. He redefined popular music in Australia. Radio stations throughout the sub-continent could now play Rock'n'Roll without fear of censorship. Bill's personal quiet manners and easy-going style had won the hearts of the Aussies. One Sydney headline exclaimed: *"The Comets are pure razzle-dazzle. Never had such unabashed enthusiasm been created for a new music."*

Australia's Festival Records' ad in the Comets' tour souvenir program booklet. Note 78, 45 and LP recordings.

"Rock, rock, rock—beats me what that Bill Haley sees in 'em!"

Australian humor gave Bill Haley a big laugh with this cartoon on a few rockers who couldn't make it to the Comets' concerts.

So great was Bill Haley's reception in Australia that Frank Sinatra, who had been booked to follow Bill, canceled his tour. He had been told *"You don't ever want to follow Haley!"* Sinatra had already flown as far as Hawaii before turning back.

When the news of Sinatra's "sudden illness" reached Lee Gordon, the promoter for both the Haley and Sinatra tour, he is said to have offered Bill Haley $100,000 in cash to stay one more week. Ralph Jones recalls that Gordon offered to fly Bill, the band, their wives and families to England, if the Comets would perform one more week. Bill refused!

Although the Australian experience was a financial and exhilarating tour de force for the Comets, it had become a private ordeal for Bill Haley. As the press acclaimed him the "Napoleon of Rock", the "King of Rock'n'Roll", the "Lord High Commissioner of the Big Beat" Bill spent most of his time locked in his guarded hotel room drinking dozens of cups of black coffee and chain smoking. He was totally exhausted, mentally and physically. He desperately needed a good long rest. Bill had flown over 3,500 miles since landing in Sydney, twenty-one days ago. Even without his strep throat, the tour had been strenuous.

Lord Jim decides to makes an "investment" for Bill and himself. He decides to venture into the exotic gem trading business. He uses a sizeable portion of the tour's profits to finance and purchase Australian opals for resale back in the States. He knows little about the semi-precious stones, but has illusions of forming an Australian-American opal cartel. Later, when he tries to sell them, Lord Jim finds there is little or no market for his "low end" exotic stones. He tells Bill later: *"Easy come . . . easy go!"*

The Comets left Australia on Sunday, January 27th at noon. Two days over the Pacific, Bill writes the following entry in his diary: *"Hit a monsoon and had a very rough trip all the way. Landed in San Francisco in a snow storm at 7 A.M. Left Frisco at 9:30 P.M. landed New York at 8 P.M. after very rough trip. Home at last . . . Thank God!"*

Unbeknownst to Bill Haley, a vicious weather system of hurricanes and torrential rain squalls would follow him from Australia, across the Pacific and right to the shores of Great Britain. His fear of flying was greatly enhanced by these bone-jarring flights and bouts of nauseating air-sickness.

His entry for Tuesday, January 29th: *"Slept all day and rested and played with the kids. Started to pack & get ready to leave for European tour. What a life!"* The next day he wrote: *"Did shopping. . .paid bills and packed. Had business meeting and got everything ready. I hate to leave, nerves are real bad."*

The Comets' British tour had been in the works for over six months. Britain's giant Decca Recording Company, under its international Decca and Brunswick labels, was enjoying phenomenal worldwide sales. No artist in the history of the firm had created so much international commotion or profit. Rock'n'Roll was still a virgin gold mine as far as they were concerned. Bill Haley and his Comets were a multi-million dollar property and company policy was to exploit their new investment to the hilt.

In early 1956, Decca officials began to press Haley to consider doing foreign tours to capitalize on his tremendous overseas popularity. Under this pressure and with many lucrative offers on his desk, Bill decides to take his Rock'n'Roll show abroad. With the Comet tour finally committed, Decca pulled out all the stops. They began to coordinate every detail of the coming tour with the British press. The Australian tour was just a warm up. They give an inside edge to the popular tabloid, "The Daily Mirror". The complex multi-city theatrical arrangements were entrusted to Lew and Leslie Grade. A top show-business press-agent, Suzanne Warner, was given the responsibility of handling all publicity. She was instructed to exploit Bill Haley's clean, wholesome image and Rock'n'Roll as a harmless fun-loving, good-time music.

Warner, a director of Associated-Television, had a reputation of being an experienced "pro" in the publicity business. She was an American who had come to England ten years before as the personal representative of Howard Hughes. She was in charge of the publicity for Jane Russell in Hughes' provocative adult western film, "The Outlaw". Liking the quiet and tranquility of Britain, she decided to make London her new home. Over the years she had represented such stars as Ava Gardner, Guy Mitchell, Johnnie Ray and Frankie Laine. However, this time her task was far more difficult. With Bill Haley came a very emotional and controversial new music coupled with the ever-present dangers of serious riots, bad press and costly cancellations. This time, Suzanne Warner was given the double-edged sword of "Hawking the Rock" without creating full scale riots. This was an assignment which could "make you or break you". Many of her British associates believed the beautiful young American was headed into a "Valley of Death", career speaking.

She knew she was given a double-edged sword. She was also well aware that Rock'n'Roll music had been adopted by thousands of tough, hell-raising Teddy Boys. This uniquely British youth-cult, dressed in oversized Edwardian double-breasted suits, settled their many arguments with a fast swing of their deadly, straight-edge razors. The "Teds" as they were called, considered the song *"Rock Around the Clock"* one of their personal anthems and rock music in general, *their sound*

When the movie *Rock Around the Clock* reached England in the late summer of 1956 the Teds used the occasion to dance in the aisles, slash theater seats and create other general displays of senseless mayhem. The large Mid-land cities of Birmingham, Liverpool, and other hot beds of teenage unrest began to ban the movie altogether.

Through Warner, the following article was printed in the Sunday Mirror in October of 1956, four months before Bill's tour to England: *"I've been reading that my movie "Rock Around the Clock" has been causing a little commotion in your neck of the woods. Now I'm sorry about that commotion. I'm sorry about the disturbances and any trouble that followed. But I want to tell the kids who've been hollering for Bill Haley and the Comets that we'll be coming their way in February."*

The usual good-natured tolerance of the British people was starting to turn an unfavorable eye to this savage new American music. With little joy, they watched rampaging Teddy Boys destroy codes of conduct and flaunt moral values which they held dear. Bill Haley's promise to "visit" Britain offered them little solace and much dread.

Suzanne Warner began one of Britain's most intensive media campaigns. She first had to reverse the public's negative image of rock music and mastermind the press' build-up of Haley's coming tour. She planted dozens of pro-rock articles and wrote full page features on the positive aspects and background of rock and Bill Haley. She played up the fact that Bill's mother was English, and Haley, like Churchill, was half British.

In one article printed in the "New Musical Express" she quotes Bill Haley: *"We've rocked around the clock; now we're rocking around the globe. To me, the most important moment in our thousands of miles of travel will come when the "Queen Elizabeth" docks at Southampton. Then for the first time, the Comets and I will see that brave and wonderous island, Britain. England is my mother's land. She was born in Ulverston, in northern Lancaster. I owe England a deep affection. It is an affection born from my mother's songs and stories of the childhood home she never forgot. When in American schools, I studied English history, English music, English literature, and I always thought; My people were part of this. English teenagers today have strengthened that bond. The Comets and I have enjoyed your letters. We are thrilled by your enthusiasm for our recordings and films. You English teenagers and our American teenagers already are partners in your liking for the happy beat of rock'n'roll. We hope we can strengthen that partnership and increase Americans' understanding of you and your understanding of Americans."*

For British Decca and its Chairman, Sir Edward Lewis, the coming tour would take on all the trappings of a medieval crusade. King Billy and his Rock'n'Rollers verses the united Saracen forces of Church, State and decent music! The usual staid Sir Edward smiled with a mischievous grin, as he reviewed the publicity campaign. This would be a bang of a show if it didn't get out of hand. The carefully planned events to come were to have all the drama and passion of a morality play.

The Daily Mirror became the vanguard of the media campaign that whipped up such enthusiasm that there were few people in the British Isles who were not fully aware that "The King of Rock'n'Roll" was coming.

Other papers took up the challenge and began their anti-Haley campaigns. They eloquently wrote with a true flair: *"Bill Haley, music's Attila the Hun with guitar and drums, plans another path of destruction across Great Britain. Theater owners and police officials quiver as he readies to lead his legions of Teddy Boys on to greater heights of wanton mayhem and civil disorder."*

Rock's sleazy reputation in England and the nightmare of major riots instigated by the hated Teddy Boys caused many to cross their fingers as Bill Haley's tour date neared. In America, the stories of rock riots and bans were on the increase. Many British tabloids waited with a fiendish delight, sharpening their poisoned pens. Some decided to create a phony, high-brow posture to protect Mother England, common morality and "good" music. They loved nothing better than a good controversy and Bill Haley and his new sound would provide plenty of that! England had no Klan to whip up mass hysteria but its rabble-rousing popular press joined with such prestigious newspapers as the "Irish Independent" and the "Manchester Guardian", to ridicule Bill Haley and his unwelcomed music.

Back at Melody Manor, Bill packs his last items, as his wife gives last minute instructions to the housekeeper. On Wednesday, January 30th, Bill, the

On board the Queen Elizabeth. Left to right: John Grande, Bill and Franny Beecher.

Courtesy© DAP

Comets, their wives, and two children—five year old Linda Grande and three year old Billy Williamson—leave for New York. Vince "Catfish" Broomall, Lord Jim and his seventy-seven year old mother also join the entourage.

Early the following morning, they board the luxury liner Queen Elizabeth and set sail promptly at ten o'clock sharp. Their American booking agent, Jolly Joyce, joins them for the historic trip as well as Noel Whitcome, a reporter from the Daily Mirror and Helen Bolstad, who represents the American press. Whitcome writes a series of articles on Bill Haley, which are telegraphed daily to his paper in London. They mark the countdown of Bill's arrival in Great Britain. On board the ship Bill notes in his diary: *"Now to rest some . . . I hope."*

Unfortunately, Bill's two day stop in Philadelphia gave the violent weather system time to catch up and play havoc on the high seas. The stormy North Atlantic can exact a cruel vengeance on mid-winter voyagers. The great ship ran head-long into the fierce hurricane on its third day out. For three battering days, the crew and the passengers are subjected to sixty-five foot waves in an ocean gone mad. Just about everybody on board was violently ill with stomach-wrenching nausea. When Ralph Jones and his wife went to dinner on Sunday night they found themselves and Catfish the only ones able to eat.

Bill writes in his diary on Monday, February 4th: *"Found out today we are going thru a hurricane aboard the Queen Elizabeth. Trip gets rougher. Can't wait till we get off this blooming boat."*

HEY, CATS—DIG THAT DOCKSIDE ROCK!!!

HERE'S Haley (picture right). And just look at those excited crowds on the dockside at Southampton yesterday.

They are seen welcoming the Rock 'n' Roll King after he arrived in the liner Queen Elizabeth. Police had to clear a path for Bill as he struggled to reach the Mirror's special Rock 'n' Roll Choo-choo which took him to London.

They call him RORY—Rory Blackwell, leader of a Rock Band which welcomed Bill Haley and his Comets when they arrived at Waterloo Station yesterday. And Rory really was roaring. Dig that crazy caper!

HERE'S HALEY! Follow the arrow, Cats! Yep, at the end of it is the Rock 'n' Roll King himself, surrounded by Cats (and caps) at Southampton yesterday as he fought his way to the Mirror's special train. Man, WHAT a welcome!

ROCK 'N' ROLL STRIP

● Rock Around The Clock skirt—worn by hep-cat Marie Imlah, of Glasgow, at Waterloo.

● Champagne for Haley? No, sir. Bill gets rockin' on MILK.

● A cop lies on Bill Haley's car roof at Waterloo. More cops sit on the bonnet. Not TOO near, please!

● Girls lost their shoes in the rush to see Bill. Now for the big sort-out after the Battle of Waterloo.

FANCY PANTS

Dig those special jeans, worn by Sylvia Wakefield, 17 (left), and Diana Thompson, 15. They said they sat up all night embroidering Bill's name on them.

Page 10 and 11, Daily Mirror, Feb. 6 1957.

The next day the ship docks at Cherbourg, France and the first part of Suzanne Warner's well orchestrated plan becomes reality. Dozens of eager newspaper reporters, photographers, and publicity people come aboard for the seven hour sail to Southampton, England. A pale and still sea-sick Bill Haley does a series of interviews and is photographed in his bathrobe and slippers. In the early afternoon, Bill, in a long winter coat, is photographed doing a dance step with his wife on the deck.

Tuesday, February 5th, about two in the afternoon, the huge ship glides into its mooring in the great harbor of Southampton.

Noel Whitcomb's full page article in the Daily Mirror quotes Bill the following day: *"THE WELCOME OF MY LIFE! by BILL HALEY!"* in bold headlines. *"Fantabulous, that's the only word for it—fantabulous. I'd heard we were going to get a welcome. And we have enjoyed some pretty crowded receptions in the past. But never in my life have I seen anything like the razzmatazz of a welcome we got at Southampton yesterday.*

"We were amazed and overjoyed. In fact . . . you really rocked and rolled us! It had all been so quiet on the ship that . . . even though Noel had warned

A seasick Bill Haley in his slippers.

Daily Mirror

WED FEB 6 1957

2D FORWARD WITH THE PEOPLE
No. 16,532

HOW THE MIRROR BROUGHT THE KING OF ROCK 'N' ROLL TO HEP-HEP-HAPPY LONDON

FANTABULOUS!!

BILL HALEY'S OWN STORY of *The welcome of my life!*

EXCLUSIVE .... PAGE 2

★ FANTABULOUS! That is the only word to describe the welcome to Bill Haley yesterday, seen here with his blonde wife (front) and fans aboard the Mirror's Rock 'n' Roll choo-choo on the way to London.

More fantabulous pictures on CENTRE and BACK PAGES

Front page of the London Daily Mirror, Feb. 6, 1957.

"Before you make off with your Bill Haley souvenir, son—those happen to be mine!"

me there would be what he called "A Derby Day turn-out"... we weren't really prepared for the fantastic scenes we saw.

"We had assembled with our baggage by the ship's gangway, ready to disembark, when I got my first surprise. There was a mighty roar that I thought must be the ship's hooter. Then suddenly, I realised it wasn't. THEY were shouting: HALEY!... HALEY! ... HALEY! from the shore! From that moment on it was unbelievable... sheer hellzapoppin.

"When we got out of the customs shed, I thought we were never going to make the car... there were so many people on top of it! Then, when we thought we'd seen everything... the real onslaught began!"

Bill and his party were welcomed with flowers during a formal greeting, but as they headed for the limousines which were to take them to the train station they were mobbed with thousands of over-excited fans. Police freed them with great effort and shoved them into the awaiting cars. Upon arriving at Southampton's railroad station, they were again mobbed trying to get from the car to the train.

Bill continues his observation for the press: *"A vast concourse of people with bands, banners, streamers, stickers, badges and balloons... they all whirled together into a fantastic kaleidoscope of colour and noise as we suddenly started floating towards the train. And I do mean floating! My feet didn't touch the ground for fifty yards... I was just carried along on the tide of people.*

"I lost my gloves, the buttons off my overcoat and a little case with my overnight gear in it. But that didn't bother me. They made good souvenirs for some of the fans. What did worry me considerably is I thought for a moment I'd lost Cuppy, my wife! She's not used to this sort of thing and it can be pretty frightening for a girl. Fortunately she was all right... though a little breathless."

Bill's wife had gotten lost in the melee, as they tried to get from the car to the train. Harmless fans were transformed into a screaming mob on seeing Haley. The huge crowd swarmed like a thousand wasps toward their hero. Several robust police officers locked arms around Bill and heaved him toward the train. A wild and desperate struggle ensued as over-excited fans fought to lay hands on their idol. Bill's wife, in tears, was found almost trampled. She was quickly escorted by police up some abandoned tracks and raised unceremoniously onto the train. She and Suzanne Warner were quite shaken, both women had their normal aplomb in tatters. Suzanne meekly asked the police: *"Can you stay with us for a few minutes?"*

Courtesy© London Daily Mirror

MIRROR ROCK 'N' ROLL SPECIAL!!

—JUST RARIN' TO GO!

Drawing from the Daily Mirror of Bill's Rock'n'Roll Express.

The train Bill mentions was the "Rock'n'Roll Special" that the Daily Mirror had chartered to bring Haley and the Comets back to London. The British Railway printed special souvenir tickets for the round trip. Part of the media blitz was this private train on which hundreds of lucky fans and coachloads of journalists and photographers from the British, American and European press traveled to Southampton to meet Bill Haley.

The eight car "Rock'n'Roll Special" had left Waterloo Station in London just after noon with a train load of colorfully dressed rock'n'rollers. Aboard was the rock band Rory Blackwell and his Blackjacks, to entertain the passengers till the train reached the southern port city of Southampton.

Bill Haley's reference to the crowds at the Southampton train station as a *"fantastic kaleidoscope"* as he was being carried through the air by British police officers' bear witness to the distortion and disorientation of his limited vision. Blind in one eye, he had no depth perception. Since Bill was also very nearsighted in his one good eye and too self-conscious to wear his glasses in public, the scene must have seemed psychedelically bizarre. The unmolested Comets watched the fast-moving events from their cars in wonder. Bill later told the band: *"You guys were lucky. . . I thought I was a gonner. . . my clothes were torn to shreads. . . they tried to pull out my hair. . . they almost killed me! God, I hope I never have to go through that again!"* One can easily see Bill's public announcements and private opinions are completely unrelated!

Once on board the train, Bill took a sedative and looked forward to several hours of peace before reaching London. He changed his tattered clothing, drank two cups of black coffee and was then informed that he was expected to walk though the train shaking hands with the passengers and participate in a series of television and press interviews. For the entire two hour journey, Bill and the Comets posed for Independent Television, plus dozens of press photographers. Their every word is written down by an army of reporters and foreign correspondents. They join in with Blackwell's group for some impromptu Rock'n'Roll and are photographed as having a *"rocking good-time on their way to a prostrate London"*. Bill stops to chat with his fans, sign autographs and shake hands with hundreds of his admirers. All along the route, thousands wave from garden windows, fields and railway embankments. Hung precariously over railway bridges were large colorful banners proclaiming: "King Haley Is On His Way", "Welcome Bill Haley and his Comets" or "Rock On-Bill Haley!".

In reality, Bill is still ill as the train pulled into Waterloo Station. His stomach was churning from his bouts of nausea from the rough sea voyage. The Comets were worried about the pressure on Bill. They knew he hated crowds and secretly prayed he would hold up till they got to the hotel.

The tremendous greeting at Southampton had been a press agent's dream. Most of the massive crowd-ballet was well orchestrated. Television coverage was extensive and no one really got hurt. Bill seemed to be able to take it all in stride. But Suzanne Warner wasn't finished yet! She planned the timing of the arrival to coincide with London's legendary rush hour to hype the effect of Bill Haley's arrival. What happened next was sheer pandemonium.

The Battle of Waterloo! Bill Haley is mobbed. Courtesy® Flair Photos

The entire forecourt of the London's huge Waterloo Station was packed with over 5,000 Haley-worshipping fans. As the train passengers, fans and press mixed with thousands of regular commuters just trying to get home, the "Second Battle of Waterloo" broke out! Eighty police officers formed a cordon to try to get Bill to his awaiting Rolls-Royce. At this point, the thousands who had waited patiently for hours to get a glimpse of Bill, feared they were going to miss him in all the commotion. Their charge was preceded by a mighty yell which, as one observer wrote: "reduced *Glasgow's famous "Hampden Roar" to a whisper"*.

Bewildered Londoners, police, ticket-collectors and anything else standing in their way were swept aside as thousands stormed the platforms in search of their idol. Babies and children were screaming as police whistles shrilled through the air. Sounds of breaking glass and the crunch of barricades mixed with cries of panic from fear-stricken commuters. The atmosphere was pure pandemonium, as Bill Haley becomes the fox in London's greatest man-hunt. The overwhelmed police drive a wedge into the mob, as Bill fights to get to the awaiting car. Nobody has any control, as throngs of over-eager fans besieged the station trying in desperation to get a look at Haley. The cry goes up that they "found" Haley! The long black limousine surrounded by ten burly English policemen was now attacked by a frenzied mob screaming: *"WE WANT HALEY! WE WANT HALEY!"* They climbed up and stood on the roof, laid over the hood and pounded its black shiny metal without mercy. Crying young girls hug and kiss the car until the windows were covered with the smears of their red lipstick. The besieged Rolls Royce, with a shaken Bill Haley within, had become an instant shrine of adoration for the screaming multitudes.

After about twenty minutes and more police re-enforcements arrive, the car began to move forward, slowly. Through the mass, ninety angry policeman formed a human snow-plow to force a path through the human ocean of mass hysteria. Crazed fans even tried to hold on to the back bumper in order to slow down the car's speed so they could spend a few more precious seconds with their beloved hero. Cuppy, who is in another limo, is also badly shaken. She breaks down in tears and holds on to a plush toy Koala bear Bill bought her in Australia. Later she tells a reporter from the Daily Sketch: *"I'm terrified of crowds"*. She will never again accompany her husband on a major tour.

Courtesy® DAP

Comets in a photo session at the Dominion Theater.

Ralph Jones and Bill at the opening night photo session.

Courtesy© Haley Family Collection

Once free of the chaos, Bill's limo speeds to the posh Savoy Hotel in London where he arrives at the back entrance. Bill has two hours before a planned gala reception begins. He writes in his diary: *"... Docked at Southampton, England at 2 PM and all hell broke out! 5000 people almost kill us!"* Late that night totally exhausted, Bill falls asleep, oblivious to the clamor about him and what's to come.

The following day the London tabloids have a field day with superlatives as they reported Haley's tumultuous arrival and what they call "THE SECOND BATTLE OF WATERLOO". The "Daily Sketch" reported; *"Five thousand hero-crazed teenagers smashed through police cordons at London's Waterloo station yesterday to give Bill Haley, master showman of the new Rock Age, the stormiest welcome any celebrity has ever received in Britain. It was 5:10 p.m. . . . bang in the middle of the rush-hour. When the train pulled in from Southampton the mood changed to a battle scene from War and Peace! The fans realized that Haley was getting away. Within ten seconds they had surrounded his car—a solid wall of bodies, hundreds deep."*

The British musical tabloid "Melody Maker" printed the following on their front page: *"Bill Haley has blitzed Britain! The biggest musical bombshell to hit Britain since the war exploded at Southampton Docks on Tuesday—and mushroomed right up to London."*

That afternoon, February 6th, the band was taken to the Dominion Theater on Tottenham Court Road. Here they are re-joined with Catfish and their instruments. They check out their equipment, don their uniforms and rehearse *Rudy's Rock* for the benefit of the press photographers. That evening would be their first concert before a sold-out audience of 6,000. The enormous publicity had focused the attention of the world on Bill Haley's first London concert. The British and European press, both pro- and anti-Haley would be there to fill the pages of their Haley-hungry papers with their opinions of Bill's new sound. Poor or ridiculing reviews could mean the loss of millions of dollars and the canceling of many of the engagements. The building pressure on Bill by late afternoon was deadly. He continued drinking coffee and giving interviews to VIP's as the band went out for a quick dinner. To media people who saw Bill the hours just before the "Grand Opening", he seemed calm and self-assured. In his notes he wrote: *"I feel awful... wish I could have gotten some rest".*

As the opening hour approached, Bill sat in his dressing room with Lord Jim, Rudy, Johnny, Billy and several Decca officials. Catfish was to say: *"Bill was as nervous as a long-tailed cat in a room full of rocking chairs".* At 6:30 P.M. he was informed the show had opened to a packed house. For about fifty minutes, Vic Lewis and his "Benny Goodman" type orchestra played a combination of swing and popular music. The kids sat through this with growing impatience, which grew into actual hostility before it was over. Lewis, being the professional he was, took the audiences taunts of *"We want Bill"* with grace and dignity and finished his set.

At about 7:30 P.M. the great curtain opened and Bill Haley and his Comets, with amplifiers on full blast, blistered the ears and numbed the minds of a cadre of music critics in the outer lobby. Within two minutes the audience of young people were clapping their hands and swaying with the rhythms and beats of Bill's sound. For the entire forty-five minutes the Comets held the rapt attention of the happy, fun loving crowd. When the curtain closed, the cries of the audience for more were only curtailed by the playing of *God Save The Queen*. Unfortunately, Bill did not give encores at this time. With his stomach-turning nausea he felt lucky to do even forty-five minutes of his act.

British teenagers had tasted their first live American Rock'n'roll music. To the thousands of kids who witnessed this performance, it was a love affair they would never forget. To the Comets who returned to their dressing rooms and stripped off their sweat-soaked tuxedos, it was the beginning of a very long night.

They all met back at the Savoy in Bill's suite. The Comets and their wives talked with Bill and Cuppy till about four in the morning. The main topic was how the show would be received by the critics and how vicious the anti-Haley press would be. Bill finally falls asleep and doesn't awaken till early afternoon. He orders coffee, as Lord Jim brings him six different newspapers. Bill spends the next hour reading the reviews with Lord Jim and a couple of the boys. The general consensus was: the music critics may debate whether rock was a music or a noise, but they all agreed, whatever you wanted to call Bill Haley's sound, the audience loved it! The press's opinions ranged from the "London Times" viewpoint: *"Extremely stimulating"* to what one tabloid considered: *"a tragic waste of energy"*.

Laurie Henshaw, columnist for the musical review tabloid "Melody Maker" wrote: *"It was precisely 7:27 pm. on Wednesday when Rock set in at the Dominion. If noise is the measure of success, then Bill Haley and his Comets are a sensation. The boom of an electric guitar behind a closed curtain heralded that the Comets were on stage. The fans took it from there. 'We want Bill!' they screamed. The cry was taken up, echoed round the packed theater, almost drowned passing traffic in Oxford Street. The six bobbies stationed at the entrance had an anxious moment.*

Al Rex "riding his bass". Courtesy® DAP

"Several more sedate members of the audience exchanged startled glances. Then the curtain rose and the Comets blasted into their first number. Blasted? An understatement. The sound from three microphones and three Comets' amplifiers hit the crowd like a battering ram. And the audience tossed it back to the tune of stamping feet and smashing handclaps. . . usually way off the beat.

"Haley, who looks like a genial butcher, led his six men through an opening number that was inaudible above the ear-shattering bedlam. And the mood of things to come was set by the Comets' antics—as uninhibited as the revelry in a German beer garden.

"Bassist Al Rex tore his trousers after a few bars. 'There's an awful draught down there,' he quipped. He threw his bass around with the abandon of an Apache ill-treating his dance partner, then rode it like a Derby winner.

"Tenorist Rudy Pompilli joined in the free-for-all. He sat astride Al, jerked his sax up and down like a pile-driver, playing it behind his back.

Rudy sits on Al Rex in a classic Comets' routine. Courtesy© DAP

"Movement is the mainstay of the Comets' act. The only man who sits still is the drummer. The rest twitch and jerk like devil dancers. Sweat poured off Bill Haley. He mopped his kiss curl with a handkerchief, meanwhile letting his guitar dangle around his neck from its sling.

"At the end of a number he whipped the instrument off, planked it down on one of the amplifiers and ran into the wings. He lurked there for a brief moment, then bounced back. The energy collectively expended by the Comets would just about propel the "Queen Elizabeth" back to the States.

"A welcomed spot of comedy broke up the fever pitch of the proceedings. It came from ex-Benny Goodman guitarist Franny Beecher and steel guitarist Billy Williamson. Announcing, Bill Haley said: 'Give him (as he waves to Franny Beecher) a nice hand before he sings . . . he never gets any afterwards'. Franny Beecher, announced as a baritone, sings in a falsetto voice to his own guitar accompaniment. Here, and elsewhere . . . din permitting, he revealed that he can really play. And, during this all-too-brief spot, so did Pompilli and accordionist Johnny Grande.

"But music throughout is secondary to salesmanship. Maybe, if Haley and his Comets just dropped the rock for one straight number, we should hear something of musical value."

This poor critic missed Bill Haley's conception altogether. He wanted the Comets to "prove" to the audience they were "real" musicians by playing some standard tune. Once again, some frustrated ex-musician reporter making a meager weekly salary is telling a millionaire bandleader how he should do his job!

Another reporter wrote this review for his paper: *"Tall and baby-faced Bill Haley, kiss curl in place, duly appeared with his Comets at the Dominion Cinema and rocked the joint with a streamline-variety entertainment lasting precisely 41 minutes, and including time for plugging his gramophone records. They made a point of getting through their foolin' early. By the time the solitary saxman among the six was playing on his back and the fellow with the big bass fiddle was riding it like a jockey, the vast audience of youngsters were gurgling with pleasure.*

"The more the din from the two electric guitars and a steel guitar, the louder they cheered and the more penetrating their whistles. These larks over, Haley and his men got down to the serious business of rock'n'roll. The audience clapped briskly on a swift beat. In "Hide and Seek", the jazzlads who knew their ritual in clapping, reached an off-beat clap and very exhilarating it was.

Courtesy Evening News

"Blimey, you're right! The emigration boom DID start about the same time as Rock 'n' Rollin' . . . I wonder if there's any connection ?"

Some British humor even blames the emigration boom on Haley's tour.

Courtesy Evening News

"Cut it, cats. Daddy's been Rockin' all night and he'd like a few bars rest."

This humorous cartoon depicts a very tired British policeman trying to get some sleep after being on duty at a Bill Haley's Rock'n'Roll concert.

"In "Shake, Rattle and Roll" the compelling off-beat would have done credit to any Spanish dance troupe. With a thunderous roar of appreciation from the fans, Haley and his men dived into "See You Later, Alligator." My seat gently rocked under me at what was surely the happiest audience in London; clapped and stamped ecstatically.

"The only sad part about this show was that Vic Lewis and his band had to stretch it out beforehand. They tried fatally to rock. It was no use . . . the crowd had paid to hear Haley."

The somber-faced anti-Haley "Manchester Guardian" printed this gem of a review under the headline: *"HALEY'S COMETS DIMMED . . . From our London Staff: The fiery trail of civic disorder that has pursued Bill Haley and his Comets throughout their rock'n'rolling journey through the American Continent fizzled sadly last night at his first London appearance at the Dominion. No one had to be doused with a hose, the seats remained firmly fixed to the floor, and the small army of attendants clustered at the back could, with sufficient introspection, pursue their own muse.*

"This is not to infer that no one was "sent". The crowded house, by no means all youngsters, stamped, clapped and roared its approval . . . but whether by order or inclination, restrained its more mobile urges admirably. The sociological and musical implication of rock'n'roll have been discussed at great length in many places—a great waste of effort if this performance is any guide. This is no more than a vaudeville act of a kind that has been known certainly since the turn of the century. The original Dixieland jazz band and Spike Jones and his City Slickers followed this pattern years ago (and equally profitably).

"Musically, of course, the thing is an abomination, a perversion of the strongly rhythmic pattern and simple chord sequence of traditional jazz and with the melodic ingenunity wrenched off and cast away. The instruments become an adjunct to the rhythm, playing up and down the chords in short, staccato phrases. Woody Herman did this and abandoned it when Haley was still beating his rattle against the cradle, in strict four-four, of course.

"The one thing that Haley probably does better than his predecessor is the production of sheer noise. The volume that he manages to get out of guitars, drums, and clavioline is sufficient to drown a tenor saxophone whose player is turned almost inside out with effort. No mean feat. Still, when you are playing against an audience as this band is, rather than to it, it behoves you to call in electronic science on your side.

"In this context it is probably the height of pedantry to deal with music niceties, but the point may as well be made, since Haley seems to have overlooked it: the fourth bar of a twelve bar blues sequence (the main basis of rock'n'roll) is a diminished seventh. Do a thing to death by all means, but don't torture it first."

Somehow you get the feeling that this critic didn't like the show. Again, Bill's music is reviewed by some third-rate jerk who's knowledge of rock 'n'roll is highly questionable. The review is reminiscent of the ding-bat mathematician who used aerodynamic equations to "prove" that a bumble bee could not fly.

Bill Haley read each day's reviews with a mixture of apprehension and exhilaration. When the critics were gracious, he glowed from within. He walked taller and smiled with a warmth that won him many friends. He so cherished a kind word from a stranger that when one was offered he excitedly wanted all his associates to read it also. However, when the critics attacked him or his music he would be overcome with sickening nausea, as if they had kicked him in the stomach. All the human emotions of fear, rejection, humiliation and ridicule would overwhelm him in a chorus of self-doubt.

Oddly, one of the fairest reviews was written in one of Britain's most prestigious newspapers, the "London Times". *"(Bill Haley and his Comets) . . . These evangelists of the cult of rock'n'roll have arrived in this country to give numerous demonstrations of their art both here and there. Their tour started at the Dominion Theater in London last night, where some 6,000 cats, alligators, and other fauna from the rock'n'roll circus had foregathered. The Comets spend their energies prodigally; they hop and shuffle and skip while they play, and signal the end of a piece by jumping in the air and raising one leg. Their sole mission is to enliven the party. Mr. Haley himself sways exuberantly from side to side, a happy smile unfading from his chubby, well-nourished face. He pounds his guitar without mercy, and sings ardently into the microphone, perspiring freely the while. But there is nothing sentimental nor morbid about his songs; his pelvis wriggles, not with care (like Elvis Presley) but with purest "joie de vivre".*

"His saxophonist, Mr. Rudy Pompilli, delights to lift not simply the bell of his instrument, but the whole golden contraption above his head as he puffs out his cheeks and pumps fierce squeals into it. Mr. Al Rex the bassist, is not satisfied with the conventional erect stance; in order to thrum the beast, he

Two tired musicians, Rudy and Franny doze for the cameras. Courtesy© DAP *sits astride it as if it were some hobby horse or lies down on top of it.*

"All the Comets' songs have texts, couched in the private alligator language that is vernacular to their admirers. They sang through microphones, and their listeners collaborated vociferously, wordperfect in the lyrics, but the words could not be distinguished for the rhythmic hand-clapping of the audience, and the shouts of the initiated. The music cannot be called tuneless; each number is based on a few melodic gestures, instantly memorable, not to say reminiscent, which are many times repeated against a lurching, highly infectious, metrical background. The parallel in concert music is Carl Orff, and the source of both is Beethoven, who built his musical structures on ideas which were striking because they were basic. Tunes and harmony mean nothing to Rock'n'roll; rhythm is all."

The London Times goes on to say: *"The acolytes describe themselves as cool but the purpose of Mr. Haley's music is to make them warm, or, in the jargon: "hep". It occupies only the second half of each programme, the earlier part being devoted to the work of another and more conventional band. Perhaps Mr. Haley's repertory is too slender to last a whole evening, but his principal virtue is his unorthodoxy and the perfect normality with which his musicians pursue it. On second thought, it is likely that he and his band are exhausted after having rocked and rolled for three quarters of an hour."*

The "Times" had spoken: there were no riots, no sex orgies, just a lot of loud but good clean fun. They found Bill Haley's music to be *"extremely stimulating."* Without pompous analysis or bluenose preaching the "Times" gave its blessing. The tour was on and an additional twelve more days were added to the schedule. Bill Haley would be rock'n'roll's good will ambassador. He seemed almost respectable, with his polite manners and soft spoken interviews. Bill would become his music's best spokesman and a diplomatic success in his drive to prove to the world rock music need not be lewd or crude to be good.

The Comets play three more days at the Dominion Theater to a sellout audience of over 24,000 fans. On Sunday, the 10th, they travel by bus to Coventry. Mobs of fans parade in the streets outside Bill's hotel shouting; *"We want Bill... We want Bill".* Clergymen denounce the holding of a demonic Rock'n'roll show on Sundays. They ask Bill to please cancel the program. But the Gaumont Theater in Coventry is sold out, and the promoters would not even consider the suggestion.

On Monday, they play in Nottingham, Tuesday, Birmingham, then Manchester, Leeds, Sunderland, Newcastle and Bradford before taking a train to Scotland. Seven cities in as many days, and all to sell-out audiences. The band continues to be welcomed like royalty where ever they go. Traveling by bus did make large formal welcomes more difficult to stage, but this was preferred to the mob scenes Bill had been encountering. The tour became a series of long trips, checking into hotels, receptions, playing a single or double concert, more back stage receptions and then a short night's sleep before starting all over again. Bill writes in his diary: *"This is nerve wracking, counting the days now till its over... Cuppy and I are really tired".*

On February, 18th Bill emerged from the Bradford train compartment to thousands of screaming fans at the St. Enoch Station in Glasgow, Scotland. He smiles briefly for awaiting photographers, waves to his excited wellwishers and quickly enters the awaiting car, before there is another Waterloo. The cars move through the throngs as Bill waves to the crowds. He and his party are booked into their hotel, where they faced another round of receptions with more photographers and reporters. That night at the Odeon Theater, Bill would give the first of four concerts to sold-out audiences of enthusiastic Scottish fans.

Once again so-called music critics try to analyze Bill's sound and Rock'n'Roll. The "Daily Reporter" printed: *"Bill Haley came to Glasgow last night and rocked the town. This is what happened when the King of Rock'n'Roll and his fabulous Comets gave two shows in the Odeon Theater: Hundreds of screaming jive-happy teenagers jammed West Regent Street, chanting: "We want Haley! We want Bill! We want Rock!'Inside the theater thousands of teenagers stamped their feet, clapped their hands to a dozen rock'n'roll numbers and almost refused to let Haley go when the Comets finished 38 minutes of hot rock'n'roll. When he played a boogie number, they cried: "Give us Rock! We want Roll! They were also boisterous and noisy—so noisy that Haley's words to rock'n'roll songs were drowned out. But they were orderly. At the end of the first show Haley had to lie down. Doctor's orders' he said. But he also said: "That's one of the greatest audiences we've ever known. Gee, they were good."*

Bill is again hit with fever and chills as he fears a return of his strep-throat. A British doctor prescribes heavy doses of penicillin and cough-syrups to keep him from losing his voice again.

Jim MacDougall, who saw the show, writes another analytical insight in his column: *"THE BEAT. HOW HALEY DOES IT"*. This article was found in Bill Haley's personal papers with the remark *"Good"* written on the margin, in Bill's own handwriting. MacDougall starts by saying: *"How do the Comets generate that powerhouse beat that by comparison makes the orthodox five-piece unit sound like it was powered by a one-cell battery? These are questions that the average jazz fan finds hard to answer, but to a student of "beat music" the answers are simple.*

"Rock" music is based on rhythm and in his line-up Haley uses five rhythm instruments. . .piano, bass, drums, and two guitars; while the melody line is led by the tenor sax. In other words, he has a rhythm which could easily sustain a 17-piece band.

"But it is when the measure in which the music is played is considered that the "rock" beat scores heavily over all others. Jazz and "pop" music is usually with four beats to the bar, with the tunes extending to 12, 16, or 32 bars. The usual approach is to accentuate the first and third beats of the bars. But if you really want to put punch into the number, you switch this routine and transfer the accent to the second and fourth beats, this is termed "off beat" playing."

"The classical term for this rhythm is syncopated, and there's nothing new about it, occasionally it was daringly used by classical composers to mildly "rock" the concert lovers. Syncopation is described in the theory manuals as "inverting the rhythm of a note by beginning on the unaccented beat." The effect is to strengthen the attack of the rhythm rather than merely hold the band together in tempo. Watch the skin bashing of drummer Ralph Jones and you'll get the idea. Bill Haley is a supersalesman in the best American tradition. The first time he put his talent into practice he scooped the pool."

After reading this intuitive review, one can almost hear Bill Haley repeating Professor Higgins' famous line from "My Fair Lady", *"She's got it! By George, She's got it!"*

For the first time Bill believes a critic really knows what his sound was all about, and it took a Scotsman from Glasgow to explain it! Haley's new sound was a very complex, highly integrated music, played by talented, skilled musicians.

That same day a rival newspaper headlined: *"ROCK SHOCK"* and went on to say: *"The H-bomb is here! Stand by for explosion when Bill Haley and his Comets streak into that socking off-beat rock 'n'roll rhythm. Haley's musical bomb has embittered and perplexed dedicated jazz musicians. Its deviation from accepted theories of music has shocked elderly professors in every conservatoire from Baghdad to Boston. But still the "rock" rolls with gathering momentum:*

"SAY THE PROFESSORS—It's primitive. Theoretically it's on the same plane as African jungle music, and it has created a generation that lives in a cultureless musical vacuum. What does Haley, at 29, (he is really 31) marshall of the H-bombers, say to this criticism? Plenty, and he throws out a challenge to the jazzmen. 'If the music is as bad as they contend, what's to stop them making it good by writing their own arrangements?' He defends his indiscriminate round-the-clock bombardment of the citizens by film, record, and radio. 'Nobody likes rock'n'roll but the public, nobody ever claimed it was good music, but the public needed it. As evidence, over 9,000,000 of my records have been sold. I belong to that public and do what they want!"

Bill's whole approach changes as he is asked, over and over, the same dumb questions, city after city, reporter after reporter. He becomes more feisty and begins to challenge some of their more stupid assumptions about the "quality" or "relevance" of his music.

When one reporter asked him if rock'n'roll was a new music, Bill shocked everyone by saying *"Rock 'n'roll is not a music! It's a treatment. A method of arrangement."* He continued: *"A good stylist could take Jingle Bells and play it on a toy eight bar xylophone with one stick or he can perform it with an eighty piece symphonic orchestra. And I can "rock it" with my Comets. That's what I mean when I say Rock'n'Roll is the "style" or the "way" you play music. Any tune can be converted to rock'n'roll. Yes even Bach or Beethoven. Now watch, tomorrow I can see the headlines already: BILL HALEY ATTACKS THE CLASSICS!"*

Bill's simple explanation of rock'n'roll as a "style" or a "treatment" for music was easier for most people to understand than all the pontificating and micro-analysis of the conservatory-trained music critics. He was also to say: *"Listening to Rock'n'Roll was like looking at a pretty girl. From six feet away she could be breath-taking, but examine her closely with a magnifying glass and you lose the whole concept!"* Bill had a unique ability, when he wanted, to cut through the bull-feathers and make his point.

After two days in Glasgow, the Comets are back on the tour again with a boisterous send-off at the train station from their fans. On the 20th of February, the Comets play to enthusiastic audiences at the Odeon Theater in Liverpool. Among the hand-clapping, foot-stomping kids were two very special

Bill with his British cousins. Courtesy© Haley Family Collection

young men; sixteen year old John Lennon and his new buddy Paul McCartney. They joined the exuberant audience with the chanting demand: *"WE WANT BILL . . . WE WANT BILL!"*

Before moving on to Cardiff and Plymouth in Wales, Bill writes in his diary: *"Met Mom's cousin today, Mrs. Anne Bannister. Crowds outside the hotel here a bit unruly, all shows sold out . . . Beautiful scenery in this part of England."* On Friday, February 22nd Bill writes: *"Cuppy went back to London today to wait for me . . . I miss her."* All the hoopla is too much for Cuppy. She is uncomfortable in the spotlight she attracts as "Mrs.Bill Haley". She shuns all interviews as Bill tries to protect her from the white hot glare of fame. Cuppy is also upset over some of the unflattering photos of her which have been printed in the papers.

On Saturday they play a matinee and two more sold-out night shows in Southampton. All during the tour getting Bill to and from the theaters required a great deal of imagination. Often Bill left his hotel in the back of service trucks, ambulances and several times dressed as a British police officer.

After the last show in Southamptom, Bill drives eighty miles back to London to be with Cuppy, at least for the night. The crowds and the constant traveling are becoming too much. He needs someone of his own to hold.

The next day they open at the giant Gaumont State Theater in London. For the next three days the Comets play before 27,000 fans. Bill's notes: *"Good to be back in London with Cuppy. Almost seems like home. Theater (Gaumont) seats 4000 people, biggest in Europe. Really tired now, wish it was over."*

On Wednesday the tour flies to Dublin, Ireland for two days and four shows at the Theater Royal. Again huge crowds form around the hotel and the theater. Bill writes in his little notebook: *"Crowds outside theater of about 4,000 people. They scare me!"* The next day he notes: *"Mobs in the streets but all seems well. . . 10 more days marooned. Two shows . . . 13,500 for two days."* Due to the ever present dangers of riots, Bill was confined to the small world of his hotel room or the stage, as the controversy of his music reached maniacal proportions. Newspapers interviewed everyone from members of Parliment, Bishops, cab drivers to Tommy Steele, Britain's own #1 rock'n'roller. Steele was to say *"Bill Haley is where it all began . . . he's the one with the most. I have all his records. . . He's the King!"*

The "Daily Mail" reported Princess Margaret, the Queen's sister, attending a rock movie in London. The paper goes on to state: *"The Princess shook off her shoes, clapped her hands, and Rock'n'rolled with the music. At one moment it seemed she was waving her stockinged feet in the air."*

From Dublin the tour moved on to the northern Irish city of Belfast. Here Bill met his bitterist criticism of the tour. The Catholic Church had banned Rock'n'Roll and the film *Rock Around the Clock* in the city. Their well organized media campaign tried to minimize Bill's concert at the Belfast Hippodrome. Bill's first show on Friday was but half full, the second was only two-thirds to capacity. In his anger, Bill writes in his diary: *"Damn it!"*

An Irish reporter, Liam Kelly, writes the following sarcastically biased review: *"What can one say but that Bill Haley and his Comets are the uncrowned kings, nay the seven little gods of Rock'n'Roll?*

"Last night the "Gonners" of Dublin society from the top and bottom drawers and all the drawers in between abandoned the wayside shrines of rock 'n'roll and went on a mass pilgrimage to the Theater Royal in order to worship at the high alter of the Dance.

"The services, which lasted for a blood-raising forty-five minutes, made even Billy Graham's fire-and-brimstone rallies seem in retrospect like so many mental-prayer meetings, and the way the creatures responded to the traditional hymns, like "Shake, Rattle and Roll," must have hurled their echoes against the vaults of heaven, causing no small discordancy in the angelic choir itself.

"Perhaps even St. Michael was tempted to take up his trumpet and join in the "Saints Rock and Roll" number. On second thought, however I feel that this was probably not the case, but that on the other hand the fallen angels laid aside their pokers for a while and took to the rhythm like alligators take to water the minute they get wind that a man has fallen overboard.

"Make no mistake about it, this is the music that goes with the mid-twentieth century, the hydrogen bomb, death, and desolation. It is the raucous brassy, inarticulate voice of sensuality. It is the loudest clarion-call to vulgarity ever heard in the civilized world. It is the chamber music of hell.

"See what it does to people. Watch their hands, eyes, trunks and limbs as they dance to it, writhing, wriggling, squirming, convulsed with passion, and ask yourself if you would honestly look forward with equanimity to your children falling prey to its malignant power. If your answer is "yes" or even an indifferent shrug, my friend, you would have been better born an ignorant Zulu." It's nice to get a Christian point of view. Too bad the Spanish Inquisition was over, this lovely fellow would have had a ball.

U.S. Cardinal Denounces "Rock 'n Roll"

HIS EMINENCE CARDINAL STRITCH, Archbishop of Chicago, in a Lenten Pastoral Letter has denounced the use of rock-'n'-roll music in youth recreation centres.

He described rock-'n'-roll music as "tribal rhythms which have a certain vogue in our day."

He added: "Some new manners of dancing and a throwback to tribalism in recreation cannot be tolerated for Catholic youths."

To re-enforce their ban, the Church reprints an American newspaper article on Saturday, March 2nd in the Irish Independent: *"U.S. CARDINAL DENOUNCES ROCK"N"ROLL"* His eminence Cardinal Stritch, Archbishop of Chicago, in a Lenten Pastoral Letter has denounced the use of rock'n'roll music in youth recreation centers.

He described rock'n'roll music as *"tribal rhythms which have a certain vogue in our day."* He added: *"Some new manners of dancing and a throwback to tribalism in recreation, cannot be tolerated for Catholic youths."*

In his Pastoral Letter he wrote *"and now I come to a matter, the very mention of which pains me. It has come to my attention that in some of our high schools and recreation centers, dancing and music are permitted which should bring the blush of shame to Catholic educators.*

"When our schools and centers stoop to such things as rock'n'roll tribal rhythms, they are failing seriously in their duty. God grant that this word will have the effect of banning such things in Catholic recreation."

That night over 10,000 Irish teenagers (they must have been a bunch of rebellious Protestants) clamored for Bill after his last show. Their ruckus created a small "riot", but the police quickly cleared the streets with their batons and the city was "saved" from the Satanic influence of Bill Haley's Rock'n'roll.

Bill answers in kind: *"I get the impression after my first week (here) that people think rock'n'roll suddenly sprang up out of the jungle and became the theme music of juvenile delinquency. I think the Comets deserve a little more credit than that. Why, I doubt if the great master Johann Sebastian Bach himself put as much work into his preludes and fugues as we did into originating this new beat."*

The tour returns to London for three days of concerts at the Royal Edmunton Theater before moving to the larger Davis Croydon Theater. At a gala reception in the ballroom of the Savoy Hotel, Bill Haley is given his first gold record by Sir Edward Lewis, Chairman of Decca Records. The award marks the sales of one million copies of the record *Rock Around the Clock* in Great Britain! It also marks the first time ANY record has sold a million copies in the British Isles. In his presentation to Bill, Mr. Lewis said: *"To mark this outstanding event in the history of the recording business I make this presentation of our first Gold Record to Bill Haley. No other company in this country has ever achieved anything like this number, and so you can imagine the feeling of pride I have in presenting this Gold Disc."* Lewis also gave Bill a solid gold watch and to each of the Comets a magnificent silver cigarette box. The gold record with the "Brunswick" label was encased in a walnut case in the shape of a wall clock. After all the critical headlines it would be Bill Haley who would have the last laugh. Rudy would tell him later while looking at the award: *"The next expert who tells us nobody listens to rock'n'roll gets whacked over the head with this!"* Bill was so proud of this recognition and this ceremony was, in his own words: *"the personal high point of the whole tour".*

The next day, March 5th another reception was held at the Savoy and the Heliodor Record Co. Ltd. on the behalf of the German record company, Deutsche Grammophon G.m.b.H. in Hanover presented Bill with his second Gold Disc for his phenomenal sales in Europe.

Courtesy© Flair Photos

Sir Edward Lewis, Chairman of Decca Records, giving Bill Haley Britain's first gold record.

For a historical note, the Rolling Stone Encyclopedia of Rock'n'Roll lists Perry Como as having received the first R.I.A.A. (Recording Industry Association of America) certified "Gold Record" in 1958. Using their criteria, Bill Haley and his Comets were already entitled to a wall full, had the awards been available.

The news coverage of these two unprecedented events seemed to have pulled the rug out from under the anti-rock, anti-Haley factions in Great Britain. Their crude pseudo-intellectual attacks had not wilted Bill Haley publicly. He was now more popular than ever. They had thrown their lies and half-truths at him with a vengeance, and he took it with grace (at least in public). Bill Haley had become an extraordinary goodwill ambassador for Rock'n'Roll. He had won a place in the hearts of millions of the British people that would be remembered for decades. He had become their "King of Rock'n'Roll"!

On Wednesday, March 6th the tour makes its last trip out into the country. They perform the last series of shows in Norwich, Doncaster, Wolverhampton, and Cheltenham before returning to London for one great last show on Sunday, March 10th. Bill and the entire crew are totally exhausted. The constant hype of the tour in their papers, maga-

TWO stampedes as Glasgow rocks

Express Staff Reporter

THREE THOUSAND teenagers mobbed police as two men were arrested at the close of the first Bill Haley rock 'n' roll show in Glasgow last night.

It was the climax to 20 minutes of near-riot as the Haley fans screamed, chanted, and danced outside the Odeon Cinema in Renfield-street.

Traffic was blocked, parked cars scratched as the mob clambered on bonnets for a better view.

Teenage girls were hurt and their

By now the rock-crazed mob were racing down Renfield-street and West Nile-street in a bid to see Haley at the hotel.

Ten youths jumped on the back of a passing lorry in Renfield-street to get there first.

Then it happened again . . . with traffic braking to a halt as chanting, jiving couples spilled across the roadway fronting the hotel.

the hotel immediately. Crowd almost rioting."

Ten minutes later the crowd was dispersed for the second time. Inside the hotel the Haley party relaxed in their private suite. The blinds were drawn. The switchboard had orders to pass no incoming calls.

That was the end of it.

This was the second mob that the police had to control and disperse inside three hours.

Queues were forming in West Regent-street for the second show when 3,000 fans from the first performance poured into the street.

POLICE ARREST HALEY

Crowd fights as 3,000 block city streets

By Daily Mail Reporter

DRAPE-SUITED youths and police struggled outside Glasgow's Odeon cinema last night while 2,000 teenagers held up traffic as they chanted "See you later, alligator." Two were arrested and charged with breach of the peace. It happened after the second performance of Bill Haley's Rock 'n Roll Comets.

BILL HALEY CAME TO GLASGOW LAST NIGHT—AND ROCKED THE TOWN. THIS IS WHAT HAPPENED WHEN THE KING OF ROCK 'N' ROLL AND HIS FABULOUS COMETS GAVE TWO SHOWS IN THE ODEON THEATRE:

Hundreds of screaming jive-happy teenagers jammed West Regent Street, chanting: "We want Haley. We want Bill. We want ROCK."

POLICE DRAW BATONS TO DISPERSE CROWDS

THERE were disorderly scenes near the Theatre Royal, Dublin, last night during and after the final performance of the "rock 'n' roll" band leader, Bill Haley, and his Comets. Some youths in a crowd which gathered in Poolbeg street towards the end of the programme, threw bottles and stones at civic guards who were trying to clear the road-way. The guards drew their batons and the crowd quickly

Patrons leaving the theatre joined the groups.

Some glass was broken in petrol pumps in Poolbeg street, and two windows in Lower O'Connell street were smashed, but no arrests were made.

Haley and his colleagues evaded the crowd's attention by leaving the theatre through a side door. They had to use a similar technique to

HALEY'S COMETS DIMMED

London performance

From our London Staff

The fiery trail of civic disorder that has pursued Bill Haley and his Comets [illegible]heir rock 'n' rolling journ[ey] [illegible] the American Continent [illegible] last night at his first [app]earance at the Dominion [Tot]tenham Court Road. No [illegible]e doused with a hose, the [illegible]d firmly fixed to the floor, [sm]all army of attendants the back could, with sufficiection, pursue their own

[illegible] to infer that no one was [illegible] crowded house, by no [you]ngsters, stamped, clapped, [illegible]s approval but, whether [illegible] inclination, restrained its [illegible]urges admirably.

[illegible]gical and musical implica[tions] [illegible]n' roll have been discussed [illegible]h in many places—a great [illegible]rt if this performance is [illegible]. This is no more than a vaudeville act of a kind that has been known certainly since the turn of the century. The original Dixieland jazz band and Spike Jones and his City Slickers followed this pattern years ago (and equally profitably).

Musically, of course, the thing is an abomination, a perversion of the strongly rhythmic pattern and simple chord sequence of traditional jazz and

Don't You Go Home Bill Haley!

BY JOHN JARRETT

London Teen-Agers Riot In Greeting Haley's Band

LONDON, Feb. 5 (P).—Thousands of teen-agers broke through strong police lines and set off a giant melee when American band leader Bill Haley arrived here today.

Many in the boisterous crowd were bruised and trampled on at Waterloo Station. One policewoman was injured seriously. Dozens of girls lost their shoes in the scuffling.

Haley and his 19-member band billed as "The Comets"

agers tried to mob Haley and strip the clothing off him. Massed police squads managed to protect him and get him to a special train for London.

At Waterloo station the scene was repeated. It took police 20 minutes to clear a path for the bandleader's car through the mob. Both headlights on the car were smashed and the mirrors, door handles and other fittings were torn off.

"I have never seen anything like it," Haley said later.

SATURDAY, MARCH 2 1957

Haley fans in Belfast scenes

R.U.C. drew batons when a disturbance was caused after Bill Haley's Rock-'n'-Roll show at the Royal Hippodrome, Belfast, last night.

The crowd, more than 1,000 strong, chanted: "We want Haley" outside the theatre, blocking all traffic.

One group of young men beat on the side of a bus while the driver attempted to make his way through

The Seven Little Gods O[f] Rock 'n Roll: BILL HALEY AN[D] HIS COMETS!

WHAT can one say but that Bill Haley and his Comets are the uncrowned kings, nay the seven little gods of Rock 'n Roll?

I could no more question their claim to divinity than doubt the genius that created "The Reclining Figure" or bestowed her ever-baffling smile on "Mona Lisa"—ask any bodgie or widgie (collectively known as cats) in the fair city of Baile Atha Cliath what he or she would like to be when they grow up or go out on pension, and it's [illegible] the answer will be [illegible] engine driver" nor [illegible]na h-Eireann."

[illegible]t the "gonners" of [illegible]ty, from the top and bottom drawers and all the drawers in between abandoned the wayside shrines of rock 'n roll and went on a mass pilgrimage to the Theatre Royal, in order to worship at the high altar of the Dance.

Neither the gods nor their creatures were found wanting. Indeed, it was sometimes difficult to know who was "entertaining" whom.

FALLEN ANGELS

The service, which lasted for a blood-raising forty-five minutes, made even Billy Graham's fire-and-brimstones rallies seem

aside their pokers for a wh[ile] and took to the rhythm l[ike] alligators take to water [the] minute they get wind that [a] man has fallen overboard.

RAUCOUS, BRASSY

Make no mistake about [it,] this is the music that goes w[ith] the mid-twentieth century, [the] hydrogen bomb, death, [and] desolation. It is the rauc[ous,] brassy, inarticulate voice [of] sensuality.

It is the loudest clarion-cal[l of] vulgarity ever heard in [the] civilised world. It is the cham[ber] music of hell.

See what it does to peo[ple.] Watch their hands, eyes, tru[nks] and limbs as they dance to [it,] writhing, wriggling, squirm[ing,] convulsed with passion; and [ask] yourself if you would hone[stly] look forward with equanimity [to] your children falling prey to [its] malignant power. Face [the] question squarely.

If your answer is "yes," [give] even an indifferent shrug, [my] friend, you would have b[een] better born an ignorant Zul[u.]

Mr. Haley was preceded on the stage of the Royal by [illegible] Lewis and his Orchestra, [no] strangers to Dublin, and the plus ultra of progressive j[azz.] Even so, by comparison w[ith] the Comets,

"There is sweet music here [that] softer falls
Than petals from blown ros[es]

£8,500 for TV peep at Haley

Daily Sketch Reporter

BILL HALEY rocked in ecstasy last night when he began to add up the profit account of his British tour, which is nearing its end.

He wouldn't say, after his Leeds concert, just how much he had made in hard cash. But in kudos the rock king agreed the tour had been "super-colossal."

TOP RECORD

For a start, publicity has earned him an all-time record bid of £8,500 to feature in an Ed Sullivan TV show in New York. Elvis Presley got only £17,000 for three shows.

And the Daily Sketch is able to reveal exclusively that when Bill returns to Britain in the autumn he

Bottles and batons in rock riots

GARDAI drew batons last n[ight] to disperse crowds gath[ering] in the streets around Dub[lin's] Theatre Royal, where "Rock ['n'] Roll king" Bill Haley and [his] Comets were appearing.

Bottles and stones were thr[own] at the Gardai, but no one [was] injured.

The crowds — mostly 'teen[age] boys and girls—began to co[llect] in Hawkins Street and Poo[lbeg] Street before eight o'clock.

8.30 p.m., when the audience f[rom] the first show began to leave [the] theatre, nearly 2,000 people w[ere] packed into Poolbeg Street.

'We want Haley'

Gathering under the windo[w]

Dublin 'rock' fans in street scuffles

IRISH PRESS Reporter

CROWDS—mostly of teena[ge] boys and girls — began to collect in the streets around Dublin's Theatre Royal before eight o'clock last night, the second night of the visit of Rock-'n'-Roll "King," Bill Haley, and his Comets at the theatre.

By 8.30 p.m., when the audience from the first show began to leave the theatre nearly two thousand people were packed into Poolbeg Street.

Gathering under the window of Haley's dressing-room they started to hand-clap and chant: "We want Haley." Fifteen Gardai had attempted to keep the milling, shouting crowds out of the

fans back into Hawkins St[reet] and Tara Street.

Before they had cleared [the] street Haley again appeared [at] the window and the cro[wd] rushed back.

There were scuffles betw[een] Gardai and youths. Hundred[s of] youths and girls came back [into] the street and for thirty minu[tes] they danced, shouted and s[ang] Rock-'n-Roll songs. There w[ere] several fights in the crowd [and] people were pushed about.

Gardai finally formed a [cordon] and with batons drawn forced [the] crowd into Hawkins St. and T[ara] St. Several bottles were thro[wn] and the glass shattered on [the] roadway near the Gardai [but] none of them was struck.

First British record to sell one million copies.

zines and on their television sets was also wearing down the hospitality of the British public. Media over-kill was setting in as promoters squeezed every last shilling from the weary fans.

On the last leg of the tour with one more show to go, Bill breaks his own "no alcohol" rule and drinks a bottle of Scotch. While doing so, he and Ralph Jones get into a heated argument over some of the finer points of jazz drumming. Both men are known to get a bit "feisty" after a few shots. Ralph, who is sitting next to Bill on the bus, joins him in killing his bottle of Scotch. He too, is soon as inebriated as his boss. The ruckus starts when Bill makes some disparaging remark about Ralph's drumming abilities. Ralph, who was a fine jazz drummer long before joining the Comets, tells Bill: *"I've forgotten more about drumming than you will ever know!"*

All the Comets are a little taken back by all the commotion. Ralph, who is usually one of the most mild mannered of the whole group, is aggressively taking on Haley in a point of music! Rudy tries to stop the argument but Bill tells him to butt-out! The two men continue to drink and argue all the way back to London. The more they drank, the more belligerent each became. Ralph calls Bill a *"dumb-ass hillbilly who can't even keep time"*. Bill calls Ralph *"a half-assed milkman that couldn't hit a drum with a baseball bat!"* Both men, usually soft-spoken and courteous, became screaming "experts" on their points of music. By the time the bus reached London, Bill had fired Ralph a dozen times and Ralph had quit a dozen more times!

The next morning Bill, sober but hung-over, went to Ralph's hotel room and quietly apologized. He said: *"This tour is getting to me Ralph. Yesterday it was just the whiskey talking—us hillbillies really don't know nuttin' about drumming—but a few too many drinks and we all become damn experts on everything."* Ralph also apologized for yelling at his boss in front of everybody. He said drinking can turn a lamb into a lion, at least in his own mind. The two men shook hands and agreed to just forget about the whole thing. Rudy would later tell Ralph what he had called Bill. The ace drummer said; *"I couldn't believe I said those things to Bill—it's a good thing he didn't remember much when he was drinking!"*

That evening the Comets play their "farewell" concert in the Dominion Theater, where they had started five weeks before. The house was packed and Bill Haley rocked London one last time.

The twelve extra days that had been added to the tour had been difficult for Bill. However, he never let it show to the 350,000 fans who had come to see him perform. The British people would never forget the hoopla and the mass hysteria generated by the mere sight of Bill Haley. The hero worship and profound adoration had impressed even the most anti-Haley critic.

In one city, two college students from Manchester University actually sold small bottles of Bill Haley's bath water at a "rag sale" for a half-crown each! They boldly went to Bill's dressing room and politely requested two gallons of his bath water! Bill told them to go ahead, anything for a good cause. After they made off with their precious liquid, Bill exclaimed to reporters: *"They got my bath water and two of my shirts!"*

Besides the concerts, the Daily Mirror had also staged dozens of giant "Mirror Rock'n'Roll Dance Parties" throughout England, Scotland and Wales. At these dances, which were attended by tens of thousands of Bill Haley fans, the Mirror held rock'n'roll dance contests. The winners received free tickets to Bill's shows and sets of his best selling records.

Bill Haley's first British tour had been a colossal success for his promoters and an incredible triumph for his music. Rock'n'Roll was no longer the lowly and despised music of the feared Teddy Boys and other misguided youths. It became fashionable. In the Febuary 25, 1957 edition of "Time Magazine", they reported that Elizabeth, the Queen herself, requested the film *"Rock Around the Clock"* to be shown in the *"Victorian splendor of Balmoral Castle itself!"*

Rock'n'Roll was now "acceptable" and at aristocratic coming-out balls and high-toned birthday parties such as the one for the Duke of Kent, it became the preferred music. Princess Margaret herself let it be well known that she "loved" Rock'n'Roll music. Many years later, the Queen herself was to tell Bill Haley *Rock Around The Clock* was one of her favorite songs.

As Bill Haley sailed home on the Queen Elizabeth, one wonders if he knew even the Royal Marine Band was playing his music aboard the Royal Yacht, Britannia. Bill Haley, by his professionalism and cool outward courage under fire, had changed forever the way Britain viewed his music. Within a year, he would also be the first to take live American Rock'n'Roll to South America and rock the concert halls and staid music foundations of continental Europe.

Gibson's ad featuring Bill Haley and his Comets

CHAPTER TEN

DREAMS OF EMPIRE: 1957-1958

"The power and the glory forever."

The long overseas tour had been brutal to Bill Haley's health. Having gotten seriously ill in Australia, Bill was never able to get back to par. The combination of bad weather, strange foods and tension plus both air and sea sickness had played havoc with his stomach, keeping him in a constant state of nausea. He told friends on his return that he felt worn-out, *"like being run over by a Mack truck"*. Rudy too had developed a high fever and was ill the last days of the tour. Upon his arrival home he underwent an emergency operation for a strangulated hernia and was laid up for the next six weeks.

Bill's intense craving for fame and fortune had now been sated to the point where he was beginning to believe he WAS something special. His associates began to notice a change in his personality. He assumed a "Big Star" complex and began to expect everybody to treat him as such. Old friends were caught off-guard with this total change of attitude. When one of the Comets walked into Bill's office to ask a question, he was told, a bit rudely, to knock first. Previously, Bill's office door had always been open to his musicians without the formalities of knocking.

The March 18th edition of Billboard Magazine noted the return of Bill Haley from an eleven week world tour in which he played to a half million fans. Actually it was more like 650,000 people, but Bill was too tired to quibble.

The slow, five day trip back to the States gave Bill a much needed reprieve. During this precious time, he makes a major career decision to get better control of his life. He decides to cut back on his touring and spend more time developing and directing his other businesses. He wants to expand his publishing companies, Valley Brook, Arcade and Seabreeze, to develop new talent and become a major force in the entertainment business. His firms had originally been formed as a tax haven to maximize profits and control Bill's and the Comets' music. By spring of 1957, the companies had grown considerably. They held the publishing rights to hundreds of rock, popular, and country-western songs. Many were from some of the best tune-smiths in the country.

Over thirty talented but relatively unknown artists were signed and promoted by Bill Haley and Jack Howard, now his Vice-President of Publishing Operations. These early Valley Brook, Arcade and Seabreeze artists included the Matys Brothers, the Morrison Sisters, Dotti Malone, Kitty Nation, Jerry Tyfer, Penny Smith, Dolores Fredericks, Rusty Keefer, Jesse Rogers, the Tyrones, the Keefer Sisters, Lou Graham and many other of Bill's old country-western associates.

About this time Bill hires Charlie Levigne to help him promote this aspect of his publishing business. Levigne had been the road manager of the very popular Frankie Lymon and the Teenagers. Raised in the tough streets of Brooklyn, New York, Levigne had impressed Bill with his handling of the Lymon group's rise to fame. His many connections within the recording industry and experience organizing major tours were badly needed by Bill.

Bill, Jack Howard, John Grande and Levigne poured a great deal of time and capital into these endeavors, as they negotiated record contracts for his stable of performers with Decca, Wing, East-West, Arcade, Mercury, Deed, and Coral Records. They used their many contacts within the entertainment industry to find bookings for their charges' personal performances.

Bill managed to get all these people recorded and several releases became regional hits. He placed full page ads in Billboard magazine to further their careers and to heighten their industry and public recognition. Bill sacrifices valuable touring time and devotes much of his energy to build Valley Brook and Seabreeze into a major music industry force. The Comets are often inactive for weeks at a time, but Bill continues them at full salary. Often, he uses them as session musicians on a wide range of recordings.

Company documents show the leasing of many songs to dozens of foreign publishers and record companies in Canada, Great Britain, France, Italy, Holland, Germany, and Belgium. The files also show Valley Brook and Seabreeze song sheets printed in French, German, Italian, Dutch, Spanish and Flemish. These were leased for $1500.00 to $3000.00 each. The files contained original international

Courtesy© DAP

THE BIG ONES ARE FROM Valleybrook

BILL HALEY and His Comets

R-O-C-K

b/w

THE SAINTS ROCK 'N' ROLL

Decca 29870 ● 9-29870

THE MATYS BROTHERS

UP THE CREEK

(without a paddle)

b/w

IN THE MOOD

Decca 29838 ● 9-29838

DOTTI MALONE

I OUGHTA

b/w

EVERYTHING BUT YOU

Wing 90060

JERRY TYFER

HOOK, LINE AND SINKER

b/w

I'M SO SORRY

Wing 90061

KITTY NATION

HALF YOUR HEART | **GOODIE BYE BYE BABY**

Wing 90059

THE MORRISON SISTERS

ROCKIN' BOOGIE SHUFFLE

b/w Teen Age Guy and Gal

Deed 1016

Midwest Representative
BOB HAYES

Valleybrook
PUBLICATIONS, INC.
112 East 5th Street, Chester, Pa. Chester 2-4105

Home Office
JACK HOWARD

On tour with the Comets. Top row, left to right: Ralph Jones, Catfish, Billy Williamson, Frankie Scott, Reds Broomall, Al Rex, fan. Front row: unknown, Dino Grande, John Grande, unknown, Bill Haley.

Courtesy© DAP

copyrights to hundreds of songs, many of which were written by Bill Haley, the Comets or his staff writers.

To further facilitate his plans for expansion, Bill purchased a corner three-story building at 129 East 5th St. in Chester. He completely renovated it into offices for his new enterprises. On the top floor he built his office and ones for his two partners, Johnny Grande, Billy Williamson and one for Lord Jim.

On the second floor were offices for Bob Hayes, Jack Howard and their staffs. On the first floor were smaller areas for more staff members; Sam Sgro, Harry West, Carol Gray, Jimmie Lynn, Charlie Levigne and others. In the basement, deep below ground, Bill constructed a complete professional recording studio. As a final touch, he inlays a blazing comet and a series of musical notes in the sidewalk outside his new "world headquarters". These sidewalk decorations are still visible today.

The renovations are completed and in May, they moved from their old offices at 112 East 5th Street in Chester, which they had been renting from William Smith, their accountant. Bill also maintains a complete office in his home at Melody Manor.

Meanwhile, Milt Gabler, wanting to cash in on Bill's growing overseas popularity, schedules a four

The Comets new offices at 129 E. 5th Street. Chester, Pa.

Courtesy© DAP

Courtesy© DAP

Postcard announcing the move to the new Comet offices, 1957.

Comets in Valleybrook recording session. Left to right: Beecher with guitar, Ralph Jones on drums, Rusty Keefer on bass and Rudy to far right.

Courtesy© DAP

The Comets gather in the basement recording studio of their new office building. Left to right: Ralph Jones, Rudy Pompilli, Erma Logan, Billy Williamson, John Grande, Al Rex and Franny Beecher. 1957

Courtesy© DAP

day recording session at the Pythian Temple. Bill wants to cut an album of popular tunes arranged with a little rock beat. Haley is now Decca's best selling recording star. His sales alone have now passed the 15,000,000 mark. He is now able to dictate to Decca what HE wants to record.

The Comets record sixteen songs, three on March 22nd: *Miss You, Billy Goat* and *Rockin' Rollin' Rover*. On the 25th, they record *Please Don't Talk About Me When I'm Gone, You Can't Stop Me From Dreaming, I'm Gonna Sit Right Down And Write Myself A Letter* and *Rock Lomond*.

Four days later they record *Is It True What They Say About Dixie?, Carolina In The Morning, The Dipsy Doodle, Ain't Misbehavin'*, and *The Beak Speaks.* On April 3rd they wax their last four songs: *Moon Over Miami, One Sweet Letter From You, Apple Blossom Time* and *Somebody Else Is Taking My Place*.

It is apparent from listening to this body of work that Bill is not at his best. His vocals seemed strained and a bit tired. Some of his interpretations are off and lifeless as Gabler tries his best to add greater variety to Bill's recording style. Rudy Pompilli does not participate in these recordings. He was still in the hospital, recovering from his operation. The sax work is done by a talented black musician, Frankie Scott. Scott also toured with the Comets with his own band and sometimes doubled with Rudy in some terrific sax duets on stage.

Franny Beecher plays some of his best support work at this session, but even his inspired playing can't save some of the tunes. His solo in *The Beak Speaks* is the best of the lot. Gabler released most of these songs on an album called *Rockin' the Oldies* later that year. The "soft rock" album is aimed at a new and wider adult audience Bill now wants to reach.

Gabler and Bill have their first serious disagreements over the direction of Rock'n'Roll. Bill wants to move into the mainstream of popular music and also record some of his country-western songs. Gabler, wishing to stick to a winning formula, doesn't believe Bill has the voice to be a good country singer and tries to discourage Bill's rekindled ambitions.

The continuing heavy criticism in the United States against Rock'n'Roll has not settled down. New and more provocative "rockers" have reached stardom. The screaming yell-sings and pounding beats of Jerry Lee Lewis and Little Richard were scaring the hell out of everybody. These fire-breathing hellions make the overt sexuality of Elvis Presley and the melodic-driven rhythms of Chuck Berry seem almost tame.

Cuppy adjusts Bill's famous trademark.

Courtesy© R. Lefavi

The debate over Rock'n'Roll had reached vicious proportions by 1958. The furor had even reached Washington and the ears of the Senate Commerce Subcommittee on Communications. This committee headed the government's investigation of widespread abuses which were prevalent, at the time, in radio and television industry.

A lobby of ASCAP songwriters charged that BMI had a monopoly on Rock'n'Roll music, and with its interlocking interests with broadcaster-owned record producers, radio stations favored BMI listed tunes over ones in the ASCAP catalog. Thus, rock was pushing their "good" music off the air waves.

Vance Packard, testifying on behalf of the Songwriters Protective Association, told the Senate Committee that *"conniving disc-jockeys and BMI was pushing cheap music on passive, uneducated teenagers."* When Packard was asked to define "cheap music" for the panel, he said he meant *"hillbilly, Latin American, rhythm and blues or rock'n'roll."* When Bill Haley read this comment he was livid! *"Don't these jerks ever give up?"*

It was during these hearings that a California attorney, Seymour Lazar, first used the word "PAYOLA" to describe the widespread hand outs of promotional funds to promote records. Public knowledge of the payola scandal would destroy the career of Alan Freed, one of Rock's greatest pioneers and promoters, and forever change the "above the table" marketing techniques of the record industry.

Bill Haley with two of his children, Sharyn Ann and son Jack. Photo taken at Atlantic City.

Courtesy© Haley Family Collection

For the anti-rock forces, the payola scandal created the myth that rock music was popularized only due to devious efforts of corrupt disc-jockeys and the under-the-table deals of irresponsible record companies. Bill Haley watched these events with alarm and foreboding.

Bill Haley feels strongly that some Rock'n'Roll had gotten out of control in America and all rock would be doomed by the "Powers that be" if it didn't "clean up its act". His many years in broadcasting taught him one thing—to fight the combined power of public morality, the Church, the Government, crazy racists, and most of the music industry was a losing battle. He could foresee the coming abyss, created by civic and religious pressures on the entertainment industry and the isolating of the Rock'n'Roll factions. The long shadows of Hoover's FBI had laid its dark seeds deep in the fertile soils of hate, greed and ignorance.

The age of the clean-cut and socially acceptable Pat Boones and their clones would soon dominate the teenage music scene. The years 1958-59 would be the swan song of the wild, exciting music of Chuck Berry, Little Richard, Elvis Presley, Gene Vincent, Eddie Cochran, Jerry Lee Lewis, Buddy Holly, and a host of other brilliant and talented early rockers. Their numbers would soon be decimated by tragic deaths, prison terms, mental breakdowns, black-balling or being conveniently drafted into the armed services.

They would be quickly replaced, almost unnoticed, by a legion of carefully selected teen idols, each one well-scrubbed, their short hair neatly combed above their smiling white faces. Each was ready to be the well-mannered, non-threatening boy next door. Talent was secondary. The "look" was essential. They all had to pass the approval of white middle-class American sensibilities. They also had to "cool it" on the raw, savage style of "colored" inspired rock'n'roll. One only needed to watch Pat Boone sing "Tutti Fruitti" to see how a song could be sung in a "civilized way".

Bill Haley's vigorous campaign for a clean, happy, have-a-good-time, music had separated the Comets' brand of Rock'n'Roll from the hell-screaming music of many other rockers.

The summer of 1957 saw the Comets' music still in demand as they continued to perform on tours all around the country. On some of the longer bus tours through the mid-West and the West Coast, Bill would often fly back to take care of urgent business, leaving the band on the bus for the three thousand mile trip home.

Bill's new superstar status requires the symbols of his new prestige. While on tour in Canada, he calls Sam Sgro, his office manager, and tells him to buy him a yacht. Bill decides to do more entertaining while playing at the New Jersey shore that summer. Sam asks Bill how much he wanted to spend. Bill just said: *"Get me something nice"*. Sam goes to Wildwood, New Jersey and buys a brand new custom-made 37′ Pacemaker with all the trimmings. Bill has it christened the "COMET IV" and spends much of his free time that summer fishing and socializing with friends aboard his new possession. He now plays the "Big Star" image to the hilt.

Chuck Berry, Frankie Lymon, Joe Turner and many other celebrities are Bill's "fishin' guests" as the COMET IV becomes one of the most sought after invitations on the New Jersey shore that summer.

On July 15th, Bill wins a battle with Milt Gabler and records his first Country-Western songs since his Essex days. His love of this music had never died and this return to his first love is one indication of his growing concern that rock music was fading. The Comets record Hank Williams' *Move It On Over*, and *How Many*, a song he picked up from a hillbilly artist in West Virginia. On this session they also record Bill's old *Twin Bar* theme song, *Rock the Joint*. But for some reason, this more polished version lacks the primitive drive and intensity of the original Essex recording.

The Comets do a very successful tour of Jamaica. Bill tells everybody to bring their wives for a company-paid "vacation". Ralph Jones remembers this time with fond memories: the warm sun, the beautiful beaches and the great seafood. His home movies show Bill and his wife Cuppy and the joking around of Johnny Grande, Rudy, and Billy Williamson. Bill's music was to have a lasting effect on Jamaica's early reggae musicians and their sound. They flocked to hear his shows from back stage to back walls and through open windows. The ancient whispers of the black rhythms and exotic cadences woven in Bill's music stirred their deepest emotions. Bill Haley's music becomes their catalyst and their inspiration.

Meanwhile, according to Jim Myers, out in Los Angeles, Myers was putting together a major television deal with Desilu Productions to showcase Bill Haley and his Comets. Myers flies back to Philadelphia with a verbal agreement. It calls for thirty-nine half-hour programs with Bill hosting the show. Bill would be allowed to invite any guest artists he wished to feature on the show. He would receive $10,000.00 per program, $10,000 to sign the contract, and ten percent of the world wide royalties. Myers recalled *"all in all the deal was worth about $400,000.00"*. Bill, with ill-advice from Lord Jim, turns down the deal. Lord Jim tells Bill, *"We don't need 'um Bill, we can make more dough than that on the road, and not get tied up for nine months"*. According to Myers, Bill doesn't inform his two partners of the offer. He fears they may want to go for the deal, but for now, Bill has no time for a full season network show. He is in the middle of too many of his own publishing and recording deals.

Jimmy Myers was furious. He had spent weeks on this deal, travelling between both coasts. His commission would have been substantial, but worst yet, he had to explain the "turn down" to network executives who believed he could get Haley's consent.

The Comets give center stage to Ralph Jones on the boardwalk at Atlantic City. Courtesy© DAP

In fact, there is some question as to whether the Desilu offer was ever a firm deal. John Grande, corporate treasurer of the Comets, has no recollection of it, and said Bill had severed his association with Myers in 1956 when Myers began supplying songs to the Jodimars. However, if the offer was made, Bill would soon regret his decision not to take it.

In September, the Comets leave for a two week tour of the midwest. They play to packed auditoriums in Minnesota, Iowa, Indiana, Missouri, Illinois and Wisconsin. They end up for a three day stand at the Casa Loma Ballroom in St. Louis, Missouri. Comet records show they played before a combined audience of over 137,000 fans.

Since his return from his world tour, Bill also wanted to do an album in which the native folk songs of many nations would be given a "Bill Haley Rock'n'Roll" treatment. He told his staff writer Rusty Keefer to work on it. For several months Keefer converted a dozen popular foreign folk tunes to Bill's style of rock. Musical arrangements were done by Johnny Grande and Bill himself. Haley called Milt Gabler and four days of studio time was set aside for the recording of the new album.

Between November 8th and the 21st the band recorded the album at the Pythian Temple. A second guitarist, Joe Oliver, is added to the Comet line-up for the session. All the songs but two were

Courtesy® DAP

Lord Jim and Bill Haley at one of Bill's famous Melody Manor backyard barbecues.

written by Bill and his staff. The album produced from this body of work was called *Rock Around The World*. It contained the following rock-a-fied tunes: *Me Rock A Hula, Rockin' Rita, Jamaica, D.J., Piccadilly Rock, Pretty Alouette, Rockin' Rollin' Schnitzlebank, Rockin' Matilda, Vive La Rock And Roll, El Rocko, Come Rock With Me, Oriental Rock*, and *Wooden Shoe Rock*. This concept was a clever idea, but unfortunately most of the tunes were weak. Excellent vocals and instrumental performances were wasted on songs that were for the most part trite. Two additional songs were also recorded that session; *It's A Sin* and *Mary Mary Lou*. These were the last recordings the Comets would make that year.

In 1957, the world-wide sales of *Rock Around the Clock* alone had reached another two million copies. In France, it had climbed to their #1 spot. The Comets' total releases for the year on Decca, London and the Brunswick labels were a staggering twenty-three singles, nine extended plays, and five albums. Their total sales now passed eighteen million records! Also, for the first time, Bill's income from record sales overseas is now greater than his American royalties.

Bill's Christmas "Party and Bash" was again a great gathering of the Comet organization. The year, with its very profitable foreign tours and record royalties, was another financially successful one. Bill had re-invested much of his earnings back into his publishing companies and into a metal fabrication company called Industrial Mechanics, Inc. near Chester.

He announces to the gathered clan that he intends to make Clymax records, his new private label, a major entertainment force in the coming year. Not content to just write and publish his and other people's music, Bill wants to actually "make the records". Since publishing and recording is the most lucrative part of the profit margin (the artist receives only one and a half to five percent of the profit), Bill's growing insistence on controlling his material and grooming other talented performers seems to make good business sense.

He also announces to everybody that he had signed lucrative contracts for tours of South America and Europe in the coming year. The estimated revenues, $165,000.00, from these two tours alone should insure another gala year. They all toast to their continued prosperity and Bill hands out his famous thousand dollar Christmas bonuses to each Comet. Again family photographs show Melody Manor adorned with holiday decorations and great tables of foods about the house. The large Christmas tree is surrounded with colorfully wrapped gifts as smiling comets pose for photographs with their wives. Bill, wearing his glasses, is happily pouring drinks for his many guests. He seemed to really be enjoying himself, surrounded by admiring friends, business associates and family. Milt Gabler is down from New York to help celebrate the occasion. Bill Haley's success has made Milt one of the highest paid executives at Decca. Since 1954, no less than 30 singles, EP's or albums had been released. If one counted Bill's total output, Holiday, Essex, Decca and the European labels, the figure came to over 130 records!

Bill's elaborate plans to extend his musical empire and diversify his assets with the promise of bold new adventures make this day specially joyous. His guests toast to new and greater horizons, to happiness and to Rock'n'Roll, may it go on forever. Bill radiated in the warm glow of admiration and genuine affection showed by his people. He was at the very pinnacle of his career. These were the days of fame and glory. Next all of Europe would dance to the magic of Bill Haley and his Comets.

However, the cruelties of fate would soon blow its frigid wind over Bill's dreams. Never could Bill have comprehended or foreseen the personal or financial disasters which he would have to endure in the coming year. Within the span of ten months he would be on the brink of ruin and bankruptcy.

The year 1958 begins with a heavy schedule of tours and extended engagements such as the Hollywood Terrace Ballroom in Brooklyn, New York. On February 6th and 7th, the Comets record five more songs at the Pythian Temple: *The Walking Beat, Sway With Me, Skinny Minnie, Lean Jean* and *Don't Nobody Move*. These were the best songs the Comets had done in some time. *Sway With Me* was a pure rhythmic "stroll" number with Rudy's sensuous sax predominant. All the Comets sang in chorus. *The Walking Beat* was one of Johnny Grande's great arrangements, heavy on his boogie-woogie piano style. *Skinny Minnie* became the hit of the session and Bill's best tune of the season, resulting in a much needed return for Bill to the U.S. top 40 charts. This song marked the sixth year in a row Bill had hits on the national charts. Decca promoted the disc with *Skinny Minnie* look-alike contests. The Comets even toured with several six foot tall gals who would dance while the Comets played the song with its infectious rhythm.

From February 20th to the 25th the Comets play four one-night concerts to sellout crowds in the largest venues in Florida: the Peabody Auditorium in Daytona Beach, the Fort Heastery Armory in Tampa, the National Guard Armory in Jacksonville, and the Dade County Auditorium in Fort Lauderdale.

They then do a whirlwind tour of Canada and the Great Lakes region in March, before appearing on Dick Clark's new nationally televised "American Bandstand" show. Bill had appeared several times earlier when Clark hosted the popular show in Philadelphia on WFIL-TV. On this telecast, March 22nd, Bill and his Comets lip-synched *Skinny Minnie* before a viewing audience estimated to be over 4,000,000 Rock'n'Roll loving teen-agers.

On April 6th, the Comets, Lord Jim, Catfish and Joe Oliver, their extra guitarist and interpreter (he speaks Spanish, French, Italian and German) begin their first leg of their first South American tour. According to the Comets' Fan Club News Letter, *"they receive a gigantic send-off at the Wilmington, Delaware train station by their fan club president, Shirley Lisowski. More than 6,000 fans cheer the band as the train leaves the old Victorian station.*

"On arriving in Miami, Loren Shayne, the local president, gave them another official fan club welcome before they drove on to Miami International Airport."

Actually the Comets leave without any fanfare. There were no fans cheering the band's departure from the train station. Lord Jim's press releases were beginning to stretch the imagination a bit too far.

The Comets leave Miami on one of Re-Al's Brazilian luxury airliners and land briefly for re-fueling in Caracas, Venezuela, before reaching their destination: Rio de Janeiro, Brazil. Here thousands of fans scream and chant for hours as the Comets make their way through customs. Shortly they board another plane and fly 250 miles to Sao Paulo, the site of their first performance.

Dick Clark with Bill Haley on American Bandstand. Courtesy© DAP

The Comets in Sao Paulo, Brazil. Left to right: Frannie Beecher, Billy Williamson, Al Rex, promoter, Lord Jim, Bill Haley, John Grande, Rudy Pompilli, Ralph Jones and Joe Oliver.

Courtesy® DAP

Joe Oliver and his Gibson. The Comets' interpreter on their South American and European tours. 1958 Courtesy© DAP

On arriving in Brazil, Bill discovers his interpreter is useless—this South American country speaks Portuguese! On the opening night at the Metropolitan Theater, Bill is mobbed and his clothes are torn to shreads, just trying to get into the theater. It takes over a hundred police officers to break through the crowd and rescue him. Here the Comets are Rock'n'Roll gods again as the public goes completely wild over Bill. Before the concert begins, Bill is presented with a large bouquet of roses from Liliano Bissi, his local fan club president. Jimmie Lynn's world-wide network of Comet Fan Clubs is completely informed of Haley's tour stops. Their Comet-worshipping presidents were always eager to greet their favorite band and be part of any publicity-attracting event.

The shows are all sellouts. The rest of the tour is summed up by an article in the Comets Newsletter by Rudy Pompilli: *"From Sao Paulo on to beautiful Rio, the garden spot of the world . . . no wonder with 200 miles of beach, the beautiful Copacabana, Sugar Loaf, the breath-taking statue of Christ overlooking Rio and more beauty than one can imagine. The crowds in Rio were "fantabulous". We played "standing room only" every night. Our fan club president, Jimenez, did the interpreting, which we were badly in need of. We did shows for TV, radio, night clubs and remote towns out in the jungle. What a thrill, riding for hours through the jungle, then coming upon a little village and all the population knew Bill and each one of the Comets by name.*

"After Rio and two beautiful weeks, we flew to Buenos Aires, Argentina . . . six hour flight. Again our fan club president Jose Levy and thousands of Comet fans presented us with a very warm welcome. We found the Latins highly demonstrative, and man, they are warm hearted.

"The two weeks in Buenos Aires were sensational and Johnny Grande went wild over the steaks. Well, not only Johnny, but all the Comets added a few pounds.

"The Argentine king of rock and roll, Eddie Pipuanino, played "The Saints Go Marching Home", as we boarded the plane for our journey home. Our South American fans really left a place in our hearts."

Bill and the Comets were very impressed with the large hand-painted portraits of them which hung out side the theaters where they played. Bill's full-length portrait was over forty feet high.

The South American tour had been arranged by the Jolly Joyce Agency and Don Ames, the promoter. The contract stated each show was to be paid in cash as they went along. All expenses were to be paid by the promoter. The Comet coffers were to receive $65,000 in total, plus side fees for personal appearances. Lord Jim was the "collector". He was supposed to wire back the large sums each week, but for reasons only known to him, he carried large amounts of cash on his person. When warned by Catfish about losing it, Lord Jim boasted; *"I've never lost a buck out of my pocket yet".* Several hours later the entire Comets' receipts for three weeks work was missing.

For the first time, Bill Haley had to ask his band to wait for their paychecks. This was an embarrassing time, as several Comets believed Lord Jim had gambled away their funds and used the "pickpocket" story to cover his losses. They reasoned that all that money couldn't have fit into his pocket in the first place.

Bill accepted Lord Jim's story and tried his best to keep hard feelings from boiling over. However, he receives more bad news on his return home. Cal Peltzmen, his new accountant, informs Bill that financial reserves were being depleted to dangerous levels. For the first time money was being spent faster than it was coming in. With over twenty

Bill Haley relaxing in an elegant Buenos Aires restaurant after a late show. Courtesy© DAP

Courtesy© DAP

The Comets the summer of 1958.

people on the payroll, the yacht in Wildwood, the recording studios, Clymax, Seabreeze, and Valley Brook all creating a costly overhead, Bill is told to cut costs or he could be in trouble soon. In fact the Comets were the only profit-making unit in the whole enterprise and Bill's pre-occupation with these other ventures had kept them off the road more than he should.

Bill decides not to cut back—Decca's second quarter royalty checks were due shortly and the band was booked weekends for most of the summer. Besides, his big European tour was only a few months away. That alone would bring in over $100,000.00. Bill reasoned that everything would be all right soon, this was just a temporary cash-flow problem.

He borrows badly-needed operating funds from Philadelphia's Fidelity Bank. His beloved Melody Manor is now mortgaged to the hilt as is his Chester office building. He lays everything on the line to help keep the dream alive until the tour revenues are received.

June 3rd 1958 the Comets return to the Pythian Temple and record two instrumentals *Joey's Song*, backed with *Chiquita Linda*. On the 9th, 12th, and 18th of June, they are back in New York to record a series of nine songs based on women's first names; *Dinah, Ida, Whoa Mabel, Marie, Eloise, Corrine Corrina, B.B.Betty, Sweet Sue,* and *Charmaine*. The album created from this body of work, plus *Lean Jean, Mary, Mary Lou* and *Skinny Minnie* is called *Bill Haley's Chicks.*

On June 6th, 1958, while in New York, Jack Howard, with Bill's permission, makes a deal with Atlantic Records to record the Comets under the pseudonym "The Kingsmen". This clandestine agreement was to be kept secret from Milt Gabler and Decca. Although not illegal, Decca's top brass would consider it unethical; their "exclusive" recording contract with Bill and the Comets still had eighteen months to go.

The "Kingsmen" record two records on Atlantic's East-West label. The first record featured the song *Week End,* an instrumental written by Pompilli, Beecher and Williamson. It was backed with *Better Believe It,* written by Al Rex, Rudy Pompilli and Ralph Jones. *Weekend* was first offered to Milt Gabler, who rejected it because it was not in the readily identifiable Haley style. The Atlantic release made it to the national charts, and was followed up with a second instrumental, *The Cat Walk* with Ralph Jones' *Conga Rock* on the flip side. All four songs were published by Seabreeze Music Inc.

On June 21st, 1958, a fourth family tragedy befalls Bill. His thirty-five year old sister, Peggy, dies of cancer. She had been ill for over a year, and although Bill knew her days were numbered, he was deeply shaken at the news. In the past four years Bill had buried his close friend Danny Cedrone, his baby daughter, his father, his mother and now his only sister.

After the funeral he called his first wife, Dottie, in despair, and asked her if she thought God was punishing him. Was his sound 'The Devil's Music' as Jerry Lee Lewis had said?

Courtesy© DAP

Jack Howard signing Clymax recording deal with Sally Starr.

Bill Haley's Clymax label Courtesy© DAP

Dottie told him Jerry Lee Lewis was crazy, didn't know what he was talking about, and he shouldn't try to question the acts of God. She reassured him of the happiness his music had brought the world. Dottie's quiet advice and reassurance was always welcomed by Bill. Feeling better, he then told her "Reds" would be by to pick up their two children, ten year old Sharyn and seven year old Jackie. Bill's two oldest children always spent part of the summer with him at the shore and several weeks with their half-brothers and sisters at Melody Manor.

By the summer of 1958, Bill's new Clymax label had released five singles, three extended plays, and one album. Their first record featured the Matys Brothers singing *Sweet Sixteen* and *I'm Alone Because I Love You*. This record was followed by Sally Starr's *Rockin' In The Nursery* and *Little Pedro*. Sally Starr was a very popular television host on WFIL-TV's "Popeye Theater". She was the wife of Jesse Rogers of Country-western fame. Both she and her husband had known Bill since his WPWA radio days. Starr promoted her record heavily on her TV program and thousands of kids in the Delaware Valley responded.

Other popular local artists Bill promoted via his publishing companies were: Charlie Gray singing *Completely Satisfied* backed with *Wastin' Time*, and Lou Graham's rendition of *Wee Willie Brown/You Were Mean, Baby*. Bill recorded the Matys Brothers again in August, singing *Crazy Street* and *Remember*. Again all the songs were published by Bill's companies, and the Comets were usually the backup band. Despite heavy promotions, however, none of these releases made the national charts.

The encouraging regional response for Sally Starr's first record prompted Bill to gamble and recorded a three record, extended-play album called: *"Our Gal Sal"*. The album contained twelve songs with the Comets backing her vocals. Produced by John Grande, this unusual collection of children's Rock 'n'Roll songs mixed with popular ballads and the beautiful *Good Night, Dear Lord*, is another example of Bill Haley's willingness to test new markets for his music. These rare kiddie-tunes were *Toy Shop In Town, Blue Ranger, Happy Birthday, Candy Bed, Cuckoo In The Clock, ABC Rock, Sing A Song Of Happiness, T.V. Pal, Little Pedro, Rockin' Horse Cowgirl, Good Night, Dear Lord*, and *Rockin' In The Nursery*. Bill also released them on a 12" long-play record with the Clymax label called: *"Our Gal Sal"*. These rare high quality records were recorded in Frank Virtue's studio, in Philadelphia. The Comets play all the musical accompaniment. When one hears this range of songs, one can appreciate the talent and versatility of these extraordinary musicians.

The large cash out-lays developing Valley Brook, Seabreeze and Clymax, however, were by now severely straining the credit reserves of the Comets. Bill begins telling creditors to be patient, his European tour would be starting in October and he was expecting over $100,000.00 in additional revenues by November.

When Bill tries to raise capital by "cashing-out" his sizeable investment in the metal fabricating company he had bought into, he is stunned to learn that his entire investment in Industrial Mechanics, Inc. is lost. The firm, which Lord Jim had so highly recommended, had gone bankrupt. However, Lord Jim is busy with his new investment scheme, the "Bill Haley and Lord Jim's Art Gallery".

He talks Bill into buying an old building on the corner of Foulk and Naamans Creek Road in Booth's Corner for $7,000.00. Another $30,000 is spent remodeling. The idea is to bring "Art" to the masses. Lord Jim has always been interested in "fine art". He plans to buy hundreds of canvases in Europe dirt-cheap and re-sell them to a new, enlightened common folk, to whom he intends to teach art appreciation This new calling becomes a passionate crusade for Lord Jim and his vision to improve the culture of Bethel Township.

Unfortunately, this get-rich-quick scheme ends almost as badly as his Australian-American opal cartel dream-deal. One wonders why Bill Haley ever got financially involved in Lord Jim's wild schemes.

Courtesy® DAP

Courtesy® DAP

The Comets headline Alan Freed's
"Big Beat" Rock'n'Roll show at the Fox Theater.

None of them ever made any money and Bill was usually left holding the bag.

That summer, Al Rex leaves the band angry and frustrated. Money is so tight that even Comet paychecks are missed. Al's wife Mary persuades him to get a regular job and come off the road. The other non-partners decide to hold out till the much talked about European tour puts the treasury back in the black. Bill promises them all that they will get all back pay plus bonuses. Rudy Pompilli gets his cousin, Al Pompilli, to fill in as the Comets' bass player.

Still believing he is close to a major breakthrough with some of his artists, Bill refuses to book any long tours and only takes engagements in the mid-Atlantic states. Most of his playing is at Widwood or Atlantic City. This schedule leaves him free, during the week, to run his publishing and recording companies. He is counting on them to turn a profit next year and help contribute to the Comets' profit margins.

Bill continues to write and arrange new songs. Over the last year and in the months to come his compositions included: *Good Night Dear Lord, Goodbye Baby, Get Off the Line, My Dream, Sway with Me, I Should Write A Song About You, Ain't Gonna Party No More, Make Believe Waltz, Walking Beat, You Gotta Sing For The Ladies*, and *Way Down In The Bottom Of My Heart*. Probably one of the most poignant and clearly auto-biographical was the song *Life of the Party:*

Now the life of the party—is acting the clown
and everyone is happy and dancing around.
Everyone is happy and gay
because the life of the party has made it that way.
Though you may have heartaches, fears and regrets
the life of the party soon makes you forget.
He won't let troubles begin
and oh, how we all envy him.
Now the life of the party is a strange sort of chap
he cheers you up with a pat on the back.
Ah, he came to the party—that's true
but he goes home alone when it's through.
Now the party is over and all the couples pass by
and, as he watches them, comes a tear to his eye.
Now he's not so happy and gay
now the life of the party goes his lonely way.
There's no one to cry to, no one to love
he lifts his eyes skyward to the heavens above.
I know all about it—you see
because the life of the party is me.

Photo of Rudy and his cousin Al taken in Torino, Italy, 1958. Courtesy© DAP

The other members of the Comets also wrote a prodigious amount of songs, in fact more than forty-six were listed with Valley Brook and Seabreeze alone!

Finally, on September 25th, the time arrives for the Comets first tour on the continent of Europe. Due to the Comets' poor financial condition, Bill tells his staff no wives will be going along this time. The only non-band members of the staff going are Catfish, Lord Jim, Charlie Levigne and Joe Oliver, again as their guitar-playing interpreter. This time his fluent Spanish, German, French, and Italian would become indispensable to Bill on this tour. The tour's promoter Alex Valdez also accompanies the Comets when they reach Europe.

Half the group, John Grande, Billy Williamson, Catfish, Frannie Beecher, Al Pompilli and Ralph Jones board the luxury liner Queen Mary out of New York. The five and a half day sail across the Atlantic is smooth and without the torments of their first trans-Atlantic voyage. They disembark at Cher-

Posing before the Roman Coliseum the Comets are unaware of the coming disaster. Left to right, Charlie Levigne, Johnny Grande, fan and Ralph Jones.

Courtesy© DAP

bourg, France without reception. They take a train to Paris and then the Orient Express for Milan, Italy.

Bill, Lord Jim, Rudy, Joe Oliver, Charlie Levigne and Alex Valdez fly over and meet the band in Paris. Bill is very concerned over the complexity of the five week tour and the rumors of possible riots and other disturbances. He desperately wants this tour to be as financially successful as his British one had been.

While in Paris, Bill reviews the ambitious twenty-three city package with his European agents. The Comets are scheduled to play fifty-six performances and much to his dread, Bill will be hosted at countless media receptions for Europe's press, television, and radio. He will answer many of the same questions, pose for the same smiling photos and secretly wish all of the hype were less of a media circus. Many reporters still treated him and his band as if they were performing clowns.

Co-ordinating these intricate arrangements with dozens of airline, train and bus schedules, in nine different countries, not to mention the booking of scores of theaters and auditoriums, was a marvel of ingenuity.

Catfish, who is but eighteen years old, was in charge of all instruments, equipment and baggage. It was his responsibility to clear them through the complex international customs regulations. He had to keep lists of all the equipment, their descriptions and serial numbers. To prepare for any emergency, he had ordered extra Premier drum heads and sticks, guitar and bass strings, Fender amplifers and other backups for evey member of the band. The Comets' techniques and travel were very hard on the equipment. Besides, it had been known for instruments to be stolen by fans. Bill's Gibson guitars were especially prized.

Catfish also packed over thirty-five stage outfits and tuxedos which had been donated to the Comets for promotional considerations by several manufacturers. All this had been carefully drop shipped to selected cities all over Europe. All the amplifiers, instruments, and band equipment had been donated by their American and British manufacturers.

On October 2nd, the Comets gather in Milan, Italy, for their first concert on continental European soil. The band plays two powerful performances to a standing-room-only audience of excited Rock 'n'Roll fans. The Italians love Bill's American-style Rock'n'Roll and scream deliriously for encores.

The Comets create an instant bond with the Italian Rock'n'Rollers. Rudy opens the show with a few words in Italian. He introduces his fellow "paesanos" in the band. However, due to advance publicity, the audience is already well aware that half the guys—Rudy, Al and Johnny—are Italian-Americans, and shouts of "Numero Uno" and "Bravissimo" fill the great theaters wherever the band plays. This is Rudy's first trip to his parent's country since his service in the army. *"The last time I was here, they were shooting at me!"* he would remark, as he showed the band what real Italian food tasted like.

The Comets continue to play their now familiar program, with its thundering beat, to the large northern industrial cities of Turin, Florence, and Bologna. Heading south, they reach the capital of Rome in the early afternoon of October 9th.

Up to this point, the tour had been going letter perfect. Bill's early jitters had calmed down a bit. Only he knows how critical this tour is to the financial survival of Valley Brook and Seabreeze. Back in Chester, there awaited a mass of creditors, friends and families whose fate depend on this tour's success.

About four o'clock that afternoon, the first ominous news came: Pope Pius XII had died suddenly. The theater owner notified Bill and Alex Valdez that all theaters were ordered to close and "other joyous entertainment" canceled. Ralph Jones recalled the band sat in their hotel rooms and watched the funeral on television and out their hotel window. The Comets, mostly Roman Catholic, were deeply moved by the spectacle and solemn pomp of the Papal funeral.

Meanwhile, Bill and his business associates were desperately trying to re-schedule some of the Italian dates for early November, but the theaters are not available when they have open time.

All over Rome, black cloths and ribbons of mourning were draped over signs, street lights and pinned to lapels. All Italian and Papal flags were set at half-mast. The normally exuberant mood of the nation changed to somber melancholy. For Bill, this not only meant the cancellation of all four performances in Rome, but also two each in Naples and Venice. A loss of over $25,000 in badly needed funds.

The idle band members used the unexpected break to see the Roman ruins and other cultural attractions of the city. One evening they were guests of Mario Lanza at his magnificent villa. Lanza, a South Philadelphia-born singer, was in Europe making his last movie. "A great guy", recalls John Grande. John's parents had known the talented performer before his fabulous voice became world famous.

Rudy, as usual, wrote out hundreds of post cards to his fans all over the world and signed many of them with his favorite alias: "Rudy Pell". Ralph's ever present movie camera records the events for posterity. Unable to re-arrange the tight schedules, Bill and the Comets return by train to Milan where they board a flight back to Paris, their headquarters for the tour.

In Milan, Lord Jim makes his last fatal mistake in misjudging the generosity and good will of Bill Haley. Knowing funds were critical, he buys $50,000 worth of oil paintings for his art gallery and charges them to Bill's hotel account. He believes he can double his money in the States on the paintings, and then pay Bill back out of the profits. When Haley finds out about Ferguson's scheme, he fires his long time friend and manager and in a rare fit of temper sends him out on the next flight to the States! This is the first time the Comets can remember Bill openly showing his anger and frustration at his wayward manager. They had watched Lord Jim pull off some pretty fast deals at Bill's expense, but this time his "luck of the Irish" had run out. Bill Haley, who had always considered Lord Jim to be his "good luck charm", finally saw his old friend as others had always seen him.

To make matters worse, Bill also found he could not return the dubious paintings. Most were purchased from itinerant sidewalk artists. When Bill tries to resell them, he finds they are worth less than $5,000! In fact, most were considered worthless.

Furious, Bill wires Jack Howard to tell Lord Jim: *"I don't care how you raise the dough, but you had better wire $50,000 to our hotel in Paris within a week!"*

Back on their schedule, the band prepares for their opening night in Paris at the Olympia Theater. The French newspapers play up the riots in America and the "bad elements" Rock'n'Roll music seems to attract. Bill is beginning to get nervous again. He misses the pep talks and ego-massages Lord Jim was so good at. Joe Oliver is now constantly at his side.

Opening night at the Olympia confirms his worst nightmares. After the Comets' forty minute performance ends and they leave the stage, over-zealous French police and a few exuberant rockers get into a tussle. Within minutes, hundreds of keyed-up kids go to the aid of their "hassled" brothers and a full scale free-for-all breaks out. Dozens of chairs are smashed, windows broken and the first blood is spilled in the streets of Europe over rock music. Police re-enforcements arrive and the kids are driven out into the streets of Paris. For about an hour, hundreds march down the avenues yelling at the top of their lungs in French: *"ROCK'N' ROLL FOREVER", "DOWN WITH THE POLICE"* and *"LONG LIVE HALEY, THE KING OF ROCK'N'ROLL"!*

The next morning the European press have a field day, at Bill Haley's expense. He is barbecued with some of the most vicious accusations ever printed about a music personality. His other two concerts at the Olympia are canceled. Bill's protests are to no avail. The theater owners refuse to allow any more Rock'n'Roll shows. Although the actual damage is less than a thousand dollars, which Bill offers to pay, the bad publicity causes several other provincial theater owners to cancel their commitments.

The following week, the Comets play to audiences in Marseilles, Lyons, Dijon, Bourges and Bordeaux. The extra heavy police protection, with dogs and riot gear in full view, dampens the audience's normal spirited participation. Although there are some minor disturbances at these sold-out shows, the Haley concerts are quickly gaining the reputa-

30000 Mark Schaden nur durch Übermut!

Ein Anblick wie auf einem Schlachtfeld: Trümmer, Trümmer, Trümmer — so hausten die Lederjacken

Der Rock'n'Roll-Skandal im Berliner Sportpalast

rb. Berlin, 28. Oktober

West Berliners Force Haley to Flee Stage

CHESTER—Chester's Bill Haley and his. band, famed rock-n-roll group now on a European tour, were forced to fleet the stage of West Berlin's Sports Palace last night by a crowd of seat-smashing youths.

Four policemen were injured slightly in a fist-and-club fight that followed. About 500 youths were involved and 18 were arrested for defying police orders.

that he didn't think they would have any trouble in Germany.

Ferguson pointed out the only trouble the Haley group has had

Haley Sets Off Third Riot

ESSEN, Germany (AP) — Bill Haley's rock 'n roll music set off a third riot of West German teenagers last night.

This time 300 police were ready and broke up the riot before serious damage was done.

Why Rock and Roll Drive Youths 'Wild'

By David M. Nichol

BONN, Germany.

A TRAIL of destruction and disorder followed American bandleader Bill Haley on his recent tour of West Germany. In four different cities youthful fans rioted so violently that the concerts were broken off and order could only be restored by police who used clubs and water hoses among their other persuasions.

…mmungsloser Ekstase zerschmetterten …endlichen die Stühle

German headline: "30,000 marks damage due to wanton destruction!"

tion of being giant "Rumble Conventions", for thousands of rebellious, post-war teenagers. The black-leather jacket had become the unisex protest garment of choice and the most visible uniform of Europe's new young rebels.

On their return to Paris, Bill meets with officials and tour promoters. Jittery theater owners want assurances that all damages and the cost of extra police protection will be covered by the tour promoters. Law enforcement officials want to ban the shows altogether. So far the tour has barely broken even. All profits have been lost due to the unforeseen cancellations and extra security costs. Bill tells his people: *"the show must go on".* He has no choice. To quit now would be a personal financial disaster.

The next two weeks would be spent playing in nine German cities and Vienna, Austria. Bill is assured that the German kids are better behaved than the "French hoodlums", who had created so much bad press. He also reads headlines such as: *"Bill Haley, Won't You Please Go Home!"* and *"Attila the Hun Returns!"* The anti-rock press in the States also reports on Haley's embattled concert tour. They make sure the "rock riots" get full coverage, with Haley and his "Jungle" music taking most of the blame for inciting the turmoil.

On the 22nd of October the band flies to Vienna, Austria. They do two performances at the great Viennese Concert Hall. The "Vienna Courier" printed: *"The old Concert Hall shook as Bill Haley rocked... when Haley came out, the public cried out... they stomped their feet against the honorable floor so that the tiers and the managers trembled."*

The Vienna Telegraph" said: *"At the first concert you get only the "show"... the whirl. Only at the second concert you hear how much weight the music has. At the first show we strained ourselves much more, at the second one, it runs by itself."*

Vienna is a triumph for Bill's new sound. The city of Strauss and Mozart had opened its arms and its Concert House to the new music and appreciated its complexity. Both shows were sold out. When Bill climbed on board his plane the next morning, he and the Comets were given yellow chrysanthemums as tokens of the Viennese regard. Upon arrival in Paris, Bill finds Lord Jim had wired the $50,000.00 as requested. Bill seemed very surprised at how fast his former manager was able to get his hands on that much cash.

On October the 26th, the Comets are scheduled to play the first of six concerts at the massive Berlin Sports Palace. The great German arena seated 7,000 and was sold-out for all six performances. Rumors flew that East German kids were going to stage a demonstration and try to disrupt the show. Besides the usual large security force on hand, eighty extra police officers were hired and hidden in the basement with full riot gear. The American State Department suggested the show be postponed, due to a report from the CIA which hinted that there might be trouble from "certain" East German communist youth groups. The report is vague and Bill's promoter dismisses it as just "Cold War jitters".

The night before the Berlin concert, Bill Haley has a nightmare. He dreams he is attacked and trampled on stage. The next morning he is restless and very quiet. He calls home and talks to his children. His mood is a mixture of resignation and melancholy. Not even the effervescent Rudy Pompilli can cheer him up. He reads in a German newspaper a quote from Pablo Casals: *"Haley's music is a distillation of all the offensiveness of our times."* Bill writes in his notes: *"This I did not want."* Bill is also informed that should any more riots occur the entire tour could be in jeopardy.

By seven-thirty on the evening of October 26th, 1958, the youth of both East and West Berlin poured into the huge arena. For a historical note, this was before the city was divided by its "Wall of Shame". Many of the kids quickly grew restless, as an atmosphere for potential violence seemed to build almost from the start. The over-sold arena rapidly filled to over-capacity as the teenagers were packed in, shoulder to shoulder. Tempers flared as many found they had no seats. Police went on full alert; an explosive mood was evident to all. One teenager interviewed by a reporter the next morning said: *"Something was going to happen, you could feel it!"*

At eight o'clock the show opened with Kurt Edelhagen's orchestra playing some popular tunes. The kids, who were in no mood for this type of music, began shouting for Bill Haley. Within minutes, pushing and shoving led to several isolated fights. Several wooden chairs are broken and their pieces concealed as future weapons. The impatient kids now began whistling and shouting down the performers on the stage. The tension builds until a swarm of youngsters storm the stage, ending the Edelhagen part of the program prematurely.

The promoters plead with the crowd to return to their seats or the show will be canceled. Bill Haley, from back stage, sees all the commotion and is apprehensive of events to come. The sight of seven thousand kids rushing him while on stage terrifies him. His nightmare of the eve before seems to be coming true. However, his promoters plead with him to go on with the show. They naively believe only Bill Haley and his Comets could calm the

"—also while ve are making defence cuts, America is establishing in Britain ROCKET and ROLL bases!"

excited and now unruly, agitated audience.

Reluctantly, the Comets go on stage one by one. First Ralph Jones, then Rudy and his cousin Al, followed by Franny, Johnny, and Billy Williamson. Then, with a mighty drum roll, Bill Haley is announced and the audience goes wild. Thousands of pieces of paper are thrown into the air, along with hats, scarfs and clothing of every description. The Comets go right into their rendition of *Shake, Rattle and Roll.* The kids, seven thousand strong, begin to stomp and clap in a thundering response. The din is so great that no one could possibly hear a thing. Next, the hard-driving, wild drum beats of *Rip It Up* seemed like a command from the "King of Rock" and only added fuel to an impossible situation.

Within minutes, whole rows of wood folding chairs were broken for weapons. Shots were fired as rival gangs tore into one another with yells in German of *"RIP IT UP"* and *"RUMBLE-RUMBLE"*.

Bill fled the stage, quickly followed by the band and the promoters. A large group of tough-looking, black-leather jacketed East Berliners marched down the main aisle, knocking down anything in their way. They headed directly for the stage.

Over two hundred police were rushed in to gain control. However, with thousands of brawling kids, they were only able to confine the worst trouble-makers to the center rink which was surrounded by a bicycle racing track. Here the worst damage was done. The Comets' amplifiers and microphones were smashed along with all the stage lights, decorations, a grand piano and all the equipment belonging to the Armed Forces Network, who were taping the show.

As more police arrived, pitched battles of fists and clubs between elements of the audience and security officials broke out everywhere. Many are injured as bloody-faced youth and police are locked in hand-to-hand combat. Catfish, who is trapped in the melee, is almost beaten by the mob and the police and pounds desperately on the stage door. Ralph Jones and Rudy, hearing his cries, open the large sliding door and rescue the terrified young man from the chaos. Then to keep the battle from spreading, they quickly fight to close it again. Finally, the police bring in fire hoses and knock the rioters off their feet. The trashed arena is cleared only to spread its former audience into the usually orderly streets of Berlin.

Once outside, the "Second Battle of Berlin" begins. Vicious fist fighting between police and other rival gangs continue. The gangs smash car and store windows as angry and frustrated German policemen use tear gas, dogs and rubber truncheons to weed out the worst ringleaders.

It takes over two hours to restore calm to the German capital. Over twenty police officers are injured. One is permanently blinded. Dozens of club-swinging youths are arrested as scores of injured teens flee the area. The arena is trashed and the local jails are quickly filled to capacity. The next morning, the city of West Berlin was in a stage of shock.

The Communists seize Haley's "Great Berlin Rock Riot" as a new "Cold War" propaganda opportunity. The East Berlin newspaper "Neues Deutschland" attacks Bill Haley in their classic anti-Capitalistic rhetoric: *"Rock'n'roll gangster Haley produces an orgy of American uncivilization . . . (he has turned) the youth of the land of Bach and Beethoven into raging beasts".*

Under the headline *"HOT MUSIC FOR A COLD WAR"* East-German Defense Minister Herr Stoph accuses the NATO powers of using *"Bill Haley the Rock'n'roll king as a recruting agent and hot-war expert".* The ludicrous article goes on to say, *"Bill Haley had been brought to West Germany in order to whip up hatred of the East German Republic as support for a nuclear world war. . . Bill Haley's special task was to engender a fanatical and hysterical enthusiasm among German youth."*

The Lord Mayor of West Berlin, Willy Brandt, was quoted: *"Embarrassing. A disgraceful result of a youthful wish for activity. A tumult of this type is not a typical phenomenon in Berlin, but nonetheless a damage to its reputation."*

Many believed the riot was deliberately created to force a Cold War incident. Radio Free Europe was beaming Rock'n'Roll music into the Eastern block nations, and the Russians had all but outlawed the music. This "rock riot" on West Berlin soil was just another sordid event to prove how decadent the culture of capitalistism was. If the KGB had to use a few dozen East German rowdies to push over the edge the normal excitement and enthusiasm of the rockers, so be it! Any embarrassment to the officials of West Berlin was worth the minor costs of starting a riot.

Herr Kraeft, the director of the Sports Palace, canceled all further rock concerts after viewing the damage to his arena. Again the tour promoters protested, saying more police were all that was needed. However, everyone knew this was a useless gesture as Bill tries to salvage the doomed tour.

The next three days, while things cool off, the Comets are scheduled to shoot their scenes in a movie called *Hier Bin Ich, Hier Bleib Ich* (Here I Am, Here I Stay). The film, shot in Berlin, stars Katerina Valente and is directed by Arthur Brauner. Ralph Jones remembers the whole cast cracking up when beautiful Katerina came walking on the set wearing a black leather jacket and holding a long wooden club. Looking like a tough, battle-hardened rocker, she asked the crew, *"Where's the Haley rock concert?"* The whole cast broke into a fit of laughter. . . everybody that is—except Bill Haley.

Film star Caterina Valente with Bill.

Courtesy CCC/Constantin/Krau

Again cruel events and unwanted bad publicity dog the Comets' shows. The following day, during their concert at the Ernst Marx Hall in Hamburg, a small group of youths wearing the now famous black-leather jackets stormed the stage and began to dance. The German police, who were mostly out of sight, rushed forward and pulled the kids from the stage. In the ensuing confusion, another wild free-for-all breaks out. Several rows of wooden chairs are smashed to pieces as police fight to get control. Only after more re-enforcements arrive, and the liberal use of tear gas, do the kids disperse. On the first outset of violence, Bill Haley fled the stage with the Comets close behind.

Bill demands from the promoters more police and better protection. The riot and mayhem puz-

Courtesy CCC/Constantin/Krau

Bill and the Comets on set of "Here I Am, Here I Stay." Note Joe Oliver (with glasses) playing guitar with the band.

zles him, but most of all he is afraid of being injured by flying objects he can't see coming. His limited vision creates nightmarish scenes in his mind. He is still unaware of how much his music has become part of the teenage "rebel without a cause" movement. *Rock Around the Clock* has become the international anthem of rock and rebellion, and in East Germany, the word rebellion is not allowed in their vocabulary.

Bill writes: *"Had I not needed the money from this tour so desperately, I would have dropped the show in Hamburg. The threats were now becoming too real."*

In the industrial city of Essen, police officials were not taking any more chances. More than 570 policemen were on hand to control any demonstrations that might break out, planned or otherwise. West German honor was now on the line. The first two shows go off without a hitch. However, the third concert turned out to be another disaster. This time, over-zealous police officers stormed the audience at the first sign of a commotion by a few punks. Bill Haley and the band again fled the stage as these rowdies throw the theater's potted plants and other decorations at the stage. The mischief-makers are arrested and taken away. The audience of over six thousand kids now awaited the Comets return but Bill will not go back on stage. The audience is told the concert is over, but they won't leave. They begin to shout: *"WE WANT BILL HALEY . . . WE WANT BILL HALEY".* The German police order the kids to leave the hall or else! The kids refuse and continue to chant. The police form a human wedge and with clubs swinging, clear the theater. Once out in the streets, mounted officers try to break up the crowd. Failing to get control, powerful water cannons and dogs are used. Ralph Jones recalls, *"It was like watching a battle. We were up on top of the auditorium looking down on the crowd outside. I've never seen anything like it! They finally drove the kids out. The kids hated it. They felt cheated. They fought against the cops with their bare hands—but the police clubs cut them down like weeds. Slowly the kids retreated, dragging their wounded friends with them. God, it was awful to watch."*

The "Battle of Essen" was duly chronicled in the headlines as: *"New Brawl Around the Cowlick (Bill's curl) with Water Cannons in Essen".* Other papers asked, *"What kind of music turns an audience of fun-loving kids into a screaming rhythm-mad mob capable of dangerous frenzy and riot?"*

The next concert is scheduled in Frankfurt. Here, under heavy police protection, six thousand teens enjoyed themselves without resorting to violence. Ralph Jones and Catfish remember Elvis Presley coming backstage to visit Bill and the Comets. *"He was stationed at a nearby army base at the time. He and a few friends would dance . . . he loved our music. After the show, we took pictures of Elvis, in uniform, with Rudy, Catfish, Johnny, Al and myself. I remember him saying to us: 'You know, if it weren't for you boys, I'd still be driving a truck back in Memphis.'"* The Comets appreciated Elvis' compliment as they trade stories with him about some of their recent harrowing experiences. Catfish also recalled his many hours playing cards with Elvis and his back-up men when they were on the same bill with the Comets. They all laughed remembering Elvis' first trip to Ohio at Bill Randle's Rock 'n'Roll Sock Hop when the shy and unknown Elvis told Al Rex, *"I hope these yankees will like my music."* Bored with his military exile, Elvis also comes again to see the Comets' show in nearby Stuttgart, only this time he wears civilian clothing. He is invited to perform with Bill Haley on stage, but the timid local authorities will not allow it, fearing a full scale riot. Imagine, the two "Kings of Rock'n'Roll" on stage together singing *Shake, Rattle and Roll*—it almost happened. Colonel Parker would have bitten right through his fat Havana cigar.

Returning again to France, the Comets do a side tour to North Africa for badly needed cash. Although not part of the original tour, they play a show in Algiers and one in Tunis before returning to Marseilles, aboard an ancient DC3 cargo plane. Flying high over the Mediterranean Sea against strong head winds, Johnny Grande was not the only Comet very concerned about ever seeing land again. Ralph Jones recalls the unusual audiences: *"We played to veiled women and a bunch of guys wearing fezzes with red or black tassels on their sides. It was kind of a strange audience for us, but we had them rockin' before we left!"*

The Comets do several more shows in Cologne, Munich, Stuttgart, and Hanover under heavy police protection. There are few new disturbances. The badly needed income from these performances help clear up some of the band's tour expenses.

The next day the band flies to Barcelona, Spain, where they play one concert before another crisis arises. Bill receives word that the Governor of the province has ordered his show closed, even though there has been no disturbances. Bill is also informed that Generalissimo Franco, the Spanish Dictator, doesn't like Rock'n'Roll and cites edicts from the Church banning good Catholics from attending

Elvis Presley back stage in Bill Haley's dressing room.
This rare photo was taken in Frankfurt, West Germany, 1958.

Courtesy K. Denton

the concerts. The Church authorities praise Franco's order, and Bill's concerts in Seville and Madrid are also cancelled.

Alex Valdez was desperate. This action has wiped out eight more performances and funds are desperately low. While the Comets go out sight-seeing, Bill and his associates try to recover from this added disaster. To make matters worse, the Spanish authorities also impound the Comets' personal tour funds and instruments for "currency violations". It takes several generous bribes and a quickly arranged departure to France to escape from Franco's sticky-fingered police and customs agents.

For Bill personally, the tour has been a financial disaster. The combined weight of the bad press, the riots, the death of the Pope, the sinister plots of the KGB, the exorbitant cost of extra police protection and Franco's cute tricks had doomed the tour. His promoter was broke and Bill had to wire home for money to get the band back to the States. The hotel in Paris was holding their passports until all charges were paid. Without their passports the Comets couldn't leave Europe, and the publicity of the band being stranded and broke in Paris was the last thing on earth Bill wanted.

As the cold winds of November chilled the northern plains of Europe, Bill Haley's fragile self-esteem and composure were near the breaking point. He feared there was a great conspiracy against him and his music. He believed he was being attacked from all sides as a sense of paranoia fell about him. The long tour and its pressures were taking their toll. Bill paced back and forth in his hotel room. He would say over and over: *"Why us?. . . What have we done to deserve this?. . . Why do they hate us so much? For gosh sake, its only music, we haven't got the plague!"*

But most of all he dreaded the return home to face creditors and almost certain bankruptcy. Close to a mental collapse, he stops giving interviews and holds up in his hotel room awaiting the group's last concert of the tour; Brussels, Belgium. He needs the modest $2000.00 fee from this "Charity Bash" desperately.

This concert was to be unlike any performance the Comets had ever done before or would ever do again. It was hailed as a celebration of the evolution of music. The concert was billed "FROM HAYDN TO HALEY" and would be broadcasted to sixteen nations throughout Europe.

An eighty-six piece symphony orchestra would play music-ranging from Haydn, Verdi, Strauss and Handel to the popular modern sounds of Gershwin, Handy, Kern and Berlin. The promoter intended to finish the concert with Haley's revolutionary new rock sound, thus illustrating the origins of man's musical heritage and its influence on the past two hundred years. The invitation to appear on the program was considered an honor for the Comets.

The early evening of the concert, the Comets arrive at the ornate Brussels Concert Hall by taxi. Ralph Jones and John Grande remember: *"We pulled up in front of this beautiful concert hall that looked like a king's palace. We usually played in the less grand arenas, theaters or auditoriums. At first, we wondered if this was the right place. After all the bad press and trashing of our last shows, we thought, 'who would book us in a nice place like this?' That's how low we were. Well, we finally go in and find our way back stage. Here, we discover we are sharing dressing rooms with ballet dancers, opera singers and musicians from a full eighty-six piece symphonic orchestra!"*

Ralph, who is the Comets official worrier, goes on to say: *"I get dressed in my tux and go look out to see what kind of audience we got. Out in this great hall, hung with brilliant crystal chandeliers, were a couple of thousand people seated in plush velvet seats. They were all wearing elegant evening gowns and dinner jackets! I said to Rudy: 'They've got to be kidding—WE'RE gonna play after THAT ORCHESTRA, to THOSE people? They'll hang us from the chandeliers!'*

"Sure enough, we wait in the wings as some of the most beautiful music I've ever heard is played. They do a part from "Swan Lake" with the ballerinas and all. I kept saying to myself, I'm glad my family isn't here to see this. That audience was the cream of Belgium society. I wonder if their good manners will keep them from murdering us. Bill just waited in his dressing room quietly, drinking coffee. His heart wasn't in it tonight. His thoughts were back in Chester.

Elvis Presley back stage with the Comets, Stuttgart, West Germany, 1958. Left to right: Rudy Pompilli, Al Pompilli, Elvis and Ralph Jones.

Courtesy R. Jones

Something Rocks and Rolls Every Minute

A German newspaper gives a minute by minute description of a Bill Haley Rock and Roll show:

8:56 P.M. — Bill Haley comes on stage and starts out with his first number in a terrific tempo.

9:00 P.M.—Haley starts his show number, "Shake, Rattle and Roll." About 2000 teenagers start to sway with the rhythm and the first ones start to get up.

9:05 P.M.—The sax player rolls over the stage blowing a frantic chorus. In the aisles couples start to dance.

9:06 P.M.—The bass man lies next to the sax player on the stage, while playing some crazy sounds. The group of dancing couples in the aisles grows.

9:13—Haley goes off stage to change clothes and is greeted by an ovation as he comes out again.

9:19 P.M.—Haley plays the number that sold millions, "Rock Around the Clock," and now 6,000 people get out of their seats and jump around from pure enthusiasm.

9:31 P.M.—Haley goes off again and when he comes out 400 teenagers are in front of the stage screaming, "Haley, Haley, Haley."

9:33 P.M.—Haley is in his last number and all at once there are 10, 20, 30 teenagers on stage crying, "Bill Haley," with a choir of 6,000 joining in.

9:36—Haley and his musicians have left the stage. The crying and whistling for encores grows and grows. The stage is full of young people trying to get autographs, and barricaded in his dressing-room Bill says: "How in the world will we ever get out of here?"

Ralph continues: *"About ten o'clock, it came our turn to do our thing. We are introduced as 'a vigorous new innovation in sound having a great influence on modern music.' I thought that sounded kinda nice, but I was still more than just worried. We went into our first number, then the second and third. I think they were; "Shake, Rattle and Roll", "Rock A Beatin' Boogie", and "Saints Rock and Roll". These were some of our best stuff, but the audience just sat there like they were shell shocked or something. They didn't move a muscle! Then we ended with our theme song, "Rock Around the Clock". We played our hearts out. Rudy was terrific. Frannie and Billy were really cookin'. Al danced with his bass while I cracked the rim shots like bullets across the high vaulted hall. Grande pounded the piano as Bill belted out the lyrics in perfect precision to our rhythm. We never played the "Clock" better. When we finished the last note, usually the audience would be on their feet screaming for more.*

"But not this house . . . the place was as quiet as a tomb. You could hear the plants growing in the outer lobby. Nobody even breathed. Puzzled, I looked at Rudy. Bill looked at Johnny. We all looked at each other. This had never happened to us before. It seemed forever, the audience just sat there and stared at us, like we just came in from the moon or something. Then it began. First the famous conductor of the orchestra rose and with his white-gloved hands, began to applaud. He was followed by his musicians, in standing ovation. Slowly, one by one, then by groups, until the entire audience was on its feet in applause. We bowed and walked off that great stage still puzzled. Later when we realized what had happened, we were proud that the first to appreciate the complex nature and difficulty of our sound were fellow musicians. But I think we shocked the blue-bloods so bad they needed the conductor to inform them that they had just heard the best rock 'n'roll music in the world."

The tour, which had begun with so much promise, ended at least in one last quiet triumph. Bill and the band returned to Paris and packed their belongings. On November 9th, they sailed home on the Queen Mary, unaware of the dire financial problems facing Bill and his dreams of a musical empire. Bill Haley would never forget this experience. He writes in his journal *"I now know how Napoleon must have felt in 1812!"*

Bill's return home was as melancholy as the cold, dreary winter night he arrived. A sense of coming doom surrounded him like the chilling fog which rolled in off the Delaware River. As he turned into the large horseshoe driveway of his beloved Melody

Manor, he passed the shabby little chicken house that had once been his boyhood home. Was this his future as well as his past?

The smoke from the burning logs in Melody Manor's large fireplace filled the damp night air as Bill parked his car and slowly walked to the back door of his home. His family warmly greeted him as he handed out the little gifts he always brought home after his long tours. He hugged and kissed his children and answered their excited questions, the big one being, *"Daddy, are you going to be home for a long time now?"*

The ordeal of the five week tour had left him once again dog-tired and exhausted. He soon fell asleep and didn't awake until late the next afternoon. While he slept, the phone never stopped ringing, but Bill was not disturbed. The following morning, he called for a meeting of his partners and his accountant. Could the dream be saved?

Ten days before Thanksgiving, Bill Haley met with John Grande, Billy Williamson and Cal Peltzman. He is informed that the accounts payable of all of his corporations are in serious arrears, and unless new revenues were forthcoming within thirty days, lawsuits would be filed and the banks would start demanding the full payment of interest and principal on all the overdue loans. And for the record, all loans were past due. Bill was also informed that all his real estate assets and their equities had been borrowed against to their maximums and Fidelity Bank had flatly refused any more extensions on all loans. Any new loans from any other bank were also out of the question.

John Grande, the corporate treasurer, asked Peltzman: *"What do we need to pull us through the next couple of months and keep us out of bankruptcy?" "A miracle"* was the accountant's sarcastic reply.

Bill had no time for jokes. He had poured too much sweat, time and money into his career and publishing companies to let a few riots led by leather-jacketed punks destroy him. *"Cal, what do you need, right now, to hold off the law suits?"* The accountant looked him right in the eye and said: *"$100,000.00 and don't forget we're sitting on about $4,500.00 in bounced checks right now. Also I don't know how much longer the creditors will wait, they're already getting very nervous...they've read about the European disaster."*

One of the unique qualities about Bill Haley was that it was easy to get him down, to totally depress him with criticism, bad luck or some other misfortune. But you could not keep him there. Maybe it was his tough Kentucky-Irish or English bulldog heritage, but Bill always found a deep inner strength

Bill with two of his children. Courtesy© DAP

which would come forth and save him in his darkest hours. Today he needed that special strength to save the Comets and his dreams.

As the others in the room saw only gloom and ruin with in a month, Bill saw a possibility. With uncharacteristic boldness, he suggested a plan to save the organization. First, he recalled several major foreign and American music publishers had offered some big bucks for rights to songs in the Valley Brook and Seabreeze catalogs. Bill told Jack Howard to make arrangements to sell the tunes to the highest bidder and fast.

Second, he told Grande to get advances for the two coming tours to South America and India. Third, he would personally call Milt Gabler and get a $35,000 advance from Decca. Bill's records were selling like hot cakes in Europe. The havoc and bad press of the just completed tour had one good side effect; it had made the Comets one of the best known and best selling rock groups over there.

Fourth, if necessary, the three partners would have to loan some more of their personal money to the corporation to keep the company going.

The last thing the three partners decided was to officially replace Lord Jim with Robert Hayes as their personal manager. Bill's former manager and long time crony had apologized to Bill for charging the $50,000.00 to his account in Milan without asking. The two long time friends talked about the old days when fifty grand was a weeks work and using

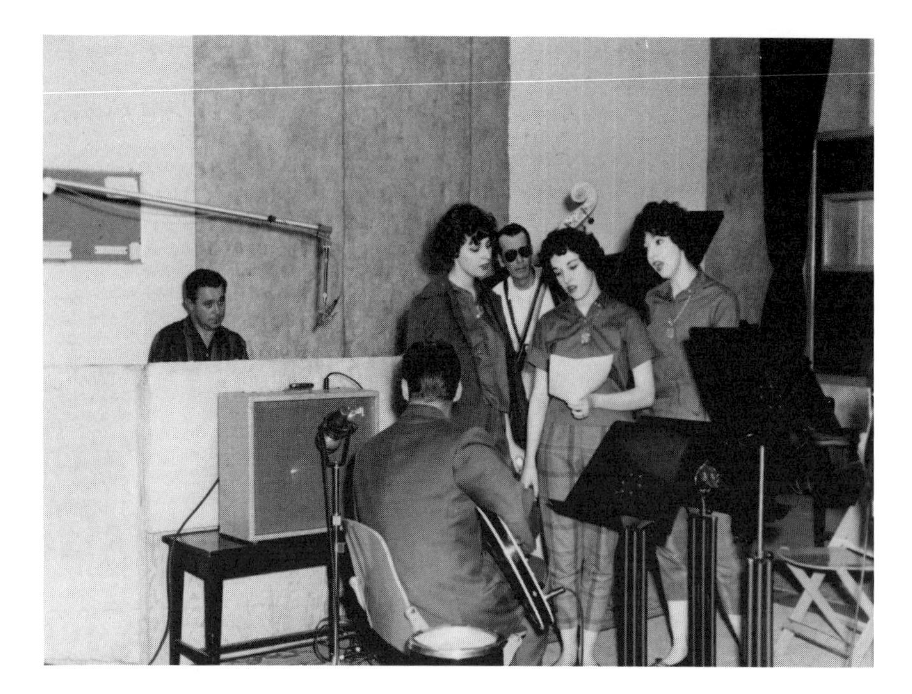

A Valleybrook recording session with the Keefer Sisters. Ralph Jones on the drums, Beecher on guitar and Rusty Keefer on the bass.

Courtesy© DAP

his best Irish charm, Ferguson made one last bid for his job back. *"Bill, ya' know I wouldn't hurt you for nothing in the world. I just made a mistake, I got a little carried away with all this art stuff."*

Bill accepted the apology but didn't ask Lord Jim back. He could no longer afford the luxury of Jim's carelessness or conniving ways. When Bill asked Lord Jim how he got together the $50,000.00 so fast, he found out his old manager had borrowed it from the mob's loan sharks. He had pledged Bill's good name as collateral! Bill went into apoplectic shock. In his last act as manager, Lord Jim's colossal stupidly had once again jeopardized the Comets. Bill had kept an arm's length from the mob ever since the old days, when he felt they were ripping off his royalties with their juke box tricks.

Half in panic and half in anger Bill tells Lord Jim he had better have a fire sale and sell every damn painting in his gallery. . . fast, because he's not going to get one red cent from him, and when Vito Carlucci comes to collect his vigorish (interest), he had better tell Vito neither Bill Haley nor the Comets had anything to do with any of the borrowed money. The street-smart Haley knew once you let the mob in as a financial partner, they will suck you dry with their 10% to 20% interest per month!

Vince "Catfish" Broomall, Bill's fishing partner, band boy, and unofficial "son" left the band that week. The constant travel and rigors of the road made the eighteen year old boy long for a home and his new wife. He had spent his honeymoon in Bill's boyhood home next to Melody Manor.

Catfish would later say: *"I wish I had a dollar for ever turkey sandwich with mayo and black coffee I brought to Bill over those five years. That was his favorite meal."* The youth had joined the band at thirteen and had witnessed all the glory years first hand, a whirlwind and rollercoaster experience he would never forget. His place as band boy would be filled by Johnny Grande's brother, Dino.

Bill cuts back on other staff and reduces overhead as much as possible. Several cars were sold as he planned to turn around his run of bad luck. He calls Milt Gabler and sets up two new recording dates for January 7th and the 29th. Another hit record wouldn't hurt either.

Christmas that year at Melody Manor had little of the gaiety and excitement of past holidays. The grounds were lighted and the house was colorfully decorated. There was plenty to eat and even more to drink. But the generous bonuses were absent. Ralph Jones showed his traditional home movies of the Comets' European tour. This time it was like watching a newsreel instead of a travelogue. Lord Jim was there, but out-of-character, as he sat in a corner saying little and drinking much. Other associates and guests conspicuously absent were Milt Gabler, Jolly Joyce and a dozen or so newly laid off staff members and their spouses. This was the beginning of what the Comets refer to as *"The bad years".*

The Christmas of 1958 ended an era of unprecedented creative energy among the Comets. The time when a small western-swing band playing "Cowboy Jive" could capture the imagination of a nation and rock the world was over. It was a time like no other before or since. It was also an end of an era, not only for the Comets, but for Rock'n'Roll as they knew it.

The relentless media anti-rock campaigns continued without mercy. Disc-jockeys would have record breaking weeks, and smash rock records on the air. The United States State Department banned Rock 'n'Roll shows on all military bases overseas. Their rationale was that rock music gave too much good propaganda to the Russians about the decadence of the West. It also became fashionable for DJ's to attack rock'n'roll with quips like: *"Here's some music to steal hub caps by"*, and other disparaging remarks.

To borrow and paraphrase Winston Churchill, the year 1958 was not the end of Rock'n'Roll, but it was the end of the beginning. Soon this exciting, captivating form of music would be over. Within months Buddy Holly, the Big Bopper and Ritchie Valens would be killed in a fiery plane crash, their just beginning careers tragically cut short. The fiery and brilliantly talented Jerry Lee Lewis would be ostracized and exiled from rock for years for being too naive to lie about his marriage to a thirteen year old third cousin. Chuck Berry, rock's greatest poet, would be arrested and sent to prison in one of the most biased court trials ever staged. Little Richard's troubled mind and his "The Devil made me do it" philosophy would soon force him to walk away from rock music and seek salvation in his church. Even the greatest rock king of them all, Elvis Presley would mark his time in military exile. He too would never again return to the raw, earthy rockabilly that had catapulted him to international fame just three years before. Strangely, it is believed by many in the music industry that Tom Parker arranged to have Elvis "put on ice" in the Army during the frenzy of the anti-rock hate fest. And when Jerry Lee Lewis became a major contender for Elvis' temporary vacant throne, insiders felt it was the devious Parker who used his considerable influence to derail Lewis' career by feeding him to the anti-rock press. Others believed it was more J. Edgar Hoover's style to use press leaks to destroy another hated rocker.

Anti-rock forces would even destroy Alan Freed, rock's greatest impresario. While other equally guilty payola-pals charmed the Congressional committees and walked free, Freed would be cut down by the vicious anti-rock movement and offered as a sacrificial lamb to the government's discjockey payola scandal. And like another Jewish kid two thousand years before, Alan's blood would wash away the sins of the many who shared his "crimes".

Bill Haley and the above young men were the embodiment of classic Rock'n'Roll. Their passion and rebellion against the status quo of the old musical order had created a new, vibrant world of sound. They had the genius to gold-plate pure trash and the audacity to trash pure gold. Never in the history of music had so much blind hate and malice been hurled at its performers. Bill Haley's dreams of a musical empire slowly crumbled to despair, as he tried to find his way in the fast changing quicksands of the treacherous politics which were the music scene of the late fifties.

Bill Haley under extreme pressure, Fall 1959. Courtesy® DAP

At thirty-three, he was too old to be a "teen idol", too controversial to be welcomed into adult popular music, and too proud to quit while he was down. Over the next few years, Bill Haley and his Comets played to smaller and smaller audiences, for less and less money. It seemed the public had forgotten or was no longer interested in the raw power and excitement of real rock'n'roll.

The Age of the Teen Idols ruled the air waves. Teen music was now dominated by the "beautiful people" and they never sang anything offensive. An era of general musical mediocrity and blandness descended on the world. The new popular music would be devoid of the cry of the fiery rock singers and the wild, hypnotic rhythms of blatant sexuality. Gone too was the almost savage, pulsating beat of the Haley's have-a-good-time music that the mid fifties was all about. The coming years, 1959 to 1963 became classic Rock's first "Dark Age".

Passport problems on board the Queen Elizabeth. Lord Jim looks on as government agents inquire about Bill's missing passport.

Courtesy® Haley Family Collection

CHAPTER ELEVEN

EPILOGUE: 1959-1981

"Yesteryear's nostalgia—today's classics."

Over the next two years, Bill Haley fought a valiant battle to preserve his style of music and keep his companies solvent. However, the changing taste in American popular music and Rock'n'Roll in general was the main culprit for the serious decline in the Comets' American income. Their still popular overseas tours and record sales became their chief source of revenue.

On top of these problems, and his other strained financial commitments, Bill finds out Ferguson's $50,000.00 loan from the mob is also his responsibility. Lord Jim had not been able to sell the works of art as quickly or as profitably as he had planned. Bill was forced to pay off his ex-manager's loan and non-tax-deductible "interest payments", which were sometimes as high as $5,000.00 a month! This was the one payment which took priority over all others. The "late charge" could be very painful. Month after month, this steady drain on Bill's dwindling income caused the slow or non-payment of other essential bills. The large cash outlays without receipts also created a bookkeeping nightmare.

When the Internal Revenue Service, acting on an F.B.I. suggestion, questioned the Comets' "business deductions" in their 1958 tax return, a new pressure was added to the already cash-poor treasury. After three separate attempts to audit the Comets' books and their unfortunate and mysterious disappearance, the Comets were in deep trouble. The failed I.R.S audit created a crisis. The frustrated and angry revenue agents disallowed all deductions and taxed the Comets' entire 1958 gross income. To collect the estimated $140,000.00 owed, the I.R.S. attached Bill's real estate holdings plus his record and publishing royalties in the late summer of 1959. Desperate for funds and cut off from his present and future record royalties, Bill countered the freeze on his income by signing a recording contract with Warner Brothers where he received a badly needed advance of $50,000.00 in September 1959. Warner was not aware of Bill's tax problems.

Bill's dreams for Valley Brook and Seabreeze to become profitable enterprises died slowly. Pressed for badly needed funds, he leased six of his Clymax tracks to Coral Records: Rusty Keefer's song *Aintcha* and *Rock-A-Way*, the Matys Brothers' *Remember* and *Crazy Street* and Lou Graham's *You Were Mean, Baby* and *Wee Willie Brown*. Later he leased Valley Brook's tracks of *Wedding Bouquet* and *Wee Willie Water Dilly* by the three Keefer Sisters to the Lawn label. The Keefer Sisters were the three oldest daughters of Rusty Keefer, Bill's long-time friend and most gifted staff-writer. Rusty also played along with the Comets on most the above recordings. These and many other valuable studio tracks, the results of countless hours of rehearsals, were now being sold off wholesale to other record labels. Bill's publishing firms were now just holding companies for about a hundred and ninety songs belonging mostly to the Comets. By 1960 Bill had suspended all publishing and recording for his companies.

The birth of Scott Robert, his fourth son in January of 1960, was one of the few joys Bill would receive that year. Twenty years later, Bill Haley's love of sports, which he had not been able to participate in, manifested itself within this son. Scott became an outstanding football player for Temple University, a source of great pride to his father.

Pressed for funds, Bill takes the Comets on tour to India, South Africa, Canada and again back to South America. The long overseas tours created added difficulties for the Comets on the home front. Bill and several other band members received ultimatums from their angry and frustrated wives to quit and come home or else! Many of the wives realized the Comets' days of glory were over. However, Bill Haley believed strongly Rock'n'Roll was only in a lull in America and if he could hold on until its popularity returned, he might still be able to continue his dream. The foreign tours still provided the bulk of the revenues for the band and their record sales, out of the reach of the I.R.S., were still strong in Europe, Asia, Australia and South America.

Still trying to placate the I.R.S. Bill asks Ruth Sipps, a Booth's Corner bookkeeper he has known since boyhood, if she would "fix" a set of books for him. He gives her all the receipts, invoices and

Bill Haley and his Comets (Y Sus Cometas) playing behind a high-stepping troupe of chorus girls in a Mexico City night club, 1961.

Courtesy© DAP

other documents he can find. Several days later she returns everything and tells him: *"Bill, you better get out of the country, cause they're gonna put you in jail!"*

Unfortunately, the final blow came in 1960 when Bill's wife Cuppy filed for divorce. Gone were the servants, the always available spending money and the glamour of being Mrs. Bill Haley. Now only the loneliness of Melody Manor, the mounting bills and the deep resentment due to Bill's frequent absences kept her company. Unaware of the full extent of Bill's financial problems, her lawyers claimed Melody Manor and sizeable child-support and alimony payments. Faced with broken fidelity and a painful legal battle from within, Bill's spirit was broken. Now cut off from his family, his home and all his American income, Bill Haley became a homeless exile in the land of his birth. He shuffled about in cheap motel rooms till finally too broke to afford even them. His last refuge was a blanket on Rudy Pompilli's couch in the front room of Rudy's Parkside home.

Hunted by lawyers, creditors, the I.R.S. and the mob, Bill ran out of solutions. Angered, bewildered and exhausted mentally, physically and financially, Bill Haley sought the sanctuary of Mexico. True to his boyhood day-dreams, like the cowboys of old, he headed south across the border to escape the tribulations of his failed dreams. Behind him lay seventeen years of remarkable accomplishments—in ruins.

To make ends meet, Bill and his Comets played "for living money" in the opulent nightclubs of Mexico City, where their celebrity status was still appreciated. The outlaw-renegade band would often dart over the U.S. border for a quick tour in the States and then back again before the ever-watching I.R.S. could step in and confiscate their performance fees. Bill's cat and mouse game with the revenuers would last for almost a decade. More than once his entire box office receipts were confiscated when local F.B.I. or I.R.S. agents discovered he was playing in their region. Bill's name had been added to the international list of tax fugitives

During the early sixties, Bill and his Comets recorded over a dozen records for Warner Brothers, Gone, Roulette, Newtown and Orfeon. The always diligent I.R.S. also confiscated most of these royalties, except for Orfeon.

Orfeon was a major Mexican recording firm which seemed to appreciate Bill's brand of classic rock and his new sound. In the United States, a new dance craze called the Twist had captured the imagination of the nation's youth. Down in his newly adopted Mexico, Bill Haley slightly adapts his basic Rock'n'Roll sound and became the Spanish "King of the Twist". Over the next five years Bill would record more than thirty Twist and seventy other songs for Orfeon. These records would establish Bill Haley as one of the most popular recording stars in Central and South America. Through Orfeon's extensive Latin American distribution, Bill once again was selling millions of records and enjoyed a new popularity. He began to rebuild his fortune and a new career as his records once again topped the Mexican and South American charts.

The Comets at the Star Club, Hamburg, Germany, 1962.

Much of the success of Bill's new rise to fame must rest on the friendship and loyalty of one man, Rudy Pompilli. Rudy set aside a promising career as a first rate jazz musician and almost single-handedly kept together a group of excellent rock musicians. When Bill called with another tour or recording session, it was Rudy who gathered together the Comets and met Bill with a complete band at the performance site; be it London, Berlin, Las Vegas or Bombay. It was Rudy who rehearsed the band during its many changes. It was Rudy who answered their questions and paid off the bills at tour's end. During these difficult years, over seventy talented musicians played with Bill Haley under the banner of the Comets. Many for a short time, just to be able to say with great pride: *"I played with Bill Haley and the Comets"*. Some Comets, like Al Rappa, Johnny Kay, Nick Masters, Dave Holly, John "Bam Bam" Lane, Joey Welz, Ed Ward, Jim Lebak, Bill Nolte, and Bill Turner, became favorites with Bill Haley's ever-loyal fans. Their talents and contributions to Bill's second career and the rebirth

One of the last photos of the Comets with Bill's two partners as part of the band. Left to right: Ed Ward, drummer, Rudy, Al Rappa, Franny Beecher, Bill Haley, Billy Williamson, Johnny Kay, guitarist, and John Grande, Mexico.

of classic Rock'n'Roll are incalculable.

While on tour in November of 1962, Bill and his Comets share the billing with the Beatles at the Star Club in Hamburg, Germany. Bill comments to Rudy after hearing the Beatles do some of Chuck Berry's work: *"Those English boys have got a real neat sound. They have a smoothness in their style of rock-'n'roll I've never heard before."*

With his rising star status, Bill makes peace with the Philadelphia mob for the unpaid balance on his debt and agrees to play three weeks a year in Las Vegas. The "Showboat", the "International", and the "El Cortez" became his Nevada club spots for the next decade. Sixty percent of his take went to pay off Lord Jim's debt. Curiously, his relationship with the mob's key bag man turns into a close friendship. The two men enjoy vacations and many fishing trips together. When Bill ran into "special problems", his unique friendship with Vito Carlucci came in very handy.

The long spells in Mexico and their other world tours were hard on the families of the Comets. One by one Bill's faithful musicians began to leave the band. Ralph Jones in the summer of 1960 followed by Franny Beecher in 1962. John Grande, Bill's Partner of twelve years signed over his one-third interest in the Comets and left the band in October of 1962. Billy Williamson followed a few months later. By mid 1963, only Rudy Pompilli was left of the old globe-trotting Comets.

To many Americans unfamiliar with the international rock scene, this was the end of Bill Haley and his music on the American charts. Classic Rock-'n'Roll was asleep and John F. Kennedy was the new President of the United States.

By 1964, the Beatles would bring a "musical renaissance" to America and the world. The mid-1960's would witness a rebirth and a new appreciation for the dimemsions of rock music on a grand scale. The new sounds became more technical and more electronically engineered than anything ever imagined by its earlier practitoners. The unique sounds of the Rolling Stones, the Yardbirds, the Who, the Hollies, the Animals, the Beach Boys, and Manfred Mann would create new gods in the Parthenon of Rock.

Bill Haley's sound became the mother of a host of musics, whose fast changing hybrids fed off one another like a barrel of cannibalistic snakes. Rock enthusiasts were as unpredictable as the music they listened to. Rock became the sound most listened to by the young soldiers fighting in the steaming

Wednesday, June 10, 1964

VARIETY

BERLINERS STILL DIG HALEY'S ROCK 'N' ROLL

Berlin, June 9.

Rock 'n' roll isn't dead—at least not in Berlin. This was evidenced last weekend when Bill Haley & the Comets plus Little Richard gave two "concerts" at the Waldbuehne, the local amphitheatre. Haley drew about 16,000 juveniles Saturday (30) and around 14,000 Sunday (31). That's six times as many as British teenage idol Cliff Richard got here three weeks ago. Richard, who gave his concert at Deutschlandhalle, mobilized only 5,000.

Odd thing about the substantial difference in attendance is that Richard songs have often appeared in local disk seller charts these past months while either Haley nor Little Richard has had a best-seller for a long time here.

Hundreds of police were at the Haley concert to calm down "rioters." (When Haley appeared at Sportpalast back in 1958, there were riots which led to heavy damage and many arrested youngsters.) This time there were only "harmless incidents."

hell of Viet Nam...and by millions of their peers, marching for "Peace" across America.

Rock sub-divided its rhythm and energies time again, always bewildering its detractors with the paradox of its simplicity and its complexity. Rock became psychedelic rock, blues rock, progressive rock, folk rock, punk rock, country rock, acid rock, jazz rock, disco rock, new wave rock and a dozen other genuine and dubious handles. Within a single decade, Rock music grew into a multibillion dollar, world wide industry. In the 1960's, Rock music became the sound on which an awesome new drug culture soared its victims'minds beyond infinity-while jamming their bluejeaned knees into the urine-soaked mud of a hundred Woodstocks. Like the proverbial junk-yard dog, every time the establishment thought it has tamed or "mainstreamed" Rock's irreverent sounds, it turned and bit it's handlers in their proverbial ass. It seemed Rock's detractors had happily celebrated its funeral a bit too soon. Bill Haley's hybrid sound would have the last laugh, as Rock's defiant epitaph became: "NEVER SAY DIE".

Down in Vera Cruz, Mexico, a rested Bill Haley was planning his next major European tour. The warmth and slower pace of southern Mexico had now become his permanent home. He had also fallen in love and married a beautiful and talented young Mexican woman named Martha Velasco. Bill loved to hear her sing and being an entertainer herself, she was probably the best equipped of all his wives to understand the rigors of stardom. She was also the first of his wives to accompany him on most of his tours. This moral support was greatly appreciated by Bill.

While the Beatles dominated the American charts in 1964, Bill Haley and his Comets were filling stadiums and playing to huge audiences of 30,000 classic Rock'n'Roll fans in Germany. In his English tour that year, he shared the bill with Manfred Mann, then one of the top rock bands in Great Britain. Bill's classic style of Rock'n'Roll stole the show and Manfred Mann's band was heckled when they tried to follow the Comets' set. Later he would do the same to the Spencer Davis Group, the Walker Brothers and other popular bands. In fact, blowing away top rock bands became almost a tradition for the Comets over the next fifteen years. Few bands in the world could compete with the hypnotic rhythms and classic genius of Bill Haley and his Comets' rendition of *Rock Around the Clock* or *Shake, Rattle and Roll.*

The British press was the first to call Bill Haley the "Father of Rock'n'Roll". He spearheaded in the sixties the first Rock'n'roll revivals, first in Europe and then in the United States. He began to fill theaters and arenas around the world with new generations of classic rock enthusiasts and was hailed as the "Dean of Rock" by millions of his older fans.

Bill's three month summer tour of Europe in 1968 saw the Comets perform in Holland, Ireland, Austria, West Germany, Denmark, Sweden and Great Britain. By fall, Bill's songs were again on the British and European charts and *Rock Around the Clock* returned to the top 20 on England's charts. Crowds once again cheered him at his arrivals and departures. In Stockholm, an armored truck is required to get him to the stage at an open air show.

On May 1, 1968, Bill Haley plays to 7,000 at the Royal Albert Hall. The enthusiasm is so great that eight beats before the end of his closing song, *Rock Around the Clock* Bill had to run off the stage to avoid an over-excited mob which overran the stage. Beatles John Lennon and Paul McCartney were among the audience that night, and later when interviewed on British radio, said: *"fantastic...a great show from the father of Pop music"*. Bill's one man crusade for the 50's Rock'n'Roll sound created a new wave of European nostalgia which soon caught on around the world.

Bill receives a tribute from the Wild Angels Rock'n'Roll Appreciation Society. London, April 28, 1968.

Courtesy© R. Lefavi

Rudy Pompilli, Bill Haley and his wife Martha on tour in Rome, 1965.

rtesy© Haley Family Collection

On June 20, 1968, Bill signs an exclusive recording contract with the Swedish Sonet label. Under the direction of Sam Charters and other Sonet producers, Bill records dozens of new and classic Rock'n'Roll and country-western songs. These tunes are released on a series of albums and singles around the world over the next two decades.

On October 18th, 1969, Richard Nader produced the first major American "Rock'n'Roll Revival" at Madison Square Garden's Felt Forum in New York City. He had seen Bill's show in Europe, and asked Bill Haley and his Comets to be his headliner. Bill, who had not been in New York for eight years, was anxious about what kind of reception he would get in the Big Apple. Still fearful of the bad memories and ghosts of the nearby Chester area, Bill almost declined the offer.

To his credit, Bill Haley walked on the stage that night and brought the house down. The response was electric as he played his classics. The New Yorkers clapped and stomped to the power and rhythm of Bill's original rock'n'roll, just like their counterparts in London, Paris and Berlin. When it was over, the audience of first and second generation rockers gave Bill Haley an eight and a half minute standing ovation. Tears streamed down Bill's cheeks as he took his bows. He was to later say in an interview: *"That ovation was one of the greatest moments in my life. I'll never forget it. New York, I love you!"*

The New York Times printed: *"(Bill Haley and his Comets) played with great energy and talent, making a relatively simple, shuffling style sound as exciting as almost anything heard lately."* Bill was also quoted saying: *"When I'm seventy-five, if I can still hold a guitar, I'll still play rock'n'roll."*

Over the next decade a wiser Bill Haley invested his growing wealth in Mexican real estate, fisheries, a hotel, and three large ranches.

In 1969, tired of not being able to live and legally work in his native land, Bill asked the I.R.S. if he could make a settlement of his back taxes. In June of 1971, after two years of effort by Rudy Pompilli and tax specialist Andrew Hoesch, he settles his long-standing account with the government tax collectors. Ironically he finds out that his ten year exile was unnecessary. His Decca and other recording royalties and the proceeds from the forced sale of Melody Manor and his three-story office building in Chester had more than paid off his tax debt years ago! His world-wide record sales had passed an incredible 75,000,000 mark, and it was the U.S. Government that owed HIM a huge refund! With a renewed sense of self-esteem, Bill planned a major comeback with his brand of Rock'n'Roll.

In 1972, he rocked London's massive Wembley Stadium before tens of thousands of rock fans. Wherever Bill and his Comets played, they established a new sense of wonder and awe for his style of music. Stuart Colman, one of Great Britain's foremost rock critics and historians, wrote of the Wembley concert: *"Bill Haley and his Comets made another triumphant return to London in 1972 for the biggest ever rock'n'roll festival held in England. Even in the face of what could be described as the ultimate competition, it was a walkover for Bill and the Comets. In a show of total professionalism, they roared through a set of classics with the slickest presentation of the day. Judging by the reception he received, it was yet another reminder for the music*

The Comets, 1969: Rudy Pompilli, John "Bam Bam" Lane, Bill Haley, Nick Masters and Al Rappa.

Courtesy© R. Lefavi

industry that the traditional Haley sound was as durable as ever."

The tired, worn-out critique that the many returns to popularity of Bill Haley's sound was just a "nostalgia" kick were put to rest forever. Haley's rock had joined Strauss' waltzes and Mozart's concertos as classics to rock fans the world over.

It had been widely known within the music community that Bill had developed a serious drinking problem after the collapse of his marriage and career in 1960. Bill fought a constant battle with the bottle until the early 1970's. A loving and understanding wife, a religious conversion and the return of respect, without the media ridicule of his earlier career, helped greatly in his temporary victory over alcohol.

Bill continued making albums and doing an occasional tour if it were lucrative enough. But in the early 1970's he mostly loved to ride about his ranch in Vera Cruz, fish the crystal clear waters of the Gulf and watch his three children, Martha, Pedro, and Georgina grow. Mexico had been good to him, and when everything else had fallen apart, it was down here he found the peace and sanctuary he so desperately wanted.

The mid-seventies brought back *Rock Around The Clock* to the top 40 in the United States. Fueled by the popular television series "Happy Days" and the Oscar winning movie "American Graffiti", Bill's classic Rock'n'Roll roars back in appreciation.

His 1974 British tour is climaxed by a standing-room only crowd at London's huge Hammersmith Palais. In Britain's heated political battles of that year, a major newspaper printed across their front page the photographs of the three party leaders of Great Britain: Jeremy Thrope, the Liberal; Harold Wilson, the Socialist; and Edward Heath, the Conservative. Below their photos were their doctrines for curing the country's serious ills. Above their pictures was the headline in large bold type: *"WHAT THIS COUNTRY NEEDS IS...BILL HALEY AND THE COMETS!"* Bill treasured this tongue-in-cheek editorial and had it framed for the benefit of future critics.

With a new life before him, Bill also buys a beautiful home just across the border in Harlingen, Texas. Here with his large swimming pool, his beloved fishing boat and a three car garage filled with two Lincoln Continentals and a Trans-Am, he finds some of the happiness and privacy he had

In concert at the Hammersmith Palais, London, 1974. Bill had just returned from a tour of New Zealand and Australia. Courtesy© R. Lefavi

sought for so many years. However, once again, the serenity wouldn't last.

The death of Rudy Pompilli in February of 1976 sent Bill Haley into a long period of mourning. His legendary sax player, who had fought with General Patton during the Second World War and had played at his funeral, had lost his own battle with cancer. He had been a Comet for 21 years, longer and more faithful than any other. His talents, his warm humor and his courage would be remembered by all the people who knew him. When word got out around Chester of Rudy's condition, his new Scottish wife Ann was to see first-hand the high regard many people had for her husband. So respected was this musician that at his last performances at the Nite Cap tavern near Chester, even the nuns came to hear him play. To ease the strain on his weakened body Rudy was provided with a stool and an electric pick-up for his sax. A cot was set up backstage for him to rest between sets. Night after night, his many friends turned out to support him. Shortly before his death he was honored by the Chester Musicians Union as "Man of the Year" in a moving tribute that will never be forgotten by those who were in attendance.

One of Rudy's last requests reflects his warm sense of humor and irony: *"Will you guys please see that they spell my name right in the papers: POMPILII. Its got one L and two i's on the end. You've been misspelling it for twenty years!"* When Rudy was asked why it took twenty years for him to say something he quipped: *"Bill said my name looked better with the two l's. The other way looked like the printer had misspelled it! Bill never wanted*

Courtesy© DAP

Keyboardist Joey Welz, far left, takes John Grande's place on German tour in late 1962. Other Comets: Johnny Kay, Al Rappa, Rudy Pompilli and John Lane.

Bill Haley with his lead guitarist Bill Turner in concert at the Sportshalle, Linz, Austria, Nov. 7, 1976.

Courtesy: B. Turner

Rudy Pompilli, the heart of the Comets.

Courtesy© Haley Family Collection

Queen Elizabeth compliments Bill Haley "It was great to hear that music again..." Theater Royal, London, Nov. 26th 1979.

to look unprofessional!" To fans around the world, Rudy's brilliant instrumental masterpiece *Rudy's Rock* would forever be one of his memorials.

The death of Rudy was soon followed by that of Bill's only other life long friend, Jack Howard. From Philadelphia, Howard had secretly continued to run Bill's publishing companies for all these years. To protect much of Bill's publishing royalties from being seized by the I.R.S., Howard transferred many of the tunes from Valley Brook (A.S.C.A.P), and Seabreeze (B.M.I.) catalogs to Jack Howard Publications (B.M.I.) and Arcade Music (A.S.C.A.P.) of which 75% was owned by Bill as a silent partner. Faithfully, he mailed to Bill, down in Mexico, his royalty checks from B.M.I., A.S.C.A.P and dozens of other international music publishing companies who continued to record hundreds of Bill's songs. To carry on the running of his American based firms, Bill appoints Rosario Lefavi. Lefavi, a close Howard associate and Philadelphia publisher, owned the Rex Zario Music Company and the Arzee record label. He also had taken over Jack Howard's two publishing companies and record label.

In 1979, Bill came out of a self-imposed retirement to tour Great Britain for the last time. On November 26th, the tour was climaxed by a Royal Command Performance at London's prestigious Theater Royal. This long standing dream of Bill's became one of the most appreciated and bittersweet events of his thirty-six year career. Back stage after the concert, Queen Elizabeth shook Bill's hand and said with obvious admiration: *"It was great to hear that music again. I grew up on it and it reminds me of when I was young. It takes one back a bit and I enjoyed it".* To which Bill replied: *"It reminds me of when I was young too, Ma'am!"*

After this supreme compliment to his music, Bill Haley starts to write his biography. The story would read like an unbelievable rags to riches saga, on an international scale. It would tell, in his own words, his incredible and most unlikely journey from a poor, terribly shy country boy, to the birth of Rock-'n'Roll, and on to wealth, glory and international acclaim. He would now tell the world how much he loved country-western and rhythm and blues music. He would list the 158 songs he wrote or co-wrote,

Courtesy© R. Lefavi

Bill Haley appoints Rosario Lefavi (above) to run his Valleybrook, Seabreeze and Arcade publishing companies.

Bill Haley and the "Last Comets". Fame Studios, Muscle Shoals, Alabama, 1979. Photo by Kenny Denton.

Courtesy K. Denton

Kenny Denton in studio 1979.

and print an incredible discography, listing his 500+ records. Last, he would list the names of his musicians, who shared his victories and his pain. Yes, it would be quite a story, from the sweaty, smoke-filled beer-joints like Luke's Musical Bar to the grand concert halls of Europe.

In the Spring of 1979, rumors of Bill's deteriorating health spread through the music industry. Rod Buckle, the flamboyant, creative genius at Sonet's London studios, asks his Swedish boss Dag Haeggqvist for permission to do one more Haley album. He assigns one of Sonet's youngest and most talented producers, Kenny Denton, to oversee the project. In preparation, the twenty-seven year old Denton spread the word among Britain's best song writers that he wanted some new material for the album. The young man is very excited about the opportunity to work with the already legendary Bill Haley. Raised in the tough East End of London, Denton represented all the energy and magic of Britain's late-seventies rock scene. With ten years of recording experience behind him, he set out to create a Haley masterpiece. Ironically, Denton had been working with Bill Haley's old mentor, Dave Miller for years. Rock history had now turned full circle. Miller gave Denton some hard won advice, *"Don't let Bill's managers screw up your sessions... let Bill do what he does best and let him do it his way."*

On March 26th, after a bitter battle with Bill's manipulating managers, Denton assembled seven veteran rock musicians; Steve Murray, Jim Lebak, Gerry Tilley, Pete Spencer, Ray Parsons, Geoff Driscol and Pete Wingfield at Music Center, Wembley, and recorded four tracks. The following day Geoff Daily rerecorded the sax work on *Hail, Hail, Rock-'n'Roll.* The other tracks recorded this session were *I Need The Music*, *The King of Rock'n'Roll* and *God Bless Rock'n'Roll.* After listening to the playbacks of *The King Of Rock'n'Roll* Bill tells Denton he did not want this song on the album. The song is great but in deference to newly departed Elvis, Bill feels it is innapropriate. The recording session is broken off and resumes on June 28th at the Fame Studios in Muscle Shoals, Alabama.

Kenny Denton completes the last nine tracks with a completely new band of young, southern-country rockers. These "Mississippi Young'uns" as Bill called them, were a new breed of musicians. Their enthusiasm and energy greatly impressed the old master and unknowingly, they became Bill's "Last Comets". Their names were recorded for posterity on the album: Ed Logan, Owen Hale, Chalmers Davis, Jimmy English, Walt Aldridge, David Baroni and Wanda Hale.

Denton's twelve tracks recorded in London and Muscle Shoals would be Bill Haley's last work. Titled "Everyone Can Rock'n'Roll" this Sonet LP would be Bill's final gift to the world of music he loved so much. One song on this albun, *God Bless Rock-'n'Roll* written by Ronnie Harwood especially for Bill, would become Haley's favorite. Bill would say it captured his story as in no other song he had ever known.

GOD BLESS ROCK'N'ROLL
(First Verse)

Lookin' thru' my window
My memory serves me well
I go back to the places
And all those happy faces
Under your spell

I remember my first guitar
That made me a Rock'n'Roll star
I traveled the whole world over
With fame and fortune in my hands

I want to thank you Rock'n'Roll
From the body, from the soul
God bless Rock'n'Roll
Thank you Rock'n'Roll
God bless Rock'n'Roll

This session also marks the end of Bill's last months of total reality. For the next ninteen months, he would live in a world of tormented confusion and severe personality changes. He was often hospitalized for bizarre behavior and horrible, debilitating headaches. At times friends and family become almost strangers to him as he failed to recognize even long time associates. His periods of insanity mysteriously came and went. In 1980, while on a tour of South Africa, he confided to a trusted friend he had a brain tumor. He said he had been to the best doctors there were and nothing could be done. He also said he was told by a specialist in Los Angeles that the tumor was inoperable.

Publicly, Bill denied the rumors of his fatal illness and became very angry when his European manager leaked them to the German press. The talkative manager quickly received the dubious honor of being the last of a long series of frustrated associates to be fired by Bill.

In his last terrible months, Bill would call friends and family with long rambling conversations in the middle of the night. To one friend he said: *"I'm only fifty-five, ...and that's too young to die! I don't want to go like Rudy, I don't want to just waste away!"*

In the early morning hours of February 9th, 1981, Bill Haley called two of his sons, Scott and Jack, and had his last known conversations. He died in his sleep of an apparent heart attack about 6:30 that morning, at his home in Harlingen, Texas.

God had answered Bill Haley's last request. Death had been quick and merciful. He had not wasted away like Rudy, or his father, mother and sister. Unfinished beside him were the neatly typed pages of his manuscript. He had written only the first six chapters. The story of his triumphs and his failures, the revelations of the brave new worlds his music had opened and his darkest fears were unalterably mixed with myth and fiction. No longer could even Bill Haley tell the difference.

True pioneers seldom receive the mantle of "greatest". Even fewer are fortunate enough to see their discoveries appreciated. William John Clifton Haley was one of these rare individuals. The excitement generated by his music had the awesome power to rock the world and the ability to send chills of fear to an up-tight status-quo.

Born of slaves and sharecroppers—of hillbillies and cowhands, rock'n'roll had come of age. No longer confined to the ghettos or the mountains; no longer just another American pop music, rock now belonged to the world. Bill Haley's sound had opened the door.

With all his shortcomings and human phobias, he was always larger than life to his fans. He was simply unique in the world of music. In Stuart Colman's book "They Kept On Rockin'" he writes: *"Leaders in the music world are always predestined, and Bill had every right to be a star. His mere presence in a room commanded respect and that old but accurate description of someone having charisma was never more appropriate than when ascribed to this most amiable man of pop music.*

"Whatever any pretentions or criticisms of the Haley's style of music, the fact remains that the slick three chord pop songs at which he so excelled, have always been the hardest to write successfully.

"Rest assured, any future songwriter would give his eye teeth to unlock the secret of some of the all-

Courtesy© DAP

Bill Haley 1925-1981.

A rare German poster from "The Tour That Never Was". Bill Haley lay in a Texas hospital, too ill to perform. He died three months later.

Courtesy© DAP

time greats created by Bill Haley and his Comets."

On his death certificate, in a space marked: "occupation," someone wrote in "singer" I guess there wasn't room to put in: composer, band leader, musician, discjockey, rancher, fisherman, laborer, truck driver, lyricist, producer, movie actor, writer, factory worker, janitor and international corporate executive. Some are born to make us think, or laugh, or to cry. Others to lead us and give us new goals and greater horizons. Bill Haley was destined to make us dance and sing a clap. He was driven by a force greater than himself. A force which he himself never understood completely but always found within.

Bill paid his dues with over 10,000 live performances played before more people than any other artist of his time. He fought the hatred of racism long before it became popular. He bore the criticism of ignorance with great dignity. He withstood the fear and pain of failure like the professional he always strove to be.

The next time you are privileged to hear Bill Haley's 1952 version of *Rock the Joint*, or his 1954 classic *Rock Around the Clock*, or his haunting 1979 rendition of *God Bless Rock'n'Roll*, remember the shy, half-blind country boy from Booth's Corner, who, with little more than an old, cracked guitar and a lot of grit, challenged the world's concepts of popular music and somewhere along the way became the "Father of Rock'n'Roll".

Courtesy D. Hirschberg

The Comets in performance at the 20th International Rock'n'Roll festival in Burnham, England, Nov. 4, 1989. Left to right: Joey Ambrose, Frank Beecher and Marshall Lytle.

BILL HALEY'S DISCOGRAPHY 1946 to 1989

This listing contains most of the known recordings of Bill Haley and his bands for a period of forty-four years. We have also listed recordings in which Bill used his band to accompany other artists and are so noted. To date, collectors and music historians have identified over 650 records associated with Bill Haley and his musicians of which over 350 are LP albums or extended play records. The remarkable number of reissues of Bill Haley's music on more than 130 labels world-wide attests to the timeless quality of his sound.

With the improved technology of the compact disc and the growing popularity of classic rock, we believe this discography will continue to grow as a tribute to the "Father of Rock'n'Roll".

Label	**Number**	**Title**

**The recordings of Bill Haley with the Downhomers: 1946/1947*

Vogue	R736	Who's Gonna Kiss You When I'm Gone/ Out Where The West Winds Blow
"	R786	Boogie Woogie Yodel Song/Baby I Found Out All About You (Bill Haley plays bass or rhythm guitar)

-1948-

**The recordings of Bill Haley and the Four Aces of Western Swing 1948-1949*

Cowboy	CR12O1	Four Leaf Clover Blues/Too Many Parties Too Many Pals
"	CR12O2	Candy Kisses/Tennessee Border
"	CR12O3?	The Covered Wagon Rolled Right Along/Yodel Your Blues Away (not released)
"	CR12O4?	Behind The Eight Ball/Foolish Questions (not released)

-1949-

Center	102	Stand Up And Be Counted/Loveless Blues (Bill Haley is listed as "Johnny Clifton and His String Band")

-1950-

**The recordings of Bill Haley and His Saddlemen: 1950-1952*

Keystone	5101	Deal Me A Hand/Ten Gallon Stetson
"	5102	Susan Van Dusan/I'm Not To Blame
Atlantic	727	Why Do I Cry Over You/I'm Gonna Dry Every Tear With A Kiss (Recorded but not released) Loveless Blues/Teardrops From My Eyes
Cowboy	CR17O1	My Sweet Little Girl From Nevada/My Palomino And I (On this record Bill Haley sings the vocals backed by "Reno Browne and Her Buckaroos". This group is the early Saddlemen.)

-1951-

Holiday	105	Rocket '88/Tearstains On My Heart
"	108	Green Tree Boogie/Down Deep In My Heart
"	111	A Year Ago This Christmas/I Don't Want To Be Alone This Christmas
"	113	Jukebox Cannonball/Sundown Boogie
"	110	Pretty Baby/I'm Crying (On this record Bill sings in duet with Loretta Glendenning, Saddlemen accompany.)
Abbey	?	Rose Of My Heart/Barnyard Special (The Saddlemen back Curly Herdman.)

Gotham	G416	Two Timin' Blues/Lone Gone Daddy (Lou Graham and the Saddlemen)
"	G429	I'm Lonesome/A Sweet Bunch Of Roses (Lou Graham and the Saddlemen)
"	G433	Please Make Up Your Fickle Mind/My Heart Tells Me (Lou Graham and the Saddlemen)

**All the above records are in 78 rpm only.*

-1952-

Essex	303	Icy Heart/Rock The Joint
"	305	Rocking Chair On The Moon/Dance With A Dolly

**The records of Bill Haley and His Comets:*

Essex	310	Stop Beatin' Round The Mulberry Bush/Real Rock Drive (Bill Haley with Haley's Comets)

-1953-

Essex	321	Crazy Man, Crazy/Watcha Gonna Do
"	327	Pat-A-Cake/Fractured
"	332	Live It Up/Farewell, So Long, Goodbye
"	340	I'll Be True/Ten Little Indians
"	348	Straight Jacket/Chattanooga Choo-Choo
Essex	?	Muskrat Ramble/You're The Moment of a Lifetime (The Matys Brothers backed by the Comets)

-1954-

Decca	29124	Thirteen Women/Rock Around The Clock
"	29204	Shake, Rattle and Roll/A.B.C. Boogie
"	29317	Dim, Dim The Lights/Happy Baby

**Brunswick is Decca's European label.*

Brunswick*	05317	Thirteen Women/Rock Around The Clock
"	05338	Shake, Rattle And Roll/A.B.C. Boogie
Transworld	718	Yes Indeed/Real Rock Drive
Essex	374	Sundown Boogie/Jukebox Cannonball
"	381	Rocket "88"/Green Tree Boogie
"	399	Rock The Joint/Farewell, So Long, Goodbye
Essex EP	102	Bill Haley's Dance Party: Rock The Joint/Crazy Man, Crazy/Pat-A-Cake/Rockin' Chair On The Moon
" EP	117	Rock With Bill Haley And The Comets: Farewell, So Long, Goodbye/Live It Up/ Real Rock Drive/Fractured
" EP	118	Rock With Bill Haley and The Comets: Stop Beatin' Round The Mulberry Bush/ I'll Be True/Jukebox Cannonball/Whatcha Gonna Do?
" EP	119	Rock With Bill Haley And The Comets: Chattanooga Choo Choo/Green Tree Boogie/Dance With A Dolly/Rocket "88"
Essex LP	202	"Rock With Bill Haley And The Comets": 12 Essex songs
Somerset	P4600	LP 12 songs, same as above
"	P1300	LP "Rock'n'Roll Dance Party" Crazy Man, Crazy/Farewell, So Long, Goodbye/ Watcha Gonna Do plus 11 v.a.

-1955-

Decca	29418	Mambo Rock/Birth of the Boogie
"	29552	Razzle-Dazzle/Two Hound Dogs
"	29713	Rock-A-Beatin' Boogie/Burn That Candle
"	29791	See You Later, Alligator/Paper Boy
Decca LP*	5560	"Shake, Rattle and Roll" 10" disc with eight songs: Rock Around The Clock/ Dim, Dim the Lights/Thirteen Women/Mambo Rock/Birth of the Boogie/Shake, Rattle and Roll/ABC Boogie/Happy Baby **Bill Haley's first Decca album*

**Ten British Releases:*

London	HFL8142	Green Tree Boogie/Sundown Boogie
"	HFL8161	I'll Be True/Farewell, So Long, Goodbye
"	HFL8194	Rockin' Chair On The Moon/Ten Little Indians
Brunswick	05373	Dim, Dim The Lights/Happy Baby
"	05405	Mambo Rock/Birth Of The Boogie
"	05453	Razzle-Dazzle/Two Hound Dogs
"	05509	Burn That Candle/Rock-A-Beatin' Boogie
" EP	0E9129	"Dim, Dim The Lights" with 4 songs
London EP	REF1031	"Rock And Roll" with 4 songs
" LP	HAPB1042	"Live It Up" 10" with 8 Essex songs

**Four German Releases:*

Decca	D17676	Crazy Man, Crazy/Whatcha Gonna Do? (MF38129)
Brunswick	12031	Rock Around The Clock/ABC Boogie (82827)
"	12041	Shake, Rattle And Roll/Dim, Dim The Lights (82844)
"	12045	Mambo Rock/Happy Baby (82851)

-1956-

Decca	29870	The Saints Rock'n'Roll/R-O-C-K
"	29948	Hot Dog Buddy Buddy/Rockin' Through The Rye
"	30028	Rip It Up/Teenager's Mother
"	30085	Rudy's Rock/Blue Comet Blues
"	30148	Don't Knock The Rock/Choo Choo Ch' Boogie
Decca EP	2168	"Shake, Rattle and Roll" with 3 other BH hits
" EP	2209	"Dim, Dim the Lights" with 3 songs BH songs
" EP	2322	"Rock'n'Roll" with 4 songs: Burn That Candle/Rock-A-Beatin' Boogie/Razzle-Dazzle/Two Hound Dogs
" EP	2398	"Music For The Boyfriend" with 4 songs
" EP	2416	"Rock'n'Roll Stage Show" Part One with 4 songs: Hook, Line and Sinker/Rudy's Rock/Calling All Comets/Rockin' Through The Rye
" EP	2417	"Rock'n'Roll Stage Show" Part Two with 4 songs; Hide and Seek/A Rocking Little Tune/Blue Comet Blues/Choo Choo Ch' Boogie
" EP	2418	"Rock'n'Roll Stage Show" Part Three with 4 songs
Decca LP	8225	"Rock Around The Clock"; Shake, Rattle and Roll/Rock Around the Clock/ABC Boogie/Thirteen Women/Razzle Dazzled/Two Hound Dogs/Dim, Dim the Lights/Happy Baby/Mambo Rock/Burn That Candle/Birth of the Boogie/Rock-A-Beatin' Boogie.
" LP	8315	"Music For The Boyfriend"—He Digs Rock'n'Roll" 4 Bill Haley songs plus 8 v.a.
" LP	8345	"Rock And Roll Stage Show"; 12 songs

**Sixteen British Releases:*

Melodisc	M1376	Why Do I Cry Over You/I'm Gonna Dry Every Tear With A Kiss

Brunswick	05530	See You Later, Alligator/Paper Boy
"	05565	R-O-C-K/The Saint's Rock'n'Roll
"	05582	Hot Dog Buddy Buddy/Rockin' Through The Rye
"	05615	Rip It Up/Teenager's Mother
"	05616	Rudy's Rock/Blue Comet Blues
" EP	0E9214	"Rock'n'Roll" with 4 songs
" EP	0E9250	"Rock Around The Clock" with 4 songs
" EP	0E9278	"Rock'n'Roll Stage Show" Part One with four songs
" EP	0E9279	"Rock'n'Roll Stage Show" Part Two with four songs
" EP	0E9280	"Rock'n'Roll Stage Show" Part Three with four songs
" LP	LAT8117	"Rock Around The Clock" with 12 songs
" LP	LAT8139	"Rock'n'Roll Stage Show" with 12 songs both above albums released in
London EP	1049	"Live It Up" Part One; four songs
" EP	1050	"Live It Up" Part Two; four songs
" EP	1058	"Live It Up" Part Three; four songs

**Thirteen German releases:*

Brunswick	12055	Razzle-Dazzle/Birth Of The Boogie (82865)
"	12059	Burn That Candle/Rock-A-Beatin' Boogie (82869)
"	12060	See You Later, Alligator/Paper Boy (82870)
" EP	10027	"Rock'n'Roll" with four songs
" LP	86044	"Rock Around The Clock" 10" disc
" LP	86036	"Schlagerparade USA" Shake, Rattle And Roll plus 7 v.a. 10" disc
" LP	86042	"Schlager aus USA" Rock Around The Clock plus 7 v.a. 10" disc
London	20032	Rocking Chair On The Moon/Ten Little Indians
"	20068	Live It Up/Rock The Joint
"	20069	Farewell, So Long, Goodbye/Real Rock Drive
" EP	F1049	"Live It Up" Teil One
" EP	F1050	"Live It Up" Teil Two
" LP	HAPB1042	"Live It Up" 10" disc

**Ten Australian releases:*

Festival	FS 841	Rock Around The Clock/13 Women 78 rpm
"	FS 919	Saints' Rock And Roll/R.O.C.K. 78 rpm
"	SP-807	Rock-A-Beatin' Boogie/Burn That Candle
"	SP-1034	Hot Dog Buddy Buddy/Rockin' Through The Rye
"	SP-886	See You Later, Alligator/Paper Boy
"	SP-1121	Teenager's Mother/Rip It Up
" EP	XP-931	R.O.C.K./S.Y.L. Alligator/Rock-A-Beatin' Boogie/ABC Boogie
"	FR12-1102	LP "Rock Around The Clock" 12 songs from the Columbia film.
"	FR12-1045	"Rock And Roll Stage Show" 12 songs including Calling All Comets/Hook, Line and Sinker, Goofin' Around/Rudy's Rock.
"	FR10-1226	10" LP "Don't Knock The Rock." Seven tunes from film.

-1957-

Decca	30214	Forty Cups Of Coffee/Hook, Line and Sinker
"	30314	Billy Goat/Rockin' Rollin' Rover
"	30394	The Dipsy Doodle/Miss You
"	30461	Rock The Joint/How Many?
"	30530	Mary, Mary Lou/It's A Sin
Decca EP	2532	"Rockin' The Oldies": The Dipsy Doodle/Miss You/Is It True What They Say About Dixie/Carolina In The Morning
" EP	2533	"Rock'n'Roll Party": One Sweet Letter From You/Please Don't Talk About Me When I'm Gone/In Apple Blossom Time/Somebody Else Is Taking My Place
" EP	2534	"Rockin' And Rollin'": Moon Over Miami/Ain't Misbehavin'/You Can't Stop Me From Dreaming/I'm Gonna Sit Right Down And Write Myself A Letter

Decca LP	8569	"Rockin' The Oldies" 12 songs listed on the above three EP's

**Nine British Releases:*

London LP	HAF2037	"Rock The Joint"; 12 Essex songs
"	HAF8371	Yes Indeed/Rock The Joint
Brunswick	05640	Don't Knock The Rock/Calling All Comets
"	05641	Hook, Line and Sinker/Goofin' Around
"	05658	Forty Cups Of Coffee/Choo Choo Ch'Boogie
"	05688	Billy Goat/Rockin' Rollin' Rover
"	05719	Dipsy Doodle/Miss You
" EP	LAT8201	"Music For The Boyfriend" 4 songs
" LP	LAT8219	"Rockin' The Oldies" 12 songs

**Nineteen German Releases:*

Brunswick	12065	R-O-C-K/Saint's Rock'n'Roll (82875)
"	12071	Rip It Up/Teenager's Mother (82877)
"	12082	Don't Knock The Rock/Choo Choo Ch' Boogie (82882)
"	12083	Calling All Comets/Goofin' Around (82883)
"	12084	Hot Dog Buddy Buddy/Hook, Line and Sinker (82884)
"	12090	Rudy's Rock/Blue Comet Blues
"	12091	Hide And Seek/Rockin' Through The Rye
"	12092	Forty Cups Of Coffee/Two Hounds Dogs
" EP	10056	"R-O-C-K" with four songs
" EP	10090	"Don't Knock The Rock" with four songs
" EP	10100	"Rudy's Rock" with four songs
" EP	10101	"Rock With Bill" with four songs
" LP	87004	"Rock'n'Roll Show"
London	DL20080	Yes Indeed/Rock The Joint
"	DL20090	Pat-A-Cake/Fractured
"	DL20091	Crazy Man, Crazy/Whatcha Gonna Do?
"	DL20092	Green Tree Boogie/Sundown Boogie
" EP	3005	"Rock The Joint" Part One
" EP	3006	"Rock The Joint" Part Two

-1958-

Decca	30592	Skinny Minnie/Sway With Me
"	30681	Lean Jean/Don't Nobody Move
"	30741	Chiquita Linda/Who'a Mabel
"	30781	Corrine, Corrina/B.B. Betty
EP	2564	"Rockin' Around The World": Me Rock A Hula/Wooden Shoe Rock/Oriental Rock/ Rockin' Matilda
EP	2576	"Rockin Around Europe": Piccadilly Rock/Vive La Rock'n'Roll/Rockin' Rollin' Schnitzlebank/Come Rock With Me
EP	2577	"Rockin' Around The Americas": Pretty Alouette/El Rocko/Rockin' Rita/ Jamaica, D.J.
LP	8692	"Rockin' Around The World" with 12 songs as listed on three EP's above.
LP	8655	"Let's Have A Party"; Shake Rattle And Roll/Rock Around The Clock plus 10 v.a.
LP	8775	"Rockin' The Joint" with 12 songs
LP	78225	"Rock Around The Clock" Same album as Decca's 1956 LP #8225 but now in "Stereophonic Sound".
East-West	115	Weekend/Better Believe It
"	120	The Cat Walk/Conga Rock (These two records are by the Comets under the pseudonym "The Kingsmen".)
Coral	61931	Wee Willie Brown/You Were Mean Baby (Comets back Lou Craham)

Clymax EP	JB140/41	Toy Shop/Happy Birthday/Candy Bed/Blue Ranger
EP	JB142/43	Cuckoo In The Clock/Sing A Song Of Happiness/TV Pal/ABC Rock
EP	JB144/45	Rockin' In The Nursery/Little Pedro/Rockin' Horse Cowgirl/Good Night, Dear Lord
Clymax	CR-10O1	"Our Gal Sal"; Three above EP records in album, twelve songs. (Comets backing Sally Starr)
Kapp	K163	Calypso Rock/Blue (Comets back Dave Day)
Kapp	K164	She Said/Walking Up Four Flights of Stairs, (Comets back Frankie Scott)

**Ten British Releases:*

Brunswick	05735	Mary, Mary Lou/It's A Sin
"	05742	Skinny Minnie/How Many?
"	05752	Lean Jean/Don't Nobody Move
"	05766	Whoa Mabel/Chiquita Linda
EP	0E9349	"Rockin' The Oldies" Part 1 four songs
EP	0E9350	"Rockin' The Oldies" Part 2 four songs
EP	0E9351	"Rockin' The Oldies" Part 3 four songs
LP	LAT8268	"Rockin' The Joint" 12 songs
London	8735	Weekend/Better Believe It
EP	1121	Conga Rock/The Cat Walk/Better Believe It/Weekend

**Seven German releases:*

Polydor EP	76748B	Spitzenschager des Jahres, Rock Around The Clock and 3 v.a.
Brunswick	12116	I'm Gonna Sit Right Down And Write Myself A Letter/The Dipsy Doodle
"	12127	Skinny Minnie/Sway With Me
"	12133	Mary, Mary Lou/Piccadilly Rock
"	12141	Lean Jean/It's A Sin
"	12149	Whoa Mabel/Chiquita Linda
"	12152	Come Rock With Me/Me Rock A Hula

-1959-

Decca	30844	I Got A Woman/Charmaine
"	30873	A Fool Such As I/Where Did You Go Last Night?
"	30926	Shaky/Caldonia
"	30956	Joey's Song/Ooh! Look-A-There, Ain't She Pretty
ABC-PARAMOUNT	1002	Everybody Out Of The Pool/Teenage Tango (The Comets under the pseudon: The Lifeguards)
DECCA EP	2615	"Rockin' The Joint" with four songs
EP	2616	"Rip It Up" with four songs
EP	2638	"Bill Haley's Chicks" with four songs
EP	2661	"Top Teen Hits" A Fool Such As I/plus three other v.a.
EP	2670	"Bill Haley And His Comets" with four hit songs list
EP	2671	"Strictly Instrumental" Skokiaan/Puerto Rican Peddler/Music! Music! Music!/ Strictly Instrumental
Decca LP Stereo	8821 78821	"Bill Haley's Chicks" with 12 songs: Whoa Mabel/Ida, Sweet As Apple Cider/Dinah/Skinny Minnie/Mary, Mary Lou/Sweet Sue, Just You/B.B.Betty/Charmaine/Corrine, Corrina/Marie/Lean Jean
Casa Blanca	5535	Teenage Tango/Everybody Out Of The Pool. (The Comets under the pseudonym "The Lifeguards").
Casa Blanca	?	The Cat/La Donna Riccia. (The Comets backing Cappy Bianco)
Coral	?	Crazy Street/Remember. (The Comets backing the Mays Brothers)
Coral	?	Aintcha/You're So Wonderful. (The Comets backing Joey Santo)

**Nine British Releases:*

London	HLF8812	Conga Rock/The Cat Walk (Comets as the Kingsmen)
Brunswick	05788	Charmaine/I Got A Woman
"	05805	Shaky/Caldonia
"	05810	Joey's Song/Ooh! Look-A-There, Ain't She Pretty
" EP	0E9431	"They Sold A Million" #15 RATC & SRR plus v.a.
EP	0E9446	"Rockin' Around The World" four songs
EP	0E9459	"Bill Haley" with four songs
LP	LAT8295	"Bill Haley's Chicks" 12 songs
Stateside LP	3011	"Bill Haley's Chick's" 12 songs

** Nine German Releases:*

Brunswick	12154	Corrine, Corrina/Marie
"	12168	Eloise/Ida, Sweet As Apple Cider
"	12171	I Got A Woman/Rockin Rollin' Rover
"	12172	A Fool Such As I/Where Did You Go Last Night?
"	12176	Charmaine/Sweet Sue, Just You
"	12179	Shaky/Caldonia
" EP	10158	"Rockin' Again" four songs
" EP	10171	"More Bill Haley" four songs
" EP	10174	"Shaky" four songs

-1960-

Decca	31030	Skokiaan/Puerto Rican Peddler
"	31080	Music! Music! Music!/Strictly Instrumental
Lawn	-?-	Wee Willie Water Dilly/Wedding Bouquet Comets back the Keefer Sisters
Decca LP Stereo	8964 78964	"Strictly Instrumental" with 12 songs: In A Little Spanish Town/Two Shadows/ Mack The Knife/Joey's Song/The Cat Walk /Music! Music! Music!/ Shaky/ Strictly Instrumental/Skokiaan/Puerto Rican Peddler/Drowsy Waters/Chiquita Linda
Warner	5145	Candy Kisses/Tamiami
"	5154	Hawk/Chick Safari
"	5171	Let The Good Times Roll,Creole/So Right Tonight
Warner LP	1378	"Bill Haley and his Comets": Stagger Lee/Shake, Rattle and Roll/I'm In Love Again/Love Letters In The Sand/Kansas City/Crazy, Man Crazy/Whole Lotta Shakin' Goin' On/Blue Suede Shoes/Rock Around The Clock/I Almost Lost My Mind/Blueberry Hill/My Special Angel
Warner LP	1391	"Bill Haley's Juke Box":Singing The Blues/Candy Kisses/No Letter Today/This Is The Thanks I Get/Bouquet Of Roses/There's A New Moon Over My Shoulder/Cold, Cold Heart/Wild Side Of Life/Any Time/Afraid/ I Don't Hurt Anymore/Detour

** Four British Releases:*

Brunswick	05818	Skokiaan/Puerto Rican Peddler
" LP	LAT8326	"Strictly Instrumental" 12 songs
Warner EP	6001	"Bill Haley And His Comets" four songs
" EP	6025	"Bill Haley's Juke Box" with four songs

** Twelve German Releases:*

Brunswick	250186	Joey's Song/Ooh! Look-A-There, Ain't She Pretty (stereo)
"	250200	Mack The Knife/Music! Music! Music! (in stereo)
"	250201	Dinah/Ida, Sweet As Apple Cider (stereo)
"	250202	Eloise/Sweet Sue, Just You (stereo)

″	12186	Ooh! Look-A-There, Ain't She Pretty/Joey's Song
″	12191	Pretty Alouette/Vive La Rock'n'Roll
″	12199	Rockin' Matilda/Rockin' Rollin' Schnitzlebank
″	12200	Mack The Knife/Music! Music! Music!
″	12210	New Rock The Joint/Rock Lomond
″	12217	Skokiaan/Strictly Instrumental
″ EP	10184	"Rockin Around The World" four songs
″ EP	10185	"Rockin' The Oldies" four songs

-1961-

Warner	5228	Honky Tonk/Flip, Flop And Fly
Gone	5111	Spanish Twist/My Kind Of Woman
″	5116	Riviera/War Paint
Apt	25051	Big Daddy/St. Louis Blues, (Three Comets: Beecher, Jones and Pompilli under the pseudonym: The Merri-Men.)
Logo	7005	Yakety Sax/another artist(B. Randolph)
″	7006	A.B.C. Boogie/another artist

** Ten Latin American Releases:*

Orfeon	1010	Twist Espanol/
″	1036	Cerca Del Mar/Tren Nocturno
″	1047	Florida Twist/Negra Consentida
Orfeon	1052	Caravana Twist/Actopan
″	1062	La Paloma/Siblando Y Caminando
″	1067	Bikini Twist/Rudy's Rock
″	1082	Mas Twist/Tampico Twist
Orfeon EP	178	"Twist Bill Haley": La Paloma/Florida Twist/Twist Espanol/Tren Nocturno
″ EP	191	"Bill Haley Y Sus Cometas, Twist Bill Haley, Vol.2 Tampico Twist/Negra Consentida/Caravana Twist/Actopan
Dimsa LP	8255	"Twist, Bill Haley y Sus Cometas": Silbando Y Caminando/Twist Espanol/ Tampico Twist/Florida Twist/La Paloma/Caravana Twist/Negra Consentida/ Tren Nocturno/Actopan/Mas Twist
Dimsa LP	8259	"Bikini Twist": Cielito Lindo/Weekend/Cometa Azul/Conga Twist/Rudy's Twist/El Twist Del Cometa/Rambuchas Twist/Bikini Twist/Twist Del Expresso/Riviera

** Two British Releases:*

London	HLU9471	The Spanish Twist/My Kind Of Woman
Ace of Hearts	LP-13	"Rock Around The Clock" 12 songs (PR)

** Seven German Releases:*

Brunswick	12221	Ain't Misbehavin'/Is It True What They Say About Dixie?
″	12226	Carolina In The Morning/Somebody Else Is Taking My Place
Warner	A5145	Candy Kisses/Tamiami
″	A5154	Chick Safari/Hawk
″	A5171	Let The Good Times Roll, Creole/So Right Tonight
″ EP	EP6	"Bill Haley And His Comets" four songs
″ LP	WS1378	"Bill Haley And His Comets" 12 songs

-1962-

Camay	3001	"Country & Western Bonanza" Bouquet Of Roses/Candy Kisses plus 10 v.a.

** Three British Releases:*

Ace Of Hearts	AH35	"Rockin' The Oldies" 12 songs same as Decca 8569 (1957)

Pye LP	GGL0282	"Rock The Joint" Twelve previously released Essex BH's tunes.
Marble Arch	817	LP "Rock The Joint" 12 previously released Essex B. H. tunes.

** Two German Releases:*

London	20495	Spanish Twist/My Kind Of Woman
Warner EP	13781	"Bill Haley And His Comets" four songs

** Seven Latin American Releases:*

Orfeon	1100	Twist Lento/Sonora Twist
"	1132	Martha/Tacos De Twist
"	1169	Jalisco Twist/Pueblo Del Twist
Orfeon EP	199	"Twist Con Bill Haley" Twist Lento/Senora Twist/One Two Three Twist/Bikini Twist
Dimsa LP	8275	"Bill Haley Y Sus Cometas-Twist" Vol.2 De Buen Humor/China Twist/Martha/ Twist Feliz/Tacos De Twist/Jarrito Twist/Twist Del Dia/Marie Twist/Lado A Lado/Ana Maria
Dimsa LP	8290	"Twist En Mexico": Jalisco Twist/Sonora Twist/Monterrey Twist/Yukatan Twist/ Mexicali Twist/Oaxaca Twist/Vera Cruz/Pueblo Del Twist
Roulette	LP203626	"Twisting Knights At The Round Table" Lullaby Of Birdland Twist/Twist Marie/ One Two Three Twist/Queen Of The Twisters/Caravan Twist/I Want A Little Girl/Whistlin' And Walkin' Twist/Florida Twist/Eight More Miles To Louisville. Recorded live at the Roundtable Club.

-1963-

Newtown	5011	Mish Mash/Let The Girls Sing (Carrie Grant and the Grandeurs, backed by the Comets.)
Newtown	5013	Tenor Man/Up Goes My Love
"	5024	Dance Around The Clock/What Can I Say
Newhits	5014	White Parakeet/Midnight In Washington
Nicetown	5025	Tandy/You Call Everybody Darling
Vocalion	LP3696	"Bill Haley And His Comets" twelve songs, three previously unreleased: Dragon Rock/ABC Rock/Walkin' Beat
Arcade LP	AR1003	"Covered Wagon Caravan" Twelve country tunes backed by many early Comets.

**Seven Latin American Releases:*

Orfeon	1195	Pure De Papas/Anoche
"	1229	El Madison De La Esterella/Viajando Con El Madison
"	1243	Avenida Madison/Reunion De Etiqueta
"	1269	Limbo Rock/Ana Maria
Maya LP	10437	"El Precursor Del Rock" Maya is a subsidiary of Orfeon/Dimsa.
Orfeon LP	12339	"Madison": Puerta Verde/Madison De La Estrella/Marruecos/Madison Del Cometa/Bailando El Madison/Reunion De Etiqueta /Avenida Madison/ Madison En Azul/El Madison/Tip Top/Mi Madison
Orfeon LP	12340	"Carnaval De Ritmos Modernos": Teresa/Limbo Rock/Desafinado/Cerca Del Mar/Que Pachanga/Carolina/Pure De Papas/En Un Pueblito Espanol/Viajando Con El Madison/Anoche/El Poney/Ana Marie

**Two British Releases:*

Stateside	SS196	Tenor Man/Up Goes My Love
Columbia	SX1460	"Twisting Knights" Down By The Riverside plus nine other BH songs

-1964-

Decca	31650	The Green Door/Yeah She's Evil
"	25650	Skinny Minnie/Lean Jean
"	25751	Corrine, Corrina/The Green Door
" EP	9-38088	Webcor Eloise plus three v.a.
Guest Star LP	1454	"Rock Around The Clock King" I've Got News For Hugh /Don't Mess Around/ The Wobble/Train Of Sin/Altar Of Love/See You Later, Alligator/This Is Goodbye, Goodbye/Helena/Panic/ABC Boogie
Guest Star LP	1474	"Ten Million Sellers" BH's See You Later, Alligator plus nine other v.a.
Guest Star LP	1499	"Trini Lopez-Scott Gregory" Five songs by Lopez and five by Bill Haley under the pseudonym; "Scott Gregory".
Diplomat LP	2397	"Discotheque" ABC Boogie/I've Got News For Hugh/Panic/ plus nine other v.a.

** Five Latin American Releases:*

Orfeon	1324	Adios Mariquita Linda/El Quelite
"	1333	Mish Mash/Madero Y Gante
"	1370	El Sax Tartamudo/?
"	1429	Jimmy Martinez/Al Compas Del Reloj
Orfeon EP	550	"Presenting Joe Turner" Monkey Man/Chains Of Love/Low Down Dog/Honey Hush
Orfeon EP	533	"Presenting Joe Turner" Corrine,Corrina /Lonesome Train/Feelin' Happy/ Stormy Monday. These recordings are backed by Bill Haley and his Comets.
Orfeon EP	385	"Twist Con Bill Haley" Vol.2: El Sax Tartamudo/Madero Y Gante/Al Compas Del Reloj/El Quelite
Orfeon LP	12354	"Surf, Surf, Surf!": Surf Del Elefante/Sax Tartamudo Surf/Madero Y Gante/ Moviedose/Note Puedes Sentar/Ella Cree Que La Amo Aun/Al Compas Del Reloj /Memphis/Sur De La Sandia/Surf Del Monkey/Mish Mash/A Gusto Contigo

** Seven British Releases:*

Xtra LP	1027	"Bill Haley and the Comets" Ten songs same as Guest Star LP 1454
Brunswick	05910	Happy Baby/Birth Of The Boogie
"	05917	The Green Door/Yeah, She's Evil
Warner	133	1960 version of Rock Around The Clock/Love Letters In The Sand
" EP	WEP6133	"Bill Haley And His Comets" Vol 1 Blue Suede Shoes/Blueberry Hill/I Almost Lost My Mind/Stagger Lee
" EP	WEP6136	"Bill Haley And His Comets" Vol 2 Kansas City/Rock Around The Clock/Love Letters In The Sand/Shake, Rattle And Roll
Ace Of Hearts	AH66	LP "Bill Haley Chicks" twelve songs all previously released

** Three German Releases:*

Columbia	22586	Tenor Man/Up Goes My Love
"	83563	"Zentrale Tanzschaffe" Tenor Man plus 13 v.a.
Roulette	21151	Florida Twist/Lullaby Of Birdland Twist

-1965-

Apt	25081	Burn That Candle/Stop, Look And Listen
"	25087	Tongue Tied Tony/Haley A Go Go
DR	69	Teenage Tango/Everybody Out Of The Pool (Comets under pseudonym; The Lifeguards (reissue of 1959 ABC Paramount 10021)

** Three German Releases:*

Europa LP	E340	"Rock'n'Soul" Rock The Joint/Crazy,Man Crazy/Whatcha Gonna Do/Farewell, So Long, Good Bye, plus 14 v.a.
Brunswick	87116	LP "The Best Of Bill Haley" All songs previously released.
"	8588	LP "The Very Best Of Bill Haley" All songs previously released.

-1966-

** Seven Latin American Releases:*

Orfeon	1842	Corrine, Corrina/ by Joe Turner and the Comets
"	1894	Rip It Up/Rock Around The Clock
"	9001	Estomago Caliente/A Tierra De Las Mil Danzas
Orfeon EP	530	"Whisky A Go Go" Nueva Orleans/Estomago Caliente/La Tierra De Las Mil Danzas/La Cucaracha A Go Go
" EP	549	"Bill Haley And His Comets": Pepito Corazon/Harlem A Go Go/Baja California Sun/El Septimo Hijo
Orfeon LP	12478	"Whisky A Go Go": La Flaca Miny/Justine /Chanclas De Tacon Alto/Pancho/El Traje De Sam/Nueva Orleans/La Tierra De Las Mil Danzas/La Cucaracha A Go Go/ Harlem A Go Go/Baja California/Estomago Caliente
Dimsa LP	8381	"Bill Haley A Go Go" Ten songs all previously released

** One British Release:*

TransAtlantic	1027	LP "Bill Haley And His Comets" Ten songs all previously released.

-1967-

** One British Release:*

Ember LP	3386	"Real Live Rock'n'Roll" Ten BH songs all recorded live in New York

-1968-

United Artist	50483	That's How I Got To Memphis/Ain't Love Funny, Ha Ha Ha
Dimsa LP	8460	"Exitos Del Rock'n'Roll" Vol.2 Florida Twist plus nine other v.a.
Milan LP	A100161	"Rock Around The Clock—The Sonet Sessions" Ten new Swedish recordings of BH hits. (France)

** Five British/Swedish Releases:*

Pye	N25455	Crazy, Man Crazy/Dance With A Dolly
MCA/Coral	MU1013	Rock Around The Clock/Shake, Rattle and Roll
Sonet LP	GP 9945	"Bill Haley and..His Comets Biggest Hits" Recorded in Stockholm 6/25/68 RATC/Skinny Minnie/Ling-Ting-Tong/Rock the Joint/Rock-a-Beatin, Boogie/ SYL Alligator/Flip Flop and Fly/Love Letters In The Sand/Saint's Rock and Roll/ SRR
Sonet LP	SLP 63	"Bill Haley and His Comets On Stage" Vol 1. Recorded in Stockholm 6/24/68 Lucille/Whole Latta Shakin' Going On/Rip It Up/Skinny Minnie/Rudy s Rock/ Shake, Rattle and Roll/RATC/Caravan/SYL Alligator/What'd I Say
Sonet LP	SLP 69	"Bill Haley and His Comets On Stage Vol 2. Recorded in Stockholm 6/24/68 Razzle-Dazzle/Cryin' Time/Yakety Sax/Jenny, Jenny/Johnny B.Good/Saint's Rock and Roll/Malaguena/Guitar Boogie/New Orleans/Rock The Joint/Rock-A-Beatin' Boogie
Marble Arch	817 LP	"Rock The Joint" Twelve songs all previously released
Ember LP	3396	"The King Of Rock—Bill Haley Plays Land Of The Thousand Dances" Hi-Heel Sneakers/Hambone/California Sun/No Matter What Shape/La Cucaracha/ Mohair Sam/Harlem Nocturne/Seventh Son/Justine/Skinny Minnie/New Orleans Same tracks as Orfeon LP 12478

MCA LP	318	"Rip It Up" Twelve previously released Decca songs

** Five German Releases:*

Decca	DL80024	Rock Around The Clock/Shake, Rattle And Roll
"	DL80025	See You Later, Alligator/Rock-A-Beatin' Boogie
" LP	86043-P	"Rock Around The Clock" All previously released
Vogue LP	17154	"Explosive Rock'n'Roll" All previously released BH hits
" LP	17158	"Bill Haley And The Comets" All songs previously released

-1969-

Decca LP Stereo	MCA161 75027	"Bill Haley's Greatest Hits" Eleven songs, all previously released on Decca DL-5027
Decca LP	78225	"Rock Around the Clock" previously released on Decca 8225

** Two Latin American Releases:*

Dimsa LP	8554	"Los Grandes Anos Del Rock'n'Roll" Vol 1, Rock Around The Clock plus nine other v.a.
Dimsa LP	8555	"Los Grandes Anos Del Rock'n'Roll" Vol 2

** One British Release:*

Ember LP	3401	"Mister Rock'n'Roll" Twelve previously released songs.

** Five German Releases:*

Vogue	14757	Rock Around The Clock/Shake, Rattle And Roll
"	14758	See You Later, Alligator/Skinny Minnie
"	14759	Rock-A-Beatin' Boogie/Saint's Rock'n' Roll
"	14881	That's How I Got To Memphis/Ain't Love Funny, Ha Ha Ha
Somerset LP	667	"Bill Haley-The King Of Rock'n'Roll" All songs previously released

-1970-

Radio Active Gold	46	Shake, Rattle And Roll/Rock-A-Beatin' Boogie
"	47	Rudy's Rock/See You Later,Alligator
"	48	Saint's Rock'n Roll/Skinny Minnie
"	49	Razzle-Dazzle/Rip It Up
Kama Sutra	508	Framed/Rock Around The Clock
Kama Sutra LP	2014	"Bill.Haley's Scrapbook" Twelve songs recorded live at the Bitter End in NY: Rock the Joint/Rock-A-Beatin' Boogie/Rip It Up/Razzle Dazzle/Framed/Rock Around The Clock/Crazy Man, Crazy/When The Saints Go Marching In/Shake, Rattle and Roll/Skinny Minnie/Rudy's Rock/See You Later, Alligator.
Kama Sutra LP	2015	"Rock'n'Roll Revival" Rock Around The Clock/Rip it Up plus ten other v.a.
Decca LP	75181	"Rock'n'Roll Survival" RATC/SRR plus ten v.a.
Valiant LP	WS1831	"Rock'n'Roll Revival" Twelve previously released songs
Ambassador	98089	LP "Bill Haley And His Comets" Ten songs previously released
Alshire LP	S5202	"King Of Rock'n'Roll" Three songs (PR) plus nine v.a.
Pickwick LP	3256	"Bill Haley And His Comets-Rockin'": Ling Ting Tong and nine other songs
MCA/Coral	CP55	"Rock Around The Clock" Twelve BH Hits

** Five British Releases:*

Ember LP	3412	"Rock Blast From The Past" RATC/SRR plus v. a.
Valiant LP	VS103	"Bill Haley And His Comets" Twelve previously released songs

Sonet LP	SNT302	"Bill Haley In Sweden" Twelve BH tunes recorded in Stockholm
Hallmark LP	668	"Rock Around The Clock Biggest Hits" Ten (PR) songs
" LP	694	"Bill Haley On Stage" Crying Time/Guitar Boogie/Jenny Jenny/ plus six other BH-Sonet hits

** Ten German Releases:*

Polydor	2137019	Rock Around The Clock/Shake, Rattle and Roll
"	2137020	Razzle-Dazzle/See You Later, Alligator
Somerset LP	758	"Biggest Hits"
MCA/Coral LP	1015	"Bill Haley's Greatest Hits"
" LP	2341	"Rock'n'Roll Revival" RATC/SRR plus ten other v.a.
Karussell LP	2345014	"Live At The Bitter End"
Bellaphon LP	B-1553	Rock Around The Clock/
Mode Serie LP	9605	"Biggest Hits" (Vogue)
Vogue LP	17196	"Rock'n'Roll History Vol.2
Polydor LP	0666772	"Live At The Bitter End"

-1971-

Janus	J-162	Travellin' Band/A Little Piece At A Time
Warner	7124	Rock Around The Clock/Shake, Rattle And Roll
Warner LP	WS1831	"Rock'n'Roll Revival" 12 songs: Crazy Man, Crazy/Whole Lotta Shakin' Goin' On/Shake, Rattle and Roll/Rock Around the Clock/There's a New Moon Over My Shoulder/Detour/Blue Suede Shoes/ I'm In Love Again/Blueberry Hill/ Stagger Lee/Kansas City/No Letter Today.
Janus LP	JX25-7003	"Razzle Dazzle" Two record album with 22 BH songs all previously released.
Pickwick LP	SPC3280	"Rock'n'Roll Revival" Two BH songs plus eight v.a.

** Two Latin American Release:*

Dim LP	125DGS212	"King Of Rock'n'Roll" All previously released Mexican recordings
Maya LP	LY70437	"El Precursor Del Rock" ten previously released Mexican recordings

**Four British Releases:*

Sonet	2016	Me And Bobby McGee/I Wouldn't Have Missed It For The World
Sonet LP	SNTF623	"Rock Around The Country" Twelve songs Dance Around The Clock/Games People Play/A Little Piece At A Time/I Wouldn't Have Missed It For The World/ Bony Maronie/There's A New Moon Over My Shoulder/Me And Bobby McGee/ How Many/Who'll Stop The Rain/Pink Eyed Pussycat /Travelin' Band/No Letter Today
Hallmark	LPSHM 773	"The Golden King Of Rock" Twelve BH hit songs previously released

-1972-

Decca LP	DXSE7-211	"Bill Haley and His Comets Golden Hits" 24 BH Hit songs on two record album.

**Two British Release:*

Janus LP	JLS3035	"Travellin' Band" Who'll Stop The Rain/Pink Eyed Pussycat/Games People Play/ Bony Maronie and eight other BH-Sonet hit songs as released on Sonet LP SNTF623
Coral	LPCPS 88	"Rock'n'Roll Survival" RATC/SRR plus ten other v.a.

**Six German Releases:*

MCA MSC	6276	Shake, Rattle And Roll/See You Later, Alligator

MCA Coral	COPS4574	LP "Rip It Up"
"	COPS6289	LP "Birth Of The Boogie"
"	COPS6292	LP "The Legends Of Rock-Bill Haley" Two record album
"	COPS6585	LP "Calling All Comets"
"	COPS6835	LP "Rockin'"

-1973-

MCA	60025	RATC/Thirteen Women. Another release of Decca's original tracks.
MCA-Coral	LP 2-8001	Soundtrack of "American Graffiti" Rock Around The Clock with 41 other v.a. hits
MCA-Coral	LP CB20015	"Bill Haley And His Comets-Rockin'" Ten BH hits originally released on Decca DL8692.
Crescendo	LP 2077	"Rock'n'Roll": C.C.Rider/I'm Walking/Lawdy Miss Clawdy/Personality/Crazy Man, Crazy/High Heel Sneakers/Blue Suede Shoes/Bring It On Home To Me/ Whole Lotta Shakin' Goin'On/Tossin' And Turnin'/Flip, Flop And Fly/ Rock And Roll Music. Recorded in Nashville, all new arrangements.

**One Latin American release:*

Orfeon	LP 13-2084	"Disco Del Million de Rock'n'Roll and Twist" Bill Haley Y Sus Cometas" Ten previously released Orfeon songs

** Two British Releases:*

Sonet	SON 2016	Me And Bobby McGee/I Wouldn't Have Missed It For The World
Sonet LP	SNTF645	"Just Rock'n'Roll Music" Same twelve songs as above GNP Crescendo LP. Sonet is original label (Swedish). Recorded in Nashville

** Two German Releases:*

Metronome	LP 200129	"Rock Around The Country" Same songs as Sonet's LP 623
MCA Coral	LP 0082.011	Soundtrack from "American Graffiti" RATC plus 40 v.a.

-1974-

Bell LP	9002	"Let The Good Times Roll" sound track Bill Haley's RATC/SRR plus 8 v.a.
Pickwick	2077-2	LP "Bill Haley-Rock'n'Roll" Sixteen BH hits. Two record album.

** Seven Latin American Releases:*

Orfeon	LP JM128	"Rock'n'Roll History" Three LP set
"	LP JM136	"Vuelven Los Buenos Tiempos" BH and v.a.
Orfeon	LP 12-928	"Rock Frenetico" Vol.2 Blues Del Cometa Azul and nine other v.a.
"	LP 12-1037	"Bill Haley Y Sus Cometas-Vol.I" with ten BH Spanish hits
"	LP 12-1038	"Bill Haley Y Sus Cometas-Vol.2" with ten BH Spanish Hits
"	LP 12-1039	"Bill Haley Y Sus Cometas-Vol.3" with ten BH Spanish Hits
Orfeon	LP E-JM 117	"Bill Haley Y Sus Cometas" Three record 30 song album of above three LP's.

** Nine British Releases:*

Sonet	SON 2043	Crazy Man, Crazy/Lawdy Miss Clawdy
MCA	128	Rock Around The Clock/Shake, Rattle And Roll
MCA	142	Rudy's Rock/See You Later, Alligator
MCA LP	CDL8017	"Rock Around The Clock" Ten BH hits
MCA LP	MCF2555	"Golden Hits" 24 Decca BH-hits, two records
Antic LP	K51501	"Live In London 74": Shake, Rattle And Roll/Rudy's Rock/Rip It Up/Spanish Eyes/ Razzle-Dazzle/Rock-A-Beatin' Boogie/Caravan/See You Later, Alligator/Saint's Rock'n Roll/Rock The Joint/Rock Around The Clock
Hallmark LP	SHM837	"Rock Around The Country" Twelve BH Hits previously released

EMI LP	CRLM 1039	"Rock Around The Clock" Twelve BH songs previously released
Alshire	S-5313	"Bill Haley King Of Rock'n'Roll" Ten BH Essex songs

** Six German Releases:*

Warner	16387	My Special Angel/Rock Around The Clock
MCA Coral	C0PS7274-D	"The Legends Of Rock, Vol.#2" Two LP album, 23 previously released songs plus Summer Souvenir.
MCA Coral	C0PS7398	LP "Rockin' The Oldies" Same as Decca's 1957 LP #8569.
MCA Coral	0082.012	"More American Graffiti" See You Later, Alligator and 24 v.a
"	0082.016	"Good Old Rock'n'Rolll' RATC/Alligator plus 22 v.a.
WEA-Inter.	48001	"20 Rock'n'Roll Tops" RATC plus 19 v.a.

-1975-

** Three Latin American Releases:*

Dimsa LP	DML8704	"Los Grandes Anos Del Rock And Roll" Vol.7 Florida Twist plus nine v.a.
Guitarra	DG 14	LP "Just Rock'n'Roll"
" LP	DG 33	"Historia Del Rock'n'Roll" BH and v.a.

** One British Release:*

MCA Coral	263	Shake, Rattle And Roll/Rock-A-Beatin' Boogie/Razzle-Dazzle

** Six German Releases:*

Metronome	0040.072	LP "Golden Oldies" RATC plus 13 v.a.
Midi LP	26007	"Rock Around The Clock"
MCA	MSC8617	RATC/SRR
"	MSC9114	SYL,Alligator/Rip It Up
MCA-Coral	SM7845P 201-784	LP "Golden Favorites" Be By Me/Summer Souvenir and 10 other prev. released hits
MCA-Coral	0082.017	LP "More Of The Good Old Rock'n'Roll" Rip It Up/R-O-C-K plus 22 v.a.

-1976-

Pickwick	PDA006	"The Bill Haley Collection" Twenty-two BH songs previously released, two LP records.
Crescendo	GNPS2097	LP "Rock Around The Country" Same songs Sonet LP 623 issued 1971

**Two British Releases:*

Sonet LP	SNTF696	"Rudy's Rock": Rude The Dude/Slippin' And Slidin'/Dynamite Sax/Saxophobia/Midnight At The Oasis/Rudy's Rock/Flamingo/Groovin' At The Nightcap/Annie Bananie/Same Old Loverman. This record was recorded in Philadelphia by Rudy Pompilii and several Comets.
Sonet LP	SNTF710	"Bill Haley and his Comets" Ten previously released songs with new arrangements (Muscle Shoals) Ooh! Look-A There, Ain't She Pretty/Dim, Dim The Lights/Bum That Candle/I Got A Woman/R-O-C-K/Farewell, So Long, Goodbye/ABC Boogie/Dance With A Dolly/I'll Be True To You/Mohair Sam

** Six German Releases:*

Sonic	LP 9104	"Bill Haley's Biggest Hits"
"	LP 9105	"Bill Haley On Stage"
MCA-Coral	0062.063	LP "20 Golden Hits By Bill Haley
"	0052.051	LP "Original Oldies" Vol. 2 RATC plus eleven other v.a.
"	0052.052	LP "Original Oldies" Vol.3 Alligator plus eleven other v.a.
"	0052.063	LP "Original Oldies" Vol.4 SRR plus eleven other v.a.

-1977-

Springboard	SPB4066	LP "Greatest Hits Live in London" (Recorded at Hammersmith Palais) Nine BH songs plus unique band introduction
WINS LP	1012	"Alan Freed's Rock'n'Roll Dance Party" Vol.3 Hot Dog, Buddy Buddy/RATC plus twelve v. a.
WINS LP	1014	"Alan Freed's Rock'n'Roll Dance Party" Vol.5 Rip It Up/Saint's Rock'n'Roll plus twelve other v.a.
GrassRoots	GR1001	LP "Bill Haley's Golden Country Origins" Twelve Early (1948-49) country-western songs leased by Arzee to this Australian recording company. Same songs as Roller Coaster 300 (1978)
** Five German Releases:*		
Ariola LP	200631	"The Story Of Rock'n'Roll" Vol.4 Rock The Joint/Saint's Rock'n'Roll/Rock-A-Beatin' Boogie plus nine other v.a.
K-Tel LP	TG155	"Rock'n'Roll Show" RATC/SYL, Alligator plus 23 v.a.
Midi MID	LP20110	"Rock'n'Roll Forever-Bill Haley And The Comets
MCA Coral	0042.001	LP "The Original Bill Haley"
MCA Coral	0082.049-2	LP "Star Gold" Two LP Collection

-1978-

Arzee	AR4677	Yodel Your Blues Away/Within This Broken Heart Of Mine (From original Cowboy tracks.)
Radiola	MR1087	LP "Rock'n'Roll Radio" RATC plus 18 other v.a.
K-tel LP	18L0227-4	"Bill Haley And The Comets Original Favorites" Twenty BH hits (Spain)
** Two Latin American Releases:*		
Dimsa-Orefon LP	DML9064	"Al Compas Del Reloj" Bill Haley Y Sus Cometas with ten previously released songs
Orfeon LP	12-897	"Los Grandes Hits De Bill Haley Y Sus Cometas" Ten BH hits, previously released
**Two British Releases:*		
MCA Coral	MCF2838	LP "Armchair Rock'n'Roll" Twenty BH songs previously released
Roller Coaster	300	LP "Golden Country Origins": Yodel Your Blues Away/Rovin' Eyes/Rose Of My Heart/A Yodeller's Lullaby/Candy And Women/Foolish Questions/The Covered Wagon Rolled Right Along/Wreck On The Highway /Behind The Eightball/My Mom Heard Me Crying/Within This Broken Heart Of Mine/Cotton Haired Gal. This album is a release of some of Bill Haley's early country records circa 1948-1950
** Two German releases:*		
MCA Coral	0042.023	LP "Strictly Instrumental" All songs previously released
MCA Coral	6.22525	LP "Bill Haley's Chicks" All songs previously released

-1979-

Arzee EP	137	Why Do I Cry Over You/Ten Gallon Stetson plus two other v.a. From original Cowboy tracks.
Claire EP	4779	All I Need Is Some More Lovin'/Trouble In Mind/Life Of The Party/I Should Write A Song About You. Previously unreleased demos.
*Koala LP	AW14132	"Rock Around The Clock-Bill Haley and The Comets" Cirvana A Go Go plus eleven other BH hit songs

Bulldog	BDL2002	LP "Twenty Golden Pieces" 20 BH hits

** Five British Releases:*

Sonet	SON2188	Hail, Hail Rock'n'Roll/Let The Good Times Roll Again
Sonet	SON2194	Everyone Can Rock'n'Roll/I Need The Music
Sonet LP	SNTF808	"Everyone Can Rock'n'Roll": Hail, Hail, Rock and Roll/Jim Dandy/That's How I Got To Memphis/Juke Box Cannonball/Let The Good Times Roll/The Battle Of New Orleans/I Need The Music/Heartaches By The Number/Tweedle Dee/So Right Tonight/God Bless Rock'n'Roll (Recorded in London and Muscle Shoals, AL.)
Roller Coaster	RRC2004	Rock The Joint/Fractured
" LP	ROLL2002	"Rock The Joint" 10 Ten early BH-Essex songs

** Three German Releases:*

Polydor LP	2459218	"Rock'n'Roll Revival" RATC plus 13 v.a.
Ariola LP	200734	"The Story Of Rock'n'Roll"
MCA Coral	0042.040	"The Original Bill Haley" Vol.2

-1980-

MCA	60025	RATC/Thirteen Women another release using original Decca tracks.
Sun LP	143	"Bill Haley And The Comets Recored At Muscle Shoals" Twelve BH songs previously released on Sonet 710 (1976)
Exact LP	EX207	"Bill Haley — King Of Rock'n'Roll" with ten previously released Essex songs.

** One Latin American Release:*

Dimsa LP	JD2035	"Bill Haley-Rock Around The Clock" Two LP album with 29 songs previously released on Orfeon and Dimsa

** Two British Releases:*

Roller Coaster	ROLL2004	"The Return of Rockaphilly" Several songs written by Bill Haley and sung by his Comets.
Sonet	SON2202	God Bless Rock'n'Roll/So Right Tonight

** Two German Releases:*

Polydor LP	2485158	"The Beat Goes On" RATC and eleven other v. a.
WEA LP	28114	"Original Rock Oldies" RATC plus 11 other v.a. (WEAMID)

-1981-

Joker LP	SM3869	"Bill Haley And The Comets-Rock Around The Clock" Ten BH hit songs
Bear-Polydor LP	BFX15068-5	"Rockin' Rollin' Bill Haley" A five LP set, 102 tracks from Decca originals
Thumbs Up	103	Rocket 88/Tearstains On My Heart (Great Britain)
Laurie	LES 4033	"The Kings And Queens of Rock'n'Roll" See You Later, Alligator plus 16 v.a.
GNWM	GNW 4015	The Great North-West Music Co LP of Red Robinson's interview with Bill Haley with three all time Haley hits; Rudy's Rock, RATC and SRR.
MCA	103162	"Haley's Golden Medley" Six BH hits on German 45rpm
Silhouette	SM10006	LP "Dedications Vol.1" Recorded live at 1956 Alan Freed Shows; Rock Around The Clock/Hot Dog Buddy Buddy/The Saint's Rock'n'Roll/Rock-A-Beatin' Boogie/Rip It Up.
Score	SC08904	LP "Rock Around The Clock" Ling-Ting-Tong/Love Letters In The Sand/RATC/Flip Flop And Fly/Skinny Minnie/Rock The Joint/SRR/The Saints Rock And Roll/Rock-A-Beatin' Boogie/SYL, Alligator. French edition.

Accord	SN7125	"Bill Haley and the Comets-Rockin' & Rollin'" Ten BH hits previously released
Phoenix 10	PHX306	"Bill Haley and the Comets Greatest Hits". All previously released
Orfeon	16S0-5277	Bill Haley y sus Cometas" El Blues De Los Cometas/Mas Twist/La Tierra De Las Mil Danzas/Pure De Papas/Florida Twist/RATC/Rip It Up/Razzle-Dazzle/Ahi Nos Vemos Cocodrilo/La'Marcha De Los Santos.

-1982-

Black Tulip	EVO10 or 28008	LP "Twenty Greatest Hits" 20 BH songs All previously released. W. German
Accord LP	SJA7902	"Bill Haley-Mr. Rock'n'Roll" 8 BH songs All previously released
Lotus LP	LOP14016	"Bill Haley and the Comets 20 Greatest Hits". Mohair Hair Sam/New Orleans/ Hi -Heel Sneakers/The Seventh Son/ and sixteen other BH hits. Italy
Polydor	H019	LP "The Best of Bill Haley and the Comets" Twelve BH hits. Holland.
Old Gold	OG9220 OG9221	Rock Around The Clock/Thirteen Women Shake, Rattle and Roll/See You Later Alligator. original Decca tracks.

-1983-

Accord LP	SN7960	"Live From N.Y.C." Same songs as Ember LP 3386 from 1967
Charlie	CR30221	LP "Rock'n'Roll Stage Show" Twelve BH songs
Charlie LP		"The Essential Bill Haley" 32 BH all time great songs. Two LP's

-1984-

Charlie	CDX-5	"Mr. Rockin' Rollin'" Twelve BH songs
Br. Music	45034	Rock Around The Clock/SYL Alligator Holland.
Buddah LP	BDS69008	"Bill Haley's Scrapbook" Eleven songs recorded live at New York's Bitter End Same songs as Kama Sutra #2014 (1970)
Roller Coaster	2007	LP "Hillbilly Haley" 21 songs
Mercury	6498047	LP "Rockin' Movies" Rock Around The Clock and 11 other v.a. (German)
AFE LP	SOS5004	RATC and 19 other songs by v.a. Vol#4
"LP	SOS5006	Shake and 19 other songs by v.a. Vol#6
"LP	SOS5007	Alligator and 19 v.a. Vol#7

-1985-

Roller-Coaster	2009	LP "Rock The Joint" Twenty-two early BH's Holiday/Essex songs (England)
Picture-Disc	AR30049	LP "Rock Around The Clock" Twelve BH Decca songs on two sided picture disc. (Denmark)
MCA CD	MCAD5539 DIDX-202	"Bill Haley and His Comets" Twenty Decca hits from the original masters.
MCA LP	MCM5004	"Bill Haley's Golden Hits" Twenty songs
MCA LP	P6208	"30th Anniversary of Rock'n'Roll Bill Haley and his Comets". Twelve Decca original tracks, cover in Japanese.

-1986-

Pair LP	MSM2 35069	"Rock And Roll Giant" sixteen songs on two LP's all previously released
DeJaVu	DVLP-2069	"The Bill Haley Collection" Twenty BH greatest hits (Italy)
Doctor Kollector	DK005	LP "Bill Haley LIVE IN PARIS" Five songs recorded live in Paris in 1966, five songs recorded live in Paris in 1974 and three from a 1956 Alan Freed Show in New York. (France)

-1987-

Hallmark	SHM3207	LP "The Original Hits '54-'57" Fourteen of BH's Decca songs. (Great Britain)
Bear-Polydor	BFX15304	"Hier Bin Ich-Hier Bleib Ich" Two BH songs with Katerina Valente: Hot Dog Buddy Buddy and Vive La Rock'n'Roll. plus 15 by K. Valente. W.Germany
EMI LP	MFP5807	"Bill Haley & His Comets" 16 original Decca recordings. England.
Pickwick	SHM3207	"Bill Haley and his Comets-The Original Hits 54'57 Fourteen Decca hits. Same as above Hallmark SHM 3207
Fun LP	FUN9013	"Bill Haley & his Comets 20 Greatest Hits". Twenty all time BH hits. Belgium
Ambassador	A98100	LP "Bill Haley's Rarities" Twenty BH hits from over the years.
Look Back	120.104-2	CD "Bill Haley & the Comets" RATC/Flip Flop And Fly/Skinny Minnie/Saint's Rock'n'Roll/Rock The Joint/Love Letters in the Sand/Shake Rattle and Roll/See You Later, Alligator/Rock-A-Beatin' Boogie/Ling-Ting-Tong/. Switzerland

-1988-

Connoisseur	VS0P115	LP "Bill Haley's Greatest Hits" Twenty-four BH songs, all previously released
"CD	VS0P116	"Rip It Up Rock'n'Roll" Vol.1 Twenty-four BH hit Decca songs
"LP	VS0P116	"Rip It Up" Same as above.
Everest LP	4110	"Bill Haley and the Comets - Everest Golden Greats. Eight live concert performances of BH's top songs.
Telstar LP	2351	"The Heart and Soul of Rock'n'Roll" Bill Haley's RATC plus 44 v.a. France
MCA CD	MCAD37294	"Vintage Gold" Bill Haley and His Comets. 3"CD RATC/Burn That Candle/SYL, Alligator/Saint's Rock'n'Roll.
MCA LP	MCL1617	"Bill Haley and his Comets" Sixteen original Decca tracks.
Vogue CD	VG651	"The Best of Bill Haley and the Comets on Stage" 18 BH hit songs. W. Germany
Polydor CD	821394-2	"RATC Bill Haley and the Comets" Twelve BH hits. W. German
Europa CD	100406.9	"Bill Haley and the Comets RATC" 14 Sonet hits Previously released. West Germany.
Black Tulip	2636742	CD "Bill Haley and the Comets Twenty Greatest Hits. 20 Original recordings
EverGreen	2690512	CD "Bill Haley Greatest Hits" Ten BH Songs.
Bescol	CD-39	CD "The Greatest Hits 16 Bill Haley" Sixteen. BH hit songs.
BlackTulip	2636832	CD "Golden Treasures of the 50's and 60's" Bill Haley's ABC Boogie plus 23 v.a.
Success	2062CD	CD "Rock'n'Roll Forever" BH's Queen of the Twisters plus 15 other v.a.
Signal	50114	CD "Rock'n'Roll Classics" BH's RATC and SYL Alligator plus 17 v.a.
Rock'n'Roll	ONN16	CD "Rock'n'Roll Vol.1 BH's RATC plus seventeen other v.a.
"	ONN17	CD "Rock'n'Roll Vol.2 BH's Shake, Rattle and Roll plus 16 other v.a. Phonographic Performances UK
" CD	ONN21	"Rock'n'Roll Giants" BH's SRR/RATC plus 22 other v.a.
"CD	ONN32	"Rock'n'Roll Greats" BH's RATC/SYL Alligator/Rock The Joint plus 21 other v.a.
RCA CD	ND90085	"Rock'n'Roll The Early Days" BH's RATC plus 11 other v.a.
K-Tel CD	ONCD5115	"Rip It Up Rock'n'Roll" BH's RATC/SYL, Alligator/Razz-Dazzle/SRR plus 12 other v.a.
Maybellene	CD05503	"25 Greatest Rock'n'Roll Hits" Part 1 BH's RATC/Razzle-Dazzle plus 23 other v.a.
"	CD05515	"25 Greatest Rock'n'Roll Hits" Part 4 BH's Happy Baby plus 24 other v.a.

All Time Music CD	ATM001	"16 All-Time Rock'n'Roll Hits" Vol.1 BH's RATC plus 15 v.a.
"	ATM006	Same as above Vol.2 BH's R.O.C.K. plus 15 v.a.
"	ATM011	Same as above Vol.3 BH's Rock-A-Beatin' Boogie plus 15 v.a.
"	ATM016	Same as above Vol.4 BH's Saint's Rock and Roll plus 15 v.a.
"	ATM021	Same as above Vol.5 BH's Saint's Rock and Roll plus 15 v.a.
"	ATM026	Same as above Vol.6 BH's Razzle-Dazzle plus 15 v.a.
"	ATM031	Same as above Vol.7 BH's Rudy's Rock plus 15 v.a.
"	ATM036	Same as above Vol.8 BH's See You Later, Alligator plus 15 other v.a.
"	ATM041	Same as above Vol.9 BH's Shake, Rattle and Roll plus 15 other v.a.
"	ATM046	Same as above Vol.10 BH's Mambo Rock plus 15 v.a.
Rhino LP	RI70598	"Billboard 1955 Top Rock'n'Roll Hits RATC plus nine other v.a.

-1989-

Roller-Coaster	RCCD3001	CD "Rock The Joint" 23 original Essex and Holiday recordings
Sonet	BHEP0001	10″ 45 "Bill Haley" Three songs with Bill's vocals overdubbed to new instrumental tracks.

Bill Haley Picture Discs:

Carosello	4002	"Bill Haley" Twelve songs all previously released on the 1969 Kama Sutra album "BH. Scrapbook" Picture disc released in Italy in 1983
PD	1084	"Bill Haley and Elvis Presley" Nine hit songs by each legend. Released in Denmark in 1984
PD	AR30049	"Bill Haley and His Comets" twelve previously released hits. Denmark 1985
PD	AR30049	"Bill Haley-Rock Around the Clock" Twelve songs all previously released Holland 1987 (different picture than on Denmark release).
Maybellene	85	"Bill Haley" Rock Around The Clock, See You Later, Alligator and Shake, Rattle and Roll (45 rpm)

BILL HALEY'S MUSICIANS

1943-1980

Over a hundred musicians performed with Bill Haley in his many country-western and rock bands. This list is a small tribute to these many talented men and women who shared the stage and the recording studio with him. We regret some names are missing and lost from the memories of their fellow band members. If you know the names of any who should be included on this list, please forward them to the authors in care of the publisher. They will be included in any new editions.

It was the combined skills and professionalism of all these people that made Bill Haley's bands world renowned. Bill Haley learned and built from each band he played in or lead. Each musician, in his own way, contributed to the success of the sound that Bill used to rock the world. The musicians are listed by instrument in alphabetical order. Where known, the musician's real name is listed in brackets after their stage name.

DRUMS

Tonyo Adonii
Dave Bates
Tony Benson (Gaudioso)
Buddy Dee (Wayne deMint)
Sticks Evans
Earl Famous
Panama Francis
Billy Gussak
Owen Hale
Charlie Higler
Karl Himmel
Dave Holly
Cliff Jackson
Ralph Jones
Joey Kay
Ivan Krill
John "Bam Bam" Lane (Barrowclough)
Cliff Leeman
Art Marotti
Bobby Monk
Freddie Moore (Fusting)
Steve Murray
Bill Nolte
Don Raymond
Dick Richards (Boccelli)
Brad Skinner
Wayne Stevens
Dean Tinker
Ed Ward

BASS

Julian "Bashful Barney" Barnard
Ray Cawley
Chalmers Davis
Jim "Ed" Gorbey
Rusty Keefer
Jim Lebak
Marshall Lytle (Tommy Page)
Bill Moss
Ray Parsons
Al Rex (Piccirilli)
Joe Piccirilli
Al Pompilli
Al Rappa
Bobby Sharp
Al Thompson
Hank Thompson (Scholz)

SAXOPHONE

Joey Ambrose (d'Ambrosio)
George Baker
Al Dean (Albert DeNittis)
Geoff Daily
Geoff Driscoll
Tony Lance (Liquori)
Ed Logan
Rudy Pompilli (Pompilii)
Frankie Scott
Mike Shay
Frank Sikora
Pete Thomas

LEAD GUITAR
Walt Aldridge
James "Slim" Allsman
George Baker
Franny Beecher
Danny Cedrone
Joe DeNick
Dallas Edwards
Jimmy English
Charles "Fingers" Hess
Chuck Huffman
Johnny Kay (Kaciuban)
Tex King (Orville Mitchell)
Nick Masters (Nastos)
Bill Miller
Paul Pruitt
Art Ryerson
Bob Scales (Scaltrito)
Duke Snow (John Muntz)
Gerry Tilley
Bill Turner (Trimarco)

RHYTHM GUITAR
Ron Atwood
Pat Berg
Slim Bland
Lloyd Cornell
Neil Drummond
George Gray
Herb Hutchinson
Tom Kozer
Clifford Lytle
Marshall Lytle (Tommy Page)
Dennis McLeod
Bobby Marhu
Bob Mason
Ray McCann
Joe Oliver
Ray Parsons
Jesse Rogers
Chico Ryan
Mike Shay
Jerry Shook
Pete Spencer
Ernie Walker
Major Wallace
Ed Warminski
Jimmy Weidow

PIANO/ORGAN
David Baroni
Bill Borelli
Mike Cannon
Chalmers Davis
Johnny Grande
Ernie Henry
Hargus Robbins
Hank Thompson (Scholz)
Joey Welz
Bobby Wood
Pete Wingfield

ACCORDION
Al Constantine
Johnny Grande
Dorothy Heavlow

VIOLIN-MANDOLIN
Jimmy Collett (Colletti)
Bill Gray
Ben "Pop" Guthrie
Arrett "Rusty" Keefer
Jimmy Maise
Roy Perky
Brother Wayne (Wayne Wright)

CLARINET
Rudy Pompilli (Pompilii)

TRUMPET
Sonny Jim Davis
Al Rappa

HARMONICA
Jimmy Riddle
Wanda Hale

TRIANGLE
Dick Richards (Boccelli)

FLUTE
Rudy Pompilli (Pompilii)

DOBRO
Lloyd Green

STEEL GUITAR
Curley Chawker
Merle Fritz
Lloyd Green
Nick Masters (Nastos)
Billy Williamson

For the record, Bill Haley played both lead and rhythm guitar, the bass, steel guitar, and the fiddle.

SONGS RECORDED BY BILL HALEY AND HIS BANDS

1946 to 1990

The songs listed below were recorded and released by Bill Haley and his musicians over a period of forty-four years. The vocals were sometimes by other artists, but the back up was Bill's Comets or one of his earlier country-western bands. This list contains over 400 titles, however it is not complete.

(A)

A Little Piece At A Time
A Fool Such As I
A Rockin' Little Tune
A Year Ago This Christmas
A.B.C. Boogie
A.B.C. Rock
Ain't Love Funny, Ha, Ha, Ha
Ain't Misbehavin'
Afraid
Ages And Ages Ago*
All I Need Is Some More
  Loving*
Altar Of Love
Any Time
Apple Blossom Time
Are You Teasing Me?*

(B)

B.B. Betty
Baby I Found Out All
  About You
Battle Of New Orleans, The
Beak Speaks, The
Be By Me
Be Honest With Me*
Behind The Eight Ball*
Better Believe It
Billy Goat
Birth Of The Boogie
Blueberry Hill
Blue Comet Blues
Blue Suede Shoes
Bony Maronie
Boogie Woogie Yodel Song
Bouquet Of Roses
Bring It On Home To Me
Bundle of Kisses*
Burn That Candle

(C)

C.C. Rider
Caldonia*
Calling All Comets
Candy And Women*
Candy Bed
Candy Kisses
Caravan
Carolina In The Morning
Catwalk, The
Charmaine
Chattanooga Choo Choo
Chick Safari
Chiquita Linda
Choo Choo Ch' Boogie
Cold, Cold Heart
Come Rock With Me
Comettales*
Completely Satisfied
Conga Rock
Coquette*
Corrine, Corrina
Cotton Haired Gal*
Covered Wagon Rolled Right Along*
Crazy Man, Crazy
Crazy Street
Cute Little Brown Eyed Girl*

(D)

Dance Around The Clock
Dance With A Dolly
Darling I Want You*
Deal Me A Hand*
Detour
Dim, Dim The Lights
Dinah
Dipsy Doodle, The
Don't Knock The Rock
Don't Mess Around
Don't Nobody Move
Down By The Riverside Twist
Down Deep In My Heart*
Dragon Rock, The
Drowsy Waters*

(E)

Eight More Miles To Louisville
Eloise
El Rocko
Empty Feeling
Everyone Can Rock And Roll
Everyone Out Of The Pool

(F)

Farewell, So Long, Goodbye
Flip, Flop And Fly
Florida Twist
Foolish Questions*
Football Rock & Roll*
Forty Cups Of Coffee
Four Leaf Clover Blues*
Fractured
Framed

(G)

Games People Play
God Bless Rock And Roll
Goin' Back To Little Rock*
Good Night Dear Lord
Goofin' Around
Gonna Dry Every Tear With
  A Kiss*
Gotta Have My Baby Back*
Grandfather's Rocker*
Green Door, The
Green Tree Boogie
Guitar Boogie

(H)

Hail, Hail Rock And Roll
Haley A Go Go
Happy Baby
Happy Birthday
Harlem Nocturne
Hawk
Heartaches By The Number
Helena
Hey Then, There Now
Hide And Seek
High Heel Sneakers
Honestly*
Honky Tonk
Hook, Line And Sinker
Hot Dog Buddy Buddy
Hot To Trot*
How Many?

(I)

I Almost Lost My Mind
I Got A Woman
I Got News For You
I Dreamed Of An Old Love Affair*
I Don't Hurt Anymore
I Don't Want To Be Alone
For Christmas
I Love You So Much It Hurts*
I Need The Music
I Should Write A Song About You*
I Want A Little Girl
I Wasted A Nickel Last Night*
I Wouldn't Have Missed It For
The World
I'll Be True
I'm Alone Because I Love You
I'm Crying
I'm Gonna Dry Every Tear With
A Kiss
I'm Gonna Sit Right Down And Write
Myself A Letter
I'm In Love Again
I'm Not To Blame*
I'm Walkin'
Icy Heart
Ida, Sweet As Apple Cider
In A Little Spanish Town*
Is It True What They Say About
Dixie?
It's A Sin

(J)

Jamaica D.J.
Jenny, Jenny
Jim Dandy
Jim Dandy Got Married
Jingle Bell Rock**
Joey's Song
Johnny B. Goode
Jukebox Cannonball
Justine

(K)

Kansas City

(L)

Land Of A Thousand Dances
Lawdy, Miss Clawdy
Lean Jean
Let The Girls Sing
Let The Good Times Roll Again
Let The Good Times Roll, Creole*
Life Of The Party*
Ling-Ting-Tong
Little Pedro
Live It Up
Love Letters In The Sand
Loveless Blues*
Lucille
Lullaby Of Birdland Twist

(M)

Mack The Knife
Malaguena
Mambo Rock
Marie
Mary, Mary Lou
Me And Bobby McGee
Me Rock A Hula
Midnight In Washington
Mish Mash
Miss You
Mohair Sam
Moon Over Miami
Move It On Over
Music, Music, Music!
My Bucket's Got A Hole In It*
My Dream
My Easy Rockin' Chair*
My Kind Of Woman
My Mom Heard Me Crying*
My Palomino And I*
My Special Angel
My Sweet Little Girl From
Nevada

(N)

New Orleans
No Letter Today

(O)

One Has My Name*
One Sweet Letter From You
One-Two-Three Twist
Ooh! Look-A-There, Ain't
She Pretty
Oriental Rock
Out Where The West Winds
Blow

(P)

Paper Boy, The
Panic
Pat-A-Cake
Personality
Piccadilly Rock
Pink Eyed Pussycat
Please Don't Talk About Me
When I'm Gone
Pretty Alouette
Pretty Baby
Puerto Rican Peddler

(Q)

Queen Of The Twisters

(R)

Rappin' The Bass*
Razzle Dazzle
Real Rock Drive
Red River Valley*
Remember
Rip It Up
Riviera
R-O-C-K
Rock A Beatin' Boogie
Rock And Roll Music
Rock Around The Clock
Rock Lomond
Rock The Joint
Rocket 88
Rockin' Chair On The Moon
Rockin' Eyes
Rockin' Horse Cowgirl
Rockin' In The Nursery
Rockin' Matilda
Rockin' Rita
Rockin' Rollin' Rover
Rockin' Rollin' Schnitzlebank
Rockin' Through The Rye
Rocking Around The Christmas
Tree**
Rose Of My Heart*
Rovin' Eyes*
Rudy's Rock

(S)

Saints Rock'n'Roll
See You Later, Alligator
Seventh Son, The
Shake, Rattle And Roll
Shaky
Sing A Song Of Happiness
Singing The Blues
Six Year Olds Can Rock'n'Roll*
Skinny Minnie
Skokiaan
Slippin' And Slidin'
Slippin' Around
So Right Tonight*
Somebody Else Is Taking My Place
Spanish Eyes
Spanish Twist
Stagger Lee
Stand Up And Be Counted
Stop Beatin' Around The Mulberry Bush
Stop, Look And Listen
Straight Jacket
Strictly Instrumental
Summer Souvenir
Sunday Down In Tennessee*
Sundown Boogie
Susan Van Dusan
Sway With Me
Sweet Sixteen
Sweet Sue, Just You

(T)

T.V. Pal
Tamiami
Tandy
Tearstains On My Heart*
Teenage Tango
Teenager's Mother
Ten Gallon Stetson*
Ten Little Indians
Tennessee Border*
Tenor Man
That's How I Got To Memphis
There's A New Moon Over My Shoulder
Thirteen Women
This Is Goodbye, Goodbye
This Is The Thanks I Get
Tongue Tied Tony
Tonight's, The Night
Too Many Parties, Too Many Pals
Tossin' And Turnin'
Toy Shop
Train Of Sin
Travelin' Band
Trouble In Mind*
Tweedle Dee
Twist Marie
Two Hound Dogs
Two Shadows

(U)

Up Goes My Love

(V)

Vive La Rock And Roll

(W)

Walking Beat, The
War Paint
Wastin' Time
Weekend
Wee Willie Brown
What Can I Say After I Say I'm Sorry
What'Cha Gonna Do?
What'd I Say?
Where Did You Go Last Night?
Whistlin' And Walkin'
White Parakeet
Wobble, The
Whoa Mabel
Whole Lotta Shakin' Going On
Who'll Stop The Rain?
Who's Gonna Kiss You When I'm Gone?
Why Do I Cry Over You?*
Wild Side Of Life, The
Within This Broken Heart Of Mine*
Wooden Shoe Rock
Wreck On The Highway*

(Y)

Yakety Sax
Yeah, She's Evil!
Yes Indeed
Yodel Your Blues Away*
Yodeller's Lullaby*
You Call Everybody Darling
You Can't Stop Me From Dreaming*
You Were Mean, Baby

**To be released on the German Hydra label.*

***To be released on the "Rock Star" label.*

Songs Recorded By Bill Haley But Not Released

There exists many demo acetate discs and tapes of songs recorded by Bill Haley and his many bands. These listed below are a few which are in the hands of collectors at the present. Many more exist, and they, with their many different arrangements, are in the inventories of recording firms in Sweden, Mexico, England and the United States. One day, we hope they will all come to light, as appreciation for Bill's music continues to grow.

Cherry Tree Lane
Jealous Heart
Prairie Pioneers
Rock On Baby
Six Year Olds Can Rock'n'Roll
Sweet Bunch Of Roses
Take Me In Your Arms
Teardrops From My Eyes
Whispering
You'll Come Walking Back

Bill Haley's Mexican Records

Bill Haley also recorded over a hundred songs on at least four different Latin American labels; Dimsa, Orfeon, Maya and Dim. Many were sung in Spanish, while others were instrumentals with a strong Spanish flair. These records sold in the tens of millions throughout Latin and South America where "Bill Haley y sus Cometas" remained very popular during the 196O's and 1970's. The list below unfortunately is not complete:

A Gusto Contigo
Actopan
Adios Mariquita Linda
Al Compas Del Reloj
Alrededor Del Reloj
Ana Maria
Anoche
Avenida Madison
Baby Elephant Walk
Baja California Sun
Bikini Twist
Caravan A Go Go
Caravan Twist
Cardlina
Cerca Del Mar
China Twist
Cielito Lindo
Cirvanna A Go Go
Comet Boogie
Conga Rock
Conga Twist
De Buen Humor
Desafindo
El Blues De Los Cometas
El Expreso
El Madison De La Esterella
El Pony
El Quelite
El Sax Tartamudo
Ella Cree Que La Amo Aun
En Un Pueblito Espanol
Estmago Caliente
Florida Twist
Happy Twist
Hey Nos Vemos Cocodrilo
Jalisco Twist
Jarrito Twist
La Cancion De Jose
La Cucaracha
La Paloma
La Marcha De Los Santos
La Tierra De Las Mil Danzas
Lado A Lado
Limbo Rock
Madero Y Gante
Madison Del Cometa
Marie Twist
Marruecos
Martha
Mas Twist
Memphis
Mexicali Twist
Mish Mashed
Monterrey Twist
Moviendose
Negra Consentida
No Te Puedes Sentar
Nocturno De Harlem
Oaxaca Twist
Pepito Mi Corazon
Puerta Verde
Pueblo Del Twist
Pure De Papas
Que Pachanga
Rambuchas Twist
Reunion De Etiqueta
Riviera
Rudy's Twist
Rue Pachanga
Silbando Y Caminando
Skokian A Go Go
Sonora Twist
Surf Dez Elefante
Surf De La Sandia
Surf Del Monkey
Tacos De Twist
Tampico Twist
Teresa
Tip Top
Trece Mujeres
Tren Nocturno
Tuxedo Junction
Twist Del Cometa Azul
Twist Del Dia
Twist Del Expresso
Twist Espanol
Twist Feliz
Twist Lento
Vera Cruz
Viajanbo Con El Madison
Weekend
Yucatan Twist

BILL HALEY FIRSTS

Bill Haley, as a pioneer in the development of a new musical format, earned the title *"The Father of Rock'n'Roll"*. This tribute was bestowed due to his many early accomplishments of which some are listed below:

1. First band leader to form a "Rock'n'Roll" group.
2. First Rock'n'Roll star to write his own music.
3. First Rock'n'Roll star to reach the national charts with music he wrote and recorded.
4. First Rock'n'Roll star to own his own music publishing companies.
5. First Rock'n'Roll star to own his record label and recording company.
6. First white artist to be elected as the "Rhythm and Blues Personality of the Year".
7. First Rock'n'Roll star to sell a million records.
8. First Rock'n'Roll star to receive a gold record.
9. First Rock'n'Roll star to go on a world tour.
10. First Rock'n'Roll star to sell a million records in England.
11. First Rock'n'Roll star to star in a full length motion picture.
12. First White Rock'n'Roll star to tour with all-Black supporting artists.
13. First Rock'n'Roll star to appear on a network television show.

Courtesy Universal Press Syndicate

Even America's foremost curmudgeon knows his classics!

Courtesy© DAP

In concert, left to right, Johnny Grande on keyboard, Dick Richards on drums, Marshall Lytle on bass.

Courtesy© DAP

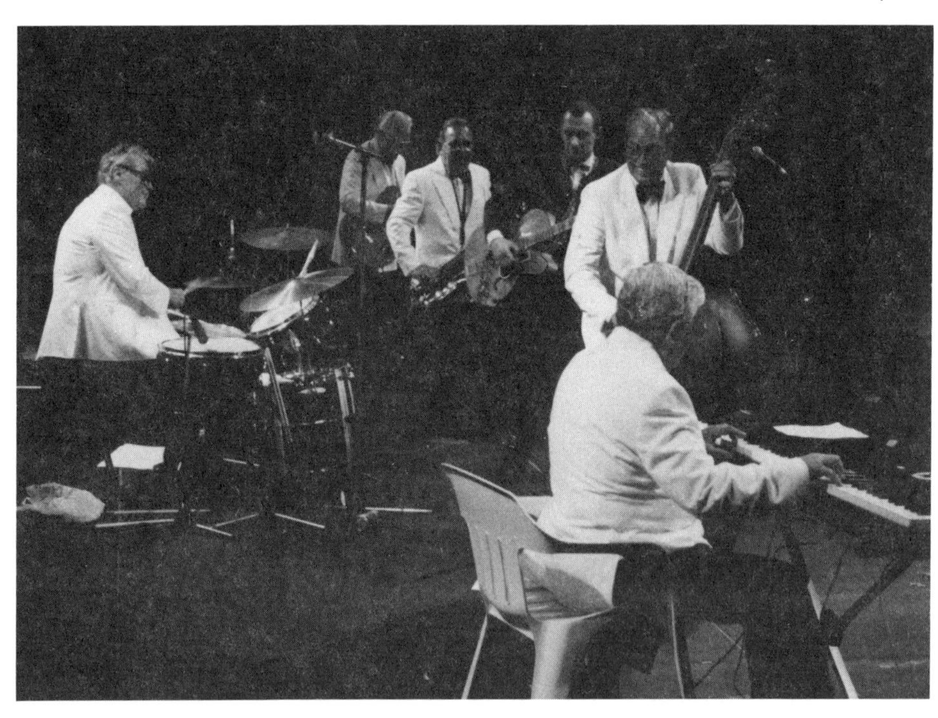

On stage left to right, Dick Richards on drums, Franny Beecher on lead guitar, Joey Ambrose on sax, Jacko Buddin lead singer, Marshall Lytle on bass and Johnny Grande on keyboard.

STILL ROCKIN'

The Comets at the London Astoria
June 10, 1990

In a historic demonstration of their unique musicianship, Bill Haley's original 1950's Comets rocked thousands in an incredible concert on June 10, 1990 at the London Astoria, just eighty yards from the Dominion Theater, where thirty-three years before, Bill first introduced live American Rock'n'Roll to the British people.

Courtesy© DAP

Rockin' with the classics. The Comets show they haven't lost any of their punch. Left to right, Johnny Grande on keyboard, Marshall Lytle on bass, Dick Richards, drums, Jacko Buddin singing in Haley's style with rhythm guitar, Joey Ambrose on sax, Franny Beecher on lead guitar and Peter Davenport replacing Billy Williamson on steel guitar.

BIBLIOGRAPHY

Belz, Carl. The Story of Rock. Oxford University Press. 1969.

Clark, Dick. Rock, Roll & Remember. Thomas Crowell Company, New York, N.Y. 1976

Colman, Stuart. They Kept On Rockin'. Blandford Press, Poole, Dorset, U.K. 1982.

Cotten, Lee. Shake Rattle & Roll. Pierian Press, Ann Arbor, Michigan. 1989

Gruen, John. The Party's Over Now. Viking Press 1972.

Malone, William. Country Music U.S.A. University of Texas Press. 1968.

Miller, James. Illustrated History of Rock & Roll. Random House/Rolling Stone Press 1980.

Ochs, Michael. Rock Archives: Doubleday & Co. New York 1984

Rolling Stone Rock Almanac. Collier MacMillan Publishers, London, U.K. 1983.

Romanowski, P and Pareles, J. The Rolling Stone Encyclopedia of Rock'n'Roll. Summit Books. New York 1983

Shaw, Arnold. The Rockin' 50's. Da Capo Press. 1987

Shaw, Arnold. The Rock Revolution. What's Happening in Today's Music. Crowell-Collier Press. 1970

Swenson, J, Bill Haley. The Daddy of Rock'n'Roll. Stein and Day. New York 1983

Tosches, Nick. Country. (Revised Edition) C. Scibner's Son, New York 1985

Magazine Articles

Billboard Magazine. New York, N.Y. Numerous articles from 1949 to 1981.

Comet Fan Club News Letter. Chester, PA. 1955 to 1959

Goldmine Magazine. "Bill Haley—the Orfeon Years" by Denise Gregoire. April 1980. Fraser, MI.

Goldmine Magazine. "Bill Haley—Personal Memories" by Kenn Petzke. November 1984. Iola, MI.

Guitar Player. "Rock Around Again" by Fred Stuckey. October 1970. Los Gatos, CA.

Guitar Player. "Franny Beecher Story" by Bob Berman. Sept. 1973. Los Gatos, CA.

Hillbilly & Western Review. The. Various articles 1949. Ithaca, N.Y.

Hit Parader. "Bill Haley in England" by Nick Logan. November 1968. Derby, CT.

Howard Publications. "Jack Howard—Friend of the Stars" 1962. Phila., PA

Howard Publications. "Bill Haley—A Biography" 1949 Phila.

Les Modelles. "Jimmy Myers—Portrait of a Rock'n'Roll legend" Phila., PA. May/June 1989

M-G-M Press Book for "Blackboard Jungle—A Drama of Teenage Terror. 1955. Los Angeles, CA

National Hillbilly News. Various articles, Oct. 1945 to May 1946. Huntington, W. VA.

New Kommotion. "Bill Haley—Don't Knock the Rock" by Rob Finnis, Vol 3 #4 1980. Wembley U.K.

News & Views. "Rock Around The Clock Marks 33rd Anniversary" Vol. 2 Issue 54. March 1986

Now Dig This Magazine. "Calling All Comets" by David Hirschberg. June/July 1988. Tyne and Wear, U.K.

Now Dig This Magazine. "The Jodimars Story" by David Hirschberg. Issues 75, 76 and 77. June, July and August 1989. Tyne & Wear, U.K.

Record Roundup. Various articles written by Jack Howard in his column "Philadelphia Patter". Oct 1947 to April 1949. Cincinnati, OH

Record World. "From Two Presses to Miller International" by Parnes. Jan. 30, 1965

Record Whirl. "Why Bill Haley and His Comets Are Soaring!" by Edith Schomberg. Nov. 1955

Record Exchanger. "The Brightest Comet Of Them All—Bill Haley" by Rick Whitesell. Issue 20

Rock and Roll Magazine. "Hip Kats Honor" and "The Daddy of Rock'n'Roll. May 1956. New York, N.Y.

Rock & Roll Revival. "The Man Who Started It All" October 1969. New York, N.Y.
Rock and Roll Roundup. "Rock Sensation" and "A Salute to Alan Freed" Feb. New York, N.Y.
Rock Revue. 1978. "The Bill Haley Story" by Herbert Kamitz and Rudolph Urban.
Rockin' 50's Magazine. "Special Tribute to Bill Haley" by Kenn Petzke and Denise Gregoire. Issue 4. Lubbock, TX
Rockin Around Magazine. "The Comets Story" by John Grande 1955. New York, N.Y.
Super Attractions Souvenir Pictorial Album. "The Biggest Rock'n'Roll Show of 1956"
Valley Brook Publications. "Bill Haley and His Comets" 1956. Chester, PA

Unpublished Works

Allsman, James. Personal papers and files.
Beeks, Ronald. Personal papers and files.
Buzzell, John. Personal files
Ferguson, James. Personal papers and letters.
Gardner, Chris. The Bill Haley Story.
Haley, William J.C. Personal papers and diaries.
Hirschberg, David. Personal papers and files.
Hoover, J. Edgar. F.B.I. archival files on Bill Haley.
Howard, John. Personal papers and letters.
Manganaro, Michelle. Personal files and letters.
Myers, James. Personal papers and files.
Pompilli, Ann. Personal papers and letters.

INDEX

INDEX

INDEX

INDEX

INDEX

INDEX